Conce

This comprehensive and authoritative statement of fundamental principles of sociological analysis integrates approaches that are often seen as mutually exclusive. John Scott argues that theorising in sociology and other social sciences is characterised by the application of eight key principles of sociological analysis: culture, nature, system, space-time, structure, action, mind, and development. He considers the principal contributions to the study of each of these dimensions in their historical sequence in order to bring out the cumulative character of knowledge. Showing that the various principles can be combined in a single discip-

ONE WEEK LOAN

Conceptualising the Social World

Principles of Sociological Analysis

John Scott

CAMBRIDGE
UNIVERSITY PRESS

CAMBRIDGE UNIVERSITY PRESS
Cambridge, New York, Melbourne, Madrid, Cape Town,
Singapore, São Paulo, Delhi, Tokyo, Mexico City

Cambridge University Press
The Edinburgh Building, Cambridge CB2 8RU, UK

Published in the United States of America by Cambridge University Press,
New York

www.cambridge.org
Information on this title: www.cambridge.org/9780521884495

First published 2011

Printed in the United Kingdom at the University Press, Cambridge

A catalogue record for this publication is available from the British Library

Library of Congress Cataloguing in Publication data
Scott, John, 1949–
    Conceptualising the social world : principles of sociological
    analysis / John Scott.
        p.   cm.
    Includes bibliographical references and index.
    ISBN 978-0-521-88449-5 (hardback)
    1. Sociology–Research.   2. Sociology–Methodology.   I. Title.
    HM571.S36 2011
    301.01–dc22   2011013370

ISBN 978-0-521-88449-5 Hardback
ISBN 978-0-521-71136-4 Paperback

Contents

Figures

1   Diversity and Continuity in Social Theory

A diversity of theories and perspectives is widely seen as an essential characteristic of sociology and, perhaps, an especially marked feature of contemporary sociology. For many observers, this diversity is a sign of chronic intellectual failure and as an indication of the chaotic state into which the subject has fallen and cannot escape. Sociology, it is concluded, is too undisciplined to be counted a social 'science' and cannot be relied upon to produce factual knowledge or to guide practical action. For the more radical commentators this state of affairs is a consequence of the over-enthusiastic establishment during the 1960s of a non-discipline taught and researched by intellectual charlatans. These criticisms of the intellectual claims of sociology have come both from those in other, purportedly more rigorous disciplines and from those outside the academic world. Many in politics and the civil service have added to this the assertion that the diversity of viewpoints is driven by political bias: intellectual choices, they argue, are made not on the basis of logic and evidence but in relation to political preferences and prejudices. Indeed, this claim is usually stated as a view that diversity occurs within a limited range of the political spectrum and that the subject as a whole is characterised by a left-wing bias.[1] Such strong expressions are less marked now than they were thirty years ago, when the British government forced the Social Science Research Council to drop the word 'science' from its title and to face a reduced level of funding as the Economic and Social Research Council. The attack against sociology was furthered through the introduction of market considerations to both research and teaching, on the grounds that only practically useful intellectual work should be supported from public funds. Fortunately for sociology, but not for the government, the subject proved one of the most popular consumer choices among students and policy-makers. The neo-liberal market strategy initiated a major expansion in sociology and helped to re-establish its position within policy discourse. Despite this change in the political context of sociology, the suspicion lingers that sociology is insufficiently rigorous and is more concerned with exploring theoretical novelty and diversity than establishing well-founded understandings of the 'real world'.

Many sociologists have themselves enthusiastically embraced the idea of diversity, though they have generally seen this in more positive terms than have the external critics. A plurality of theoretical positions – even if mutually contradictory – is seen as something to be encouraged in the spirit of the Maoist dictum 'Let a hundred flowers bloom; let a hundred schools of thought contend'. Such internal views are based on the belief that there can be no intellectual certainty about social matters – there can be no single scientific truth but rather a plurality of truths. As there is a diversity of standpoints from which to view the social world, so must there be a diversity of theoretical perspectives corresponding to these standpoints. This argument seems to lead inexorably to the view that sociologists must 'take sides' in political disputes. Intellectual controversy becomes a reflection of political choice and political standpoint.[2] Less explicitly political is a position encouraged by the growing influence of post-modernism. This is the view that, because there is no reality to the grand narratives of 'science' and 'truth', sociology can consist of nothing more than playful intellectual constructions that tell us more about their producers than they do about the external world. Indeed, the very idea of an 'external world' may be seen as a product of particular theoretical discoveries.

This acceptance of diversity, whether in radical or more neutral and agnostic form, has been widely embraced by practitioners of academic sociology and has become deeply embedded in school and university curriculums. Rival theories and theorists tend to be presented alongside each other in lectures and textbooks with students left to make their own choices from among them. Marx, Weber, or Durkheim, functionalism, structuralism, or interactionism, structure, conflict, or action: these are presented as the alternatives among which students must choose, with the criteria of choice being left largely unspecified. In this situation, the choice of an approach with which a student feels most comfortable as a way of proceeding may come to be seen as the *de facto* epistemological basis on which theoretical decisions are to be made. Not surprisingly, students may come away from their studies with the idea that all intellectual decisions are merely a matter of mere personal preference. They can be forgiven for concluding that there is a supermarket of sociological ideas from which the sociological consumer can select a preferred theory or perspective and reject all others.

The argument that I try to establish in this book is that this total embrace of diversity involves a misunderstanding and misrepresentation of sociology and of social theory. I argue that while theoretical differences are a fundamental feature of sociological activity, they are capable of resolution – in principle if not always in practice – through the collection and assessment of relevant empirical data and through rigorous logical argument (see the argument in Letherby *et al.* 2011). However, many apparent 'theoretical' differences are not theoretical differences *per se*. These are often differences in a much more limited number of ways of conceptualising social phenomena. Theories of social activity are underpinned by specific conceptualisations that are not, in general, explicitly restated in each particular theory. Any sociological argument does depend on particular conceptualisations of the social world, but these are not tied to theoretical differences in a one-to-one way. It is these 'perspectives' or 'approaches' that generally figure in courses and textbooks on social theory rather than specific theories themselves. My argument is that such conceptualisations may often be seen more fruitfully as complementary frameworks rather than rival approaches.

It is often the case that strong claims are made for one particular way of conceiving the social world, the implication being that it is the only valid point of view to adopt. However, few such claims can withstand close scrutiny. To argue for the importance of a focus on issues of social interaction, for example, does not mean that an alternative focus on group conflict or individual reflexivity must be rejected *a priori*. Alternative conceptualisations of social phenomena are *prima facie* worthy of consideration as complementary perspectives on the social world. Each illuminates what others ignore or marginalise. They enable the production of ideal-typical constructions that enter into theoretical accounts of the social world, but they never provide the whole picture – if such an idea of the 'whole picture' makes any sense at all. This view of sociological diversity rests on the argument that sociology must be, in Mannheim's (1929) sense, relational rather than relativistic. Perspectives may be related to varying intellectual standpoints but they are not simply relativistic expressions of those standpoints. A dynamic synthesis of theories rooted in diverse conceptual perspectives is the means through which a transcendence of partial theorisations and partisan commitments can be achieved (Scott 1998).

My argument is that sociology has failed to progress as rapidly as it might because of a failure of intellectual cooperation. The achievement of broader understanding and, therefore, the resolution of explanatory differences, has been inhibited by the tendency to maintain exclusive claims to particular conceptual schemes and to one-sided intellectual commitments. Individual sociologists may choose to concentrate their attention on the insights generated from within their preferred conceptualisations, but these cannot be seen as providing an exclusive pathway to the truth. Explanatory advances are more likely to result if sociologists also cooperate in a search for complementarities so as to pull together the underlying conceptualisations. Diversity co-exists with an intellectual division of labour in which the explanatory potentials of the various conceptual perspectives are pursued cooperatively as a common intellectual enterprise as the most effective means of theoretical understanding and empirical advance.

This cooperation must rest on the recognition that rival conceptualisations may articulate a common set of *principles* of sociological analysis that can be used in the construction of specific theories. These principles are essential in a discipline that aims to explore social life in all its complexity. The focus on particular perspectives to the neglect of others has meant that crucial principles of explanation have been disregarded. For example, legitimate criticisms of the limits inherent in the systemic focus of structural-functional arguments on education, crime, and religion because of a neglect of action, conflict, or change, have often led to a wholesale denial of all that structural functionalists have argued and an exclusive embrace of one or other of the rival principles. This kind of theoretical rejection ignores the fact that there *are* systemic features in social life and that perspectives based on action, conflict, or change may be equally limited or one-sided in their accounts. Similarly, criticism of individualist approaches to action theory for their neglect of societal-level facts in studies of voting, educational achievement, or mental illness may result in a rejection of action theories and a failure to recognise that individuals and their actions are, indeed, an important feature of many social situations.

A corollary of this tendency to assume the exclusive validity of particular principles of explanation is that intellectual change tends to be driven by fashion. The apparent exhaustion of a conceptual framework leads to the search for an alternative to replace it. When this, too, is exhausted the search begins again. Where intellectual choice is seen as a matter of personal preference, the succession of frameworks is limited by the range of currently fashionable schemas. Each conceptual framework completely replaces its predecessor in the work of its adherents and, as a result, the insights achieved through the use of particular conceptual principles may be lost or marginalised in the collective memory of the current practitioners. Perspectives are abandoned, intellectual fashions move on, and the partial understandings built up in earlier intellectual generations are forgotten. The history of any discipline tends constantly to be rewritten from the standpoint of current concerns, and some theorists and their ideas are written out or marginalised as a new pantheon of theorists and canonical works is constructed.

In these circumstances, it is hardly surprising that some such apparently novel positions comprise restatements (generally unacknowledged and unrecognised) of positions abandoned during earlier and now forgotten phases of criticism. 'Culture' is rediscovered as 'discourse', 'heredity' is rediscovered as 'the body', and so on. Old ideas on culture may be rediscovered by a new generation and hailed as an innovative 'cultural turn', and ideas on materiality may be subsequently renewed as an 'object turn'. Restatements of earlier arguments that do not understand themselves as rediscoveries can only reinforce the apparent chaos and diversity of the discipline and involve a considerable waste of intellectual effort. Rediscoveries and restatements, even in the guise of intellectual novelty, will often add something to the original insights, as the idea of discourse adds something to the idea of culture, but they are likely to be more powerful and productive if generated through a knowledge and appreciation of the earlier insights and with an intention to establish them cooperatively in an intellectual division of labour. Reinventing the wheel is far less productive than retaining and improving on inefficient wheels. New discoveries – new principles – are, of course, possible. Innovation is not always reinvention. The excitement of sociology lies precisely in the discovery and discussion of innovations and novel refinements of more established principles. Such advances can be recognised, however, only if they are seen in relation to the larger disciplinary conspectus from which they emerge.

These issues of fashion and rediscovery are not peculiar to sociology, though they are, perhaps, more marked than they are in other social science disciplines. The reason for this greater prevalence is to be found in the generalising character of sociology as compared with the more specialist social sciences. Sociology as a discipline is concerned with exploring all or any aspects of social life and sociologists have a great variety of conceptual schemes that they can use. Specialist social scientists focus their attention on limited areas of social life and so face fewer issues of rival conceptualisation. Explanatory disputes in those specialised social sciences are more likely to appear as purely technical questions within a shared way of conceptualising the social world.

Theorising in all of the social sciences does, however, have certain common characteristics. The theories produced by sociologists are exercises in 'social theory' rather than merely 'sociological theory'. The latter term may better reflect the disciplinary label, but the term 'social theory' recognises the crucial part played by sociological principles in the work of other social scientists. The social theories produced within sociology are used by other social scientists, and sociologists draw on the social theories produced within these other disciplines. For this reason, it is not possible to draw sharp intellectual boundaries around the various social science disciplines. The conceptual schemes developed within each of them cross-cut the various specialisms and social scientists must be seen as possessing a common set of conceptual schemes, embodied in the discipline of sociology, that provide the basis for the principles and theories developed within specialist work (Scott 2010).

It is for this reason that any discussion of social theory cannot confine its attention to the work of self-identified 'sociologists'. There must be reference to the work carried out by geographers and historians and to ideas developed within economics, political science, criminology, and numerous other specialist disciplines in so far as these contribute to social theory. Disciplinary affiliations were, of course, far less marked – and often non-existent – during the formative period of the social sciences, from the mid-nineteenth century through the first third of the twentieth century, when the key principles of sociological analysis were established. The firmer disciplinary boundaries that have since been established have rarely been so tightly drawn that theorists have been rigidly confined within a particular discipline throughout their careers, and there has been a constant interchange of theoretical ideas among disciplines. The emergence and growth of interdisciplinary studies and the spawning of new disciplinary specialisms has further ensured that the production of social theory has remained a generic feature of social science and is not confined to the Sociology Departments of the universities.

In this book I aim to draw out the forms of conceptualisation that I believe to be central to a comprehensive social theory. I uncover and outline the main concerns of sociologists and other social scientists as they have developed within disciplinary discussions and try to show how they can be seen to relate to each other as elements within a broad framework of social theory. I try to show that arguments often treated as pointing to fundamental alternatives can actually be seen as complementary to each other. I argue that the degree of complementarity in social theory is actually much greater than many have assumed. Theoretical diversity is not a sign of confusion and lack of discipline but is a reflection of the complexity of the social world and of the need to approach its understanding from a number of different, but equally valid, directions.

I take a historical approach to documenting these principles of sociological analysis. I have tried to show when and where particular ways of conceptualising the social first emerged and crystallised as means of sociological explanation, using the ideas of their originators and pioneering investigators. My aim, however, is not to repeat the comprehensive history of sociological analysis that I have provided elsewhere (Scott 2005; and see Scott 1995). Rather, I aim to establish the baseline principles from which subsequent developments have taken place, drawing on later work in so far as it adds significantly to the earlier discussions. This means that some familiar writers who reiterate or rediscover earlier ideas are given less attention than is often the case in other discussions, especially where they merely amplify or elaborate on already established principles. My aim has been to place this work within its often unacknowledged historical lineage and context so as to bring out the extent to which sociological understanding has, or has not, been advanced. Where distinctively novel ideas have emerged, their originality is recognised in relation to the departures made from already established ideas. It is in this way that the continuity and development of sociological knowledge and ideas can be brought out and the context of theoretical differences can be better understood.

Such an approach could be criticised for its 'presentism', for assuming that there are fundamental and unchanging issues which all theorists, regardless of their historical context, must be addressing. This is only partially valid as a comment on my method. It is self-evidently the case that the world addressed by Durkheim, for example, is fundamentally different from that faced by Foucault, and that they must, of course, be expected to employ different concepts and arguments in order to understand and explain the varying features of their worlds. The same point would apply even more strongly to the work of Durkheim and that of Plato. To this extent, the arguments of differentially located social theorists are incommensurable and it would be foolish to expect them to be integrated into a single theory with the same theoretical object. To the extent that Foucault may, in some of his work, have been concerned with the late nineteenth century and early twentieth century of European history, we might expect some convergence of his concerns with those of Durkheim. However, that would be a trivial response to the claim of 'presentism'.

The claim underpinning the argument of this book is rather different. It is the view that there are, indeed, some fundamental features of social life that are true universals and that theoretical ideas to explain these will have an enduring relevance. As I will show, Durkheim developed, among other things, the idea that social phenomena exhibit a 'structure' and that the social structure is one of the key 'social facts' that define the nature and purpose of sociological explanation. Foucault shared this view. Though generally regarded as a 'post-structuralist', he showed that social phenomena were connected in chains of interdependence such that the observable 'archipelago' of individuals, groups, and agencies are connected at a deeper level by relations of power. Foucault's concept of structure – notwithstanding his eschewal of the word – is continuous with that of Durkheim and can be considered as an elaboration of it. Indeed, the development of structural thinking can be traced from Durkheim through Radcliffe-Brown, Parsons, Lévi-Strauss, and others who fill the sequence from Durkheim to Foucault. It is in this sense that I see the introduction and elaboration of the idea of structure as a fundamental sociological discovery and as a universal feature of social life which all these writers can be considered as having contributed to. Similar considerations apply to all the principles of sociological analysis that I discuss in this book.

I have identified eight fundamental principles as currently underpinning the core concepts required in sociological analysis and as defining a disciplinary conspectus within which a sociological division of labour can operate. These principles are culture, nature, system, space-time, structure, action, mind, and development. Chapter 2 is concerned with *culture*, with the idea that human populations can be seen as formed through processes of enculturation or socialisation into a shared world of symbols and meanings that inform their social activity. This is not an insight achieved in any recent 'cultural turn' but is a deeply rooted feature of sociological understanding. I trace the emergence of an idea of culture from earlier notions of 'spirit' and trace the ideas of social constitution and social construction as they have developed through a variety of theoretical lineages and with varying political inflections.

Chapter 3 looks at those material conditions of *nature* that comprise the human body itself and the environment in which it lives. I trace the ways in which ideas of environmental conditioning and determination have been developed into ecological models of social change that comprehend the effects of physical conditions, modes of material production, and technologies on human ways of life. The biology of the body is an adaptive response to changing environmental conditions, but it is shaped and channelled by cultural formation to produce those variations that are so apparent as features of social life. Human activity cannot be understood in the manner of evolutionary psychology and sociobiology, as an outcome of genetic differentiation alone. This argument is illustrated through considerations of gender and kinship, neighbourliness and community, race and ethnicity, and life and death. Structures of action and forms of consciousness are shown to be products both of cultural and natural processes.

Chapter 4 shows that social processes cannot be understood without the use of the principle of *system*. Systemic relations among social phenomena are generated, reproduced, and transformed by structured processes of action. While they have holistic principles of their own, social systems have never been understood as entities distinct from the activities that sustain them. I trace the gradual refinement of systemic ideas from early organic analogies through structural-functional and living-system models, to more dynamic non-linear views of systems as dispersed fields of activity.

Chapter 5 turns to issues that have sometimes been seen as the topics of, respectively, history and geography. These are issues in *space-time*, understood as comprising fundamental categories of human understanding. Space is understood as an abstract, formal system materially expressed in the physical conditions that comprise the environments in which human populations live. Human activity is organised in such a way that social structures exist as spatial structures and human populations can be seen as social morphologies. Physical concepts of time are related to conceptions of social time and to the idea that social activities must be understood as occurring over time and can, therefore, be seen as processes of social change. I show that temporal processes have been conceptualised at a number of levels.

Chapter 6 considers the idea of social *structure*. Although this is often seen as closely linked to the idea of culture (and some have equated social structure with 'cultural structure') I show that structure is not a purely cultural phenomenon and that the concept highlights the ways in which the activities undertaken in human populations are constrained in ways that may reinforce socialisation but equally may run counter to it. Behaviour can rarely be seen as completely determined by the socialisation of individuals, and they should not be seen as mere 'oversocialised' cultural dopes. Rather, culturally formed motivations to act must be channelled by distinctively structural factors that constitute the limits and potentialities through which actions are constrained. Culturally formed normative expectations held by those with whom we interact and the relational forces inherent in human association together comprise the constraining structural features of any human society.

The principle of *action*, described in Chapter 7, highlights the fact that individuals retain a freedom of action – agency – despite the joint effects of culture and social structure. Human agents reflexively construct their own actions as pragmatic, strategic responses to their circumstances and as expressions of commitment to their values. I trace the emergence of various strands of action theory and I show how individual actions can be related to social structure. I take up the argument of Chapter 6 – that social structures can be seen to be the products of human action – and demonstrate the mutually supporting features of explanation in terms of both structure and action.

Chapter 8 is concerned with the *mind* that is formed as a socialised subject and as an integral aspect of a socialised body. I look at the ways in which a distinctively social understanding of psychological processes emerged and provided concepts that allow a close articulation with contemporary views of consciousness. I look at the development of ideas of imitation and identification, and at the socialisation of the unconscious, and I examine how group processes can produce cognitive consistency. Returning to issues of time and change, the chapter explores ways in which the cognitive and emotional development in individual human agents has been conceived.

Chapter 9 is concerned with social development, understood as a specific temporal process of change in social systems. I trace the ways in which evolutionary accounts of the endogenous structural development of human societies have been modified into more flexible views of open-ended development in which exogenous processes of diffusion and conflict contribute to the triggering of the social potentialities and tendencies through individual and collective action.

These eight principles of sociological analysis emerged and have developed within sociology and the other social sciences since the formative period of the nineteenth century. This is why the pioneering ideas of the formative theorists remain of fundamental importance in sociological understanding, despite the many changes that societies have undergone since their time. The theoretical ideas that they initiated provide the conceptual means through which a variety of diverse theoretical arguments have since been constructed. Taken together, the principles comprise the essential tool kit for conceptualising social phenomena. It is not a matter of choosing among the perspectives they inform in order to select the one and only basis for doing sociology. Rather, it is necessary to recognise them all to be essential, even if of variable importance, in the intellectual division of labour through which the social sciences have and can continue to develop. The aim of this book is to elucidate these principles and to show their complementarity. This complementarity may often be unrecognised, but it is real nevertheless, as I hope to have demonstrated. The principles may not yet fit together into a coherent and perfectly integrated scheme. Many areas remain for further work and full integration may be a long way off, if it can ever be achieved. Their joint use, however, is the basis on which sociology can advance and within which more detailed explanatory work can fruitfully be undertaken.

2   Culture: the Socialisation of Meaning

'Culture' has long been seen as central to the constitution of human subjectivity and action.[1] The word originated in an analogy with the 'cultivation' of farm land as an object of 'agri*culture*'. Roman thought had linked *cultura* to the cultivated or educated way of life through which rational and intelligent ways of thinking are developed[2] and this underpinned the Renaissance discourse of human difference in which the cultivated 'reason' of the 'ancients' and the 'moderns' was contrasted with the 'savagery' and 'barbarism' of the middle ages and contemporary non-European societies. This discourse allowed the observable differences in customs and practices uncovered through European colonial expansion and travel to be described and explained. Kant (1790) popularised this idea of *Cultur* and the view that a cultured, or refined, way of life is superior to the coarse and uncultivated ways of the primitives and the uneducated.[3] Culture is the origin and mark of a truly human existence that goes beyond the merely 'natural' condition of animals and 'savages'. Culture comprises the shared ideas, meanings, and values that were understood as 'spirit' (*Geist* or *ésprit*) or 'soul' (*Seele* or *âme*), the active mental and moral force in human life. Montesquieu (1748) held that a 'general spirit' – a 'moral spirit' or 'national spirit' – inspires the religion, language, custom, and form of government of a population.

The availability of more reliable ethnographic reports led to an appreciation that primitive societies may be as cultured as their more 'civilised' neighbours. Emerging in the historicist writings of von Herder, von Ranke, and Droysen, a wider and non-evaluative idea of 'culture' was developed by Burckhardt (1860) in Germany, Danilevsky (1869) in Russia, and Tylor (1871) in Britain. Tylor gave the word something close to its current meaning of 'that complex whole which includes knowledge, belief, art, morals, law, custom, and any other capabilities and habits acquired by man as a member of society'. It comprises the 'opinions and habits belonging in common to masses of mankind' and so the 'special dress, special tools and weapons, special laws of marriage and property, special moral and religious doctrines' of a society (Tylor 1871: 1, 12, 13).

Herder (1784–91; see also 1770) had been among the first to see culture as the essential element in a systematic explanation of human life. The collective ideas and feelings of a people (*Volk*) comprise a shared mentality or *Volksgeist*. This is carried and reproduced through language, the vehicle of thought that sustains a distinctive worldview and the identity that constitutes a people as a 'nation'. Von Humboldt (1836) held that a language is the basis of a cultural 'tradition' through which individuals are influenced by past generations as well as those with whom they interact in the present. These ideas underpinned the 'folk psychology' – the ethnic psychology, or the psychology of peoples – of Lazarus and Steinthal (1860), who identified a spirit of the people (*Volksgeist*) or collective spirit (*Gesamtgeist*). In a similar vein, Bastian (1860) wrote of folk ideas (*Volkergedanken*). Dilthey (1883) used these ideas as the basis for defining the 'sciences of spirit' (*Geisteswissenschaften*) and the hermeneutic methodology for 'understanding' (*Verstehen*) spiritual objects as a cultural tradition.

This view was most fully elaborated by Wundt in the ten volumes of his *Völkerpsychologie* (see the summary in Wundt 1912).[4] Wundt held that ethnology, anthropology, and sociology study the collective mental *products* of human association (language, myths, customs, etc.) while folk psychology studies the individual-level mental *processes* through which these are reproduced and transformed. His own concerns were with the 'psychological' processes, but he also had much to say about popular mental products. The individual mental processes involved in thoughts, sentiments, and dispositions are, in Hegel's terms, aspects of 'subjective spirit'. The mental products have been externalised and objectified as 'objective spirit' – as conceptual systems, works of art, customs, and practices – that confront their producers 'externally' as fixed and given conditions.[5] Such cultural products are real supra-individual objects analogous to physical objects and therefore able to be directly observed and conceptually grasped (Wundt 1897). The culture of a people, then, comprises the mental elements common to interacting individuals and that are virtually present in objectified form as customs and practices and in the linguistically formulated myths and religions that give identity to a people and are the means through which their intellectual, aesthetic, and moral concerns are explored and elaborated. This external 'mental environment' is the milieu within which individual minds arise. It comprises a 'complex of psychic elements' (Dilthey 1883: 104): a sphere of value, meaning, purpose, and self-consciousness that, as a 'cultural system' (*ibid*.: 101–2), provides the ideas, feelings, and will through which individuals acquire a sense both of 'inner obligation' and of personal freedom. These meanings are 'created by a community of human life and are, therefore, inexplicable in terms merely of individual consciousness, since they presuppose the reciprocal action of many' (Wundt 1912: 3). They are the results of intersubjective communication.

The idea of *Geist* or culture as collective spiritual or mental products was central to the sociologies of Sombart (1902) and, Weber (1904–5), who explored the 'spirit of capitalism' and its impact on material life, while Müller-Lyer (1908) saw human history as a sequence of cultural phases. In France, Le Bon (1895b) saw the 'soul' of a people as the shared and inherited psychological characteristics that are the basis of their institutions, art, beliefs, and politics, while a group of writers around Durkheim, most notably Halbwachs and Lévy-Bruhl, drew on Comte's view of the autonomy and objectivity of cultural products as 'social facts'. In the United States, the German émigré Boas supervised the work of Kroeber, Sapir, Linton, and White and developed a strong interpretation of cultural relativity. In Britain, idealists and evolutionary writers, including Bosanquet, Hobhouse, McDougall, and MacIver, developed Spencer's idea of the 'social organism' as a mental system. Tylor's definition had become central to the emerging disciplines of sociology and anthropology, where culture rapidly displaced the word 'spirit'. Rickert (1910) came to see culture – the sphere of valuation and meaning – as the specific object studied in the human or cultural sciences, while Boas (1911) popularised this view in American social thought. By the 1940s this was firmly established as the accepted social science usage in both Europe and North America. Individuals were seen as becoming specifically human beings through their enculturation (Kluckhohn 1949: 23).

Culture, language, and meaning

Culture, then, defines the unique individuality of particular societies, highlighting the diversity resulting from their distinctive customs and ways of life (Bauman 1973: ch. 1). It consists of linguistic signs or symbols organised into the ideas, evaluations, and feelings, into mental constructs, or representations, held in verbal and non-verbal form. It is 'the *signifying system* through which necessarily (though among other means) a social order is communicated, reproduced, experienced, and explored' (Williams 1981: 13). Culture comprises 'patterned or ordered systems of symbols which are objects of the orientation of action ... [C]ultural elements are elements of patterned order which mediate and regulate communication and other aspects of the mutuality of orientation in interaction processes' (Parsons 1951: 327). It consists of the shared ways of orienting, thinking, feeling, evaluating, and acting through which people are able to organise their actions and the choices they make. It is the pool of common meanings belonging collectively to a group or set of groups and that provide explanations, judgements, and other orientations towards objects and are the means through which people give meaning to their experiences. Formulated into the body of commonsense knowledge that orients people in their everyday encounters, it is also formed into the more systematic knowledges of religion, art, science, and political belief. It both shapes behaviour through the learned dispositions that constitute personality and 'character' and provides a repertoire of justifications that allow people to make sense of and account for the choices they face (Mills 1940; Scott and Lyman 1968; Swidler 1986; Boltanski and Thévenot 1991).

Durkheim (1898) saw cultural factors as the 'collective representations' that originate externally to particular individuals and confront them as things that 'constrain'. Such 'representations' are ideas, images, and models of action held in the mind that enable a person to visualise the world, to construct an image of it, and to formulate plans of action. Representations allow people to go beyond mere sense perception to *interpret* the causes of those impressions and to act in relation to them (Peristiany 1965; and see the essays in Pickering 2000). Durkheim aimed to show that human experience of the world is necessarily social and that mental representations must always have a decisively collective character. With the possible exception of feral children, all human experience is mediated by linguistically formulated collective representations to become communicable signs. A purely individual consciousness would be little more than 'a continuous flow of representations which are lost one in another, and when distinctions begin to appear they are quite fragmentary' (Durkheim and Mauss 1903: 7). The mind would be limited to this disconnected, chaotic understanding of the world 'if education did not inculcate ways of thinking ... which are the result of an entire historical development' (*ibid.*). While each individual may draw on and formulate these collective representations in particular ways, making individual minds unique in their mental content, the constitutive elements in all individual knowledge and understanding are collective in origin (Durkheim 1883–4: 398). The world encountered in thought and action is only ever known as a represented world, a world constructed from these mental elements.

Through cultural systems of meanings humans interpret their experiences, define their situations, and guide their actions and interactions. It is through cultural representations that they acquire a sense of order and predictability – of familiarity – in their understanding of the world (Moscovici 1984: 37). Culture is the means through which people interpret the raw materials of their existence and make sense of their experiences. It tells people what the world is like, provides them with a selective orientation to the external world and to other people. The cultural contents available to people serve as the templates or paradigms of thought and judgement that they employ for action within that world.

Wundt had followed Herder in recognising the importance of language as the means through which the spirit of a people is formed and preserved. Because language is the vehicle of thought, he argued, differences in language lead to 'divergent directions and forms of thought' (1912: 53). For example, he suggested there were differences between the 'concrete' thinking of primitive societies and the more abstract conceptual reasoning found in more advanced ones (*ibid.*: 73; see also Lévy-Bruhl 1921). This approach to language was set out by Durkheim: 'Language is social in the highest degree: it has been elaborated by society, and society transmits it from one generation to the next. Furthermore, language is not merely a system of words: each language implies a particular mentality, that of the society which speaks it' (Durkheim 1912b: 69). This was further developed in the writings of Sapir and Whorf, who saw languages as systems that shape the world views and experiences of those who speak them. Sapir (1921) held that the so-called real world is unconsciously built up through the language habits that predispose people to interpret their experiences in specific ways. Whorf added that it is the grammatical structure of speech (principles of tense, gender, number, and so on) that gives individual words and, therefore, whole utterances their meaning. The systems of classification inherent in a grammatical structure constitute the world of experience and the ways in which it can be thought about (Whorf 1936: 66–70; 1937). A language, therefore, embodies a distinctive worldview, a distinctive perspective on the external world through which people construct particular models of reality (Whorf 1941: 47):

We dissect nature along lines laid down by our native languages. The categories and types that we isolate from the world of phenomena we do not find there because they stare every observer in the face; on the contrary, the world is presented in a kaleidoscopic flux of impressions which has to be organised by our minds – and this means largely by the linguistic systems in our minds. We cut nature up, organize it into concepts, and ascribe significances as we do, largely because we are parties to an agreement to organize it in this way – an agreement that holds throughout our speech community and is codified in the patterns of our language. (Whorf 1940b: 213)

For this reason:

users of markedly different grammars are pointed by their grammar toward different types of observations and different evaluations of externally similar acts of observation, and hence are not equivalent as observers but must arrive at somewhat different views of the world. (Whorf 1940a: 221)

The structure of a language shapes the basic worldview of its speakers by providing them with the linguistic habits that predispose them to particular ways of thinking.

Culture as collective mentality

Central to the emerging concept of culture was the idea of culture as a collective mentality shared by a population within a region that, therefore, comprises a 'cultural area'. Boas and his students stressed that the inhabitants of a cultural area share the thoughts and feelings that define their way of life (see Kroeber 1923: 187–93; Linton 1936: 348). They highlighted the reality and autonomy of culture as a 'superorganic' system of meanings (Kroeber 1917; see also White 1949), echoing Spencer's view of the social as something that goes beyond the organic level of individual people. A similar view was taken by Hegelian writers in Britain, who held that there is no isolated individual to counterpose to collective processes: the individual *is* a social product. 'Social organisms' are formed through the association of individuals united by 'inward' bonds of membership in a community – by the obligations and duties inherent in shared and established sentiments of membership (Bradley 1876: 9; Jones 1883). The 'moral' bonds that unite individuals are to be understood as a 'social mind' or collective mentality formed by the meeting of the many individual minds that comprise its 'constituent elements' (Bosanquet 1899: 276). This social mind – 'the social spirit of a people' (*ibid.*: 38) – is a feature of a system of intercommunicating minds, and it is through this means that a 'community of thought' can exist and can sustain a community of language, beliefs, and values (Jones 1883: 27). From a related philosophical standpoint, Cooley (1909: 21) set out his view of culture as a 'social mind' (see also Dealey and Ward 1905: 55).

Undoubtedly the strongest, clearest, and most influential statement of this view was that of Durkheim, who took directly from Wundt the idea of social reality as a 'social conscience' that shapes individual actions (Durkheim 1887). The integration of a cultural system, he argued, cannot result simply from individual attempts at psychic integration. It occurs, rather, as a collective – and largely unintended – product of the circulation of cultural meanings as they pass through a variety of individual minds and generate strains and tensions among the various components of the culture (Durkheim 1897: 299). Following Montesquieu, he held that the focus of sociological attention must be on the coherence or interdependence of institutions that results from their permeation by a common 'moral' element. Human association produces a collective mentality, or system of representations, with a reality *sui generis*, and society comprises a distinct psychical or mental entity that exists as a specifically 'social fact'. Each institution derives its particular character from its dependence on others and on the structure of the whole of which it forms a part (Durkheim 1892: 56). This *conscience collective* (Durkheim 1895: 145) can be quite diverse. Although fundamental categories and concepts may be widely shared, being deeply embedded in its linguistic forms, actual propositional knowledge may vary a great deal among individuals and social groups. There need be no monolithic consensus of knowledge or belief across a whole society, despite the fact that its members share a common language and system of concepts.

There is a lingering suspicion that the postulation of culture as *conscience collective* or social mind involves the claim that culture exists as a substantial entity separately from individual minds (see, for example, Turner 1994). Durkheim's argument was not intended to hypostasise the social mind as an entity separate from individual minds, and it was for this reason that Durkheim, in his later work, preferred to avoid the term *conscience collective* and so avoid any substantialist interpretation of his argument as advocacy of a separate 'group mind'. Nevertheless, it remained his view that representations constitute a separate and distinct aspect of reality that is irreducible to the physiological processes of individual brains or the mental processes of individual minds (Durkheim 1898: 27–8).

The influential work of McDougall did, indeed, use the misleading term 'group mind' (1920: 7, 9, 12). What he meant, however, was that those who live within a particular milieu share certain ideas, beliefs, and values that comprise their common resources and their sense of collective identity. The 'group mind' comprises the common mental life of an aggregate of people, but it is contained only in their individual minds. As Linton argued:

Although the ideal patterns are carried in the minds of individuals and can find overt expression only through the medium of individuals, the fact that they are shared by many members of the society gives them a super-individual character. (Linton 1936: 102; see also Ingold 1986: 231)

Hobhouse was among the first to show clearly and explicitly that the idea of culture as a social mentality refers simply to a system of individual minds in communication. It is 'the order formed by the operation of mind on mind, incorporated in a social tradition handed on by language and by social institutions of many kinds, and shaping the ideas and practices of each new generation that grows up under its shadow' (Hobhouse 1913: 12). A social mentality, then, exists as 'a mental network or reticulum', a network of minds that sustains and is sustained by a network of actual social relations:

In this network there will be a certain equipment of ideas, modes of judgement and action, by which the inner life of the group, the mutual relations of its members and also the relations between the group as a whole and the outside world, will be determined. This is the group mentality. This mentality is conditioned not only by the nature of the constituent minds as they would be apart from the group relations – e.g., as they may actually function in other groups – but also by the relations constituting the group, and through these often enough by situations in which the group happens to find itself. (Hobhouse 1924: 186)

Similarly, Ginsberg argued that society exists only as 'a sum of habits, dispositions, ideas effective in a group of interacting minds' (Ginsberg 1929: 53). It is:

a mental condition widely effective in a group of interacting minds. Such a group constitutes not a mind or will, but rather a network of minds, related to one another in a thousand different ways, each conscious of himself but only dimly aware of the nature of the interaction between himself and his fellows, and certainly not aware of the whole in all its complexity. (Ginsberg 1929: 53)

The social mentality, then, can be understood as a system of circulating ideas that constrain individuals through the social pressures exerted as they circulate and through the sense of obligation and compulsion that, in consequence, individuals experience. It was for this reason that McDougall (1920: 9) defined collective mentality as 'an organized system of mental or purposive forces'. The individuals involved as members of a group communicate expectations to each other and these others feel compelled, obliged, or constrained to act in relation to them. The various collective representations (representations of the group, of its members, of their anticipated thoughts, feelings, and actions) are held within individual minds, yet each individual experiences them as a subjective field of psychic forces derived from their attachments, commitments, and repulsions to others. Individuals learn cultural meanings from those others with whom they interact, but they also creatively contribute to the production of those cultural meanings:

Every individual is born into a culture which already existed and is independent of him. Culture traits have an existence outside of the individual mind and independent of it. The individual obtains his culture by learning the customs, beliefs, techniques of his group. But culture itself has, and can have, no existence apart from the human species. (White 1949: 285–6)[6]

Cultural patterns are collective yet dispersed among the individuals that comprise a society. The contents of a culture are contained in individual minds, and this is what enables people to think, feel, and act in culturally formed ways. Culture is an 'ideal substance' that has no material existence of its own and is existent only in individual minds. It is the interlocking reciprocal representations held by people that gives an objectivity to their shared mental constructs. Individuals are the carriers or bearers of culture and sustain it through their ongoing communications with each other. Cultural meanings are formulated in speech and in other forms of communication and so can be transmitted from one actor to another. Communication is a mechanism of diffusion within and between societies. Cultures are complex, differentiated systems of meanings whose contents are dispersed among the minds of the myriad individuals whose interconnected activities in networks of differential association sustain the meanings through their communication with each other.

The elements of a culture are dispersed among the individual members of a population, but this cultural material is not, of course, identical in each individual mind. Rather, the contents of the culture are differentiated across the various members of a population, and each individual possesses only a part of the total stock of knowledge available in a society. Each individual is unique, sharing some but not all of his or her cultural material with the numerous and varied other members of their society. Individuals may share relatively similar 'copies' of the cultural 'software' that they acquire through inferences from the manifest content of the communications they receive and which they store in their memories for use in later communications (Balkin 1998: 14).

A social mentality consists only in the sameness or uniformity of thoughts, feelings, and actions among the members of a population. There is no need to assume the existence of either a single group mind nor a myriad of identical individual minds. All that is implied in this view is that individuals infer and interpret frames of meaning and habits of communication that are stored in unique ways in each individual mind but collectively comprise a structured system of communication. Uniformities are the result of 'identification' with the group and its members: people act in terms of the idea or representation of the groups of which they regard themselves as members and so feel themselves, in some sense, as bound by the thoughts and feelings of other members. It is, therefore, the existence of concepts defining a group (but held in individual minds) that gives other shared representations their distinctively social character (Greenwood 2004: 79).

As a collective system, a culture may nevertheless exhibit an overall 'pattern', 'ethos', or 'inner form' (Kroeber 1948; Shapiro 1962; Benedict 1934). Drawing on Popper (1968) and Sorokin (1937–41), Archer (1988: 104) defines any cultural system as a 'corpus of existing intelligibilia', of 'things capable of being grasped, deciphered, understood or known'. She argues that although there is no necessary tendency towards coherence or harmony among its various elements a cultural system can be assessed for its logical integration and consistency with established principles and criteria of aesthetic taste and morality, and there will normally be various inconsistencies, contradictions, and incompatibilities, reflecting the diversity, plurality, and syncretism through which cultures are built.[7] In drawing upon the ideas made available to them within their culture, people are constrained by its particular state of system integration. Parsons' 'pattern variables' were designed to grasp this integration analytically, though even he recognised that any ethos or coherent integration is purely contingent. Although individuals may think and act within the cultural resources available to them and may strive to establish a degree of consistency in their thoughts and actions, the diversity of individuals and groups is such that the intersection of individual courses of action is as likely to generate inconsistency as it is to generate consistency.

It is, nevertheless, important to recognise the interdependence between individual, culturally formed actions and the state of cultural integration. People work within the forms provided by the cultural patterns that they have internalised, however contradictory these may be. Ideas are worked out as logical implications or consequences of other accepted ideas, and it is in this way that cultural innovations and discoveries are possible. New ideas are discovered through logical reasoning, but such discoveries are inherent in and integral to the conceptual system and are made possible only because of the acceptance of its premises. For example, the discoveries of new prime numbers are 'real' consequences of the particular number system employed. Thus, cultural ideas show 'advances' and 'developments' because they are outgrowths of previous ideas. The cumulative work of many individuals produces a corpus of knowledge within which certain 'discoveries' become possible or more likely. Such discoveries are 'ripe' and could not have occurred earlier and are also likely to be made simultaneously by numbers of individuals (White 1949: 299; Merton and Barber 1958).[8]

Culture can also be understood as a collective memory. This idea was elaborated by Halbwachs (1925a; 1950) and in the work of the *Annales* school through Braudel (1949), Ariès (1963), and Le Goff (1988). Collective representations comprise a cultural heritage stored in individual minds and so made available for future communicative acts. As a collective memory it is a distributed memory, with no one individual holding the memory in its entirety. It is sustained, drawn upon, and reconstituted collectively as a cooperative but often contradictory act of remembering. This collective memory is:

> the integration of various different personal pasts into a single common past that all members of a community come to remember collectively. (Misztal 2003: 11)

Halbwachs showed that memories are not stored in individual minds as unconscious images of past experiences. What is stored are fragments or traces that become memories only when consciously reconstructed. These fragments are the raw materials from which memories are built (Halbwachs 1925b: 47–8).[9] Thus, remembering is always reconstructing. In 'remembering', an individual draws on social categories of understanding and ideas shared with and communicated by others. Each individual's memories are part of a pool of shared memories, and what each is able to recall is reconstructed, in part, from the suggestions of others (*ibid.*: 238). What any one individual remembers of the past is a product of their shared social experience.

Recent experiences resulting from continued interaction with others who experienced those same events form clearer and more coherent memories because they can more easily be reconstructed. Through conversations a shared account of the recent past is constructed and affirmed. Where those who interact are long-time associates, as in a family, the shared memory will stretch back a correspondingly long time. To recover memories of a long distant past, it may be necessary to mentally place oneself in the position of those with whom one interacted at the time of the initial experience and seek to understand how they, too, would have experienced the events: there may be an imagined conversation, or perhaps a real conversation with survivors, that underpins the process of recall and remembering (*ibid.*: 52–3). As a construct in the process of constant reproduction, and so of transformation, collective memory involves forgetting as much as remembering, and there may be 'collective amnesia' (Billig 1995: 38). Events and experiences cease to be remembered and may even be actively suppressed until lost to collective recall.

There is, in any society, an active and a latent collective memory. The active memory is actively sustained as a reality that is constantly renewed and reinforced through collective acts of remembrance and rehearsal. The latent memory is contained in physical form – in archives, libraries, and other depositories – and may not be consulted or drawn upon for long periods. Where the memories of a cultural heritage are held in latent form and have not been subject to comprehensive censorship or destruction, forgotten memories have the potential for rediscovery and re-entry into active collective memory.

Because of this, individuals may 'remember' things and events that they have not directly experienced and, indeed, that occurred before they were born. Many in contemporary France, for example, have memories of the French Revolution that have passed down to them over the generations as an aspect of the collective lived experience of the French as a whole. It follows that the content of the collective memory is always a product of contemporary concerns: the image of the past is part of an ongoing reconstruction of the collectivity (Halbwachs 1925b: 40). Cultural innovations may have their continuity with the past emphasised so that they, too, come to be seen as 'traditional', their novelty being obscured and soon forgotten (Hobsbawm 1983). This is the basis on which collective traditions are built, and such selective remembering is central to the imagining of communities (Anderson 1983).

The ability to retain a latent memory depends, in large part, on the introduction of a written language. This gives greater autonomy and fixity to cultural meanings and allows them to be stored in a determinate physical form and so to be recalled more accurately (Goody 1986; 2000). It is only in societies with a written language that a proper sense of history exists. In purely oral societies, the past and the present are sustained as a single reality, with memory extending only through a few generations and for very limited events. The distant past merges into the mythical past. In literate societies, events may be recorded in detail and narratives of social change can be created. Members of such societies come to understand the present as having come to be through particular processes of change, or of stasis. The cultural heritage may, therefore, become a 'tradition', in the sense of something that is valued because it is of long-standing and has 'always' been that way (Shils 1981). Such a tradition is a selective retention from the past: a 'selective version of the shaping past and a pre-shaped present' (Williams 1977: 115): 'From a whole possible area of past and present ... certain meanings and practices are selected for emphasis and certain other meanings and practices are neglected or excluded' (ibid.). These meanings become sedimented into a tradition that constitutes the history of the society and provides a context for individual memory and communication.

Communication and cultural reproduction

The paradoxical conclusion that a social mind can exist only within individual minds is resolved once it is recognised that cultures are created and sustained through communication among networks of associated individuals. Communication is the means through which cultural symbols are transmitted, intra- and intergenerationally, from one individual mind to another. For Durkheim, collective representations are contained within individual consciousnesses, but circulate among the associating individuals in such a way that the collective conscience is not confined, in its totality, to any one individual. It exists as circulating 'currents' of thought that distribute the contents of the collective conscience differentially among the myriad individuals concerned. Communication is the transmission of meaning, whether by word of mouth or through a technical medium of communication such as writing, printing, telephony, or broadcasting. Cultural transmission from person to person produces a 'chain of testimonies' (Vansina 1961: 19; Hervieu-Léger 2000). Things communicated are remembered and recalled in verbal form and may be retransmitted verbally to become further elements in the chain or network of testimony.

The communicative transmission of symbolic meanings from one person to another is crucial to cultural development, an idea that Tarde explored through the idea of 'imitation'. This is 'the mental impression from a distance by which one brain reflects to another its ideas, its wishes, even its way of feeling' (Tarde 1898b: 94). It is a means of 'inter-mental' transmission. People take into themselves a direct impression of what they hear or see and so can produce a direct copy of it: they acquire a 'negative' – a template or item of cultural software – from which they can produce a 'positive' (*ibid.*: 96).

People do not, of course, copy everything that they encounter in their associations. Tarde held that an individual may fail or refuse to imitate because some other model is more attractive and so 'neutralises' the propensity to imitate. Imitation is determined by the opportunities available in a person's patterns of association and the attractive valencies attached to particular others and their actions. These valencies are positive factors such as attractions towards those admired or identified with, and negative factors such as dislike of those towards whom there is prejudice or bias on grounds of class, race, or gender (Tarde 1890). While an infant is a pure automaton, tending to imitate everything, maturation involves an accumulation of models, templates, and sets of valencies that give the capacity for autonomous choice from among the many possibilities (Tarde 1898b: 99).

It is the 'collective forces' or tendencies generated by the circulation of collective representations that produce the tendencies and dispositions that motivate individuals to act in one way or another (Durkheim 1897: 299). These forces – the 'currents' of opinion and feeling that circulate through a society – affect individuals from the 'outside'. Each individual receives representations (often contradictory) from those with whom he or she associates. These representations combine and recombine with each other in the individual minds, where they may generate novel ideas and are reconciled into tendencies of action or inaction (*ibid.*: 310–11).

Tarde saw the spread of ideas and practices through 'rays' of imitation and chains of influence. These originate in particular individuals and constitute the social world as a network of interweaving and intersecting influences divided into zones of 'imitative radiation' (Tarde 1898a). The structure of such a network depends upon the distribution of attractions and repulsions among its individual members. The strength of the influences focused on a particular individual depends on the number of positive influences and the presence of countervailing or repulsive influences. Thus, innovations can spread 'contagiously' or they may fail or rapidly disappear, depending on the channels of influence possible (Rogers 1962; Coleman *et al.* 1966). The diffusion of ideas through a network shapes the mental contents that combine to constitute the social mind and to form states of opinion (Tarde 1901).

The cultural heritage is rarely uniform or static. The members of a society are each involved in numerous intersecting chains of transmission, and both errors and innovations can occur at each link in the chain of transmission. Cultural meanings mutate as they pass from one person to another, and the resulting mentality will, to a greater or lesser extent, be diverse and contradictory, in a state of constant flux. Where consensus exists, it is likely to be partial and precarious unless strongly reinforced by ritualised mechanisms of reproduction and strong mechanisms of legitimation. Organised instruction and the ceremonial repetition of narratives, for example, may involve rhythmic or mnemonic devices that help to ensure their accurate and unaltered reproduction. The attachment of strong sanctions to effective storytelling will further reinforce this (Vansina 1961: 31–8). Where these mechanisms are weak or absent, consensus will be weaker or more limited, and cultural flux will be more apparent. A cultural heritage will, therefore, tend to change continually over time, though at varying rates of change.

Cultural differentiation and diversity

The ideas of culture and enculturation developed initially as accounts of 'national culture' and national character. National cultures were seen as resulting from the fusion of formerly separate and autonomous local cultures as patterns of communication and systems of activities were extended along with the establishment of territorial boundaries and state systems. Cooley (1909), for example, held that communication is constrained by the territorial extent of interaction and association, and for much of human history the limited territorial extent of human groups meant that communication was confined to relatively localised face-to-face contexts. The introduction of writing, printing, postage, mechanised transport, and electronic media made possible the building of more extensive chains of communication across larger spaces and allowed communication to occur with far greater rapidity and over much greater distances. Immediate face-to-face communication was supplemented by mediated and more extended communication. Cultural areas thereby became more extensive and, with the formation of nation-states, took on a 'national' form.

For Cooley, these extended forms of communication at a national level were the basis on which 'public opinion' could be formed as a distinctive aspect of culture concerned with 'national' matters. In the large, extended masses that comprise modern national societies, opinion is no longer tied exclusively to unreflective custom and tradition, but can embody a wider concern for public affairs and a 'democratic mind' that allows more rational reflection on established institutions and practices (Cooley 1909: 107 ff). While Cooley may have drawn rather optimistic views about the 'mature political judgement' of the masses, he correctly traced a growth of rationality and conscious self-determination in public opinion to the changing structure of social interaction and communication and the 'larger mind' that this generates.

Much cultural analysis has tended to take British, French, German, and other national cultures as a focus. A number of early cultural analysts, however, recognised that these are invariably embedded in wider systems of meaning resulting from transnational interchanges and processes of diffusion. A recognition of the importance of transnational communication in European systems led to the view that many of the national cultures of Europe could be seen as elements in a looser and more extensive 'European' or 'Western' culture that differed from 'Oriental', 'Slavic', and 'Eastern' cultures (Spengler 1918–22; see also Toynbee 1934–9; Huntington 1996). The growth of transnational political and cultural integration was seen as indicating a decline in national culture and a growing 'cosmopolitan' outlook (Branford 1916) with significant consequences for conceptions of citizenship (Hobhouse 1911; and see the rediscovery of this idea in Beck 2006).

Much greater attention has been given to the internal differentiation of national cultures. Although cultural traits may be widely shared among the members of a national society, individual minds are formed on the basis of patterns of differential association (Sutherland 1939) that sustain more or less dense clusters of intercommunication. A national language, for example, may exist in numerous local and regional dialects, each characterised by its own vocabulary, style, and grammatical forms. More generally, cultures tend to be differentiated around the varying experiences of their members as they enter into structurally specific spheres of association with their distinctive clusters of cultural elements. Cultural forms may therefore be organised around distinct patterns of association as partially autonomous 'subcultures' linked to class, ethnic, gender, and other aspects of social experience. Variant forms of the more widely shared cultural meanings can be maintained and distinctive and specific meanings formed within these cultural formations.

The idea of the subculture developed from the 1940s to refer to these cultural variations within a population (Lee 1945; Gordon 1947; Komarovsky and Sargent 1949). Subcultures are distinct and relatively autonomous cultural pools of meaning on the basis of 'smaller, more localised and differentiated structures, within one or other of the larger cultural networks' (Clarke et al. 1976: 13). They are structurally distinct 'sub-universes of meaning' (Berger and Luckmann 1966: 85) and are sustained by, and in turn sustain, specific yet intersecting networks of social relations and patterns of individual and collective action. Subcultures are associated with particular subgroups within a population and occur wherever the differential association of subgroups leads to a differentiation of opportunities and interests that generates specific cultural traits and orientations. Commonalities of experience and, therefore, of memory occur by religion, class, and nation, where collective mentality and memory are due to frequent and recurrent association with particular others and not simply to their membership in a social category. Subgroups can develop distinctive ways of thinking, acting, and feeling organised around specific 'focal concerns' (Miller 1958) that underpin variant norms and values and that enjoin, encourage, or permit activities that are different from, and often deviant from, the standpoint of the overarching cultures.

Subcultures may arise within a particular parent culture through a differentiation of association and experience within its corresponding social structure. Examples might be the occupational subcultures of isolated mining and fishing communities and the subcultures of segregated or excluded religious communities. Other subcultures may originate outside the parent culture. This might be the case with second or subsequent generations of migrants who have maintained cultural traits from the original migrants. Subcultures may alter because of the influence of a dominant, mainstream culture or other subcultures. Cultural variations may become so great that a variant becomes, in effect, a distinctive culture, especially where a degree of physical separation occurs. Thus, French, Spanish, and Italian all became distinctive languages from their origins as dialect variants of Latin as a result of the migration and territorial separation of their speech populations within Europe. It is on the basis of such linguistic differences that wider 'national' differences eventually developed.

Early work on subcultures explored the 'delinquent' subcultures of young, working-class males in street and neighbourhood gangs. Gang behaviour was seen as an expression of adherence to values and norms that diverge from mainstream middle- and working-class values and through which gang members pursue their distinctive goals and way of life (Cohen 1955; Cloward and Ohlin 1960; see also Yinger 1960). Various other subcultures of criminal and deviant groups were identified on the basis of their differential patterns of association (Downes 1966: 9). In the mid-twentieth century, Clarke and his colleagues documented the existence of distinctive youth subcultures, rooted in the generational experiences of working- and middle-class life. Youth cultures share cultural elements with the mainstream culture but express these differently and combine them with other elements specific to their class contexts (Clarke *et al.* 1976: 53; Murdock and McCron 1976). Working-class youth cultures were organised around specific focal concerns and carried a number of more or less transient cultural 'styles', such as those of the 'Teds', 'Mods', and others, relating to clothes, posture, speech, leisure, etc. (Hebdidge 1979).

Subcultures remain integral parts of wider parent cultures, and intersecting clusters of association bring subcultures and mainstream cultures into complex relations. A subculture may be constructed in relation to – and perhaps in opposition to – mainstream values and styles, the subculture being an intentional construction of difference or resistance. This may involve what has been referred to as a 'value stretch', a situation in which subcultural values are formed as stretched, exaggerated, or extreme variants of the dominant values (Rodman 1965). A culture may thereby include certain 'subterranean values' that are permitted expression in certain circumstances but are given especially high priority within certain subcultures (Matza and Sykes 1961). Masculinity, for example, may be a widely held value that is interpreted in particularly hard and aggressive ways by those in certain subgroups. Similarly, leisure values of hedonism and excitement may be held in check in normal, everyday life but be permitted full expression at other times (Young 1971a).

Subcultures are nested in and overlap with larger environing cultures. Thus, a participant in a criminal subculture may also be a member of the working-class subculture within which it is embedded and of larger regional and national cultures. It is equally possible, however, for different subcultures to co-exist within the same physical space yet have only minimal interconnections because of their distinct networks of differential association. Thus, migrant ethnic groups may maintain their inherited cultural traditions through the perpetuation of reciprocal patterns of exclusion and closure directed against other migrants and representatives of the dominant culture. Such a subcultural enclave may show little influence from wider cultural forces. In other circumstances, of course, associational patterns may comprise an 'ethnic melting pot' and generate a great deal of cultural penetration and overlap with more established migrants and their descendants. Cultures must, therefore, be seen as 'complex and many sided, including a wide variety of interrelated traditions' (Matza 1964: 37, 60), as disparate and, perhaps, contradictory manifolds that contain both dominant and subterranean traditions and numerous differentiated elements, some traditions and elements being formed into more or less autonomous subcultures sustained by the differential association of the participants.

Cultures, then, exist as complex hierarchies of levels. They are dispersed systems of differentiated and interpenetrating bodies of knowledge, customs, and traditions. No one level can be regarded as fundamental or as providing the base point from which others can be seen as 'sub-' or 'supra-'. Such terms make sense only in very concrete contexts, and what is subcultural in one context may be supracultural in another. A working-class culture, for example, may be considered as a subculture of an overarching national culture, but also as a parental culture for various adolescent and delinquent subcultures. The key question in cultural analysis and in using these terms, therefore, is to identify the natural boundaries of the particular cultural area under consideration, recognising that such boundaries do not rest upon hermetically sealed barriers to association and communication. Cultural influences invariably flow across apparent social boundaries. This is especially apparent in the growth of transnational cultural connections that result from the globalisation of social relations and practices. National cultures become less distinct as cultural units: they show lower levels of integration and fewer signs of unity, becoming embedded in transnational processes that tie their elements differentially into global cultural structures (Lash and Urry 1994).

Symbolic systems and cultural codes

Once the sociological view of culture had been established by Tylor and the processes of cultural organisation and enculturation had begun to be explored, attention also turned to the need to analyse cultural elements themselves and their forms of combination. Pioneering attempts at this were analyses of language as a system of words connected through rules of grammar and meaning into coherent utterances and forms of discourse. De Saussure (1916) drew on these ideas as a means for constituting a general theory of cultural signs that he called semiology and that he saw as a contribution to the emerging science of collective mentality. Independently of this, Peirce (1877; 1878) had set out a pragmatist view of cultural signs that he called semiotics and that he saw as contributing to a symbolic interactionist account of communication.

Communicated thoughts are more or less complex combinations of symbols. The social evolutionist Keller (1915) took the radical step of seeing the symbol as analogous to the recently discovered gene. The biologist Alfred Emerson also took this view in private discussions with Parsons, who developed the idea that where the gene is the unit of heredity in biological systems, the symbol is the unit of inheritance in cultural systems. The symbol is an 'internalized object ... which can be transmitted with minimal change from one personality to another' (Parsons and Bales 1956: 397). In apparent ignorance of these earlier views, the biologist Dawkins (1976) took up the analogy and argued that the basic unit of cultural transmission is the 'meme', a suggestion enthusiastically taken up by advocates of so-called memetics (Blackmore 1999). This extension of the basic analogy, however, depends on a spurious parallel. Where the sign or symbol is a discrete and precise cultural element, a 'meme' has been claimed to be anything from a single letter of the alphabet to a whole song or complex text. Dawkins' argument can more realistically be seen as a partial and limited restatement of the earlier thesis of cultural transmission already considered.

Far more productive have been those writers who have relied on the narrower idea of the sign or symbol. Lévi-Strauss (1958; 1960) specifically returned to Saussure's use of the linguistic sign – the word – as the model for all cultural signs and developed a general theory, structuralism, that could show the grammatical and lexicographical rules through which the cultural discourses of myth and religion are organised through symbolic communication. Saussure's work had developed the pioneering linguistic ideas of Humboldt (1836: 54, 214), who had recognised that a language comprises two distinct elements. These were the internal or 'inner form' of mental processes that comprise the intellectual meanings of 'thought' and the external or 'sound form' through which these are made perceptible to the senses of others as sounds. The language of a society comprises its culturally specific system of ideas and sounds. Saussure summarised this in the claim that language is the use of vocal signs to convey messages. Aiming to distinguish the cultural aspect of language from the purely physiological aspects of the human faculty of speech, he saw linguistic semiology as the science of the specifically *social* fact of spoken communication.

Communication depends on the individual capacity for thought, itself a product of linguistic rules and conventions. Human consciousness is shapeless and indistinct without language, and it is only through the possession of a language that people are able to formulate meanings and to think creatively. The concepts used to organise thought are not formed extra-linguistically and only then expressed in language. Rather, the linguistic form is a condition for the formation of concepts (von Humboldt 1836: 214).[10] Language constitutes cultural contents in individual minds and is the mechanism of cultural transmission. It is language that unites the shapeless stream of consciousness with specific sounds and so allows the contents of consciousness to be manipulated as 'ideas' in the individual mind and so to be communicated from one person to another (Saussure 1916: 111–12). Thought, as argued by Sapir and Whorf, is the silent use of language, and the use of language is, in a real sense, 'communal thinking with others' (von Humboldt 1836: 27).

Language exists in the two dimensions that Saussure referred to as the 'diachronic' and the 'synchronic'.[11] Diachronic analysis is concerned with historical changes in language and had been the exclusive topic of many descriptive linguistic studies in the nineteenth century. It was the basis, for example, of the long debate on the origin and development of the Indo-European languages (Meillet 1903; Renfrew 1987; Mallory 1991; Anthony 2006). On a micro-level, diachronic analysis focuses on the individual speech acts (*paroles*) through which language is used to communicate particular ideas. Oral and written speech involve the formation of sequential or spatial combinations of linguistic elements to convey messages from one individual speaker to another. Each individual communicative act involves a selection and mental combination of linguistic signs from the vast pool of possibilities inherent in the language. Language use is creative and speech can generate an infinite number of combinations from a finite number of elements.

Recognition of synchronic or 'structural' analysis was Saussure's most distinctive innovation. This focuses on the 'social fact' of language or 'tongue' (*langue*).[12] A tongue is a linguistic system as it exists at a particular moment and from which diachronic combinations of signs are drawn. A tongue is the collective property of a 'speaking mass' (*masse parlante*).[13] It is a linguistic 'code' comprising the 'collection of necessary conventions that have been adopted by a social body' (Saussure 1916: 9), and a synchronic analysis of a tongue is, at its most general, a study of the collective rules and principles that comprise the 'grammar' govern-ing the use of a specific set of linguistic signs. A grammar encompasses the morphology, syntax, and lexicography (vocabulary) of a language and permits the members of the social body to exercise their faculties of speech. As shared social facts, tongues consist of 'interpersonal signs', and understanding a newly encountered sign involves relating it to other signs that are already known and understood through processes of coding and decoding (Morris 1964: 20–1).

A linguistic code is distributed among the individuals that comprise the speaking mass: it is a 'social product deposited in the brain of each individual' (Saussure 1916: 23, 77). It exists only in the separate minds of the constituent individuals and in the textual records (such as books of grammar) that these individuals produce in their attempts to reflect on their own language. It both constrains and enables the creativity of the members of the speaking mass. The variant and fragmentary 'copies' that each individual possesses are, from the standpoints of the individuals, the necessary conditions for any individual act of speaking.

From a diachronic point of view, linguistic codes are seen to be highly 'mutable'. In using a language, its speakers both reproduce and transform it (Freyer 1924: 87). Both representations and their sound images tend to be transformed very slowly, over the long term, as small, and generally unintended, innovations and 'mistakes' accumulate across the speaking mass and become sedimented as 'given', taken-for-granted elements in the shared linguistic code. As such, tongue is both an instrument and a product of speech (Barthes 1964: 16): speech is possible only because a tongue provides the means on which speech can draw; and speech is the means through which modifications to its rules are made.

Saussure referred to the 'inner' collective representation or concept as the 'signified', while the 'external' sound image or sign-vehicle (com-monly termed the 'word') is the 'signifier'.[14] It is the signifier, as a pat-tern of sounds, that allows representations to be communicated vocally from one person to another. One speaks and another hears, and it is the 'psychological imprint of the sound' on the mind of an individual, the impression made by a sound on the senses, that allows a heard sound to generate or conjure up a particular idea (Saussure 1916: 66). Signifiers exist on what Hjelmslev (1943) called the 'plane of expres-sion'. Signifieds, on the other hand, exist on the 'plane of content' and embody specific cognitive and emotional meaning. Language is, there-fore, a process of 'signification': the signifier indicates or evokes a signi-fied concept or meaning (Barthes 1964: 48). This meaningful binding of a signifier to a signified is why Mead referred to the sign as a 'signifi-cant symbol' (Mead 1927: 44–5).

The link between a signifier and a signified is logically 'arbitrary' or contingent because it is purely conventional: there is no intrinsic or necessary link between a signifier and its meaning. Speakers could, in principle, use any one of a number of alternative words or sounds to express a particular idea. However, concepts do not derive their meaning simply from their use to refer to external objects. A symbol acquires value or meaning because of the culturally defined ways in which it is used by a speaking mass. Speakers are creative and can 'freely, actively, and arbitrarily' bestow value or meaning upon things (White 1949: 29). This creativity is constrained only by the linguistic code that speakers have acquired as members of their society. It is only by using the signifiers defined in the particular rules and conventions of their language that they can be understood by the others they encounter. The rules and conventions of the code are inherited as social facts, and their socially sanctioned character constitutes the logically arbitrary features of signification as obligatory or necessary for socialised speakers. The actual choice of signs in communicative interaction is not, therefore, arbitrary for any individual speaker of a language.

Mead followed Peirce in seeing the meanings communicated in interaction not as mere abstractions but as dependent on the contexts of their use. The shared possession of a linguistic code allows the members of a society to understand each other, through coding and decoding practices – but it is also necessary for the participants in a communicative encounter to establish a reciprocal orientation towards each other. Each must take the attitude of the other towards his or her own communicated signs as they negotiate a shared definition of the situation (Mead 1927: 47). In using a word such as 'dog', a speaker assumes that it will evoke the same range of responses in the minds of others as it does in him or herself (*ibid.*: 71; and see also Parsons 1953). The meaning of a sign is found in its pragmatic relevance to an actor, and the situated meaning of a concept consists of the tendencies of those interacting to respond to it in one way rather than another.

Bernstein shared Saussure's view of cultural codes as central factors in the transmission of cultures, showing that linguistic codes are articulated into the 'speech codes' through which actual discursive utterances are formulated in *parole* or linguistic performance. The effects of particular speech codes depend on how they are embedded in particular educational practices that are themselves governed by specific 'educational-knowledge codes'. These are the codes through which curriculum and pedagogy are organised in schools. They organise the ways in which words and phrases are combined into the organised discourse of education and are an integral aspect of its power relations (Bernstein 1971;

1996). The 'decoding' of school knowledge (in 'learning') depends upon the possession of an appropriate communicative *competence*, an ability or capacity to 'understand' what is said and implied in a particular situation and, therefore, to learn from it. This competence rests on the particular cultural codes acquired during socialisation.

Lévi-Strauss used this idea in the four volumes of his *Mythologiques* (1964; 1967; 1968; 1971), where he explored the myths of central Brazil and neighbouring tribal areas. He saw myths as collective attempts to make sense of the world and held that the various myth narratives of a particular cultural area (such as those of the Indians of central South America) will all disclose the use of a cultural code specific to the population living there. The code reflects the grammar and range of meanings available in the language(s) of that speaking mass. He saw mythical thinking – like all thinking – as dialectical. In myths people identify and resolve dualisms, with each resolution becoming an element in a new dualism. Lévi-Strauss's later studies ranged increasingly widely as he drew his examples from many different cultural areas.[15] The purpose behind this extension of the method beyond a particular cultural area reflected Lévi-Strauss's view that the human mind operates according to certain universal mental principles that constitute a universal code for all myths: the dialectical structure of mythical thinking, he held, is a consequence of the binary structure and operation of the human brain. Not all structuralists have followed Lévi-Strauss in this final step. Barthes held that primary level myths also draw on secondary codes that are specific to particular activities or functions. Though these codes may sometimes relate to universal or very general aspects of human existence, their form and content are always specific to a cultural area and its primary cultural code.

Barthes (1964) extended this approach to the discourses and texts of politics, economics, and the mass media. He argued that symbolic representations can have a variety of external physical forms of expression. In addition to the spoken word, symbols can be signified as marks, alphabetical writing, military semaphores, and Morse code, as well as through the artefacts and activities involved in religious rites, interactional deference, economic production, and other social activities. Just as the analysis of speech may be extended to writing, so semiological analysis may be extended from linguistic communication to communication through the compilation of symbolic messages and narratives through religion and mythology, mass media advertising imagery, the gestures and road markings of the highway code, and numerous other cultural codes that permeate everyday life. Through these ideas it became possible to uncover the processes of 'coding' and decoding through which cultural and subcultural values and themes are formed and sustained

(Hall 1973). Lévi-Strauss identified gustatory, astronomical, and cosmographic codes within South America. In contemporary Western societies, Barthes identified garment, fashion, furniture, and architectural codes. From a different basis, Luhmann (1970; 1975) recognised monetary and power codes, also recognised by Parsons (Parsons and Smelser 1956; Parsons 1963b), as well as legal, religious, and mass media codes (Luhmann 1965; 1996). The particular type and numbers of codes within any cultural area reflects the differentiation of distinct cultural spheres and subcultures.[16]

The key assumption behind a structural analysis of myth is that each myth can be interpreted in association with similar and related myths, which may then disclose a common set of 'hidden' meanings. Particular sets of myths, drawing on a variety of codes, exist as permutations of these common themes and elements (Lévi-Strauss 1964: 77, 136), and myth narratives offer a variety of alternative and complementary ways of thinking about common issues. Thus, human relations of sexuality, friendship, and status may all be represented, in transposed ways, as relations among animals, types of food, sounds, plants, landscape features, and so on (Leach 1970: 66). By identifying the myths of a corpus as permutations or transformations of similar elements, a structural analysis can uncover 'deep' messages that are 'absent' from the surface narratives of any particular myth.

A hidden message in a corpus of myths, Lévi-Strauss argued, is not to be seen as a historically original form of the narrative that has subsequently spread through a cultural area. Myth diffusion undoubtedly does occur, but it is not the process that interests Lévi-Strauss. The deep structure of a set of myths is, rather, a mental structure presupposed in all the variant forms. This hidden message is not, in general, immediately accessible in consciousness to the people who learn and transmit the myth, though they may be able to access its elements at an unconscious level. As an unconscious mode of thinking, the hidden message drives the production of further myth narratives and informs the practical activities and relations into which people enter. Lévi-Strauss owes a great deal to the psychoanalytic interpretation of dreams and dream narratives, which Freud (1900) had seen as an expression of repressed unconscious desires. He had adopted Jakobson's argument that the mind, as a brain, operates digitally through the combination of binary oppositions. The permutations and transformations that he produced in his studies were all organised around such dichotomies. While this may, indeed, be an important aspect of human thinking, thought is not merely digital, and the messages disclosed by Lévi-Strauss actually point to more complex modes of thought.

The hidden message behind a myth corpus is a 'poetic' truth that contains and may embody contradictions that are difficult to resolve consciously or practically, or even to think about. This contradictory or paradoxical character of the hidden message was explored by Derrida and other 'post-structuralists' as something to be uncovered through a 'deconstruction'. This approach was termed 'post-structuralist' in order to distinguish its method of deconstruction from Lévi-Strauss's emphasis on the universal binary oppositions that he thought he could find in the biology of the brain. Central to this was the psychoanalytical method, and this method (though not specifically psychoanalytical explanations) was taken up most forcibly by Lacan (1966b) and Derrida (1967) in analyses of the virtual structure of texts. The structural analysis undertaken by Barthes was also less tied to the identification of binary oppositions, but Derrida's method takes this further. Post-structuralism, then, offers a more open and flexible method of structural analysis, though its mode of presentation often masks this simplicity of purpose in a complex verbiage.

Culture, discourse, and power

While many discussions of cultural formation have implied that culture is a free-floating sphere of ideas, this is not the case for the majority of cultural theorists. Montesquieu's earliest writings held that national cultures had to be seen in relation to the specific material conditions with which they are associated, and writers on subculture have shown their class, gender, and ethnic bases. The relation between cultural and other social factors was closely examined by Marx (1859b) and Marxist writers, who looked at this in terms of the relationship between class and consciousness. Mannheim (1925) generalised this from classes to all differentiated social groups: to generations and age groups (1927), associations and organisations, ethnic and national entities. Hartsock (1983b; 1983a) and Smith (1987; 1990) have explored its implications for gender divisions and identities, while Guha (1982; 1983) and others have extended it to colonial relations and 'subaltern' groups.

Cultural 'forms of social consciousness' are the 'sentiments, illusions, modes of thought and views of life' that comprise the 'psychology' of an epoch or social group (Marx 1852; Plekhanov 1908: 58). Marx also looked at the intellectual, aesthetic, and moral elaborations of this 'psychology' in the form of mythology, religion, and philosophy. These form part of a social 'superstructure' that reflects the economic 'base' of class and power relations. Thinking is determined by 'social being', by the 'real life process' of 'real, active men' that constitutes the material conditions of which consciousness is the 'reflex' (Marx and Engels 1846). Culture is an 'ideological' expression of those material conditions: it obscures or distorts them and contributes to their legitimation in the eyes of those who are disadvantaged by them (Plekhanov 1897). It was in this same vein that Barthes (1957: 149) saw the 'mythological' aspects of meanings as the outcome of narratives that 'naturalise' given social conditions and so provide the imagined circumstances in which people live their everyday lives (see also Althusser 1971). As such, they are discursive expressions of the power relations among groups (Foucault 1982).

Marxists have attempted to uncover the causal links in this relationship without resorting to a crude economic determinism that reduces culture to a mere reflex of economic conditions, reflecting Weber's (1904–5) argument that the link between social conditions and social consciousness is only ever one of 'elective affinity'. There is a 'causal link' between the technical level attained in material existence and the 'world outlook' of a society or group because social forms of thinking draw their content from the material or practical way of life that is the origin of all immediate experience (Plekhanov 1908: 60). Nevertheless, culture has an autonomy that allows it to exercise a reciprocal influence on the material way of life (Engels 1894). Economic conditions are, therefore, determining only 'in the last instance' (Engels 1890: 480–4).

The causal influence of material conditions is at its strongest in forms of society where the need to secure material subsistence is so pressing that the patterns, rhythms, and concerns of material life predominate over all others and the intellectual expression of any ideas beyond the purely practical can occur only 'after' material needs have been met. In exploring such intellectual concerns, the horizon of experience is limited by the restricted material conditions under which the members of the society live and it cannot easily escape these limitations.

In more complex forms of social life, the range of experience and, therefore, the possible sources of intellectual expression are more varied and so the possibilities for autonomous cultural expression are greater. An increased range of experience allows a greater variety of intellectual exploration and social imagining. Cultural expression can pursue a direction set by the particular cultural traditions or social heritage, and a number of different forms of expression may be associated with any particular set of material conditions. Nevertheless, cultural expression remains limited – ultimately and in the last instance – by these material conditions. The most general categories and forms of understanding are limited by the most general characteristics of the material mode of production.

These most general characteristics, for mainstream Marxism, are the class relations of the society. A class position comprises a particular structure of advantage and disadvantage that defines the range of experiences open to its occupants. Class-conditioned experiences and interests constitute the 'standpoints' from which people view the world and from which all refinements and elaborations of their 'class consciousness' take place (Plekhanov 1908: 73). Bernstein (not himself a Marxist) has shown that this applies to the speech codes through which forms of consciousness and discourse are organised. Speech codes are of two broad types according to whether they are 'restricted' or 'elaborated' in relation to the social contexts that give rise to them. Restricted codes require their users to select from a limited range of alternatives tied to particular social contexts for their meaning. They are associated with the segmented structures of mechanical solidarity found, in the contemporary world, in working-class communities. Elaborated codes, which allow their users to select from a much wider range of items and are more 'universalistic' in the meanings they convey, are associated with the differentiated structures of organic solidarity characteristic of middle-class ways of life and the dominant social institutions (Bernstein 1962). Those whose language use is structured by a restricted code, Bernstein argued, may experience difficulties in dealing with knowledge structured by an elaborated code, and he showed that the possibilities of inter-class communication are constrained by the differentiation of speech codes along class lines. This is a principal basis for the class differentiation of discourse and consciousness.

Lukács (1919) argued that the ideal typical consciousness that can be 'imputed' to a class, defined by the possibilities of action available to it, sets the limits on the possible consciousness that class members can attain.[17] The actual consciousness of class members at any particular time, as embodied in its collective mentality, is a partial realisation of this potential and combines its historically achieved insights into its own capacities with elements of the actual consciousness of other classes that have been imposed on it or otherwise acquired. All actual consciousness is therefore, to a greater or lesser degree, 'false consciousness'. It is adopted despite the fact that it does not correspond to the standpoint and interests of the class but has been imposed or inculcated by a dominant or more powerful class. Subordinate classes do not escape the categories and forms of their society, but adopt ideas that are not directly reflective of their *particular* standpoint. The subordinate class adopts, in whole or in part, the 'ruling ideas' (Marx and Engels 1846).[18] Gramsci (1929–35) saw this in terms of the 'dual consciousness' that combines autonomous perspectival insights with imposed, hegemonic distortions.

Lukács (1923b) saw the full extent of potential consciousness as only ever approximated in the greatest artistic and literary products and in religion, where those with the freedom to engage in intellectual exploration can escape the bonds of material constraint. Those forms of consciousness most closely linked to practical concerns (consumer preferences, attitudes towards property, etc.) are likely to be most tightly constrained by immediate class concerns. However, Alfred Weber (1920) and Mannheim (1932) made similar points about the ability of the relatively unattached intellectuals to, in part, transcend their class positions and social locations. The more complex and diverse a society, the more likely is it that some groups may be able to escape the limits of their situation and move towards a broader viewpoint by reflecting upon the partial viewpoints and the conditions responsible for them. In a process of 'dynamic synthesis' they can construct more generalised ideas.

In this chapter I have set out the concept of culture that developed in sociology and related disciplines and that came to form a key principle in the construction of the leading conceptual frameworks of the social sciences. Human individuals are culturally formed through their membership in populations that constitute linguistic communities and that sustain a shared yet diverse and differentiated system of meanings into which newborn and developing members are socialised. Cultural systems are dispersed in individual minds and in material artefacts, and are communicated from individual to individual in chains of influence and dissemination. As such, cultures comprise collective forces that shape and control individual behaviour. Cultural formation and communication involves processes of encoding and decoding in terms of the shared linguistic and other symbolic codes that comprise a culture. Cultural codes are integral elements in structures of power and, as such, have an 'ideological' character as discursive forms of power relations.

3   Nature: Conditions and Constraints

Human beings are the products of their culture, but they are also the products of their nature. They exist as biological organisms that live in particular physical environments on which they depend and which they transform. Human behaviour cannot be understood without taking account of this natural basis, and some have argued that nature must be seen as the primary determinant of human behaviour. For these material determinists, culture is all-but irrelevant as human freedom of choice is so tightly constrained by the material conditions under which it is exercised. Against this, most cultural analysts have held that culture is able to transform nature through its 'cultivation'. Some have gone so far as to suggest that culture has the capacity to override nature altogether and that all human life is a result of processes of social construction operating alone. Neither form of determinism – material or cultural – can be sustained, and I seek to show in this chapter that social theorists have moved towards a recognition of the interdependence of nature and culture and an explanation of the mechanisms of interdependence.

Human beings exist and act within a geographical world – a world formed by global physical, chemical, and biological processes. This world comprises geological and landform structures together with the atmospheric, hydrospheric, lithospheric, and biotic systems that jointly set the natural conditions faced when acting. This geographical world is not primordially given, existing independently of human activities. It is encountered always as the outcome of the transformative capacity of prior human actions. The 'natural' world is a culturally formed nature, a nature that embodies, though rarely directly or transparently, the purposes and plans of human actors.[1] Thus, it must be seen not only as geophysical, geochemical, and geobiotic, but also as geocultural.

It would be more accurate to refer to nature as much more than a merely *geo*graphical world. The earth was formed within a developing solar system, and terrestrial physical, chemical, and biological processes are influenced by processes in that wider solar system. There are, for example, gravitational effects on geomorphology, radiation effects on global climate, and extra-terrestrial origins for many chemicals and, perhaps, even for life itself. Human activity is no longer confined to the earth: technological devices are sent to other planets, humans travel in space and visit the moon, and the possibility of extra-terrestrial settlement and expansion is becoming a reality (Dickens and Ormerod 2007). From this point of view, it would be more appropriate to describe the world as heliographic or even astronomical, rather than simply geographic. For most sociological purposes, however, extra-terrestrial influences can be treated as background influences that make themselves felt through terrestrial processes and a more precise terminology is both unnecessary and pedantic. I write, therefore, of the 'geographical' world, but with these qualifications in mind.

As an environment the world comprises the physical, chemical, and biological conditions that constitute the range of potential 'habitats' in which human existence is possible and that determine, to a greater or lesser extent, the kinds of activities and social relations that can be pursued. The possibilities for securing subsistence, shelter, and defence, for engaging in production, distribution, and consumption, and for participating in the myriad other activities that constitute a way of life depend upon the material resources and opportunities available in particular environments. Human activity within an environment produces the 'places' within which people live and through which their experiences of both the natural world and other people are organised. An investigation of the 'placing' of human activities within an overall geographical environment must consider the 'site' of settlements or activities and their 'situation' relative to both their proximate surroundings and their more distant environmental settings. It must also examine the particular ways of life engendered and sustained by this placing. A place, then, is somewhere a particular way of life is pursued, under definite environmental conditions, and that is the focus for the experiences of the people who live there. It is a location constituted through human practices that has a material base and is an experienced and imagined relational structure (Casey 1993; 1997; Pred 1986).

As a product of nature, the human body has definite biological characteristics and is often considered, along with the physical environment, as something immutable and to which social forces must simply adapt. A key question, then, is the extent to which the body can be shaped and transformed by those social forces: are human activities the product of 'nature' or 'nurture'?

There has been a massive growth over the last two decades in publications variously described as 'sociobiology' or 'evolutionary psychology'. Basing their arguments on Darwinian evolutionary ideas (and generally laying exclusive claim to them) these theorists have set out a number of criticisms of what they see as the prevailing social science view of human behaviour. Established social science perspectives, it is argued, have ignored, or even suppressed, any recognition of the importance of the biological factor in human development (Pinker 1994: 411). Their counter-claim is that all human behaviour must be explained in terms of innate traits and capacities that have been shaped by processes of natural selection and adaptation to the material environment operating over millions of years. Culture and social structure, from this point of view, must be seen as mere derivatives of human biology.

This view has been advocated in evolutionary psychology and sociobiology as a more viable alternative to what is described as 'the standard social science model'. This was first characterised and named by Tooby and Cosmides (1992) and was seen as originating in the work of Durkheim. Tooby and Cosmides give only a single citation to one page in Durkheim (1893), and later writers have echoed the critique of social science by repeating or alluding to this same source. This suggests a reliance on Tooby and Cosmides rather than any direct consultation of the original source or, indeed, any other sociological work. Even the sustained criticisms made by Pinker (2002; 1994; 1997) are developed through innuendo rather than through critical engagement with sociological ideas. This lack of familiarity with what social scientists have actually written does not prevent Pinker from concluding that the 'standard social science model' has been the uncritically accepted paradigm for classical and post-structuralist sociologists alike.

Pinker argues that the standard social science model rests on a position of 'social constructionism' in which infants are seen as born without fixed instincts or character traits and as acquiring all their socially relevant attributes through socialisation into a given culture. Against this, Pinker argues that biology offers the most comprehensive basis for an explanation of human behaviour. This strong claim for biological determinism implies a denial of any significant autonomy for culture and social structure and sees sociology as virtually irrelevant in any account of human activity. In the long term, biology must always prevail as biological conditions are immutable and cultural factors are plastic. This assumption leads evolutionary psychologists to propose a universal human nature rooted in the fundamental genetic differences that distinguish human beings from other animals.

This argument misunderstands and misrepresents sociological arguments. Sociologists have argued for the importance of cultural factors and the social construction of bodies, but this does not mean that they regard these as the *only* important factor in human development. Claims for the importance of a sociological perspective do not require that human biology be disregarded. Almost all those sociologists who have considered the human body have treated culture and biology as interdependent factors in the development of human behaviour, neither being assumed capable of telling the whole story alone.

Environment and way of life

All living entities are bound to their physical environment. The recognition of human differences, physical and cultural, and of their geographical distribution led many early writers to seek out the causal connections that generate the observable associations between environmental conditions and ways of life. Some held that environmental features exert a direct causal effect on the physical and mental attributes of human individuals and that, for this reason, individuals must adjust to their environment and will change only when their environment changes. The main limitations to this adjustment were found in the more or less immutable characteristics inherited from previous generations. The evolutionary theory of Darwin (1859) recognised the relationship between variations in inherited characteristics and the selective or 'adaptive' constraints inherent in environmental conditions. The interplay and relative importance of 'heredity' and 'environment', of 'nature' and 'nurture', was much debated over the following century.

The idea of 'adaptation' to environmental conditions has been central to this discussion of heredity and environment. Adaptation is not a simple causal effect of exposure to a particular environment but is, rather, a matter of the 'fitness' or 'appropriateness' of individual attributes to a specific environment. Physical conditions are such that those with particular attributes are better able to prosper and reproduce. Adaptation occurs as individuals within a species inherit biological variations that improve their ability to survive in a particular environment.

Sociological forms of evolutionary theory, especially those described as 'Social Darwinist', recognised that only the 'fittest' (those who are adapted to their environment) will survive and prosper, but they saw fitness to survive as dependent also on social factors. The culture, social relations, and technology of a human population constitutes both a 'social heritage' that enhances or limits adaptation and a 'social environment' to which individuals must adapt. These social factors, however, were seen as providing the potential for human influence and control over the physical environment. Tools such as the plough, for example, could be used to transform the agricultural potential of a habitat and so allow a human population to survive and prosper under otherwise less favourable conditions. What Marxists refer to as the 'means of production' can comprehensively transform the capacity of social groups to live in and from particular environments.

The emerging disciplines of physical geography, geology, oceanography, and meteorology in the nineteenth and early twentieth centuries showed that rocks, landforms, climate, soils, and vegetation were causally connected and that their geographical distributions are the results of long-term processes of terrestrial development. Reports on the rocks and soils found in particular districts, combined with a growing awareness of the erosive effects of flood, rainfall, and glaciation, meant that nineteenth-century geologists could not fail to realise that systemic processes were at work and that the action of water and wind on the rock layers of the earth's surface had produced its distinctive geomorphology (Lyell 1830). Observation showed that these processes were cyclical or involved definite patterns of recurrence. Land is formed into mountain ranges and extensive plains that are subject to erosion by wind and water, with the eroded material being carried by rivers and deposited as sand or clay sediments that subsequently become compacted under intense heat and pressure to form hard 'metamorphic' rocks. Movements of the earth's surface uplift and fracture these rocks to produce mountain chains that are subject to renewed processes of erosion and deposition. This 'cycle of erosion' is variable across different terrains and is modified as a result of the specific local properties of arid, maritime, and other environmental zones.

Developing largely separately from geology, oceanography discovered processes at work within the water mass of the seas and explored the underlying rock of the seabed to produce accounts of the origins of islands and the evolution of coastlines that extended this understanding of physical change. This understanding was further complemented by work in meteorology and climatology that looked at atmospheric processes resulting from the movement, heating, and cooling of air masses. Local weather conditions and broad climatic variations were shown to intersect globally and over time, and these varying climatic effects were seen as the basis of the 'weathering' of the landscape by wind and rain. Weather and climate denude and shape the landscape in ways made possible by geology (see Monkhouse 1954). Classifications of plants, organisms, and soils, often stimulated by agricultural concerns, were the basis of a view of the land surface and its vegetation as a combined product of both geomorphology and climate.

By the middle of the twentieth century, geographers had arrived at a fully developmental understanding of the formation of mountains, river valleys and drainage systems, coastlines, and the 'solid' geology of land surfaces (e.g., Holmes 1944; Dury 1959; and the popularised accounts of British geology in Stamp 1946; Trueman 1949). Earth history had been shown to be the outcome of a sequence of variant and intersecting cycles of physical change. From the mid-twentieth century, this had begun to be reformed in recognition of the working of larger global processes. It came to be realised that the now-familiar processes of geomorphology and climate show a pattern that reflects physical variations at a global level. Soil and vegetation were recognised as influencing and being influenced by wider physical and organic processes, and these came to be recast, from the 1930s, in the idea of an 'ecosystem'. This provided a model of the superficial surfaces of the earth as zones or systems with dynamic properties of their own and as shaped by the effects of human activity on the earth. These zones gradually came to be seen as interdependent elements in a composite global ecology (see Trudgill 1977). At the same time, geomorphologists came to see continental land masses as vast rock plates that move across the earth as a result of a global circulation of convection currents that forces volcanic material to the surface along junctions between the plates. The new science of plate tectonics studied the thermal dynamics of the earth's mantle and the consequent 'continental drift' that produced not only earthquakes, tsunamis, and volcanic activity but also the processes of mountain uplift and faulting that are the central concerns of geomorphology (Tarling and Tarling 1971; drawing on the earlier suggestions of Wegener 1912).

The physical structure of the earth, then, is a global system of processes and not simply a collection of isolated cycles and events (see Summerfield 1991). This global awareness has also been reinforced by new understandings of the interdependence of atmospheric processes in different parts of the world. Studies of long-term global climate change, for example, have shown that periods of glaciation and aridity have been integral elements in shaping the global system, and, as a result, fundamental global shifts in climate have occurred. Most significantly, it has come to be realised that human activity is now having a major impact on global climate distribution and is likely to have major consequences for terrestrial environments in the near future. Thus, geomorphology and climate can be seen as forming a complex global system subject to constant change and driven by its internal processes (Moore et al. 1996).

Contrary to some recent claims (Catton and Dunlop 1978), social theorists have not ignored environmental conditions. While the separation of geography from sociology during their development may have led sociologists to concentrate their attention on cultural influences, a concern for nature and the environment never completely disappeared.

Early investigations by social theorists did, however, tend to take a rather simplistic view of the effects of environmental factors on human societies, generally focusing on the effects of a single factor – typically climate – seen as having direct and determinate consequences for human beings (see the overview in Thomas 1925: ch. 5). Aristotle and later Ibn Khaldun (1377) had suggested that the political superiority of the civilised world was due to the psychological advantages resulting from life in a temperate climate. Montesquieu (1748) was the first to develop this systematically as an account of climate and soil, seeing variations in cultural spirit between nations as results of variations in climate and other factors of nature. The influences of climate on blood flow, breathing, and nervous energy, he held, shape the body and its organs and determine the mental faculties and endowments of a people, giving them a distinctive 'spirit' or character. Assuming that climate directly determines character, a mapping of human populations by latitude and altitude into their climate zones would also map the resulting distribution of character types.

Montesquieu followed Aristotle in identifying three climate zones: the 'hot' (the torrid or tropical), the 'cold' (the frigid or polar), and the 'temperate'. The temperate climate found in much of Europe, he held, produces mentally active, emotionally phlegmatic, and courageous people. Although their emotional coolness means a lack of imagination and an aesthetic weakness, their courage makes them brave protectors and defenders of freedom. Montesquieu saw this temperate spirit as expressed in the progressive attitudes responsible for the institutions of liberalism and democracy. The emotional excess and the predisposition towards submissiveness and servitude that result from life in a hot climate, on the other hand, are expressed in political conservatism and a tendency to despotism.

Similar views were developed by other writers. Buckle (1857–61), for example, contrasted the lassitude of hot climates and the desultory habits of cold climates with the invigorating effects of a temperate climate. Similarly, Ratzel (1887–8: 36; see also Semple 1911) suggested that temperate climates are conducive to thrift and seriousness, while hot climates engender an easy-going emotionality. Peschel (1875: 315–17) drew different conclusions, holding that a subtropical climate is especially conducive to mental activity and intellectual speculation because the 'sultry hours' in the middle of the day make productive manual work impossible. This made the subtropical zones the seed beds of civilisation. This claim was echoed by Spencer (1873–93: vol. 1), who saw all the major civilisations as having originated in the tropics and concluded that humidity is more important than temperature: a warm and dry climate is far more conducive to both mental and manual effort than a warm and wet one. Some statistical studies claimed to show the impact of seasonal variations on human activities within the temperate zone. For example, the spring and summer months in Europe, when melancholy, restlessness, and irritability are especially marked, were held to be associated with higher rates of suicide, violent crime, rape, murder, riot, and illegitimate conception (Leftingwell 1892; Dexter 1904).

These suggestions were refined by Huntington (1915; 1924), who argued that the optimum daily temperature for both manual and mental activity is around 50°F and so the optimum working conditions are found where there are mild winters, summers that do not exceed 75°F, and continual but moderate storms and variations in weather.[2] Britain, Western Europe, and eastern and central United States correspond most closely to this optimum. Climate zones least suitable for sustained activity, Huntington held, are Amazonia, central and southern Africa, India, and South East Asia. Huntington saw climatic variations since the end of the last Ice Age as explaining why it was that ancient cultures had developed in areas that are now climatically 'unstimulating' (Huntington 1924: 295, Fig. 3; 358, Fig. 48). He went on to identify a global system of climatic zones or belts as contiguous tracts of land with similarities of climate, and therefore of vegetation (Huntington 1940: 73).

More sophisticated investigators had sought to uncover the mechanisms responsible for these effects. Reclus identified latitude and altitude as the crucial physical factors: latitude (a measure of inclination towards the sun) is the principal determinant of air temperature, while altitude determines both temperature and air pressure (Reclus 1905–8: vol. 1, 42; see also the later view in Lamb 1982: ch. 3). Ratzel argued that correlations between character and climatic zones could be explained by the acclimatisation or adaptation that results from living for long periods in a particular climate. Adaptation occurs through bodily changes and the formation of habits of behaviour, and this adaptation may limit long-range migration and settlement (see also Draper 1867–70: vol. 1). Ratzel saw these bodily changes as inheritable, relying on the Lamarckian view of the inheritance of acquired characteristics. Some subsequent writers even held that adaptations to a particular climate can be inherited as 'racial' characteristics (Le Bon 1895b: 11; Kidd 1898; Ripley 1899). While all such deterministic ideas have now been abandoned, it is not impossible that, over the very long run, some minor genetic traits that enhance adaptation may be selectively retained within a population and that the socialised habits acquired by a particular population will, indeed, be passed on from one generation to the next as part of its social heritage.

Despite their obvious problems, climate theories did prepare the way for more comprehensive and satisfactory theories of variations in environment and habitat. It is now generally recognised that climate is simply one variable factor in the complex ecological systems encountered by human beings. Igneous forces, the elevation, subsidence, faulting, and folding of rocks, the atmospheric phenomena of precipitation and wind that shape relief and surface geology, the solar heating of the atmosphere and the crust that produce changes in temperature and air pressure and generate climatic and weather effects, and the terrestrial forces of rotation and gravitation, all operate together to condition biological processes and so to form the surface of the earth into distinct zones with specific and distinctive physical characteristics (Bernard 1925). The causal effects of environmental conditions operate conjointly and interdependently, as ecological systems.

Reclus (1868; 1869) focused on climate, topography, and oceanic effects in his model of global geographical zones. Climates, following Aristotle, were classified into tropical, frigid, and temperate; topography was classified into plains, plateaux, and mountains; and oceanic effects were classified as maritime, insular, and continental. These three factors, Reclus argued, combine and intersect, as well as operating alongside such secondary factors as variations in soil and mineral resources and the effects of the 'subterranean forces' of volcanism and earthquakes. Global zones and the smaller tracts into which they are divided come to be characterised by particular types of minerals and soils. The minerals (coal, oil, metal ores, nitrates, etc.) are integral features of the rock types characteristic of a tract, while the soil types (the mix of alluvial deposits with sand, clay, and chalk as forms of tundra, podzol, laterite, and greyerth, etc.) are consequences of the climatic and hydrographic erosion of rocks. The climate and the fertility of the soil allows, encourages, or prevents the spread of vegetation of various kinds, while the pattern of vegetation is a powerful determinant of the distribution of animal species, including humans. Such biological systems comprise interdependent elements of flora (plants) and fauna (animals) – they are 'ecological' systems within a globally connected structure. As a result, the world is formed into a vast kaleidoscope of natural regions, each more or less conducive to particular ways of life.

Various attempts have been made to improve on Reclus and to identify the climate/vegetation zones that have prevailed in the crucial period of human history since the end of the last Ice Age. The classification most widely used today is that of Köppen (see Köppen and Geiger 1928), which has undergone a series of revisions since it was first published. This classification distinguishes five climatic zones: tropical humid, dry, moist mid-latitude (temperate), cold mid-latitude, and polar, to which has been added a 'highland' zone to recognise the effects of altitude. Subdivisions of these categories, reflecting variations in temperature and precipitation, have led to the overall categorisation of twenty-four climate zones now in standard use (Trewartha 1968; and see Huntington 1940: 573; Forde 1934: Fig. 2). This classification is often combined with separate classifications of soils and vegetation cover in order to produce geographical maps of the kind found in contemporary atlases. These typically focus on seven principal zones – rainforest, savannah, prairie, desert, woodland, taiga, and tundra – to which may be added various mixed and subtypes such as the tropical monsoon zones and the subtropical or 'Mediterranean' zones.

Febvre has summarised the broad features of this global distribution of ecosystems:

> In the centre is a forest vegetation, so overpowering that it stifles all life except its own, bordered by regions more suitable for human settlement. Then comes a gap, with the belt of sub-tropical deserts following on one another slantwise from continent to continent, beyond which possibilities of settlement again appear, gradually reach their maximum both in quality and variety, then fade away again in the frozen lands of the North and South. (Febvre 1922: 137)

Determinism and possibilism

Adaptation to environmental conditions, for many theorists, was understood in highly deterministic terms. It was seen as the passive response of organisms to material conditions. Natural forces were seen to operate directly on human bodies and minds to produce specific and environmentally invariant effects: people are born with and conditioned into temperaments and habits of acting that necessarily lead them to grow certain crops, raise certain animals, and construct certain types of dwelling. A one-to-one relationship between environmental conditions and way of life was assumed: human choice was seen as irrelevant, and a determinate and exact correlation between physical conditions and way of life was assumed.

Other writers have recognised that human activity had the potential to transform given environmental conditions and that environmental influences condition and limit social facts rather than determine them. This is even apparent in the arguments of Montesquieu. Much as he emphasised a climatic explanation of the spirit common to a population, he recognised that climate exercised its influence alongside 'moral' factors. These are the customs and practices that have been acquired and built up over previous generations under this self-same combination of determinants. Similarly, Reclus held that while human groups 'have been compelled to reflect the innumerable phenomena of the continental outline, their rivers and sea-coasts, and their circumjacent atmosphere', their modes of adaptation are long-term consequences of the interplay of human choices and will in the face of shifting environmental conditions. Thus, 'man is incessantly engaged in a conflict with the globe on which he dwells' (Reclus 1869: 435). Humans attempt to control natural forces but are also shaped by the tendency of these forces to sustain or undermine the choices made (Forde 1934: 3–7).

Even a strong determinist like Huntington recognised that climatic and other natural factors work alongside other factors to make outcomes less determinate. The failure of civilisation to develop in areas that were climatically favourable, for example, was seen as showing the effects of factors other than climate:

Even if our climate ideas are correct, it will still be true that the ordinary events of the historical record are due to the differing traits of races, the forces of economic pressure, the ambition of kings, the intrigues of statesmen, the zeal of religion, the jealousy of races, the rise of men of genius, the evolution of new political or social institutions, and other similar circumstances. (Huntington 1924: 369–70; and see Huntington 1945)

Despite his strong emphasis on now-discredited racial ideas, this statement shows that Huntington did not adopt a rigid environmental determinism. He noted, in particular, that the significance of climate varies with the state of cultural and technological development, and this led him to suggest that technology may be a means through which the effects of climate can be offset.

It was Vidal de la Blache, however, who advanced this view most systematically, arguing that adaptation occurs through the complex interplay of a number of factors:

every area with a given relief, location and climate, is a composite environment where groups of elements – indigenous, ephemeral, migratory or surviving from former ages – are concentrated, diverse but united by a common adaptation to the environment. (Vidal de la Blache 1922: 10–11)

Vidal held that human beings and the way of life they follow are to be seen among the 'elements' that mutually co-exist within this adaptive system. Plants, animals, and humans are active elements whose existence, activities, and interdependence transform the nature of the environment faced by each of the constituent elements. In the case of humans, hunting and agricultural activities can transform material circumstances through 'cultivation', but 'civilised' ways of life have greatly increased the human capacity to affect the environment. The means of technical intervention and the social capacity to employ them make human beings a major influence on the ability of all beings (humans included) to adapt to their environment. They are able to transform one 'natural economy' of plants, animals, and activities into another. Regions are not fixed and given but are the result of continual environmental transformation. For Vidal, geography deals not with a simple one-way determinism of physical conditions on human life but with a complex and dynamic ecological system of interdependent elements, mutually adapted and adapting to each other.

Lucien Febvre drew out the implications of this position by contrasting simplistic determinism with what he called 'possibilism'. He held that 'It is not true that four or five great geographic influences weigh on historic bodies with a rigid and uniform influence' (1922: 89–90). Rather, diverse geographical influences push people in various and often contradictory directions, while humans, as active agents 'endowed with initiative' (*ibid.*), attempt to resolve and mediate these influences through their actions. Thus, there *is* an effect of climate on human activities, but this is indirect rather than direct. What is crucial is the effect that climate has over time, especially over long periods of geological time, on other environmental factors to produce a topography of distinct zones, understood as 'climatico-botanical unities' (*ibid.*: 115) that shape the distribution of animal species and their varying chances of survival and prospering. Human beings construct their actions as more or less intelligent responses to their environmental conditions. An environment is a location in which various things are possible, but no one thing is uniquely determined, least of all by a single causal factor. It is for this reason that even a matter as simple as the distribution of population across the globe does not show a perfect correlation with the distribution of environmental conditions: there are 'favourable' zones with little or no population and 'unfavourable' ones that are occupied. There is no 'exclusive and tyrannical compulsion from external conditions' (*ibid.*: 172).

Causal mechanisms in nature must operate alongside human agency and choice and so everything 'bears the mark of contingency' (Vidal de la Blache 1917 cited in Febvre 1922: 144). 'Wherever "man" and "natural products" are concerned, the "idea" intervenes' and 'Between the desires and needs of man and everything in nature that can be utilized by him, beliefs, ideas, and customs interpose' (Febvre 1922: 167):

We admit regional frames in a general sense, but in the collection of physical features it represents we see only possibilities of action. (Febvre 1922: 173)

Human responses to environmental conditions depend on culturally shaped and socially structured choices that are able, within limits, to transform an environment and produce novel conditions for those who will act in future. The growth of technology and other cultural advances have increased the possibilities for human control and have allowed societies to achieve a degree of liberation from 'the tyranny of the natural regions' and have increased the autonomy of human choice and deliberation from their physical conditions:

the nature which intervenes to modify the existence of human societies is not a virgin nature, independent of all human contact; it is a nature already profoundly impregnated and modified by man. There is perpetual action and reaction. (*ibid.*: 361)

The role of technology was initially recognised in archaeological and anthropological arguments on 'material culture' and the 'stages' or 'ages' with which it is associated: such as the technological advances of the 'Iron Age' as against the 'Stone Age' (Lubbock 1865). Environmental conditions that result from technological intervention must subsequently be responded to in the same creative and socially constrained way as any 'primordial' environmental condition. This is the way that human societies have developed from the 'unconscious products' of nature found in the 'primitive' state to being the more or less conscious products of increasingly active and purposive agents.

When exploring beyond the limits of their immediate environment, human populations learned more about the world and began to introduce and develop ways of moderating the effects of the physical forces of nature (Reclus 1869: 467). Agriculture transforms nature by altering the fertility of the soil and by affecting the distribution of animal and vegetable species. Agricultural technologies such as the use of irrigation channels and wells, the drainage and reclamation of land from swamps, marshes, lakes, and inlets, and the building of dykes and embankments, modify the terrain and the range of cultivation. Weather forecasting and the ability to modify the effects of local climate through specific forms of cultivation allow societies to cope with potentially hostile conditions. Improvements in communication through the construction of canals, roads, and railways, using bridges, viaducts, and tunnels, allow improvements in trade that intensify and transform agriculture and the terrain. Last but not least, the industrial powers and manufacturing capacity introduced by machine technologies allows higher levels of autonomy than ever before (Reclus 1869: chs. 21–8).

The most systematic statement of this position is found in Marxist materialism. This asserts the dependence of consciousness and ideas on 'real individuals, their activity and the material conditions under which they live' (Marx and Engels 1846: Part I, 42). The claim was that the securing of material subsistence is the fundamental – infrastructural – element in human social activity: social structures originate in and are trans-formed through the life-processes of individuals 'as they operate, prod-uce materially, and hence as they work under definite material limits, presuppositions and conditions independent of their will' (*ibid.*: 46–7). By 'developing their material production and their material intercourse, [they] alter, along with this their real existence, their thinking and the products of their thinking' (*ibid.*: 47).

The basis of this claim is that 'men must be in a position to live in order to be able to "make history"' (*ibid.*: 48). People must eat, drink, and be clothed and housed if they are to engage in any other social activities. The production of subsistence is a need that 'must daily and hourly be fulfilled merely in order to sustain human life' (*ibid.*: 48). This production of the means of subsistence is conditioned by physical circumstances as these have been modified by human activity over the generations, and so any account must begin from the social activities through which people relate to nature. Any particular way of life depends upon the mainten-ance of a specific and 'corresponding' mode of production that is the basis of the 'mode of life'.

A mode of production combines specific 'productive forces' with defin-ite relations of production. The productive forces comprise labour power (characterised by its strength, skill, knowledge, etc., as embodied cap-acities), raw materials and other objects of labour, instruments or tools of production, and space.[3] They are the means through which nature is appropriated and transformed and comprise capacities or social powers of production organised in particular forms of allocation or division of labour and, thereby, of ownership. These technical and class relations of production are the means through which access to raw materials, tools, and products is regulated.

The mode of production within a specific environment has been con-ceptualised by Marxists as an 'infrastructure', and the overall structure of a society is seen as an articulation of this 'infrastructure' with a lar-ger and encompassing 'superstructure'. The superstructure comprises the representations, institutions, and relations through which political, legal, religious, and other social activities are organised. As I discuss in Chapters 4 and 6, the superstructure has a 'relative autonomy' and can exercise a reciprocal determining role on the mode of production. Because the effects of the superstructure are significantly determined by the infrastructure, however, Marxists have stressed that the latter is the ultimate determinant – the determinant 'in the last instance' of the overall structure (Althusser 1971: 129–30). For all their autonomy, the institutions of any society that continues to exist must be adapted to its material environment.

Material conditions set 'limits' to the variation in the social relations they can sustain and there is normally a 'correspondence' between infrastructure and superstructure: 'Given a certain level of development of the productive forces, or expansion of human power and its material extensions, a certain set of production relations, or social form, is appropriate as a framework for the use and further development of that power' (Cohen 1978: 97). Social determination is such that the productive forces 'select structures according to their capacity to promote development' of their productive powers (*ibid*.: 160, 162).

Marxism depicted a growing technological mastery of the material environment such that there can be a more intensive utilisation of its resources and an enhanced ability of human populations to adapt to a variety of environmental conditions. It was held that under some circumstances, as shown in Chapter 6, the productive forces can come into contradiction with the social relations that constrain them. When the social relations no longer allow the continued expansion of the productive forces, they become a 'fetter' on those forces, which can develop further only if the social relations are transformed (Marx and Engels 1846: 88–94).

An alternative view is found in theorists for whom technology itself may develop to the point at which its effects undermine the social relations of production and the associated superstructure. This was alluded to by Reclus (1869: 522), who saw early agriculture in the Middle East as having resulted in an over-farming that reduced the once fertile land to a desert. Similarly, he saw the Brazilian rain forest as being destroyed by farming. This view has been elaborated in recent writings on globalisation and the limits to growth. The growth in interregional linkages reinforces, and perhaps completes, the detachment of human activities from specific physical conditions and increased time-space distanciation makes it possible to transfer activities from one place to another without great regard for prevailing physical conditions. Beck (1986; 1988) has argued that the creation of a global ecological system in which regions have an increased autonomy from their environment creates conditions in which the very technology that produced that autonomy has itself become a source of global environmental risks.

What has been established, therefore, is that environmental conditions are 'systems of possibilities'. The causal mechanisms of nature are not absolute determinants – 'there is nothing synchronous, necessary or pre-determined in them – but constant variations and mutations, periods of dormancy and sudden awakenings' and all subject to subjectively mediated human activity (Febvre 1922: 181). Environmental zones vary in the possibilities that they open up, or close off, for human action.

Material conditions constrain the exercise of choice and the outcomes of those choices. They are crucial conditions for the practical success likely to follow from particular courses of action and, therefore, of the chances that those actions will be reproduced in the future. Human activity, especially as mediated by technology, can increase the range of possibilities through a technical mastery of nature to which, nevertheless, there may be definite limits.

Habitat, place, and way of life

This possibilism and a recognition of the transformative potential of productive activity was the basis for the most compelling accounts of the relationship between regional habitats and human ways of life. Initially found in the local and regional studies of Le Play (1855), an approach to these issues was systematically drawn out by Geddes and his associates (Geddes 1904b; 1905; 1915; Branford and Geddes 1919a; 1919b) and developed in the work of Herbertson (1905; Herbertson and Herbertson 1920) and Fleure (1918; 1919) and the 'ecological' studies of Semple (1911) and the Chicago sociologists (Park and Burgess 1925). A number of important regional 'community studies' developed this approach (Lynd and Lynd 1929; 1937; Williams 1956; 1963; Littlejohn 1963; Rees 1961; Dennis et al. 1956; Stacey 1960; and see the discussions in Frankenberg 1967; Vidich et al. 1971; Bell and Newby 1976). The development of large-scale survey research helped to undermine this style of work, resulting in a period in which the ideas of locality, region, and community were less central. Although most studies continued to be locality-based,[4] the location was treated as of secondary importance to the general processes of social change being investigated. Only from the late 1970s did the region and the community once again become prominent concepts (Massey 1978; 1984; Hudson 1986; 2001; Clout 2003).

Geddes set out a framework according to which the habitat in which people live shapes the subsistence activities they can undertake. The resulting work relations set constraints that limit the possible choices that can be made in other areas of life. The habitat is transformed through work and technology and sustains a particular way of life among a people. The cultural outlook that develops among the people is the basis on which they develop and transform their patterns of work and so transform the habitats in which they live. It is within their habitats that people can create a distinctive way of life.

People define the situations in which they live, and in giving meaning to the world around them, they accord a human significance to those aspects of interest or relevance. The objects and entities encountered and

experienced are defined through the cultural matrix shared with (
and enter into the collective activities through which people oper
their environment. The social heritage, therefore, becomes an ir....
part of the 'total environment' (MacIver and Page 1949: 117–18). This
total environment is, then, socially constructed, but it is not merely a
social construct any more than it is merely a physical reality. It is, nevertheless, 'man-made':

> When man turns a territory into a country or a plot of earth into a home, he is
> fusing into one the physical and the social environment. His own activity, as
> he clears and cultivates the spoil, dams rivers, builds roadways, and so on, in
> time makes it impossible to tell where the geographical or nature-given envir-
> onment ends and the man-made environment begins. The physical becomes
> at the same time the symbol of the social. It is charged with human memories,
> human traditions, human values. Much of it becomes the external aspect of
> social institutions. (MacIver and Page 1949: 118)

It is in this way that a habitat becomes a true 'place'. Phenomenologically,
'place' is the location of specific human experiences. It is a location
defined by its geological and climatic distinctiveness, with more or less
clearly defined boundaries and economic and cultural particularities. As
such, it is a 'humanly meaningful loci of spatial specificity' (Massey and
Thrift 2003: 275). The sense of place is the basis for a sense of 'community' within a particular location. It is the lived environment in which
people undertake their everyday activities and in which they construct
and reconstruct the meanings through which they live these activities.

For each individual, their own body is the focus of 'their' place – it
is the standpoint from which their subjective experiences originate and
from which they look out across their place to its boundaries. It was the
view of Husserl that the body provides a sense of 'here' and of the surroundings and environs within which an individual occupies a focal position. 'Here' is the centre of a person's experience of their surroundings,
the place from which they look out to the wider world (Husserl 1905;
1907; and see Merleau-Ponty 1945). Place is the material location of
a person's being-in-the-world. It is a centre of experience and memory
within which arise forms of bodily activity, cognitive and normative gratification, and emotional attachment:

> Space opens out before the body and is differentiable in terms of front/back;
> left/right; vertical/horizontal; within hearing/beyond hearing; within sight/
> beyond sight; here/there polarities. (Tilley 1994)

Individuals see their world from the standpoint of their own location
within it. They perceive, identify, and classify its features to form their
definitions of their situations (Golledge and Stimson 1987; Kitchin and

Blades 2001), and these cognitive schema become the basis on which they organise their actions in relation to their world. They understand their environment in terms of personal mental maps that emphasise those features that are important and salient to them (Gould and White 1974).

In towns and cities, the street becomes an immediate focus of everyday social activity. It is a place of movement and circulation and of transient encounters. It is a place of consumption and its cafes and bars develop as more regular meeting places. As a place for strolling and for the passive contemplation of displayed merchandise in shops, the majority of its human encounters have a transient and anonymous character (Simmel 1903; Benjamin 1940). As a lifeworld, however, it is increasingly dominated by the car and the consequent requirements for signage, routing, and parking, as well as by such distinctively urban phenomena as congestion and pollution (Buchanan 1963).

Beyond the house, neighbourhood, street, and place of work is the wider territory that forms the indeterminate boundary of a place (Casey 1993: 293). A familiar territory has distinctive and meaningful characteristics for those in a particular place. The territory occupied by a population and in which they build their lifeworld is always encountered and experienced as a cultured or 'cultivated' environment and not as a primordial physical environment (Sauer 1925). The environment of a population is perceived by its members as a 'landscape'. A sense of place is, through a 'landscape gaze', the basis of an aesthetic conceptualisation rooted in a relativistic and perspectival way of seeing the world (Tuan 1977; Cosgrove 1984; see also Gregory 1994; Sharma 1995). Cultural representations of a landscape – landscape imaginaries – are integral elements in wider frameworks of signification through which people give meaning to the places in which they live, and in complex societies landscape imaginaries are ideological expressions of gendered, classed, and racialised relations (Cosgrove 1993; 2001). As a humanised environment the cultural landscape, rural and urban, is a continually developing and changing product of human activity as it adapts a population to the conditions encountered (Darby 1951; Hoskins 1955).

Geddes (1915) was a pioneer analyst of the consequences of urbanisation. Migration into expanding urban areas results in a cultural mixing of those from diverse rural environments, generating a distinctive and dynamic cultural creativity: 'synergy' was the term for this introduced by Geddes. The synergy of a city gives it a distinctive spirit that comprises its capacity to shape perceptions and the activities they inform. Writers of the Chicago school explored the internal differentiation of large cities into diverse urban habitats. Localities with communal solidarity are incorporated into the expanding city and are transformed into districts and suburbs in which the mobility of the city population results in a 'loss of community'. Such impersonal localities are places of irregular and transient encounters. Migrants into large cities such as Chicago settled where their class or ethnic compatriots had already settled and each 'zone' developed, through differential association, its own cultural, political, and economic characteristics and communal solidarity or lack of solidarity (Park and Burgess 1925).

The places in which people live cluster together as 'regions', an idea explored in the writings of the Vidalians in France and in classic formulations by Hartshorne (1939) and Dickinson (1947). As they grow in size, cities become dominating centres of wider areas, and Fawcett (1919) identified regions by the dominance of particular large cities as the focus for economic activity. Dickinson, his student, held that a region is more than simply a contiguous collection of environmentally conditioned activities. It is an area where interdependent social factors result in a homogeneity of social conditions. Its residents follow common and interrelated economic activities, often confined within the region itself, and they participate in a regional system of politics. As a more or less distinct population grouping within a larger population it may sustain a distinctive regional subculture: it may have characteristic regional ties and practices, traditions, habits, knowledge, and skills, and these may be associated with particular educational practices and with the circulation and readership of newspapers. It is 'an area of interrelated activities, kindred interests and common organizations, brought into being through the medium of the routes which bind it to the urban centres' (Dickinson 1947: 11; 1964: 7; see also Odum and Moore 1938). An area becomes a region because the activities of those in its villages and towns are integrated and interlocked and its inhabitants are able to sustain a sense of community. This can arise wherever interdependent individuals occupy a shared place in which they act and encounter each other. People experience *being* in a place; *becoming* a part of it. The place is their lifeworld and from their experience of their lifeworld they can imagine a community with others in the same place (Tuan 1977; 1974). Community is the 'imagined' solidarity of those who live in a place, whether local, regional, or national (Anderson 1983; Cohen 1985).

The towns and villages of a region maintain extensive economic and political linkages with a focal city, and Geddes introduced the term 'conurbation' to describe such all-pervasive cities (and see Mumford 1938). In conurbations and their surrounding regions, the distinction between rural and urban became less meaningful. A 'rural' place is one where consumption and production activities are significantly shaped by the available resources and given physical conditions. An 'urban' place, on the other hand, is one where technology has made possible the minimisation and perhaps elimination of any immediate physical constraints. In the city region the rural is incorporated into the urban, making the rural/urban distinction almost meaningless (Castells 1968). The countryside, like the town, becomes an almost exclusively 'created environment' (Giddens 1984: 184, adopting the terminology of LeCorbusier 1925).[5] This dissolution of the rural through technological and cultural advance makes it more difficult to speak of a natural region in the sense implied by early geographers such as Vidal. Human activity remains regionalised, but the large city-regions are defined in cultural, political, and economic terms as concentrations of activity in which environmental conditions become of secondary or minimal importance.

Bodies and the genetic mechanism

The people who inhabit particular regions are, of course, biological organisms that must adapt to the physical conditions of their environment. If their construction of these as places in which to live are relatively free cultural creations, they cannot simply be seen as the products of biological adaptation. Evolutionary psychology, however, presents just such a deterministic model of human behaviour, arguing that evolutionary processes are such that human beings are mere products of the environmental selection of the genetic variations resulting from sexual reproduction. From this point of view, cultural freedom is a product of genetic factors that limit the freedom that humans have to construct their own bodies and behavioural responses. Genetics and the physical environment set definite limits to the range within which social behaviour can vary.

Organisms are composed of cells, millions of which are clustered into the various specialised organs and other units that comprise their bodies.[6] Cells consist largely of proteins and nucleic acids, and most particularly of the deoxyribonucleic acid (DNA) that carries the information for building body parts. This information is stored in genes, units of coded information stored on the intertwined 'double helix' molecules of DNA. The totality of all the genes within a cell comprise its 'genome', and all 40,000 genes in the human cell have now been modelled, gene by gene. As the cells of an organism divide and multiply, these DNA chains are replicated, ensuring that each cell in a body contains identical genetic information to all others. The information coded in the cell comprises the recipes for the production of the enzymes and, most importantly, the proteins that are the physical expression of the genetic information.

The various proteins work together to build specific body parts, to digest food, to fight infections, and to undertake all the other functions and activities that shape the organism and its activities.

Darwin (1859) had recognised that the members of a population vary from each other by small but sometimes significant traits that can be transmitted to offspring. He showed that environmental conditions create pressures to 'select' those traits that are adaptive. It was subsequently discovered by Bateson (1902) that these selective pressures operate on genes within the cells, as it is the genes, or combinations of genes, that produce the traits that may be more or less adaptive. Competition for food and other necessary resources is such that organisms having the particular genes that give them the best chances of survival – those that are best adapted to their environments – are most likely to reproduce. Individuals that are adapted to their environment have a greater chance of survival and, therefore, of having offspring with similar traits. Conversely, those lacking the adaptive traits are less likely to survive and will have fewer descendants. Over a series of generations, then, the distribution of genetic material in a population alters in response to changing environmental conditions and the competitive struggles among organisms that result. In some of his later work, Darwin followed Lamarck (1809) in postulating the direct effect of the environment on biological traits and the ability of individuals to pass on these 'acquired characteristics' to their offspring. Although some recent research has suggested that this is not completely wrong and that some inheritable traits may result directly from environmental pressure, it is now accepted that inherited variations are the results of fixed genetic elements that may mutate at random and are subject to environmental selection.

It is inherited genetic combinations within an organism that determine its chances of operating successfully in specific environments. Sexual reproduction is the only means through which genes can be transmitted from one generation to the next.[7] Genes that improve an organism's survival chances in its specific environment are likely to be perpetuated in a given population, as those organisms with these particular genes are more likely to prosper and, therefore, to reproduce. Conversely, those genes that hinder an organism's survival are likely to disappear along with their carriers.

Genes are linked together as chromosomes, each chromosome consisting of many thousands of genes, and each cell in a human body consists of two sets of chromosomes. Offspring are not biological clones of a single parent but inherit one set of chromosomes from each of their parents and this is the source of their genetic distinctiveness. The genes inherited may not be perfect copies of parental genes. Cellular replication of DNA can result in random copying errors, most of which are insignificant or have effects that are limited by in-built control mechanisms. Ageing and death in an individual organism are consequences of a long-term accumulation of errors that results in a reduced capacity for cellular regulation and so leads to bodily breakdown. Organisms that reproduce will pass on at least some of their genetic errors to their offspring and so sexual reproduction is responsible for a continual change in the genetic materials available in a population. This genetic renewal and variation provides the raw materials on which the 'natural selection' of adaptive traits occurs.

Genetic variation and natural selection are the means through which new species of organism can appear and evolve. In large-bodied and long-lived species these biological mechanisms of evolution operate over millions of years, and few significant changes have taken place in human genetic structure during the thousands of years that humans have existed. Current genetic traits are results of those long evolutionary processes that produced organisms biologically well-adapted to environmental conditions that existed thousands of years ago.

From what is known of human origins, the human genome is an adaptation to a hunting and gathering life on the African savannah. These specific adaptive biological traits made it possible for some human groups to spread out of Africa into other environments. The cultural abilities made possible by this genetic inheritance gave human populations a highly flexible adaptive capacity and virtually eliminated any significant environmental pressures towards further genetic change. As a result, human biological evolution all but ceased many thousands of years ago. Changes in technology and social relations since the beginning of the Neolithic period have occurred over far too short a period (around 10,000 years) to have had any significant selective effect on the human genome.

Evolutionary psychologists have drawn particularly strong conclusions from this lack of genetic change. Ardrey (1961; 1970; 1967), for example, held that the innate and instinctual characteristics of contemporary human beings remain those of their Palaeolithic ancestors and are shared, in fundamental respects, with many pre-human species. This is combined with a strong claim that almost all human characteristics, physical and mental, are genetically determined and that the effects of culture are purely superficial. This leads them to conclude that the basic elements of human biology and mentality have remained unchanged through 100 millennia of cultural change and so will continue to make themselves felt as determinants of cultural change. The original human characteristics persist and continue to manifest themselves under the new conditions, despite being, in some respects, inappropriate (unadapted) to the new environments in which humans now live: 'No child of ours, born in the middle twentieth century, can differ in birth in significant measure from the earliest *Homo Sapiens*. No instinct, whether physiological or cultural, that constituted a part of the original human bundle can ever in the history of the species be permanently suppressed or abandoned' (Ardrey 1961: 12).

The evolutionary argument becomes problematic and contentious whenever it is claimed that the effects of culture are secondary and unimportant relative to genetic factors. Evolutionary psychology, for example, sees mentality and behavioural dispositions as genetically determined and sees only a very limited role for culture in shaping or changing them. Human beings retain fundamental biological traits that may clash with cultural tendencies. Wilson (1975), for example, holds that the basic biological traits of humans can be identified by inspecting those that are most typical and persistent in the primates most closely related to humans. These traits include:

aggressive dominance systems, with males generally dominant over females; scaling in the intensity of responses, especially during aggressive interactions; intensive and prolonged maternal care, with a pronounced degree of socialization in the young; and matrilineal social organizaton. (Wilson 1975: 551)

There is, Wilson holds, a strong likelihood that these traits have persisted, as biological traits, in human beings, and this is why they vary so little from one human society to another. Ardrey took the particularly strong line that humans are an individualistic, aggressive, and violent species marked by sharp sex differences. While those in the direct line of the contemporary apes and monkeys are inoffensive, non-aggressive, and largely vegetarian, humans have evolved from 'terrestrial, flesh-eating, killer apes', the *Australopithecines*.

The problems with this overly rigid and deterministic view have been shown by Maryanski and Turner (1992), who have presented a judicious and balanced view of the biological inheritance of human beings. They start out from the widely accepted recognition that there are significant variations at the genetic level between humans and other primates and they relate these to observable social characteristics in order to infer what humans share as a species. They show that it is plausible to conclude that primate evolution led to palaeolithic hunter-gatherers with genetic predispositions towards certain distinctive social ways of behaving. While humans share tendencies for group formation and territoriality with monkeys and apes (see especially Ardrey 1967: 5; 1961: 86; 1970), other human characteristics are quite distinct. Palaeolithic humans were predisposed to live with others but were individualistic and formed

small and shifting hordes, rather than the large and permanent groupings found among monkeys. The only strong relationship was the bond
between a mother and her dependent child. This was the basis on which
members of the horde maintained a very loose sense of belonging or 'kinship' that links individuals of common descent to a particular territory.
The stronger and more organised levels of sociality that appeared from
the Neolithic can be seen as cultural products imposed on a more or
less recalcitrant biological nature. The range in forms of social organisation is far greater among humans than among other primate species. In
addition to their large brains, humans do seem to have particular genes
that give them great flexibility in social behaviour, especially those that
make culture possible. There are, as a result, great variations between
human populations in such matters as group size and cohesiveness,
territorial defensiveness, and the involvement of males in parental care.
Humans live in a 'social cage' that contains and controls their genetic
predispositions, but human societies vary in the extent and form of this
control, resulting in greater or lesser degrees of 'repression' and consequent stress. The individualism of contemporary capitalist democra-
cies, Maryanski and Turner suggest, allows for a greater expression of
the individualistic tendencies of human beings than is typically the case
in pre-modern societies.

Tool use, sociability, and communicative abilities emerged in all
hominid species as adaptive traits on the African savannah and humans
evolved with particular well-developed linguistic and technological abilities. These abilities made possible the building of complex cultural
systems and, therefore, complex and highly variable social structures.
Engels (1876b) was among the first to recognise the importance of tool
use in human evolution (see also Kroeber 1917) and to see its cultural
elaboration as the basis of complex technologies that enhance environmental adaptation. Cultural variation co-exists with the fixed biological
foundations that may, in the long term, set limits to those cultural forms.
Nevertheless, technology has meant that great cultural diversity has been
possible:

> During the past ten thousand years or longer, man as a whole has been so
> successful in dominating his environment that almost any kind of culture can
> succeed for a while, so long as it has a modest degree of internal consistency
> and does not shut off reproduction altogether. (Wilson 1975: 550)

Sociobiology has taken the lead in emphasising the possibility of a clash
between human biology and culture. Wilson holds that humans are so
well adapted to Pleistocene conditions and the hunter-gatherer way of
life that, without the help of technology, they may be unadapted to most

subsequent environments. Cultural patterns are sustainable over the long term, he argues, only so long as they do not run radically counter to a fundamental human nature.

Cultural and social construction

Evolutionary psychologists and sociobiologists rely on a caricature of social science. As should be apparent, there is no wholesale rejection of biological factors and a number of sociologists have actually contributed substantially to the evolutionary account of human nature. To argue for the importance of cultural formation and social construction is not, in any sense, to argue against the importance of (or even the fundamental importance of) genetic and biological determinants. The fact that sociologists may not routinely explain social phenomena in terms of biological factors is simply a recognition of an academic division of labour and expertise. Indeed, this is the implication of Durkheim's arguments that are so frequently quoted, and distorted, by evolutionary psychologists. Durkheim's (1893) statement that sociology studies social facts and not the individual facts of psychology and biology was not an attempt to reject individual facts *per se*. It was to reject these as the basis of a sociological explanation. Psychology and biology can contribute to the explanation of human phenomena, but they can never provide the whole explanation unless there is a consideration also of social facts. It is the job of the sociologist to study these specifically social facts and causal influences and, in doing so, contribute to a more rounded understanding of human phenomena.

In this section I will show how sociological work on culture and social construction has complemented investigation into the biological determinants of human behaviour. The key to this is provided by Parsons, the principal inheritor of the Durkheimian perspective on social facts and often seen as the paradigmatic advocate of an 'oversocialised' view of human action (Wrong 1961). Parsons saw socialisation as the mechanism relating the social to the biological and the psychological levels of explanation. His most developed reflections on the topic (Parsons 1978) presented the culture-nature relationship as fundamental to the human sciences. A human being is simultaneously an actor and a living being, the purposive action of human agents taking place within a physical and biological environment. Action is effected through an organic system that depends upon the physical system for the material and energy that allows the building and maintenance of bodies and that co-exists with other, equally dependent, organisms. The ways in which an agent relates to an environment, however, depend also upon the cultural meanings through which purposive activity is organised. Adaptation to the environment cannot be studied without reference to the symbols and representations internalised in an actor's personality.

Parsons concluded that social actions are never simply 'triggered' by hereditary factors. Human infants must, on the basis of their given biology, follow a process of learning if they are to participate in their society (Parsons and Bales 1956: 42). Infants who do not learn are unable to act socially: 'What has sometimes been called the "barbarian invasion" of the stream of new-born infants is, of course, a critical feature of the situation in any society' (Parsons 1951: 208). Infants are born with capacities and dispositions that must be shaped through socialisation. They lack biological maturity at birth, and the maturation of their capacities occurs hand-in-hand with their learning of cultural expectations. Infants – and adults – have 'needs' and instinctive responses, but these must be given social expression. Some needs require satisfaction in very specific ways, while others can be met in a variety of different ways. Culture shapes inherited biological characteristics, but the 'range of variability open to actors and cultural definition always has some limits':

We assume then a set of needs which, although initially organised through physiological processes, do not possess the properties that permit those physiological processes to be exclusively determinative in the organisation of action ... Moreover, the needs themselves can be modified, or at least their effect on action is modifiable, by the process of becoming embedded into need dispositions. (Parsons *et al.* 1951a: 9)

There is an interdependence between culture and 'viscerogenic' needs as socialised 'need dispositions'. Human action is oriented by these need dispositions rather than by pre-social biological needs *per se*. Far from ignoring organic conditions, then, Parsons emphasised that human action could be fully explained only through an awareness of the part played by socialisation. It was for this reason that he continually stressed the need to see sociology within an explicitly multidisciplinary framework.

Marx (1844a) set out a similar view of human nature as 'species being', the essential and fundamental element in what it is to be a human being. This is a species essence or species nature that involves not merely biological characteristics but also the self-conscious understandings that people have of being members of a particular species and of their distinctiveness from other species. Human beings are conscious of their physical circumstances and must take account of them in their actions in order to achieve the things they desire (*ibid*.: 112). They are part of nature, but have the ability to distinguish themselves from nature and so to relate to it in unique ways:

Man is directly a natural being. As a natural being and as a living natural being he is on the one hand endowed with natural powers of life – he is an active natural being. These forces exist in him as tendencies and abilities – as instincts. On the other hand, as a natural, corporeal, sensuous, objective being he is a suffering, conditioned and limited creature, like animals and plants. That is to say, the objects of his instincts exist outside him, as objects independent of him; yet these objects are objects that he needs – essential objects indispensable to the manifestations and confirmations of his essential powers. (*ibid*.: 181)[8]

Embodied tendencies of behaviour are oriented towards objects that offer resistance because they have an independent reality that is unknown – and perhaps unknowable – by the human agent. Instincts are not automatically expressed and satisfied but involve an active struggle in relation to the objects that will satisfy them.

Marx's view on this point parallels Parson's analysis of 'needs'. Through their sensual and practical relation to the world (through hearing, smelling, tasting, feeling, thinking, observing, experiencing, wanting, acting, and loving) people orientate themselves outward and *construct* the objects on which they operate. They do not simply take over given objects to meet fixed needs, but 'appropriate' nature in their sensual and practical activity – and, above all, in labour (Marx 1844b: 121–3). Thus, the senses always involve a 'theoretical' or cultural element:

The eye has become a *human* eye, just as its *object* has become a socially human object – an object made by man for man. (Marx 1844a: 139)

Labour as a 'free, conscious activity is man's species character' (Marx 1844a: 113). It is 'Conscious life activity [that] distinguishes man immediately from animal life activity' (*ibid*.). Labour, and therefore species being, is *social*, and individual thought and consciousness is an expression of this social being (*ibid*.: 138).

This view of the social construction of the body has been especially developed by writers influenced by Foucault, a theorist who has many unacknowledged affinities with Durkheim and his school. Foucault (1971) saw language and discourse as the principal structuring or governing factors in social life. Where Parsons held that values are central to the cultural formation of the body, Foucault showed that these values must be imposed on the body through specific communicative acts. Linguistic forms are, therefore, central to the practices of power through which bodies are disciplined or trained to behave in specific ways. This kind of discursive control may be supplemented by direct, repressive controls, which were the dominant way in which the powers of states and other collective agencies were exercised in pre-modern societies (Foucault 1975: 8). In modern societies, however, social control occurs principally through communicative acts that recognise and interact with agents as 'mindful bodies'. The subjectivity of the person is an essential element in bodily control as meanings and intentions are explored through language.

Foucault provided a powerful supplement to the Parsonian emphasis on primary socialisation within the family. Values and knowledge, he argued, are socially organised through discursive communities that promote and implement them, and this is most marked in the formation of specialised groupings of 'experts' in the handling of the body: doctors, psychiatrists, criminologists, teachers, religious leaders. From childhood, human agents are subject to the disciplinary practices of organised experts. Births take place under medical supervision and behaviour is constantly subject to medical intervention. Social conformity is maintained through the actions of teachers, while deviance is controlled and corrected by psychiatrists and social workers. Each expert group constructs images of social types that are integral elements in their assessments of normality and deviance, and they discipline individuals into conformity with these social types. Foucault showed, for example, how experts involved in the production of a discourse of sexuality assumed the normality of the 'Malthusian couple', and used categories such as the 'hysterical woman' and the 'homosexual' to organise their actions in relation to perceived normality and deviance in sexual intimacy and marital behaviour (Foucault 1976a: 105). Foucault stressed, in particular, the increasing pervasiveness of a medical definition of reality such that the expert 'gaze' increasingly takes a medical form (see also Illich 1977). Poor performance at school, criminality, and sexual expression all come to be seen as matters that can be resolved and 'treated' in medical terms through disciplinary practices on the body. Central to this medicalisation, he argued, is the psychiatrisation through which medical intervention on the mind is seen as the means through which the body and bodily actions can most effectively be controlled.

Some credence is given to the misperception of 'social constructionism' in evolutionary psychology by the fact that Foucault did not step outside the analysis of discourse to examine the physicality of actual bodies. His concern is exclusively with discursive representations of the body and their impact on human courses of action through bodily disciplines, displays, and movements. As a result, real bodies tend, as Shilling (1993: 80) argues, to 'disappear'. However, the Foucaultian position does not explicitly deny the physicality of human bodies or their independent causal influence on behaviour. Physical bodies are, as they were for Durkheim, the objects of the biological sciences and not of sociology. The concern of the sociologist is with the practices of power through which attempts are made to shape and organise the body. Unlike Parsons, Foucault did not theorise the relationships between culture and nature across the disciplinary frontier.

This is apparent in Butler's rejection of any universal category of 'the body' as an inert thing that exists in fixed physical form prior to its discursive construction (Butler 1990: 175–6). She recognises that physical bodies exist, of course, but not in a universal and essential form as *the* body. Bodies are, from the moment of conception, 'surfaces' or 'scenes' of cultural intervention and inscription. They necessarily appear as signified objects, as objects that have been given meaning and can be displayed, utilised, and perceived only in culturally specific ways. The importance of these insights is partially undermined (from the standpoint of hostile critics) by a failure to explicitly note that cultural formation through discursive social construction works on real physical entities that have their own causal effectivity and are, to a greater or lesser degree, recalcitrant to inscription.

An emphasis on the social construction of bodies and bodily displays was elaborated somewhat earlier in the work of Goffman, whose writings concerned not the shaping of the body *per se* but *bodily performances*. The social meanings accorded to a body underpin the construction of the particular displays, performances, and forms of impression management that are discussed in Chapter 7. Goffman argued that people rely on 'shared vocabularies of body idiom' (1963a: 35). These are cultural codes that organise comportment, dress, facial expressions, manner of talking, and so on, through techniques of body management. Even earlier, Mauss (1934) showed how ordinary, everyday activities such as walking, sitting, and digging are performative acts that depend upon the training and practising of culturally acquired skills. These 'techniques of the body' are essential aspects of the production of apparently 'natural' ways of behaving. For example, MacAndrew and Edgerton (1969: 88) have shown that the effects of alcohol on the body are not direct physical expressions of physiological intoxication but are culturally mediated. 'Drunken comportment' is an essentially learned affair:

Over the course of socialization, people learn about drunkenness what their society 'knows' about drunkenness; and, accepting and acting upon the understandings thus imparted to them, they become the living confirmation of their society's teachings. (MacAndrew and Edgerton 1969: 88; see also Lemert 1967; Becker 1953)

Similarly, sex differences in bodily form are produced through gendered practices of training and discipline. The encouragement given to boys in contemporary Western societies, in their families and in schools, to engage in such 'masculine' activities as sport and physical exercise cultivates their physical strength and magnifies innate differences of musculature and stature. By adulthood, average measures of size and strength differ considerably between men and women (Lowe 1983). In the same way, cultural emphases on feminine attractiveness encourage many women and girls to exercise and diet in ways that not only reinforce physical differences in body size but also lead many young women into eating disorders, such as anorexia nervosa, that result in physical emaciation and changes in bodily function (Orbach 1978; Chernin 1985).

The cultural codes and techniques of the body are central to what Elias (1939) and Bourdieu (1972) have called 'habitus'. Elias showed that modern ways of behaving are the results of a long process of 'civilisation' in which eating, defecating, and sleeping became the objects of disciplined cultural regulation. Unrestrained behaviour was subjected to social controls that were gradually internalised as 'self control'. Bourdieu saw people as occupying places in cultural, institutional, and relational structures that form their bodies (and their minds) in such a way that the 'embodied structures' (López and Scott 2000) generate actions that tend to reproduce the social structures. Bodies are differentially shaped according to the class, gender, age, and other social positions occupied. Thus, Elias showed that processes of state formation produced patterns of upper class and courtly behaviour that were slowly imposed on those in lower classes. Bodily habitus comprises the internalised and embodied systems of cognition and motivation that predispose people to act in certain ways. It comprises specific socialised orientations, dispositions, and tendencies of behaviour.

Discursive constructions of bodies and bodily performances occur through cultural representations and their formation into sanctioned institutional structures. However, the social relations in which people are involved are also important constraints upon their bodies. The principal contributions to an analysis of the bodily effects of social relations have begun from the view of Marx in the *Economic and Philosophical Manuscripts* (1844a). In addition to whatever natural characteristics human beings may have, they are always involved in definite social relations. It is 'the ensemble of the social relations' that exists at any time that gives the human essence. The essential characteristics of human beings, therefore, are historically specific (Marx 1844b). The social relations in which people live are the means through which they appropriate nature, and so it is impossible to distinguish the merely physical from the non-physical aspects of this appropriation. Species being involves the capacity for both subjectivity and objectivity. There is a subjective consciousness of the characteristics of one's own species and also a human objectivity in the cultural creations through which humans produce and through which they act (Meszaros 1970).

Marx's analysis of 'alienation' disclosed the conditions under which the socialised character of species being is distorted and human action falls below the truly 'human' level. When labour takes the form of 'work', as it does in capitalist society, it ceases to be a free and creative social activity. It is fragmented by the requirements of private property and commodity production, becoming itself a commodity. As such, it is purely instrumental, a means to an end, and the human agent is estranged from his or her product, from the process of production, and from the other people involved in the production and distribution of the commodity produced. Instead of being experienced as an affirmative expression of human physical and mental energy, productive activity is experienced as something 'external' and coerced. Eating, drinking, and procreating, for example, all come to be experienced as activities that have no meaningful connection to the satisfaction of human needs. People are, under capitalist relations of production, alienated from their own species being: their 'nature' is no longer a distinctively 'human' nature.

For Marx, then, human beings are natural, biological organisms that have, as an essential characteristic, the ability to reflect upon their own needs. As a result of specific relational factors, however, they may become alienated from their human characteristics and so able to satisfy only the most basic of their animal needs. Their ability to reflect on their own circumstances, however, makes possible the overcoming of this alienation and the establishment, or re-establishment, of a truly human existence (see also Kropotkin 1902).

Having set out this view of human nature, Marx set it to one side as a taken-for-granted aspect in the rest of his work. His work from the late 1840s was concerned (as was the work of Durkheim and Parsons) with the specifically social causes and consequences of economic and political change. Having established the relationship between nature and culture, he saw little need to refer to it in any detail in the kinds of investigations that he carried out in the rest of his work. There is in Marxism, then, no neglect of biological nature. Marx's recognition of the historically variable character of human beings leads him to challenge any idea that particular sets of social relations are natural, necessary, or universal. His view of human nature gave him a critical recognition of the possibility of *change* in human affairs.

These general ideas on the social construction of the body have been developed in discussions of three central processes through which socialised beings are produced: race and ethnicity, sex and gender, and the ageing and deterioration of individual bodies. These are discussed in each of the following three sections.

Race and ethnicity

The idea of 'race' emerged in various European languages between the fifteenth and nineteenth centuries. Race became the basis of a discourse of racial differences through which individuals and populations were classified according to their bodily characteristics and had psychological, social, and moral attributes imputed to them. This racialisation of differences became the basis of forms of exploitation and oppression that systematically disadvantaged those deemed to be of 'inferior' races.

Spanish colonists coined the term *raza* to refer to the indigenous peoples they encountered in the Americas and it was subsequently adapted into English, with references to the Irish and to indigenous North Americans and slave peoples as races (Smedley 1993). The word was slowly given a more general usage, referring to those seen as sharing a common lineage. It was equivalent to ideas of population types, varieties, or stocks and was often treated as interchangeable with the idea of a 'nation'. New connotations were acquired in both English and French from around 1800, when observable and specifically biological differences between populations came to be seen as racial markers. Influenced by the work of Linnaeus (von Linné 1806) on the systematic biological classification of plants and animals, scientists began to use 'race' as a virtual equivalent of the word 'species'. Linnaeus himself had identified various species of 'Homo', including the orang-utans among these, following the similar approach of Lord Monboddo (Burnett 1779: 135). Instead of recognising a single 'human race', distinguished by its natural characteristics from all other animals, these and other writers held that there is a plurality of biologically constituted races. They identified a limited number of permanent biological types behind the observable variations in human bodily form (Banton 1977: 89; and see Banton 1987: chs. 1 and 2).

One of the earliest formulations of this idea of biological race was that of the Baron de Cuvier (1834), who developed a classification of animal species as biological types and went on to extend this to human beings. Drawing on work by Johann Blumenbach (1795) he recognised three principal human species, which he called the Caucasian, the Mongolian, and the Ethiopian and that he identified by skin colour and other external characteristics. In addition to these, he recognised a number of lesser species such as Malays, Eskimos, and American Indians. The races were regarded as subspecies of a single inter-fertile human species, but 'hybrids' were believed to be infertile or to result in a 'degeneration' of the species.[9] Subspecies were identified by differences in anatomy and physiology, which Cuvier held to be also associated with psychological and cultural differences. Numerous writers, including Hamilton Smith (1851) and Knox (1850), who introduced the word 'Negro' to replace 'Ethiopian', elaborated on this idea of biological race. De Gobineau (1853) developed a systematic racial classification on the basis of the classification of cultural differences produced by Klemm (1843). Central to this racial discourse was a belief in the physical and cultural superiority of the Caucasian or 'Aryan' race. This race was the supposed creator of the major civilisations of world history: Hindu, Egyptian, Greek, Chinese, Roman, and contemporary European. The cyclical decline of each of these civilisations was seen as an inevitable consequence of increased racial mixing during their later stages. For some, such as Gobineau, the extent of interbreeding in the modern world made it more difficult to find any pure races.

The early racial theorists tended to take a 'monogenetic' and theological view of human development. From this point of view, all human populations are descendants of Adam and Eve and so have a common geographical origin. Variations between populations were seen to result from the spread of human beings to environments that shaped their biology in different directions. Many adopted Lamarck's ideas on the inheritance of acquired characteristics, seeing the migration of populations to colder climates, for example, as encouraging the development of paler skin colouring. There was, therefore, a close association with the environmental ideas developed by theorists such as Montesquieu (1748). Some, however, abandoned the religious view and advocated a 'polygenetist' view of the plural origins of human beings. Agassiz (1869), for example, held that black African Americans were a completely separate species from white Americans, and his views reinforced the sociological justifications of slavery put forward by Hughes (1854) and Fitzhugh (1854).

More sophisticated racial theorising saw races in narrower and more concrete groupings that comprised various national and territorial populations and that they saw as resulting from cross-breeding and localised adaptations over the generations. They were ready to adopt Darwin's ideas (1859) on natural selection rather than Lamarck's. Rejecting the theological account, Darwin nevertheless challenged the polygenetic approach to race by showing that there was, indeed, a single human species and that biological types were not fixed and given for all time but evolved transgenerationally through variation and natural selection (Darwin 1871). 'Race' referred simply to any species, variety, or kind of living being, whether vegetable or animal. As the products of natural selection operating in specific environments, human races are loose and ill-defined. Most influential among the Darwinian theorists of race was Haeckel (1879), who saw the various races as subject to natural selection. Less well-adapted races were unable to develop further and were on the road to eventual extinction. Racial differences were a 'recapitulation' of evolutionary processes: the mammal embryo, for example, developed through stages equivalent to those of the fish and the reptile. Similarly, Haeckel held that after birth the Caucasian child develops through Negro, Malay, American, and Mongolian stages as it recapitulates social development from the stage of savagery through barbarianism to civilisation.[10] Related ideas were the basis of Gumplowicz's (1883) views on racial struggle and conquest as a struggle for survival. The conflict of human populations, he held, is a biologically determined necessity inherent in the existence of racial differences. These biological constraints drive the social conflicts that underpin state formation and expansion (see also Robertson 1912).

The dominant point of view remained that which reduced social difference to biological conditions. Ammon (1895), Vacher de Lapouge (1896), and Beddoe (1862) all used measures of head size, eye colour, etc., which they saw as the correlates of racial difference. For all these writers, physical differences were expressed in mental and cultural differences. In some cases, fine distinctions were made, especially within the Caucasian category. Commentators recognised the struggles of Celts, Anglo-Saxons, and other subdivisions (Robertson 1897; 1911). These views were influential in the development of the Eugenic movement in the works of Galton (1881) and Pearson (1909), who advocated the rigorous artificial selection of 'fit' breeding populations in order to maintain the cultural superiority achieved by the Anglo-Saxon race and, in particular, its middle-class members.

Racial thinking permeated commonsense and scientific discourse, leading to a widespread acceptance of the idea of biologically grounded racial differences. This was apparent in the development of anthropology as a discipline. The cultural differences between populations that constituted its subject matter were seen as 'racial' groups. Boas, however, recognised that the material environment had a great effect on human mentality and argued strongly against any view of fixed racial traits. Human nature was remarkably similar across the globe and was also highly plastic. Cultural differences among human populations bear no direct or uniform relationship to any obvious 'racial' differences in physique. Biological traits, for the Boas school, were – at best – superficial markers of cultural difference. Kroeber (1923: 41) used the established classifications of racial types to identify variations in secondary characteristics, such as skin colour and hair texture, that he saw as unproblematic markers of difference in body type. Linton (1936) saw these characteristics as selectively retained variations that had emerged under various environmental conditions. However, he argued that migration and population movements had brought divergent populations together and had reduced the extent of these racial differences. The range of variation within the human species, he argued, is far less than in most other species, and he found no evidence that the persisting differences in secondary characteristics were associated with significant differences in strength, intelligence, or personality. Indeed, it was concluded that people exhibit the cultural characteristics of the populations with which they live, and not those of the populations with which they share a genetic origin. A child born in Japan to Japanese parents but taken to the United States at birth and brought up by American parents grows up 'American' and not 'Japanese' (Benedict 1946). What others have interpreted as racial character the Boas school saw as an effect of the social environment.

The tension that existed between cultural variations and racial difference was partially resolved through a separation between physical anthropology and social or cultural anthropology – a resolution for social anthropologists that involved a repudiation of the problem of biological determinism. The issue was made somewhat easier to handle when the implications of the discovery of the genetic mechanism of inheritance were worked through. A new understanding of race was summarised in an influential UNESCO report, which argued that races should be defined as 'geographically separated varieties of a species' of plants, animals, or humans (Dunn 1951: 270). All human beings draw their genes from a common pool and so form a single species. They are able to reproduce with all others who share this same gene pool, but they cannot reproduce, and so cannot exchange genes, with members of any other species. Within the single human species, however, there are relatively separate and isolated populations that have little or no reproductive sexual intercourse with other populations. These populations have relatively distinct gene pools and so tend to show varying frequencies in the appearance of biological characteristics. They differ, for example, in terms of skin colour, hair type, and other superficial anatomical characteristics. These are the groups to which the term 'race' had conventionally been applied and, if used only in this sense of geographically separated varieties with a concentration of particular inherited characteristics, the word can realistically continue to be used.

Such 'races', however, are neither fixed and permanent, nor sharply and exclusively defined. There is no such thing as a pure, completely distinct race. Races differ in degree rather than in kind. They are distinguished by the relative frequency with which certain inherited characteristics appear, not by the complete absence or exclusive presence of any particular characteristic. These frequencies change over time, albeit slowly, as a result of environmental changes:

Biologically, 'race' is a result of the process by which a population becomes adapted to its environment. The particular array of traits which come to be the most frequent, and hence to characterize the group, are probably those which now or at some past time proved to be successful in a particular environment. (Dunn 1951: 272–3)

What is transmitted through reproduction is 'a set of specific potentialities to respond in particular ways to the environment' (Dunn 1951: 264). That is, people inherit a tendency to exhibit particular skills or characteristics. Each individual inherits many potentialities, and some of these, such as blood type and eye colour, will be exhibited in any environment in which a human being can exist. A number of different genes must work, quite independently, to produce the various proteins whose net effect is to make an eye or a hair of a particular colour. In the more controversial area of skin colour, at least six different genes are involved in producing the skin pigmentation. However, hair and skin pigmentation also depend upon exposure to the sun, and so the direct genetic factors are never expressed in their 'pure' form. Genetic factors provide, at best, the *potential* for certain forms of behaviour, but the realisation of these tendencies depends upon the presence of specific factors in the physical and social environment (see Jones 1993). These develop very early in life, and often within the uterine environment. Other potentialities, such as resistance to certain diseases and particular emotional and cognitive responses, are realised only in certain environments and so may develop, if at all, more slowly and much later in life.

There are, therefore, biological differences between human populations, but these are not as sharply defined as early racial theorists thought. The deterministic assumptions often based on the differences that mark out subpopulations of humans have been shown by genetic theory to be unsustainable. The genetic differences between human populations are slight, and variations *within* a population are generally greater than any variations *between* populations. Evidence so far suggests that variations in mental characteristics (for example, the distribution of specific emotional responses and cognitive abilities)[11] are minor and reflect the effects of environmental differences far more than they do inherited differences. The twentieth-century experience of racial genocide has, quite understandably, led many to repudiate the language of race, and the phrase 'relatively genetically distinct populations' may now be more accurate and to be preferred to the term 'race'.

At the same time, however, the size of interreproducing populations has increased throughout the contemporary world and there has been a corresponding decline in the significance of 'racial' distinctions. Europe and North America, for example, are especially diverse in their genetic pool and the corresponding range of biological potentialities. It makes increasingly less sense to attempt to delineate biological races on the basis of observable biological differences. Races no longer coincide with discrete national, religious, and other social group boundaries, and the term 'race' is very misleading if used outside a strict biological context. Visible physical markers may be employed by groups to identify and label each other and to establish the social barriers that create ethnic groups, but these groups cannot be described as 'races' without invoking unwarranted biological ideas that have now been discredited. While scientific theory has largely abandoned the attempt to describe and explain human differences in racial terms, commonsense racial discourse persists. The observable differences between human populations are widely regarded as 'racial' differences and are assumed to be closely linked with mental and moral differences. Use of the word 'race' to describe ethnic groups rests upon racist assumptions that perpetuate ethnic disadvantage.

For all these reasons, it is scientifically inappropriate to expect to find sharp differences of race in human populations. Minor genetic differences that result in obvious differences of skin colour, hair type, and facial structure may, nevertheless, be associated with populations in which the tendency for intra-group sexual preferences tends to be substantially stronger than that for inter-group sexual preferences. Cultural developments within these populations have often given rise to the judgements of identity and otherness that contribute to the formation of specific 'ethnic' identities. Ethnic groups are racialised when their identities are based on actual or assumed racial differences and these differences are elaborated through a racial discourse.

This dependence of a sociological understanding of race on a concept of ethnicity rather than stark biological differences was recognised in early work by Du Bois (1903; see also Robertson 1897), who was among the first to show that the physical characteristics of human beings were not strong enough in their effects to explain the cultural diversity of human populations.[12] He held that races can be seen only as specific historical cultural formations. The cultural patterns of African Americans at the turn of the nineteenth century were a product of the historical experience of slavery and the subsequent social exclusion of black people from white society. Slavery itself had to be seen as a feature of European imperial expansion. 'Race' is a folk concept that labels ethnic differences in deterministic, biological terms and reflects the contradictory forces at work in American society.

It was on the basis of such views of ethnicity that Gumplowicz (1883) had suggested that conflict between racially defined groups was a driving force in social change, though he accepted the prevailing view that bio-logical race differences underpinned ethnic differences. Cox (1948), Rex (1970), and Smith (1986), however, have developed accounts of ethnic conflict that recognise the racialisation of ethnic differences as a product of specific discursive practices. Their work is an important contribution to the view of collective action discussed in Chapter 7.

Sex, gender, kinship

Ideas of sexual difference have a much longer history than those of racial differences, and they have a correspondingly stronger reality as biological differences. Male and female bodies develop because of distinctive fea-tures in one pair of chromosomes, the 'X' and 'Y' chromosomes, that help to generate distinctive reproductive organs and other 'secondary' sexual characteristics. The chromosomal differences between males and females produce a sexed body.

The sexed body was not ignored in early sociology, but it was treated in rather superficial terms. Comte (1851–4: vol. 1, ch. 4) recognised a sharp differentiation of physical, psychological, and emotional differ-ences between males and females and argued for equality of women as the means of ensuring that their essential and distinctive characteristics are represented in public life. Women, he held, had a stronger emotional and aesthetic orientation than men and were oriented towards caring for the well-being of others. These qualities, central to their domestic pos-ition, could play a major part in building a more altruistic social order (see also Tayler 1904). A radical view on the rights of women was tem-pered by an acceptance that currently prevailing sexual differences are universal and essential.

This has been seen in far less radical terms by many evolutionary psychologists. Ardrey, for example, held that differing social construc-tions of men and women must conform to fixed and innate differences between males and females if psychological problems are to be avoided. A social order that imposes expectations on women that run counter to their natural tendencies and inclinations will result in strains, tensions, and personality disorders. Contemporary 'emancipated' women, he argued, must be unhappy and neurotic because the social demands placed on them deny their instincts and natural bents:

The emancipated woman of whatever nationality is the product of seventy million years of evolution within the primate channel in which status, territory, and society are invariably masculine instincts, in which care of children has been a female preserve, and in which social complexity has demanded of the female the role of sexual specialist. Yet she must somehow struggle along in a human society that idealises in her behaviour every masculine expression for which she possesses no instinctual equipment, downgrades the care of children as insufficient forms for feminine activity, and from earliest girlhood teaches her that a rowdy approach to the boudoir will bring her nothing but ruin. Should she attain the analyst's couch walking on her hands, it would be little wonder, for she lives in an upside-down world. (Ardrey 1961: 165)

Such views, whether politically radical or reactionary, were rejected by other theorists in whom a more strongly feminist viewpoint was found. Ellis (1894), for example, opened up the whole question of the relationship between human biology and differences in sex and sexuality, and it was on this basis that Schreiner (1899) and Gilman (1898; 1911) advanced their views on the historical variability in constructions of men and women. This was taken up in the 'second wave' feminism of the 1970s in a fundamental distinction between sex and gender. 'Sex', it was argued, refers to the genetic differences responsible for the production of specific hormones and the various primary and secondary sexual characteristics. 'Gender', on the other hand, refers to the psychological and cultural meanings attached to sex differences. It designates the social differentiation of men from women through constructions of masculinity and femininity. While sex differences are determinate biological conditions, feminists saw them as neither immutable nor universally constant. Environmental factors, including those of the social environment, play a great part in shaping the forms taken by sexual differentiation. The crucial point, however, was that the gendered meanings attached to sex are far more variable than sex itself. The biology of sex does not uniquely determine or require particular differences of gender.

Recognition of gender variability owes a great deal to the work of Margaret Mead, a student of Boas who developed his view of the relationship between culture and nature. The starting point for her discussion of gender is most clearly expressed in the words of her friend, mentor, and fellow student, Ruth Benedict:

All over the world, since the beginning of human history, it can be shown that peoples have been able to adopt the cultures of people of another blood. There is nothing in the biological structure of man [*sic*] that makes it even difficult. Man is not committed in detail by his biological constitution to any particular variety of behaviour. The great diversity of social solutions that man has worked out in different cultures in regard to mating, for example, or trade, are all equally possible on the basis of his original endowment. Culture is not a biologically transmitted complex. (Benedict 1934: 13–14)

Mead held that societies develop around ideas and values that are elaborated over time as specific cultural traditions that need take little account of biological differences: 'it may bend every individual born within it to one type of behaviour, recognising neither age, sex, nor special disposition as points for differential elaboration' (Mead 1935: xiv; and see her 1950). Many of the differences between men and women accepted as natural and innate in Western culture are neither universal nor necessary.

In her studies of three societies in New Guinea, Mead showed that sex differences had been developed in very diverse ways and that the various roles attached to sex differences are 'social constructs' (Mead 1935: xvii). Arapesh men and women were accorded different economic, political, and religious roles, but no temperamental differences were recognised. Both men and women were gentle, caring, and mutually supportive, and were, in Western terms, 'womanly' and maternal. Among the Mundugumor, however, both sexes had what Westerners would see as 'masculine' traits: social relations were distant, competitive, aggressive, and highly individualistic. Tchambuli society showed clear sexual contrasts between men and women that were quite the opposite of those normal in Western society: men engaged in domestic activities, body painting, and personal decoration, while women held all positions of power, controlled the land, engaged in fishing for food, and were dominant in sexual relations. Mead concluded that:

If those temperamental attitudes which we have traditionally regarded as feminine ... can so easily be set up as the masculine pattern in one tribe, and in another be outlawed for the majority of women as well as the majority of men, we no longer have any basis for regarding such aspects of behaviour as sex-linked. (Mead 1935: 279–80)

Behavioural differences between the sexes, then, are 'cultural creations' or arbitrary 'social fictions' (*ibid.*: 313). Mead's conclusion is rarely sustained in this strong form, and some doubts have been placed upon the reliability of her fieldwork data (Freeman 1996; but see Orans 1996). Nevertheless, she did undoubtedly establish that the range of variation in gendered behaviour is far greater than most evolutionary psychologists allow.

Although they are critical of purely cultural explanations, radical feminists have produced arguments that help to sustain Mead's broad conclusions. The basic position was stated by Firestone (1970), who held that socialisation into gendered forms of behaviour rests on the biological conditions of sex. However, her position is that the crucial factor is not biological difference *per se*, but the varying social experiences made possible or likely by these experiences. Thus, it is the ability that women have to give birth that is the basis of their differential experience and knowledge and that involves them in power struggles with the men who control their labour and their children (O'Brien 1981). The social construction of gender is constrained by male and female biology, and the gender characteristics that prevail in a society depend on the typical experiences encountered by males and females in that society. Biology does not result in a fixed and given fate, but generates conditions of life that may be alterable. Techniques of medical intervention in reproduction and child-birth and practices of child rearing may alter the biologically conditioned experiences of women and so alter their cognitive and emotional capacities and responses. An important strand in feminist theory linked such biologically conditioned variations to broader ideological formations rooted in unconscious psychological processes. Ideological forms of subjectivity result from gendered patterns of socialisation and the means through which people experience and understand the world (Mitchell 1974). Socialisation results in a universalised 'patriarchal' system of male domination, though the specific forms of this patriarchy can vary from one society to another. No strand of feminist thought denies the need to consider both biology and society in a comprehensive explanation of sex-gender systems in social life (see the important review in Price and Shildrick 1999). Liberal feminists and many Marxist feminists, however, hold that the dualism between sex (nature) and gender (culture) requires the use of distinct principles of analysis and explanation appropriate to each (Oakley 1972). In Marxist feminism, this dualism of sex and gender has been formed into a 'dual systems' view of the interdependence of patriarchal gender relations and capitalist class relations. Marxist feminists use the concept of ideology to explore the ways in which a hegemonic pattern of patriarchy has been established in capitalist societies through specific patterns of class and sex socialisation (Barrett 1980).

The range of variation possible in sex and gender relations has been most graphically explored in the work of post-structuralist and postmodernist feminisms during the last couple of decades. Like their non-feminist counterparts, they stress the cultural construction of all social differences, including those of sex and gender. Inspired by Foucault, they see the human body as a plastic container for discursive representations. Butler has rejected the universal and essential categories of 'patriarchal' and 'woman' that are often seen to pre-exist particular political processes. Gender, she argues, is discursively constructed and always intersects with other discursively constructed identities such as those of class, race, ethnicity, and sexuality (Butler 1990: 4–6; and see Hill Collins

1990). Thus, 'sex' does not pre-exist particular processes of social formation as a determinate and fixed category. People are not divided into separate and distinct categories of being by their biology (Butler 1993). It is in this sense that de Beauvoir could argue that 'one is not born a woman, but, rather, becomes one' (de Beauvoir 1949: 301).

What is important to note, however, is that the rejection of essentialist *categories* does not require rejection of the very idea of biological *facts*. The point is that the range of biological variation in the distribution of biological traits across a population is such that people can be divided into sex categories only if cultural representations are used to interpellate them as specific subjects: as 'male' and 'female'. Thus, both sex and gender are social constructs. Although Butler rejects the distinction between sex and gender, on the grounds that both are cultural constructions, it remains a useful distinction: sex is a construction of biological difference and gender is a construction of the forms of behaviour and character seen as appropriate to the members of the various culturally constituted sexes. Sex and gender are, however, to be seen as mutually constituting constructions. Unintentionally echoing Goffman, Butler (1990: 185) sees sex and gender as 'performative': they are produced in and through the enactment of scripts that constitute them through performances in gestures, movements, and words. It is through similar processes of performativity that sexuality is constituted.

Sex relations are constitutive of the relations through which children are born and brought up and through which, as a result, adults acquire 'kinship' relations to each other. Though kinship is commonly seen as a direct expression of the innate biological relatedness of males and females, this relatedness is always selectively constructed as culturally variable relations:

A kinship system does not consist in the objective ties by descent or consanguinity between individuals. It exists only in human consciousness; it is an arbitrary system of representations, not the spontaneous development of a real situation. (Lévi-Strauss 1945: 50; see also Gellner 1973: 171)

In other words, kinship systems 'are cognitive systems employed for the ordering of social relationships which have reference to some aspect of "physical kinship"' (Harris 1990: 31–2). People in all societies recognise and construct biological relations of parenthood and siblingship (whether actual or assumed), compounding these terms (or their linguistic equivalents) into more complex classifications of biological relatedness (Barnes 1998: 298).

Biological relatedness, rooted in sex and reproduction, is a feature of human biological evolution that derives from the forms of relatedness found in other animal species. Recognition of biological relatedness is found in all primates, though its form varies considerably. All apes live in permanent family-like groups structured by age and sex.[13] They have evolved with a tendency to form small societies characterised by low levels of sociality and that predispose their members to solitary activities. Gibbons are 'monogamous', mating for life, and form elementary family units of dependent infants and juveniles. There are few sexual divisions in gibbon activities and mature individuals leave their natal groups to find their own mates. The only stable group among orangutans is that of a mother and her dependent offspring. Male orangs live a largely solitary life and tend to mate promiscuously. Mature juveniles adhere to temporary bands until adulthood. Gorillas form larger stable groups comprising, usually, one mature male with several females and their offspring. Several such groups may co-reside within a particular territory, perhaps with some solitary males, though there is only limited interaction between groups. Chimpanzees, the closest genetic primate to humans, live in large groupings of 25–100 members and engage in promiscuous sexual activity. The only strong bonds are those between females and their dependent offspring.

This evidence on sociability and biological relatedness led Maryanski and Turner (1992) to conclude that the last common ancestor of apes and humans was a creature that lived in promiscuous hordes in which strong female-offspring ties persisted until puberty. These hordes were likely to have been relatively unstable and would probably not have persisted intergenerationally. Early hominids lived on the open savannah, where there were adaptive advantages for primate species with the ability to communicate through language and symbols. Despite their limited genetic predisposition for large and cohesive groups, such species could cooperate in large groups for defensive and foraging purposes. These groups could maintain themselves through the recognition of larger networks of biological relatedness and so developed characteristic systems of kinship classification (Maryanski and Turner 1992: 32; Dickens 2000b: 87–8).

Thus, early human societies established institutionalised relations of 'marriage' and 'parenthood' that allowed the formation of relatively stable family, band, and kinship relations. This was first recognised by Westermarck (1891), though he overemphasised its genetic basis. Somewhat later, Murdock (1949) recognised the overriding importance of the cultural basis of regularised fatherhood:

The universal participation of the father in the human family would thus seem to depend mainly upon economic specialization and the development of the body of traditional lore to be transmitted from one generation to the next. Since both are products of cultural evolution – indeed, amongst the earliest of such – the human family cannot be explained on an instinctive or hereditary basis. (Murdock 1949: 11)

The biological relations of sex are culturally formed and relationally constrained through representations of kinship that organise practices of caring and socialisation. It is through these practices that definite ideas of gender roles and identities are produced. Variability and change in cultural definitions and in the structural organisation of the division of labour are the mechanisms responsible for variability and change in gender relations.

Matters of life and death

The social construction of the body is apparent in the most fundamental matters of individual life and death. Birth, maturation, illness, incapacity, ageing, and death are biological conditions and processes that occur in and through definite social conditions and processes. However 'natural' their biological basis, they are socially constructed bodily performances.

Although age was recognised as an important factor in early sociological analysis, as a significant social fact alongside 'sex' and 'race', it was generally seen as a simple numerical variable. Not until fairly recently has this reliance on a Western, chronological measure of age been seen as problematic (Riley 1987). This has involved an explicit consideration of the relationship between the biological facts of life, ageing, and death, and the cultural constructions of the stages of life.

Human life begins, to all intents and purposes, at the moment of conception, and human beings follow a limited life span during which their body ages until the point of death.[14] Considered biologically, ageing is an inevitable consequence of the cellular deterioration that occurs within any living organism (Kirkwood 1999). This deterioration hinders tissue repair and metabolic processes, resulting in increasing difficulties in responding to environmental influences and, therefore, reduced capacity for homeostasis. Ageing is manifested in the greying of hair, wrinkling of the skin, and reduced functional ability – there is likely to be, for example, reduced muscular strength, lowered reaction time, and impairment of memory. The effects of ageing are compounded by the effects of illness, impairment, and injury, with death typically occurring at an earlier age than might be likely in the absence of these contingencies. Conversely, there is evidence that susceptibility to certain diseases increases with age.

Recent research has shown that age, and the subjective experience of ageing, is influenced not only by conditions in physical environments but also by the social contexts in which they occur. The human life course is marked by various conventional (and culturally variable) stages: infancy, childhood, youth, adulthood, old age, and so on. These stages are social constructions that reflect prevailing cultural imagery and are associated with age-specific norms. Age was first properly recognised sociologically by Mannheim (1927), who highlighted the crucial importance of generations or birth cohorts. Stages are formed through institutionalised definitions of the schedules and sequences of the stages themselves. Conceptions of childhood and old age, for example, have been shown to vary considerably during the development of Western modernity (Ariès 1963; Cole 1992). Death itself is a socially constructed passage (Ariès 1977) surrounded by complex social understandings (Glaser and Strauss 1965; 1968). These meanings and conceptions may crystallise as social positions and their associated roles. Passing from one to another varies by class, ethnicity, and other social conditions, and involves the following of socially defined styles of life as rites of passage (Van Gennep 1909). When applied to individuals, age classifications open up or close off opportunities for action.

Illness is generally treated as a simple biological condition, but it, too, is subject to social construction and is structured by social processes (Parsons 1951: ch. 10; 1958b). The susceptibility of males and females to different diseases, and their consequent variations in longevity, for example, are accentuated or diminished by the effects of cultural representations of sex and gender and the relational structuring of sex differences (Arber *et al.* 2003). Similarly, ethnic differences in illness are modified by racialised ethnic identities and their structural consequences. This is not to deny, of course, that physical illness *is* a biological condition, or that some illnesses and impairments may be almost exclusively determined by biological factors. There is much evidence that random genetic differences and errors in DNA replication can produce abnormal bodily states. Many evolutionary psychologists, however, have held to overstated models that stress the genetic basis of illness and impairment. Research in human biology has, indeed, shown the effects that genetic variation within a population can have on the distribution of individual traits and attributes: sex, hair colour, height, susceptibility to certain diseases, and a number of other physical characteristics have all been shown to be genetically determined, in whole or in part, whether resulting from direct genetic inheritance or from 'faulty' genetic replication. Genetic factors are central to the aetiology of autism and Down's syndrome, for example, and there is also evidence that specific genes may be responsible for cancerous growths, cystic fibrosis, Alzheimer's Disease, and haemophilia. In these latter cases, however, cultural differences shape the particular ways in which these conditions are expressed. Some simplistic presentations of genetic research have claimed to have discovered 'the' gene responsible for particular adaptive or non-adaptive capacities and for such behavioural patterns as homosexuality (Hamer *et al.* 1993), alcoholism (Blum 1992), and rape (Thornhill and Palmer 2000). This view sees genes as mechanical programmes or blueprints for the production of specific and invariant attributes and behaviours. They are seen as containing detailed instructions for generating fixed and inescapable outcomes and behavioural performances.

The mechanisms of genetic determination, however, are far more complex than these simplistic presentations allow. While there is strong evidence for a direct one-to-one relationship between particular genes and such disorders as Huntington's Disease, this is far from typical. More typically, genes have their effects only in combination (Ridley 1999; Dickens 2000a). Most genes are highly non-specific so far as particular macro-outcomes are concerned. They involve very simple instructions that are applied recursively in open environments and are involved principally in the production of quite specific micro-outcomes such as muscle building and disease resistance. The chances of finding a strong correlation between the presence or absence of a particular gene and a specific condition, without taking account of other factors (including social factors), are low. Macro-outcomes are not pre-given in specific genes but result from the application of a whole array of genetic instructions under specific environmental conditions. Environmental effects are often of crucial importance in deciding the consequences particular genes will have in particular cases. If the environment changes, then the results of the genetic instructions are likely to be very different. Typically, then, the normally observed human traits and attributes are the results of the combined effects of a large number of genes. At the same time, this combined effect may produce atypical organic outcomes under certain environmental conditions.

In this chapter I have shown that cultural formation must always be considered in relation to natural conditions. It is undoubtedly true that much remains to be resolved in our understanding of the relationship between culture and nature. If there is a problem in the view of the relationship between biology and culture held in mainstream sociology, this does not involve a denial or rejection of biology (as held by its evolutionary psychology critics) but an over-sharp disciplinary division of sociology from biology and psychology that comes from Durkheim's insistence on the disciplinary autonomy of sociology (Benton 1991). I have shown that humans live in reproducing populations within specific natural environments and must draw on their natural and cultural resources to construct the habitats in which they can thrive. The particular way of life that is followed reflects the environmental conditions and technologies available, and underpins the cultural systems that facilitate or hinder the ability of humans to adapt to diverse environments. The cultural responses that people are able to make to their environments produce the regions and localities within which they lead their everyday lives and through which their culture can be perpetuated. The human body itself must be adapted to its environment, though cultural representations and the technologies they inform allow considerable scope for variation in human characteristics. There is no fixed and given human nature, though there are genetic and organic conditions that limit the range of possible cultural variation. Ethnic differences and gender differences, the kinship relations through which these differences are organised, and the life course followed by socialised individuals, must all be seen as the complex outcome of this interdependence of the natural and the cultural.

4   Systemic Processes: Regulation and Control

Many of the earliest attempts to conceptualise social phenomena invoked ideas of what would now be regarded as 'system' thinking. Theorists variously stressed the holistic, organic, or systemic properties of socially organised populations. These systemic ideas promised a dynamic rather than a static approach to social phenomena. Indeed, Comte (1851–4: vol. 2, 1 ff) made the distinction between 'statics' and 'dynamics' the central feature of his new science of sociology. Despite the claims of some social theorists, the holistic properties of societies, as I show in Chapters 6 and 7, are real and irreducible to the individual acts from which they result. In this chapter I will look at what is added to the sociological viewpoint by using the idea that social phenomena can be conceptualised as social systems.

The earliest system models in sociology used ideas from classical mechanics to build a 'social physics'. The mechanistic viewpoint saw the causal relations among the basic units of analysis as analogous to the impact of one billiard ball on another. That is, objects were seen as moving or changing position because of the direct effects brought about by the impact of other objects on them. Mechanics focused on 'hard particles whamming into one another' (Martin 2003: 7) and so on the local physical, mechanical contact of objects possessing extension and mass. The impact of an object generates a force that pushes other objects in the direction of this force, and a mechanical system is the result of these causal, force relations. For some sociologists, the advances made in mechanics seemed to suggest a way of arriving at determinate laws of individual behaviour, these laws summarising the causal effects that individuals have on each other as they move around the world.

The treatment of individuals and their actions as inert objects engaged in purely external and atomistic reactions had obvious limitations. While it showed the systematic connections that could be found in social life, its deterministic assumptions seemed unrealistic. While some critics of mechanistic theories of action counterposed an emphasis on 'free will' to the mechanical system model, others sought a more flexible concept of the social system. Within physics itself, discussion moved beyond these classical ideas to explore what were called thermodynamics and energetics. Thermodynamics introduced the concept of the field of potential that results when objects move relative to each other in such a way that system-level processes can maintain states of equilibrium among the objects and their forces. Once again, social scientists turned to these ideas as ways of overcoming the major limitations of the earlier social physics.

Thermodynamics seemed to produce a better understanding of emergent properties and processes and, therefore, to allow more dynamic system models. Marginalist economists (Menger 1883), the velocity theory of money (Fisher 1911; Pigou 1927), and the later economics of Keynes (1936), for example, saw systemic concepts such as employment, savings, investment, aggregate demand, national wealth, and money supply as aggregations of individual-level variables that stood in dynamic states of equilibrium.

In parallel with this move towards thermodynamics was a growing interest in biological ideas of organic systems. The biological idea of the organism as a system of interdependent, functioning parts seemed, also, to offer the chance of properly dynamic models of emergent social processes. The focus in biological system theory was on the *flow* between elements rather than on direct physical contact. It was, therefore, much more compatible with the thermodynamic models being constructed in physics, though the two initially had little contact. Social theorists saw linguistic communication among individuals as creating the channels through which ideas flow, and a 'social organism' was seen as an entity tied together through this communication of associating individuals. The key theorist of the social organism was Spencer, but the idea reverberated through the sociologies of Schäffle (1875–80), Lilienfeld (1898), the Oxford idealists, de Roberty (1904), and the work of Worms and the Durkheim school (see Barberis 2003). It achieved a powerful empirical expression in the ethnographic studies of Malinowski (1922) and his followers.

Reactions to crude organicism led, in the 1930s, to the attempt to draw again on physical ideas to supplement biological concepts. Henderson (1938–42) turned to the earlier work of Bernard (1865) and connected these with the organicist ideas of Cannon (1932) on 'homeostasis'. This work reflected the emerging ideas of von Bertalanffy (1940) and Wiener (brought together in Wiener 1948), writers who had begun producing general theories of living systems. This work gave rise to a general system theory that combined physical and biological principles into a general framework that, it was argued, offered great potential for the development of theories of social systems. Parsons (1961a), Luhmann (1977), and others began to recast their theories in terms of these new 'cybernetic' ideas.

The most recent developments in theories of social systems have returned to physics, where theorists have incorporated an analysis of the 'chaos' and 'complexity' that result from the concatenation of individual effects into unpredictable system-level phenomena.

Motion, forces, and fields

Mechanical models of social systems took an atomistic approach in which individuals were seen as forms of matter that move under the influence of forces of attraction and repulsion. This followed the Cartesian view that the force of motion was the product of mass and velocity. Individuals gravitate towards each other as a result of these forces, and this gravitational motion is the source of change in social systems. Quesnay's *Tableau Economique* (1758) was, perhaps, the earliest such model, showing the relations between production, distribution, and national wealth, but its basis was first set out by Quetelet (1848), inventor of the term 'social physics'. It was taken up more systematically by Dühring (1873) and Carey (1872). Even Spencer (1862)[1] saw motion as the first principle of all scientific enquiry. The mechanism of force was basic to Engels' (1876a; 1886) dialectical materialism, according to which:

The whole of nature accessible to us forms a system, an interconnected totality of bodies ... In the fact that these bodies are interconnected is already included that they react on one another, and it is precisely this mutual reaction that constitutes motion. (Engels 1886: 71)[2]

For Engels, mechanical force, heat, chemical force, light, electricity, and magnetism are mutually convertible forms of matter in motion. Organic processes and social processes are similarly reducible to patterns of matter in motion. Motion brings about a change of place through forces of attraction or repulsion,[3] and a mechanical standpoint sees the convergent patterns as the 'resultants' of these forces. Thus, systems at each level of analysis could be understood in terms of distinct laws of causal relations, even if they are ultimately reducible to matter in motion. Specific forces are secondary factors – mere consequences of motion – and the language of force can ultimately be abandoned and all phenomena redescribed in terms of motion alone. This was the basis that Engels proposed for Marx's discussion of the laws of motion of the capitalist mode of production.

Similar views were developed by Pareto (1896–7), initially as a theory of economic variables that he later extended to include 'non-rational', 'non-economic' variables (Pareto 1916). The generalisation of mechanics from economic theory to a fully social theory was also explored by Ward (1883), Patten (1896), and Haret (1910). As these theorists developed their ideas they began to take account of the more recent developments in physics that centred on a recognition of the key role of 'energy' in physical systems. This led to a reconceptualisation of mechanical systems as 'fields' within which variations in energy levels produced by matter in motion generated the very forces that produced this motion. These views focused far more directly on emergent system-level processes than did their more atomistic predecessors.

Joule, von Helmholtz and other physicists of the mid-nineteenth century had introduced the idea of 'energy' (*Kraft*) as a fundamental force in the physical world. Helmholtz (1847) set out a view of energy as a cause of all motion and, therefore, of the dynamic properties of matter. Energy is a virtual substance, a 'potential' that is manifest only in the various forms of heat, magnetism, electricity, etc., and is convertible from one form to another. It was held that any system comprises a fixed amount of energy that can merely be converted from one form to another. As a result of this conservation of energy, energy can neither be increased nor decreased, though it can be stored up in a material form that can be released through mechanical 'work' (*Arbeitskraft*). Later work in thermodynamics suggested that energy can be lost, though not gained, and that there is, therefore, a tendency towards increasing 'entropy' in all systems (Clausius 1885). Helm (1887) and Ostwald (1892) took up the idea of potential energy as the available capacity of an entity to produce effects, seeing matter as spatially distinguishable quantities of energy.

Helmholtz developed this into the idea of a vital force found in all organic beings and he extended this idea to human activity. Human labour power as a form of energy, he argued, is the means through which energy is supplied in social activities and is the material base for these activities.[4] These ideas were taken up in the economic theories of Gossen and Podolinsky, the latter seeing food intake as the means through which the solar energy stored in agricultural produce can be transformed into the physical work of human beings (Gossen 1853; Podolinsky 1881; 1883; see also Sacher 1881). Podolinsky assumed that basic human needs can be measured in energy terms (as calorie requirements) and held that each calorie of human work must produce at least ten calories of available energy if it is to ensure basic survival at a subsistence level. He saw this as a basis for reformulating the labour theory of value and proposed the construction of energy budgets in order to measure the value of labour power (Martinez-Alier 1987: 49, 52).[5] This basic idea had been implied, but not formally stated, in the collection of household budgets by Le Play (1855), and it was developed more systematically when Clausius (1885) and Ostwald (1909; 1912) in Germany, and Geddes (1884), Branford (1901), and Soddy (1922; 1926) in Britain, began to construct the input-output models of energy flows that became the basis of contemporary ecological economics.[6] Such arguments suggested a way of understanding the view of Marx (1859a; 1864–5) that the flow of value through circuits of capital in an economy is measurable by the quantities of labour power expended. This became the basis for Marxist views of systems of energy in equilibrium (Bukharin 1921).

A key innovation made in this work was the development of the idea of the field. This was introduced by Maxwell, who saw a field as a spatial distribution of energy and defined the electromagnetic field as 'that part of space which contains and surrounds bodies in electric or magnetic conditions' (1865: 34; 1877). Maxwell assumed the existence of a 'medium' capable of receiving and storing energy and in which an 'electromotive force' can communicate motion from one part of the medium to another in a pattern of 'undulations' (1865: 37, 39). This idea of the materiality of space as a medium replaced the classical idea of action at a distance with a contiguous field of energy in which wave-like interactions occur. Where the classical mechanical model had seen motion in terms of a billiard-ball model of causality, the new theories saw systems as fields with the potential for the creation of force as a result of the presence of an object within the field (Hesse 1962). The 'internal relations' of a system comprise the arrangement of its parts into an 'assemblage' of relative positions (Maxwell 1877: 2) that shape the movements of objects, and the actual forces found in any system are the result of the presence of objects whose properties interact in such a way as to result in a change of a state in the system. Gravity, for example, describes the tendencies of movement apparent in objects as a result of their motion relative to each other. These field theories modelled potential forces as 'vectors' or 'valences', as slopes or gradients in a space of objects in motion. The state of tension in a field generates the tendencies of behaviour manifested in objects placed in that field. The field, therefore, is a dynamic system in which each object induces forces on all other objects, creating a system of forces that can affect any other susceptible object that enters the field.

Fields and their properties are built around the emergent properties of lower-level mechanical contacts, even though these lower-level processes may be unknown or bracketed-off from consideration. Thus, electromagnetic field theory proved successful in terms of the relations postulated among particles, while 'magnetism', as a force, was understood as an emergent effect of unknown processes within the particles. It was not until much later that quantum mechanics began to provide an account of the lower-level mechanisms on which the emergent properties of the electromagnetic field depend. This recognition of emergent properties made it possible for theorists to see applications to biological and social phenomena, where distinct emergent processes could be studied in their own right. A striking elaboration of these views that anticipated many later advances was the politically suppressed 'tectology' of Bogdanov (1913–22) in the Soviet Union.

Pareto was, perhaps, the most influential exponent of this view of the social system as a social physics. He had originally studied equilibrium in elastic solids and drew on this to construct an equilibrium model of supply and demand under conditions of perfect market competition (1896–7). Equilibrium is a state of balance or adjustment among a plurality of forces. It is a state in which the vector sum of all the forces acting on a body is equal to zero (Russett 1966: 2). In this state there is no tendency for the system to change unless external forces impinge on it and impel it to change. In an equilibrium state in the economy, supply is equal to demand in all markets and the distribution of resources is optimal. A market equilibrium concerns changes in the price of a commodity in response to changes in its conditions of supply and demand, together with the consequent changes in supply and demand that result from the altered price. Price, supply, and demand fluctuate until a point is reached at which there is no further tendency for any of the variables to change. Equilibrium is produced wherever rational agents are constrained by the market competition of a large number of small producers, no one of which has the power to affect market price, to operate according to the principle of diminishing marginal utility.

The construction of models describing single markets, such as those devised by Alfred Marshall (1890), is termed *partial* equilibrium analysis. Walras and Pareto, however, described *general* equilibrium models that apply to a whole system of markets. In such a general equilibrium model, equilibrium occurs when there is a set of prices that will clear all markets.[7] Pareto saw economic markets as explicable by the simultaneous variation in the analytical elements of the system. An economy could, therefore, be modelled as a set of simultaneous equations in which the prices and quantities that comprise the solutions to the equations define its equilibrium conditions. Simultaneous equations are sets of two or more linear equations that are true at the same time.[8] Two simultaneous equations with two unknown variables generally have a unique solution. These relations can also be graphically represented by supply and demand curves whose point of intersection is the solution to the simultaneous equations and forms the equilibrium point of the system. Simultaneous equations are typically constructed in quantitative, numerical form, but the relations among variables may equally be described in algebraic or other qualitative terms. In economic theory, the use of money as a measure of value allowed the quantitative formulation of equilibrium models.

Pareto (1916) constructed an analogous theory of the 'non-rational' elements in social life that were excluded from the equations of economic theory and treated by it as purely residual terms. These were the emotions, instincts, and prejudices that Pareto referred to as the 'residues' (sentiments), interests, 'derivations' (rationalisations), and heterogeneity of individuals. The concrete equilibrium in any social situation is, therefore, a combination of analytically distinct economic and social models. Pareto held that a social group comprises a number of mutually dependent elements in a bounded set or closed system that is isolated from environmental effects except in so far as they are purely exogenous sources of disturbance (Henderson 1935: 13, 17–18). 'Natural' environmental factors such as climate and physical conditions were seen as such exogenous factors. This assumption of a closed system allows the social scientist to ignore extraneous factors and analyse the system within its definite and known limits. Systems can be described by laws of equilibrium because the state of the closed system is such that it returns to its initial state if disturbed.[9] Within such systems, variation in any one element leads to variation in the others. The interdependence of parts is such that when any one is disturbed a chain of reactions ensures that the system returns to its initial state. Pareto saw these social and economic equilibria as dynamic rather than static, but was unable to formulate laws of moving equilibrium and modelled social change as a series of static equilibrium points (Pareto 1896–7).[10]

Lundberg (1939) was heavily influenced by Pareto and worked in parallel with Dodd (1942) to use field theory and statistical mechanics to define equilibrium states as the *most probable* of the many possible outcomes of the flows of energy and information generating a current system state. He saw the balance of forces in a system determining the 'direction and vigour' of the flow of energy, with individual behaviour being the resultant. One of the few examples of the explicit use of such field theories in sociology is that of Lewin (1936). Drawing on the *gestalt* psychology of Wertheimer, Koffka, and Köhler,[11] Lewin was able to build subjectivity into his scheme. Where earlier mechanical models had treated the individual as an atom to be analysed in purely external terms, Lewin saw the subjectivity of the agent as an essential element in a sociological system model. He began at the psychological level and constructed a model of the psychological field, seen as the totality of mutually dependent elements within the mentality of a particular individual. It is a person's mental map of the world in which they move. As a field, it comprises the dynamic processes between consonant and dissonant elements that establish the psychological strains and tensions to which the individual is subject. The individual person is seen as moving around in terms of a 'phenomenological lifeworld', the world as experienced and lived by that person. People construct definitions of the situations encountered and anticipate and interpret changes in the world brought about by their own acts and by those of the others on whom their actions impinge and whose actions affect them. In Lewin, the relationship between the psychic field and the interpersonal social space was treated unproblematically, though he gradually gave more attention to the independent group dynamics of the social field (Cartwright and Zander 1953).

Organisation, emergence, and function

Mechanical system models provided the foundations for a number of important sociological theories. The most important advances in the longer term, however, combined mechanical ideas with those they found in the work of social theorists who drew on the system models that had developed in biology. Chief among these theorists had been Spencer. Despite his methodological and political individualism, Spencer had recognised that societies are not simply collections of individuals but are distinctively social entities with persistent relations among their individual participants. Societies persist as systems of relations, despite the constant replacement of their individual members through birth, death, and migration (Spencer 1873: vol. 1, 435–6, 444). Although social entities are products of matter in motion, they must also be understood as having properties similar to those of biological organisms. A society is a self-sufficient 'system of organs', each of which is specialised around a particular activity to which it contributes. The separate organs are 'functionally dependent' on each other as the constitutive parts that comprise the internal structure of the society (Spencer 1873: 439–40; 1860: 397).

Spencer's key point was that an organism has properties distinct from and irreducible to those of its parts considered in isolation because the constituent elements are altered by the relationships they have with each other. The behaviour of the organism cannot be predicted from a knowledge of the attributes of its parts considered in isolation. Its properties 'emerge' from the interrelatedness of the parts. Mechanical systems have some similar features, but there are important differences. A screw can be removed from an engine and remain a screw, able to be used in a variety of other objects. A heart, on the other hand, cannot exist as a heart outside a body within which it is related to lungs, a blood supply, nerves, and other organs. A body cannot live unless its parts complement each other effectively (Bradley 1893: 513 ff; Hegel 1812–16: 350). The philosophical basis of this organicism was most clearly formulated by the Hegelian writers who developed Spencer's insight (see Mackenzie 1895: ch. 3). The elements that make up an organism, it was argued, have certain properties only because they are parts of a specific whole.

The organs of biological organisms are specialised around such functions as breathing, eating, and excretion, and Spencer aimed at a comprehensive list of the 'functions' that must be met by a social organism. He held that any relatively complex social system must be organised around three distinct functional systems: a sustaining system concerned with production; a distributing system concerned with the transport and communication that allow the circulation of people, goods, and information; and a regulating system concerned with offensive and defensive activities. The various groups, organisations, and institutions of a society, he held, tend to be specialised in relation to one or another of these three functional activities, and the structures of a society are the means through which these functions are fulfilled. The structures associated with the sustaining system are those concerned with the internal requirements of the society. These structures result from adaptations to the physical environment of the society: 'the material environment, yielding in various degrees and with various advantages consumable things, thus determines the industrial differentiations' (Spencer 1873–93: vol. 1, 492). The structures associated with the regulating system, on the other hand, result from activities that have adapted to external relations of conflict and cooperation with other societies (*ibid.*: vol. 1, 506). Holding an intermediary position between internal and external adaptation, the structures of the distributing system are jointly shaped by both the producing system and the regulating system (*ibid.*: vol. 1, 526 ff).

Spencer developed this basic functional schema through a series of comparative and historical explorations into domestic, ceremonial, political, ecclesiastical, professional, and industrial institutions, though he did not systematically relate each of these back to their functions. He did, however, depict the specifically governmental and military aspects of the regulating system primarily undertaken through political institutions as the key to social order. These institutions may be concerned with governing the internal sustaining and distributing activities (mainly undertaken through economic institutions) or with governing the external relations themselves. Either subset of institutions and their associated functions can be dominant in a society, and this was the basis for

Spencer's distinction between 'industrial' and 'militant' societies. A few years earlier, Hughes (1854) had made a similar distinction between 'free' and 'warranted' social orders.

This organicist view was further developed in the functionalist anthropology of Malinowski (1944) and the more structural variant of functionalism in Radcliffe-Brown (1937), but it was in the general and analytical methodology for investigating social systems set out by Parsons in his pioneering work *The Structure of Social Action* (Parsons 1937) that it found its most systematic expression. Parsons relied on the methodological ideas of Henderson and Whitehead, discussed in the next section, but he felt that, in the mid-twentieth century, sociology had not reached the stage at which it was possible to construct that kind of theory. Instead, he argued (Parsons 1945: 216 ff; 1951: 20), it is necessary to make do with what he self-consciously described as the 'second best' form of a 'structural functionalism', a form of theorising that reconstructed Spencer's organicist ideas using both Durkheim's sociology and the advances made in biology by Bernard (1865) and by Parsons' Harvard colleague Cannon.

In *The Wisdom of the Body*, Cannon (1932) had set out a novel understanding of the mechanisms responsible for the stability and growth of organisms. Organicist system models had recognised that organisms show certain constancies of structure relative to their environment and so could be considered as 'boundary-maintaining' entities. He saw this stability as a state of 'bounded equilibrium' that allowed organisms to follow a path of patterned growth over time. His key innovation was to provide a mechanism able to explain how this is possible. An organism, he argued, is an 'open' system engaged in a continuous exchange with its environment. It receives or acquires 'inputs' from its environment and transfers its own 'outputs' to the environment. This exchange allows an organism to acquire the resources needed for environmental adaptation through processes of 'learning':

> Organisms, composed of material which is characterized by the utmost inconstancy and unsteadinesss, have somehow learned the methods of maintaining constancy and keeping steady in the presence of conditions which might reasonably be expected to prove profoundly disturbing. (Cannon 1932: 21–2)

What Cannon meant was that an organism that persists must have built up mechanisms through which it is able to respond, actively and intentionally, to disturbances in its environment. Cannon defined this ability to achieve equilibrium through a coordination of system parts as self-regulation or 'homeostasis' (*ibid.*: 24). Because the parts of a system are interdependent, a change of state in any one part is followed by changes in all other parts, and the change feeds back to the initial point of change. Once initiated by an exogenous disturbance, change can reverberate through the system. An organism is involved in constant 'self-righting adjustments' (*ibid.*: 25; see also Lilienfeld 1898: 10) through which a constancy of structure can be maintained, despite the continual replacement of the material that exhibits that structure. It is able to restore an equilibrium state that is disturbed only by exogenous change. By maintaining their structure,[12] organisms are able to resist tendencies towards change induced by external circumstances unless these are so extreme that the limits of self-regulation are exceeded. An equilibrium state is one in which there is no tendency for any unit to change its state, and so all change is exogenous.

Parsons later summarised this argument:

A system ... is conceived as 'programmed' to behave in a planned way within a range of developing contingencies, without the necessity of predicting the specific contingencies in advance. As the process of 'behavior' of the system develops over time, there is a feedback of information about developments in the environment, including the consequences of the preceding operations by the system. This feedback information is evaluated in its relation to the program and the outcome is the setting in motion of a new set of operations which are 'adapted' to the new situation. (Parsons 1970a: 234)

This highlights the crucial way in which an organic system model goes beyond the insights of a purely mechanical system model. Mechanical models focus on the energy flows inherent in the movement of individuals and resources, but organic system models focus also on the information flows inherent in the communicative acts of those individuals. This advance was integral to Spencer's view of the social as a 'super-organic' sphere of linguistic communication and intersubjectivity rooted in culture. Social systems have the capacity for self-regulation because the communication of information allows situations to be defined and activities to be monitored, so enabling individuals and groups to convey their perceptions and evaluations of system states to each other.

The general basis on which this homeostasis is achieved is shown in Figure 1. A system that maintains its equilibrium state must be structured in such a way that its environment is monitored for changes so that these can be detected and tested against a pattern or template to discover whether the change is sufficiently disturbing to threaten the persistence of the current system state. When change goes beyond the limits of the pattern, 'strains' are experienced and centres of control set in motion adjustments that operate on the environment in such a way as to offset the change and restore the stability of the system (Cannon 1932: 289). A system responds to strains by monitoring and regulating its processes.

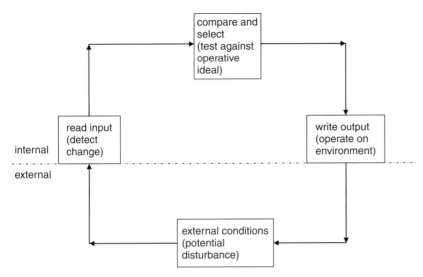

Figure 1 Homeostasis in a social system
Source: adapted from Fararo (1988: 165). See also Stinchcombe (1968).

A homeostatic system, then, operates through the 'feedback' of environmental information to the control centres.

Cannon had suggested that his model of the organism could become the basis of a general model of 'complex systems', among which he included social entities (*ibid.*: 305).[13] It was Parsons, however, who carried this forward. A structural-functional model of a complex system, Parsons argued, involves an analytical simplification. It is one in which certain variables or combinations of variables have been abstracted from the totality and treated as if they were constants, making them fixed points of reference for the analysis of the system. Specifically, the structural components or *parts* of the system, which are relatively fixed combinations of the fundamental elements from which the system is built,[14] are used to define the overall structure of the system. The remaining, dynamic processes of the system are then related to the social structure and its constituent parts. Processes are considered only in so far as they have a 'functional significance' for the system as a whole, i.e., in so far as they contribute to or detract from maintaining the integrity of the structure. The concept of function provides 'criteria of the *importance* of dynamic factors and processes within the system' (Parsons 1945: 217), and the function of any particular process is defined as its relative importance for the ongoing operation of the system.

From this point of view, processes can be either functional or 'dysfunctional', according to whether they make a significant contribution to the maintenance of the system or significantly detract from its maintenance (*ibid.*: 218). Functional processes are 'those observed consequences which make for the adaptation or adjustment of a given system' (Nagel 1956: 83). They are mechanisms that stabilise the system by responding to external disturbance and confining change within certain limits. They maintain the current state of the system within these limits or allow it to develop in a patterned way over time. Dysfunctional processes, on the other hand, are those consequences that lessen the adaptation of the system and tend to destabilise the system and so to bring about the breakdown or radical structural transformation of the system.[15]

Parsons saw adaptation as occurring in response to 'strains' that put pressure on a system to change. The mechanisms through which strains lead to corrective responses are understood by analogy with the pressures inherent in a spring:

The less adequately it is met, the more 'pressure' it will take to realize certain patterns of social action in the face of it, and hence the less energy will be available for other purposes. At certain points for certain individuals or classes of them then the pressure may become too great and the spring may break. (Parsons 1951: 28–9)

When this occurs, the system breaks down. Processes are dysfunctional when they prevent a system from responding to pressure and so lead to its breakdown.

Parsons' argument was that systems of action are organised into three levels that he called the personality, social, and cultural systems. As a bounded system, a psychological system comprises a 'personality' with its distinctive 'character structure' and its distinctive memory, perceptual, and other subsystems. A bounded cultural system comprises particular 'patterns of culture' that permeate its religious, scientific, and other subsystems. A bounded social system comprises a 'society' with its kinship, economic, political, and other subsystems. Each of the three systems of action can be analysed independently by treating the other systems as elements within its environment. Thus, the environment of a social system comprises the personalities or minds of its constituent individuals and the shared cultural meanings sustained by these individuals, as well as the physical conditions that make up the material environment. A social system constitutes a society in so far as it 'contains within itself all the essential prerequisites for its maintenance as a self-subsistent system' (Parsons *et al.* 1951a: 26). This framework allowed Parsons to begin to conceptualise the ways in which cultural factors – meanings and information – can shape the flow of energy through a system. This relationship between information and energy became a central element in later developments of system theory.

Parsons developed his work through an account of the social system, a view that he developed in his book of that name (Parsons 1951) and in the associated collection of papers published as *Towards a General Theory of Action* (Parsons and Shils 1951). The institutions that are the parts of a social structure are seen in Parsons' system model in their various relations to the functional needs, prerequisites, or imperatives of the social system. A functional process is one with consequences that meet, or contribute to, a functional prerequisite, and these are the 'goal states' necessary for the survival of a system (Nagel 1956). A comprehensive list of prerequisites provides a definition of the equilibrium state of the system and, therefore, of the generalised conditions for system maintenance.

Spencer, as I have shown, identified sustaining, distributing, and regulating functions in organic systems, and he used these to classify institutions. Structural functionalists have subsequently proposed various classifications of functional prerequisites and corresponding institutions. An early attempt to follow Spencer's initial proposals was that of Hughes (1854: 48–9), who saw societies as consisting of separate organs concerned with subsistence, security, health, education, enjoyment, morality, and religion. Almost a century later, Malinowski (1939; 1941) recognised three broad categories of functional need: biological needs related to nature (needs for food, reproduction, safety, health), 'derived' cultural needs (production, regulation, education, authoritative control), and 'integrative' needs (relating to cultural symbolism *per se*). A subsequent summary statement by Aberle and his colleagues listed nine functional requirements ('things that must get done in any society if it is to continue as a going concern' (Aberle *et al.* 1950: 100)) relating to productivity and sexual recruitment, role definition and assignment, communication, shared cognitive orientations and goals, and the regulation of the means of action or emotional expression, socialisation, and social control (*ibid.*: 104 ff).

The most influential statement has been that of Parsons, who began from Malinowski's identification of physiobiological, psychological, and cultural imperatives, and added the internal integrative imperatives of the social system itself (Parsons 1945: 229). He concluded that a structural-functional analysis of a social system must be concerned with:

- the biological prerequisites of individual life through nutrition and physical safety;

- the conditions for minimum stability of personality, i.e., for the socialised capacity to secure adequate motivation;
- the cultural imperatives of adequate communication through language, knowledge, and beliefs;
- the integrative imperatives relating to the limits on the incompatibility of its constituent roles (Parsons *et al.* 1951a: 25).

Parsons' most general account rephrased these prerequisites in terms of a more general organicist distinction between 'internal' and 'external' processes. The structurally distinct parts of a system comprise its 'subsystems' (Parsons *et al.* 1951b: 196), and the two principal subsystems identified by Parsons are those involving the internal processes through which system parts can be integrated into a cohesive whole and those involving the external processes through which the system can adapt to its environment.

The external processes of a system are those related to the situational needs of the system within its environment. They typically involve instrumentally oriented expectations concerned with securing the means and resources (as 'facilities') necessary for given social activities. He saw this as a question of 'allocation', of the distribution of people to tasks in a division of labour that ensures people have the facilities needed for these tasks. Parsons argued that economic and political structures are typically and principally concerned with the instrumental meeting of situational needs and adaptation to the environment. Facilities are organised into 'power' relations, such as the purchasing power accorded by money and the political influence given by authority relations. The adaptation of a system refers to its ability to secure required resources from its environments and to operate in such a way that it does not disturb the ability of these environments to continue providing these resources. Thus, any effectively functioning system comprises structural 'mechanisms of adaptation' and of integration that allow it to maintain its boundaries relative to its environment (Parsons *et al.* 1951b: 196).

The internal processes of a social system are related to the integrative needs of the social system itself and concern the avoidance of conflict and contradiction through the establishment of the solidarity and cohesion that constitutes social order. System integration is the degree to which the parts of a system fit together into a relatively stable and enduring whole (Lockwood 1964). Expressive structures of kinship and community are those typically concerned with meeting integrative needs and maintaining the internal order of the system by building up its level of solidarity. This solidarity is rooted in 'prestige' and social status.

Spencer and the early organicists saw social organisms as tightly integrated entities. This was apparent in the argument of Radcliffe-Brown that the parts of a society are connected into an integrated and coherent whole that is the 'total' society or social structure – in Malinowski's terms it is the 'integral system of culture' or the 'culture as a whole' (Malinowski 1926: 133, 135). The function of any recurrent activity is the contribution that it makes to the maintenance of this unity. All the parts work together to produce an internal consistency or harmony and to minimise conflict. Parsons is often seen as having assumed the perfect integration of social systems. For Parsons, however, the model of perfect integration was an ideal type with which actual societies could be compared. In arguing this he was recognising the importance of critical remarks made by Merton (1949), who had noticed that early approaches had tended to assume that *all* social items have an indispensable part to play in relation to the *entire* culture or social structure and, as a result, complete functional integration was taken as axiomatic. Merton argued that this strong form of functionalism overstated the degree of integration, which has to be treated as empirically variable (*ibid.*: 27). It is important for the sociological analyst to assess the overall balance of functional, dysfunctional, and non-functional consequences of the items in any system. Thus, while there may be certain unavoidable functional 'needs', there are no indispensable social structures: functional needs may be met through a range of 'structural alternatives' and they may even fail to be met altogether.

Some critics of structural functionalism and system theory have held that they involve unwarranted teleological claims by assuming that systems act purposively in relation to a goal of increasing their own equilibrium. Credence has been given to this view by some users of the biological analogy. Mackenzie (1895: 160), for example, held that organic systems have internal ends concerned with self-conservation or structural maintenance. The critics recognise that some systems (such as human personalities) do indubitably act purposively, but they hold that most systems do not have the consciousness required to sustain and pursue such purposes. Nagel (1956) countered this criticism using the arguments of Merton (1949) to construct a more formal language for describing a 'functional' account of homeostasis without implying any reference to purposes, goals, or group minds. He argued that while a homeostatic system may involve a tendency to self-perpetuation, this is the outcome of specific mechanisms that causally maintain or develop its equilibrium state. So long as the reading, comparison, and writing of activities of the system (see Figure 1) can be described in causal terms and without invoking vitalist processes, functional models are scientifically acceptable. Functional needs are not *de facto* societal goals unconsciously and automatically pursued by the members of a social system.

Parsons recognised that functional prerequisites do not exercise a direct mechanical influence on actions but have their effects only in so far as they are taken account of, in some degree or another, in the subjectivities of agents. Individual actions must be 'oriented' (or adapted) to the meeting of those needs in some more or less direct way. Any particular functional prerequisite has causal effects only *via* the individual actions that implement it, or that fail to implement it. Individuals act under given conditions and subject to the limits set on the outcomes of their intentional actions by these conditions. Agents are always, to a greater or lesser extent, aware of the conditions under which they act and will reflect on the possible constraints that impinge on the need to act in one way rather than another and on the actual success or failure of their actions.

Thus, the reproduction of those structures that meet functional needs depends upon the existence of particular commitments and patterns of motivation (Parsons 1945: 234; 1951: 22, 42). If these patterns of motivation are not secured, then social order is endangered and the structure of the system will change or break down. It is for this reason that Parsons saw the key mechanisms of homeostasis as the complexes of motivational commitments through which deviance and disruptive tendencies can be minimised. These are the mechanisms of internalisation, support, tolerance, restriction, and sanctioning. He recognised, however, that there is no necessity for these motivational orientations to actually occur: they are contingent outcomes of mechanisms of socialisation and social control. Socialisation may not result in the inculcation of the required motivational mechanisms, and social control may inhibit innovations or ignore deviance. 'Perfect', socially stabilising socialisation and social control is an analytically important case to explore, but it must not be assumed that all real societies will correspond to this ideal type. It follows that the institutional integration of a social system as a boundary-maintaining entity is not inevitable but is, rather, highly problematic. Rather than seeing equilibrium as a necessary and inevitable feature of social life, Parsons saw their establishment as a contingent consequence of the emergence of mechanisms of adaptation and integration. Actual societies may fail to establish effective homeostatic mechanisms of adaptation and integration and so may fail to achieve the equilibrium that will allow them to persist without structural change or total collapse.

Parsons saw actual societies as falling at various points along a continuum between the two extremes of the 'fully institutionalised' social system and the 'anomic' social system (Parsons 1951: 39). A society is in a state of anomie when its patterns of socialisation and social control are such that the necessary cognitive and evaluative commitments have not been built up within individual actors and so are not secured through regulatory norms. In such a situation, social order is precarious and is likely to collapse or to undergo radical change. Parsons held that a clear discussion of the fully institutionalised case, such as he set out in some detail in *The Social System*, was a necessary analytical yardstick for investigating those actual societies that have not fully institutionalised their social activities. With such a point of reference it is possible to determine the conditions required for stability and order to exist. An empirical investigation of any particular society can show whether or not these conditions are actually met and what might be the consequences of any failure to meet them.

Information, integration, and autonomy

Structural-functional analysis of social systems can achieve a great deal, but it is only the first step towards a more analytical sociology. The move towards a more analytical and precise system theory in social science owes a great deal to exploratory work undertaken by Henderson in the 1930s. Writing from a background in physiology, and especially from his reading of the physiology of Bernard (1865; see also Hirst 1975), Henderson set out a sophisticated formulation of the idea of the biological system. Discovering the methodological ideas of Pareto, Henderson (1935) began to use these to extend his own ideas from physiology to sociology and to synthesise mechanical and biological analogies into a dynamic equilibrium model of the social system.

Pareto's aspiration to build general equilibrium theories of social systems had been unsuccessful because the level of quantification possible in most areas of social science would not permit the construction of the kinds of simultaneous equations discovered in economics. On similar grounds, Henderson held that the main limitation to the development of these ideas in the social sciences was the absence of and the difficulty in attaining the kind of data needed to manipulate all the relevant system variables. System theory would be developed to the extent that this situation improved in other fields of social science. Nevertheless, the logic of system analysis could be followed even in the absence of such quantitative rigour.

Henderson defined a system as a 'persistent aggregate' of elements in which changes in any one element depend upon changes in all other elements (Henderson 1938–42: 86–7). The relations among the elements are neither chaotic nor random but are constituted by the constraints inherent in the myriad forces connecting the elements:

the properties and relations of persons exist not in a changeless state, but in a state of flux. However, the instantaneous states and the changes are not chaotic or random states and changes. On the contrary, they are, in general, subject to connections and constraints of a kind that may be referred to, or considered as in a measure determined by, the condition of equilibrium. (*ibid.*: 88)

Henderson connected these ideas with the view of the organism as a bounded or isolated system then emerging in biology. The idea of the mutual dependence of parts to form what Bernard called the 'internal milieu' of the system was substituted for the more rudimentary idea of cause and effect among separate elements. The mutual modification of parts is such that everything within a system is both cause and effect. Once established, a balance among the interdependent parts constitutes an equilibrium that can be maintained or restored through the internal operations of the system: the interdependence of elements is such that a small disturbance can be controlled by forces among the elements that tend to re-establish the state of the system as it was before the disturbance (*ibid.*: 73, citing Pareto). Homans (Homans and Curtis 1934; Homans 1950; see also 1941: final chapter), a student and colleague of Henderson, drew out some implications of this view. Crucially, he held that systems do not necessarily seek and maintain equilibrium. Equilibrium is a possibility that depends on whether the initial conditions of the system are those of stable equilibrium, unstable equilibrium, or no equilibrium at all.

Henderson's recognition that a system exists within an environment was associated with an emphasis on identifying sharp boundaries that close the system off from external influences. Homans, on the other hand, argued that bounded systems may, nevertheless, be 'open' rather than 'closed'. That is to say, systems must be understood in relation to the environment to which they adapt their inflows and outflows of information and resources. This argument was an important step in moving Henderson's account into the mainstream of what came to be called general system theory. This emerged in two early papers by von Bertalanffy (1940; 1945) that were later cast as a more general statement (1956) in which he specified the characteristics of an open system:

The organism is not a static system closed to the outside and always containing the identical components; it is an open system in a (quasi-) steady state, maintained constant in its mass relations in a continuous change of component material and energies, in which material continually enters from, and leaves into, the outside environment. (von Bertalanffy 1940: 121; see also 1964)

Equilibrium conditions in open systems have some similarities with those in closed systems, but the fundamental thermodynamic assumption of increasing entropy does not hold. Instead, an open system can sustain high levels of organisation because of its exchanges with its environment. This self-regulation through metabolism is modelled through a set of simultaneous partial differential equations that take account of the rates of inflow and outflow across its boundaries (von Bertalanffy 1967: 143–4).

This view of the 'living system' as defined by an exchange of material with its environment formed the basis of Bertalanffy's general system theory, which he held to be applicable to psychological and social systems as well as to biological systems (von Bertalanffy 1968; 1956). Such a theory incorporates the ideas of 'feedback' developed by Cannon and Wiener, but instead of seeing feedback solely in 'negative' terms, as damping down tendencies to change, general system theory sees it also in the form of the 'positive feedback' that amplifies tendencies towards change and so is 'deviation-promoting' (von Bertalanffy 1967: 150). Buckley (1967: 58) saw this as the basis of processes of 'morphogenesis', the 'processes which tend to elaborate or change a system's given form, structure, or state' (*ibid.*).

Most strikingly, and importantly, these innovations build on the organicist combination of the 'energy' that had been central to the sciences of nature and the 'information' and cultural controls central to the human sciences. General system theory centres on the interdependence of the energy flows that condition system behaviour and the information flows that control it. Much use is made of information theory and theories of communication to explore the operation of control processes in sociocultural systems (Buckley 1967).

Parsons embraced this approach as allowing him to move beyond the limits of his initial system model. Following from his initial 'second best' structural-functional solution to this problem, Parsons went on to a model of action systems that endeavoured to follow the Pareto-Henderson methodology as rigorously as possible. While the many lacunae in his formulation of a system theory point to the need for further theoretical work, it does provide a general and highly productive theoretical context for research. From the 1950s he began to develop this new system theory, broadening his earlier conclusions. By the middle of the 1950s he felt that it was possible to move towards a truly analytical theory of social life. His works *Economy and Society* (Parsons and Smelser 1956) and *Working Papers in the Theory of Action* (Parsons et al. 1953) were both the culmination of his structural-functional phase and the beginning of his new phase (see Parsons 1970b).

Parsons carried forward the now-established idea that a society could be understood as the totality of all social relations and social institutions sustained by the individuals living in a particular place and so constituting a system of interdependent activities. These activities, being complex and multi-stranded, may come to be specialised around particular concerns – functions – and may also become separated over time and/or space into distinctive circuits or fields of activity. These circuits comprise functionally distinct subsytems and typically exist at numerous nested and overlapping levels. Indeed, Parsons saw societies themselves, alongside cultures and personalities, as subsytems within larger action systems. The value that Parsons recognised in the emerging general system theory was that it provided a framework for understanding system/subsystem relations without relying on the simplifications of structural-functional theory. He held to the model of the system that he had derived from the work of Cannon, but to this he added a deeper, more dynamic account of homeostasis.

Parsons' extension of the system model centred on a reworking of the 'pattern variables' that he had already used to classify cultural variations. He transformed these variables into a set of analytical categories that could grasp the functional organisation of social activity (Parsons *et al.* 1953; Parsons and Smelser 1956; Parsons and Bales 1956). Where he had previously seen social structures in relation to a loosely defined set of functional prerequisites, he now redefined these as a system of imperatives organised in relation to the dynamic variables that are the true 'analytical elements' for social theory.

These analytical elements define the multidimensional field within which action takes place. They define a mathematical space, much as the dimensions used in physics define the space within which matter and motion can be located. The relative location of units in an action system and the movement of a unit from one location to another can be specified by coordinates in this space. The assumption made is that the two dimensions define lines of continuous variation along which position and movement can be measured as variable coordinates on mathematical axes. Nevertheless, the intersection of the two dimensions define boundaries or watersheds that make it sensible, for many purposes, to dichotomise the variables. Thus, there is a more or less clear boundary between a system and its environment that makes it meaningful to distinguish internal from external processes. Similarly, there is a more or less clear boundary between an interest in the building of a stock of utilisable facilities and an interest in their actual consumption or use (Parsons 1970a: 233). Because the dimensions are seen as orthogonal or logically independent of each other, changes in location over time can be

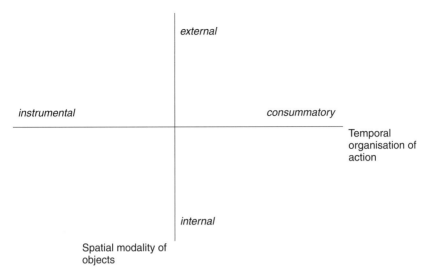

Figure 2 The multidimensional action space

described by logically independent statements that can, ideally, be represented as simultaneous equations. These equations would specify the ways in which change in any one part of a system depends upon change in all other system parts with respect to their external conditions.

Parsons rather misleadingly refers to this multidimensional action space as 'four-dimensional'. In fact, his method specifies a two-dimensional space within which four quadrants can be identified, these quadrants reconstructing the four functional imperatives that he had derived from his general argument and that are seen as forming the particular 'pulls' inherent in the polar combinations of the dimensions as a result of the forces generated in the system. The two dimensions are referred to as the internal/external dimension and the instrumental/consummatory dimension (see Figure 2). The internal/external dimension distinguishes those processes that concern a system itself from those concerning its relation to its environment. The instrumental/consummatory dimension highlights the degree to which a process operates as an end in itself or as a means to an end. These dimensions generalise his earlier arguments on system processes by drawing out the underlying variables that were implicit in references to the fixed aspects of action systems.

The quadrants defining the functional imperatives are functional 'subsystems' of the overall system or field of action (Parsons and Bales 1953: 85) and are set out in the familiar cross-classification grid of the 'Parsonian box', as shown in Figure 3.

	instrumental	consummatory
external	Adaptation	Goal attainment
internal	Latency	Integration

Figure 3 The four subsystems of action

The adaptive quadrant comprises the functional imperative of 'adaptation' (abbreviated as 'A'). Actions 'pulled' in this direction are those that can ensure the generalised adaptation of people to the environment within which they live and act. The adaptive subsystem concerns the processes through which a system becomes oriented towards an object world from which the resources or facilities required by the system can be acquired. It is concerned with the processes through which a system has learned to recognise the relevant properties of objects and so makes them utilisable as 'means' in action. The goal attainment subsystem ('G') concerns the processes through which a system can be kept moving towards its goal states. It is concerned with linking motivation to performance. The integration subsystem ('I') concerns processes through which units are held together and their operations are structured in a coordinated way. It concerns the degree to which they fit together in a coherent and solidaristic unit. Finally, the latency subsystem ('L') involves processes that are able to build up the capacities and channel the motivation needed if a system is to maintain its current state. It is concerned with the amount of 'tension' reduced or built up, as in the latent energy inherent in the tensile strength of a wound spring.

This new approach allowed Parsons to reconceptualise the relations among the personality, social, and cultural systems, to which he added a fourth functional subsystem of action that he termed the behavioural organism. These are, respectively, the G, I, L, and A subsystems of action. His main concern, however, was with the social system itself, which he had recast as the 'integrative' subsystem of action. Within the social system, a parallel pattern of four functional subsystems is specified. The A subsystem of the social system is its 'economy', comprising processes that relate to the environment through the extraction and production of the facilities required in social action and so are oriented to want satisfaction. It is concerned with 'producing and allocating fluidly disposable resources' (Parsons 1968b: 188). Physical objects cannot themselves internalise symbolic representations and it is through the adaptive processes of the A system that access to these resources is regulated. This view was also adopted by Habermas, who saw the economy as concerned with the appropriation and mastery of external nature through production: 'Production processes extract natural resources and transform the energies set free into use values' (Habermas 1973: 9). The social system adapts to its environment through 'forces of production' that organise labour power and technologies. As processes of strategic or instrumental action, the forces of production embody empirical, technical knowledge and tend to develop as crystallisations of rationally grounded systems of scientific knowledge. The G subsystem is the 'polity' and is concerned with forming goals that link environmental conditions to the value commitments of members and operate through powers of command. It organises and mobilises the resources necessary for the attainment of collective goals and treats conditions as 'rewards' for performance rather than as 'means' to an end. The I subsystem is the 'societal community', a system of normatively defined order that regulates activities. It carries the cultural patterns inculcated through socialisation as the skills and dispositions associated with social positions, and is the means through which the integrity of shared cultural orientations and identities can be maintained and loyalty, trust, and cohesion can be built up. Its principal structures are those of family, neighbourhood, and wider diffuse solidarity. Finally, the L subsystem carries shared meanings and definitions of individual and collective identities. It relates all social processes to general values and so maintains the cultural codes or controlling symbolic patterns of a society. The L subsystem is the focus of cybernetic control, generating the flows of information that programme the regulatory operations of the whole system. Its organised representations (most generally 'religious' representations) structure value commitments into meaningful actions oriented towards legitimate social norms (Parsons 1966: ch. 1; Schluchter 1979: 28). Parsons' model brings together the mechanical emphasis on energy and the organicist emphasis on information. There is a hierarchy among subsystems such that the L system employs information to exercise cybernetic 'control' over the 'conditioning' effects of the energy generated and distributed in the A system. This cybernetic hierarchy is apparent also in Giddens' argument concerning the complementarity of 'rules' (information) and 'resources' (energy) in explaining the structuring of social action (1976b: 121–3; 1979: 63–6).[16]

Because action systems are 'open' to their environment, they require mechanisms that can ensure that the difference between a system and its environment is maintained. Disintegration of the system boundary, Parsons argued, is equivalent to the 'death' of the system (Parsons and Bales 1953: 92). System continuity is achieved through the distribution of energy across the system's boundaries with its environment and among its various subsystems. This distribution operates like the physiology of a biological organism as circuits of interchanges between subsystems. The social system as a whole comprises a complex nexus of 'double interchanges' or 'balancing flows' of 'inputs' and 'outputs' that circulate around the system as it attempts to establish a state of equilibrium. Each subsystem depends upon inputs that must be secured from its environing subsystems. At the same time, it must provide specific 'outputs' on which these other subsystems depend (Parsons and Smelser 1956: ch. 2).

A general analytical model of the possible interchanges among subsystems highlights the specific inputs and outputs of the various functionally specialised units. These are analytically distinguishable flows of information and energy that may have a greater or lesser degree of structural distinctiveness as 'organs' or parts of the system. Flows are functional if they contribute to the ongoing maintenance of the system and are dysfunctional if they result in a deficit or excess in the input required by another subsystem (Parsons 1968b: 180). Fararo (1988: 180, 182) has begun to show how to formalise these double interchanges algebraically as simultaneous equations. Such an algebra may, where possible and appropriate, use quantitative variables, but the relationships will often be qualitative.

Thus, the economy of a modern society is an adaptive subsystem that comprises an extensive division of labour and technological apparatus of production among individuals and organisations that is organised as an occupational system of employment relations and a market system of commercial transactions. This economy requires specific 'factors of production' as inputs: it requires labour from households concerned with L functions, capital from business and financial enterprises concerned with G functions, and organisational or entrepreneurial skill from the I system. The various outputs of the economy – consumption goods, productivity, and 'new output combinations' – must be sent to units within the L, G, and I subsystems. Similarly, the polity, as a goal attainment subsystem, requires loyalty, productivity, and support, and must provide capital, allocations of power, and imperative coordination.

These interchanges are mediated by 'payments' of various kinds. In the case of the economy, for example, an exchange of labour for consumer goods is mediated through the income received for the labour and the market prices paid for the commodities. Transactions between the economy and other subsystems are handled in monetary terms. Parsons generalised this view to see money as a generalised 'medium' of exchange, an abstract or generalised measure of the value of goods and services that allows calculations and transactions to proceed more smoothly. It is a symbolic representation of the real material processes, what Giddens calls a 'symbolic token', deriving its value only from the rules governing its use (Parsons 1964b: 273–5; 1975; and see Giddens 1990: 22–7). Parsons suggested that each subsystem may generate a symbolic medium that can serve as the equivalent of monetary pricing in the economic subsystem. Power (authority), influence, and value commitments are presented as generalised symbolic media produced, respectively, in the G, I, and L subsystems. While this suggestion may be overly schematic if taken to imply precise equivalences and parallel operations, the general point is undoubtedly valid. Wherever a symbolic medium can be generated by the operations of a system, it provides a measure and means of calculation through which interactions can be coordinated and an equilibrium achieved (Fararo 1993). By regulating the communication of information from one subsystem to another, the symbolic media are the means through which a system of communicative flows can regulate a flow of energy.

Parsons saw the generalised media as measures that could be used in the simultaneous equations defining system states. This is clearest in relation to money, where monetary quantities can be analysed in equations defining the general equilibrium conditions of an economic system in the manner of the economic theories of Pareto and Walras. Parsons' argument, however, was that similar considerations apply for power and other generalised media, and he suggests that voting, for example, can be seen in relation to inflationary and deflationary circuits of power (Parsons 1959).

Echoing the law of inertia in classical mechanics, he held that a system will remain unchanged unless something external occurs to disturb its state and cause it to change. When a disturbance occurs, systems must respond to this in some way. A failure to respond or an 'inappropriate' response will result in the degradation or dissolution of the system. This is why any ongoing system will have 'mechanisms of control' that attempt, with greater or lesser success, to contain any tendencies to break down by restoring its structure or changing it in a patterned way. These homeostatic mechanisms of the structural-functional model came to be seen in terms of the balance of circular flows (Parsons and Bales 1953: 99–103). Parsons went on to specify 'laws of equilibrium' that specify how a system will respond to disturbances and re-establish equilibrium, as well as the conditions under which it may prove impossible to re-establish an equilibrium. These 'laws', however, tend to be assumed rather than derived, and they rest on an assumption that equilibrium will, in fact, be re-established. Parsons was, perhaps, premature in attempting to state such laws, and more work needs to be done to investigate the conditions under which equilibrium may, or may not, be established.

While Parsons' formulation of a theory of social systems was cast as a general system theory that treated equilibrium and integration as contingent, as system states that may not be achieved, much of his work concentrated on situations of complete integration. A number of critics of his approach have, accordingly, emphasised the importance of recognising the autonomy of subsystems and, therefore, the possibility of mal-integration and contradiction in the relations among system parts. From the 1930s his Harvard colleague Sorokin (1937–41) developed an anti-equilibrium view that stressed precisely the ways in which system parts can counteract each other in their operations. This point of view was also inherent in Merton's (1949) recognition of the part played by 'dys-functions' in system behaviour. Writers such as Eisenstadt (1965) and Wilbert Moore (1974) recognised the importance of making this explicit qualification to the Parsonian system model. According to Moore, social systems exhibit 'strains' – a 'lack of synchronization of types and rates of change' (*ibid.*: 3, emphasis omitted) – when institutional patterns in one field of activity alter and become incompatible with or undermine those in another. In complex societies, he argued, the possibility of strain is great.[17]

An influential general formulation of this argument was that of Gouldner, who recognised that 'there are varying degrees of interdependence which may be postulated to exist among the parts of a system. At one extreme, each element may be involved in a mutual interchange with all others; at the opposite extreme, each element may be involved in mutual interchanges with only one other. The former may be regarded as defining maximal interdependence and "systemness", the latter as defining minimal interdependence or "systemness"' (Gouldner 1959: 156). Where integration is low and system parts contradict one another, the strains or tensions between processes may be such that one part of a system becomes a 'friction-generating part' (*ibid.*: 163). The most powerful extension of the system model along these lines is to be found in the argument of Lockwood (1964), who sees the analysis of incompatibilities in institutional and relational patterns as central to sociological analysis and as concerning what Marx referred to as system 'contradictions'. System malintegration exists when there are incompatibilities between the patterns or principles around which specific subsystems are organised, and such malintegration becomes a contradiction when the incompatibilities occur between structurally distinct institutions or clusters of institutions. As Mouzelis summarises the point: 'The concept of system contradiction means that principles of organisation dominant in a certain institutional sphere are more or less incompatible with the organising principles operating in the other institutional sphere of the same social system' (Mouzelis 1991: 60; see also Parkin 1972). This same general point of view has been central to the 'neo-functionalism' of Alexander and others (Alexander 1988; Münch 1982a; 1982b; and see Alexander 1985).

Although Parsons recognised that any actual social system will have other social systems in its environment and that each system must adapt to the pressures imposed by these, he did not conceptualise this adequately. He saw the 'theoretical closure' involved in scientific analysis as requiring that empirically open systems be treated in isolation, within their own boundaries, and so as describable in terms of their endogenous processes. This led him to treat the influence of other societies as purely exogenous, if not extraneous influences.[18] It was this failure to conceptualise trans-societal connections and processes that led Urry (2000) and others to argue for the abandonment of the system model. However, the system model is not inherently restricted to national societies, and theorists such as Nettl and Robertson (1968) and Wallerstein (1974; 1980; 1989) have proposed models of international, global systems (see also the essays in Robertson 1992).

Complexity and chaos

A recognition of the difficulties that general system theory has with contradiction and malintegration, and therefore with change, has led many contemporary theorists to explore the implications of new developments in the theorisation of physical systems. Work on 'chaos' and 'complexity' has produced ideas that help to theorise the plurality and diversity of social systems and their tendency to radical structural transformation.

The meteorologist Edward Lorenz (1963) showed that small changes in local environmental conditions can have radical and unpredictable repercussions across the system as a whole and can fundamentally transform its overall state. More generally stated, he showed that local linear changes can accumulate to produce non-linear 'chaotic' transformations at the global level. The small changes in the system produce a positive feedback loop in which the effects of the changes are amplified through a chain reaction to the point at which the established equilibrium conditions can no longer be sustained. Concatenating changes may push the system to its limits and shift the whole system into a new and radically different state. This has been seen as a sudden 'flip' or 'catastrophe' in system state occurring at a 'bifurcation point' at which a number of possible outcomes may have been possible (Nicolis and Prigogine 1977; 1989; Thom 1972). Maturana and Varela (1972) introduced the idea of 'autopoesis' to refer to the self-organised closure that a system may achieve.

The crucial factor in this view of system processes is the state of interdependence among the system parts. The kind of change that a system can undergo is inherent in its structure, but these changes are activated only when certain kinds of local changes occur. In the absence of these local changes and the feedback they produce, no change can occur; but without the existence of the specific system structure, change would not take a non-linear form. Radical structural change is not, of course, inevitable. If potentially disruptive effects are contained within the limits defined by the structure of the system, changes can be channelled into smooth linear processes, or may lead to an oscillation in system state. This avoidance of chaotic change is said to be the result of 'strange attractors' within the system. The ability of a system to achieve a stable equilibrium state varies with the amount of energy that can be imported from the environment.

These models of complex systems enlarge the concerns of general system theories such as that of Parsons. Many writers prefer the term 'field' or, more radically, 'rhizome' (Deleuze and Gattari 1972) in order to explicitly recognise the intersection and overlap of social systems in more complex arrangements (López and Scott 2000: 87–8). De Landa's (1997; 2006) formulation of a system theory refers to systems as 'assemblages' in order to be able to recognise that they may be both dispersed and internally inconsistent. This allows them, *inter alia*, to better handle the transnational processes that, as noted earlier, have posed some difficulties for Parsonian theory.

These arguments have not yet been fully incorporated into a revision of general system theory, and they are only just beginning to be taken up in sociology (see Eve *et al.* 1997; Byrne 1998; Urry 2003). They suggest, however, ways of developing the renewal of field concepts (see, for example, Bourdieu 1989) and encompassing the recent emphases on dispersal, plurality, and contradiction in social systems that are often seen as elaborations of a distinct 'post-modern' perspective.

I have argued that a recognition of systemic processes has been central to sociological analysis. Systems thinking originated in a range of mechanistic models that focused on the natural basis of the flows of energy and resources that constitute the basis of any social system and utilised physical concepts and metaphors to understand social processes. The development of biological models allowed this argument to be broadened into an account of the transmission of information and its flow through circuits that enable self-regulation through feedback processes. With the introduction of the cybernetic processes studied in general system theory, the role of cultural meanings and symbolic communication in the transmission of information was better understood and the equilibrium and disequilibrium states of social systems came to be seen as the combined outcome of both cultural information and material energies. The most recent advances in developing the system idea have involved a greater awareness of the ways in which small-scale alterations in system behaviour can result in substantial and unintended changes in the overall structure of a system.

5 Space-Time: Forms and Practices

Space and time – or space-time – are categorical dimensions of under-standing (Kant 1781), though Durkheim (1912a) showed them to have a social origin (see also Schmauss 1994; Rawls 2004: ch. 10). Time is central to ideas of historical change and social development (Nisbet 1969). Space is fundamental to ideas of distribution, migration, and placement. Social processes such as industrialisation and urbanisation are described in terms that directly imply both temporal change and spatial location. These are routinely described in terms of their pace and acceleration (Aminzade 1992: 459) and their distribution and location. The articulation of culture and nature occurs over time in relation to the projects, plans, and strategies of agents, and it occurs in the definite places in which they live. Self-regulation in social systems involves flows of resources and information that are monitored over time and across space to provide feedback on current system states and to generate systemic change.

The ideas of time and space are, however, poorly understood and have often been employed in simplistic and problematic ways. Time is some-times treated as a mere dating system for labelling cross-sectional data. The space in which social relations are organised is often reduced to the natural environment that conditions human actions. Nevertheless, a number of theorists have set out approaches to space and time that have not received the general attention that they deserve. They have been treated, if noticed at all, as discussions of special topics within sociology that can be ignored by those concerned with other topics. The aim of this chapter is to recover these theoretical ideas and to place them at the heart of any attempt at sociological understanding.

Space

The 'environment' within which human action takes place is both a set of material conditions and a 'space' within which social relationships unfold. Material environments are spatial constructions, but the nature of space is little understood.[1] A common view (the Newtonian view) has been that space is an empty container within which matter exists: the universe is a large 'something' within which material objects happen to exist. The problem with this view is that it implies that space could exist without the matter it contains. This would imply that space has a substantial but non-material existence – a contradiction in terms. Space simply cannot be seen as an empty container. The relation between matter and space is exactly the opposite of this: matter exists as a spatially extended arrangement.

Space is not an empty container but is a product of the organisation of matter: the arrangement and rearrangement of matter constitutes the space that the matter occupies. Material objects are spatially extended (they have a size and a shape), and they exist in relation to other spatially extended material objects. The overall configuration of space is, therefore, a concatenation of all causally interdependent material objects. This view, found initially in Leibnitz, was later elaborated by Einstein (Casati and Varzi 1999). Particles and the larger physical objects they constitute are in a state of constant motion, and their movements embody and generate the gravitational and other forces through which physical matter is attracted and repulsed to form the complex arrangements that we call space. According to Einstein, space – more strictly, space-time – is to be understood as the 'curved' and dynamically changing patterns of warp inherent in the relative movement of material entities under the influence of the forces that result from their causal interdependence and movement.

Human beings exist as material entities – bodies – that move and transform the other material objects that surround them, producing a spatial arrangement of clothes, crops, cars, books, furniture, houses, and so on. For this reason, human activities, too, are spatially extended. The concept of space designates the formal properties exhibited in a pattern or arrangement of things within an environment. It is the geometry of place, abstracted from its material form (Werlen 1993: 142; Hillier and Hanson 1984). Human activity results in a distribution of people and objects in a material environment that can be understood as a set of points and a corresponding set of movements and connections among these points. A space is defined by the potential chains of connection or movement between points and that define their locations relative to each other. Spatial arrangement, however, does not exist separately from its material containment. Social relations are projected into a space at the same time as they inscribe themselves in nature, producing a lay-out of buildings, routes, and boundaries that contain and constrain human activities. Social relations, expressed in the material arrangements of objects, are extended as patterns of communication and interaction across the space they define, this space being formed into routes, channels, and media of communication and the specific boundaries, borders, and frontiers that they define. People act within space on the basis of the spatial ideas they acquire through socialisation. These are the bases for all their judgements of space and position in space. The interaction and association of individuals on the basis of the collective representations of the space within which they imagine themselves to live – lived space – is objectified as social structures.

It was Durkheim's key insight that social structures have a spatial form with properties that can be analysed *sui generis*. The specifically spatial aspect of social organisation has a material existence as a 'social morphology' distinct from the physical environment itself. Social reality comprises collective representations and attitudes, organised as the social institutions and relations that structure actions, together with the spatial arrangements of the physical objects that express those structures and activities and that are reproduced, or transformed, by them. The 'moral reality' of cultural representations is the essential mark of the social, but this moral order exists only in and through its visible and tangible physical 'substratum'.

Initially outlined in *The Division of Labour in Society* (Durkheim 1893), the idea of a 'social morphology' was a major theme of *The Rules of the Sociological Method* (Durkheim 1895) and was elaborated in a series of reviews in the *Année Sociologique*. Social morphology, Durkheim argued, is the spatial distribution of the embodied individuals and other material objects through which social life is expressed. These morphological phenomena are 'combinations of persons and things ... bound together in space' (Durkheim 1899: 521–2). Analysis of social morphology involves, fundamentally, investigations into the size and the density of a population, seen as results of demographic processes of fertility and mortality and of the migratory movements of peoples across space. These movements produce varying spatial concentrations and dispersals of population, actors with varying degrees of centrality and peripherality within that space, and the more or less definite boundaries that define the limits or frontiers of their association and communication. In addition to the composition and distribution of the population itself, social morphology comprises its patterns of land and resource use, its construction of dwellings and streets in an overall lay-out or plan of settlements, the location of walls, squares, monuments, and other public places, the routes and means of communication and transport, and so on.

Studies by Durkheim's followers, most notably Mauss (1904–5) and Halbwachs (1909), elaborated on these ideas in studies of urban land use patterns, population distribution, and seasonal variations in settlements.

Halbwachs produced the first book-length summary of the field, arguing that spatial 'form' is the material aspect of the moral 'spirit' and structure of a society. Spatial forms describe 'the manner in which population is distributed in space' and are represented in models of the extension, volume, and density of a population through which it becomes a 'collective body' with distinctive material characteristics that condition people's actions and relations with each other (Halbwachs 1938: 32). More recently, Foucault (1975; 1976b) has shown that systems of surveillance and discipline can arrange and maintain material objects and people in 'sequestered' spatial zones that allow more effective control over behaviour.

The extents, boundaries, and zones of localities, regions, national territories, and transnational agencies are not mere environmental givens. They are constituted by the activities and social relations of the people who live within them and that give them a spatial form. Spatial areas, when more or less coterminous with specific habitats, may become phenomenologically distinct 'places' by virtue of the particular kinds and combinations of activities and relations that define the space. As I have shown, those whose activities constitute a locality may feel a sense of community and an identification with that locality.

Lefebvre (1974) has shown that a spatial morphology is produced because human activities are always 'spatial practices'. A social morphology is the unintended outcome of a series of purposive acts and sets the conditions under which further actions must occur. Thus, people produce the spatial conditions under which they act, but these conditions are also *means* of spatial production (*ibid.*: 85). In the words of Soja:

Spatiality exists ontologically as a product of a transformative process, but always remains open to further transformation in the contexts of material life. It is never primordially given [as nature] or permanently fixed. (Soja 1989: 122)

Halbwachs showed that where social relations are differentiated into intersecting and specialised spheres of activity, the shapes and boundaries of these spheres may not coincide with each other. The overall morphology of a society is a result of the concatenation of political, religious, economic, domestic, and other spatialised processes at work and the 'frontiers' these define (de Greef 1886–9). Religious affiliation and participation, for example, generate a differential distribution across space of the adherents of the various religions (see, for example, Russell and Lewis 1900). Those involved in each religion organise space into the particular 'parishes', 'dioceses', and other districts associated with the churches, temples, and other buildings in which their activities are carried out. The spatial division and arrangement of religious activity is also reinforced and transformed by short-term and periodic population movements, such as the weekly walk to church, pilgrimages, crusades, and larger religious dispersals and diaspora. Similarly, states with diverse political functions generate boundaries and internal administrative districts with distinct and overlapping military, judicial, and fiscal spaces, each with its own central and subsidiary places. It is within these spaces that the members of a population are formed into subjects, citizens, officials, and soldiers (Halbwachs 1938: chs. 2–3; Fawcett 1918). These religious, political, and other spaces are, in turn, influenced by general population movements that transform the religious and political demography of a society and make possible a greater or lesser degree of centralisation and a realignment of internal and external boundaries. The idea of the 'nation' and its national territorial boundaries may express a specific pattern of political spatialisation, but these may not coincide with the frontiers defined by religious relations and economic transactions. For this reason, 'society' and 'nation' are not the same thing. The society formed by those who live within the bounds of the French state, for example, may extend in myriad ways beyond them.

Recent work has explored the cultural 'scene' as an example of such a spatial arrangement. A scene is a focused system of activities, delineated in space and time, within which people realise and express their tastes and preferences through cultural signs that may be appropriated from elsewhere but are recombined and developed in ways that express specific interests, concerns, and forms of identity (Peterson and Bennett 2004). Originating in the study of music, it refers to the ways in which people may be attracted to ideas and practices that resonate with or have an affinity with their particular experiences and so may become involved in folk, jazz, heavy metal, and other musical scenes (Straw 1991). Musical scenes are cultural spaces constructed through the interdependent activities of musicians, record producers, journalists, and audiences around particular bands or genres. A musical scene comprises a core of performers involved in overlapping spheres of performance and holding an authoritative position in relation to the defining of canonical or paradigmatic performances or styles of performance. It is centred on an audience with a shared body of knowledge concerning performers and their careers and repertoire, and it is organised through a network of magazines, websites, festivals, clubs and other performance venues, and, perhaps, recording companies and radio shows. Similarly, fashion scenes may be organised around particular networks of designers, retail outlets, magazines, and fashion shows, while sports scenes may be organised around particular teams, stadiums, television programmes, and so on.

Formal conceptions of space

The study of space was transformed when Haggett (1965) and Morrill (1970) showed that social morphologies could be formally modelled as configurations of points, the points representing the people and objects that constitute the spaces. Envisaging a space as a configuration of points allows the use of geometry – the mathematics of points, lines, distances, and shapes – to chart the relative location of people and objects within places and highlights the formal, mathematical properties of the space itself. This made it possible to analyse spatial form with concepts of dimensionality, distance, agglomeration, size, accessibility, and paths.

The dimensionality of a space is the number of logical parameters required to describe its spatial extension. Distance is the spatial proximity or separation of places, as measured by time, cost, or some other measures of similarity along the dimensions of the space. Distance is typically symmetric – the same measured in either direction – but it may vary with the direction in which it is measured. Agglomeration refers to the clustering or clumping of people and objects in relations of spatial contiguity or association as they form settlements, places of work, encampments, etc. The size of a space or region of space, as a bounded 'field' of interaction for the members of a population, refers to its areal extent (Haggett 1965). Accessibility is a measure of the centrality or peripherality of people or objects within an agglomeration or of an agglomeration within a larger space. For example, places may be more or less 'isolated' from each and show varying degrees of peripherality. Finally, the paths of movement and connection that link points into a network of channels define definite routes through space.

Recent debates among physicists over the dimensionality of space at the sub-atomic and astronomical levels have not undermined the view that, at the human level, the geographical space of the physical world can be seen in Euclidean, three-dimensional terms:

for the intermediate scale which we usually refer to as geographic and in which are located the social and physical events of the earth's surface that constitute the immediately perceived and humanly created environment, the appropriate description of physical space is that familiar abstract three-dimensional Euclidean geometry. (Sack 1980: 7)

Human activity, then, exists as a three-dimensional space. This was the view of Kant (1768), who held that a person's sense of direction and movement in space depends upon the material presence of their body at a specific location within that space. Bodily presence provides an egocentric perception of the world from which distances and directions to the various objects encountered are judged. It is the experience of bodily presence that gives a sense of front and back (before and behind), left and right, and up and down (above and below). The body is the point of origin of action and is, therefore, the basis on which human beings experience space in terms of the three dimensions of length, breadth, and depth. These dimensions have been represented in maps by the formal framework of longitude, latitude, and altitude.

The social relations produced by human activity may, however, transcend these physical dimensions and require the use of further, non-physical dimensions to represent their spatial location and extent. The unequal distribution of resources within a population, for example, can be described only if a description of the physical location of those resources is combined with a description of the degree of 'inequality' exhibited in the distribution. Thus, Bourdieu (1979) used principal component analysis to depict the horizontal and vertical dimensions within which the distribution of capital is organised. Representations of the space formed by social relations may, therefore, require many more than the three principal dimensions of physical space and so human activity must be seen as defining a multidimensional spatial reality. Bourdieu's work suggests the need for a plurality of dimensions if the distribution of all the various forms of capital (economic, social, educational, cultural, political, etc.) are to be mapped. In a more general vein, Parsons saw the need to chart the multiple dimensions of action space (Parsons *et al.* 1953). The number and character of the dimensions of social space does not seem to be an invariant and fixed property but may vary considerably from one society to another and at various levels and scales of social activity.

If points are separated from each other, people and objects must move or be moved over the distance that separates them. Movement within social space – through mobility, migration, travel, and transport – has been seen by analogy with the physical movement of objects subject to gravity. Early usage of the idea of 'universal gravitation' reduced the movement of social objects to the assumed effects of a natural force of attraction, but the gravitational analogy does not require this strong reductionism. Attraction is simply a word to summarise the kinds of spatial relations that typically occur as a result of particular forms of human motivation.

Rationally motivated strategic action has most often been taken as the basis of theories of spatial attraction. Thus, Carey (1872) extended Newton's laws to the social world and claimed that the amount of movement between any two places is proportional to the size of their populations and inversely proportional to the distance between them: the existence of a large aggregation of people exerts a strong attraction on potential migrants, but this force of attraction is offset by the effects of increasing distance. Haggett (1965: 35) summarised empirical work in this tradition as supporting a general formula according to which the interaction between two points (i and j) is proportional to the product of their populations (equivalent to their 'masses') and the inverse square of the distance between them: $M_{ij} = P_i P_j (d_{ij})^{-2}$. This formula involves fairly simple assumptions about the validity of regarding each individual person as making an equal contribution to the 'mass' of a given town or city, and more refined measures have weighted population size by, for example, mean *per capita* income to recognise the effect of wealth on the attractiveness of a place. Similarly, analysts differ about whether distance is better measured by straight line mileage or by travel time with given forms of transport. While various alternative formulae have been proposed, none has gained any general degree of recognition, reflecting the diversity of motivation in human actions and the consequent complexity of spatial relations. Nevertheless, the general point remains the case that movement in space can be seen as patterns created by forces of attraction in fields of association.

Patterns of movement through space can involve periodic and repetitious transhumance movement between places (Mauss 1904–5), nomadic circulation around a space, direct migration and settlement from one place to another, daily travel from home to work, and so on. Patterns of population movement among places of settlement, work, domesticity, and leisure may be individual or collective, may involve 'chain' or loop migration (Macdonald and Macdonald 1964), or may form waves of diffusion from particular points of influence (Tarde 1898a; Morrill *et al.* 1988). Hägerstrand (1953) has shown that a measurement of the flow and diffusion of people and objects over time allows an identification of the varying space-time trajectories followed by individuals over the course of their lives. Social life as a whole comprises a complex system of intersecting spatial trajectories.

Patterns of actual and potential movement of people and objects define the shapes and sizes of the spaces within which people live. The most widely used measure of size has been the mean travel distance for those visiting a particular place, which has been seen as defining its effective hinterland or catchment area (Tobler 1963). This travel distance varies with both the value of the object or person moved and the actual cost of travel, so improvements in transport technology can reduce effective distances and increase the rate of movement from any given point. When mapped in two dimensions, areas of population movement have been shown, at their simplest, to be roughly circular in shape, though this circularity is modified by the presence of major natural boundaries such as mountain ranges, lakes, and seas. The catchment areas for migrants have been shown to vary in shape according to the 'vacancies' available in the centre and the information that potential migrants have about these vacancies. The differential distribution of information distorts and, perhaps, fragments the total area of migration (White 1970; Chase 1991).

Spatial shape is also directly determined by political and administrative activity that establishes the normatively defined boundaries of a 'territory'. Territorial boundaries express the *power* of an agency, such as a state, and hence the spatial extent of its territorial reach and penetration (Mann 1986: ch. 1). Boundaries may become extended as originally separate spatial areas coalesce with the expansion of a central state, but they may equally be arbitrary impositions of an external power. For example, France and Germany developed as national territories through the establishment of unified political control as one state came to dominate others (Elias 1939). Colonial territories established by imperial powers in Africa and areas of white settlement in North America and Australia are examples of externally imposed boundaries (Fawcett 1918: ch. 6).

Movement is rarely distributed uniformly across a space. It normally follows specific paths or channels that are jointly shaped by natural factors and already established networks of movement to form road, rail, air, and shipping routes (Demolins 1901–3). Transport networks have typically been built according to a principle of minimum distance, the actual configuration of a network reflecting the density of its interconnections and the centrality of the various points. However, many such networks result not from conscious planning but from a continual sequence of ad hoc decisions over time (Cooley 1894). In addition to purely strategic decisions, however, routes also result from actions drawing on value commitments to, for example, the protection of sacred areas or ancient woodlands. It has been suggested that network analysis can highlight many of the formal properties of such networks (Haggett and Chorley 1969).[2]

The relative 'centrality' of places has been an important concept in studies of urbanism. The determinants of centrality have been found in marketing, the provision of services, and in transport. Rational decisions over the allocation of resources made in a space with uniform population density, such as an entirely rural society with dispersed agriculture, tend to generate agglomerations of people and service activities in the 'central places' in which transport times involved in marketing resources are optimised. The interdependence and specialisation of activities within the hinterland are enhanced and the central places develop as villages, towns, and then cities (Morrill 1970: 61–9; Haggett 1965: chs. 4–5).

The demand for a service or activity shows a tendency to fall with distance, and the study of central places has shown how equilibrium or optimum states can be established. If the distance is such that the cost for the participants is too great, pressures will build up for the agglomeration of services in more attractive locations. This has been seen as the basis for multiple centres that co-exist in a dynamic system state until the system as a whole moves towards equilibrium. The arrangement of centres relative to each other, the relations of each centre to its immediately surrounding area, and the pattern of transport or movement routes among them are results of the marketing of goods and services, but are compounded by the requirements of efficient transportation and the administrative constraints involved in servicing dispersed communities (Christaller 1933; Ullman 1941; and see Morrill 1970).

Theories of the location of industrial processing have shown its dependence on the availability of resources, both physical and human, and the ease of transporting them. Alfred Weber (1909) provided a powerful theory of the location of individual plants as outcomes of the rational choices made in strategic actions. The siting of places of production, he argued, depends on the transport costs involved in obtaining raw materials and taking the finished product to market. Industries will locate where these costs are at a minimum. Weber held that these costs reflect both the distance to be travelled and the weight of the material carried. Transport costs, of course, will vary with the mode or modes of transport available and with the pattern of transport routes, the latter already reflecting earlier location decisions. More complex versions of this theory have included the impact of the varying costs of labour at alternative possible locations (Friedrich 1929; see also Lösch 1940).

Similar arguments have been used to explain the clustering of related industries in particular places. The uneven spatial distribution of resources is such that industrial location is unlikely to show a pure central-place pattern. Where there is a regional clustering of industrial activity across a given space, enterprises may be able to achieve economies of scale in production and distribution, despite any increase in the distance over which resources have to be transported. If plants are able to achieve these economies, the location decisions of each plant or firm will depend on those of others in the same or related industries (Hotelling 1929). Overlapping markets, the substitutability of products, and brand differentiation add further complications to the resulting spatial arrangement (Morrill 1970: 91–6).[3]

Increasing attention has been given to the implications of rapid transport in fast trains and airplanes that move ever larger numbers of people at increasing speeds. In addition to huge reductions in spatial distanciation (the bringing of physically distant parts of the earth closer to each other) these means of transport constitute moving spaces in which travellers are enclosed and insulated from the surrounding spaces through which they move (Letherby and Reynolds 2005). They are temporary lifeworlds for the traveller, detached from her or his ordinary, everyday lifeworld. Complexes of terminal buildings dedicated to servicing these travellers combine to constitute distinct spaces with an anonymity that makes it plausible to describe them as non-places (Augé 1992): their transient occupants are, in effect, 'nowhere' while travelling.

New forms of electric and electronic communication have also introduced new forms of space and place. Telephony and wireless opened up possibilities for the more extensive spatial distanciation of those engaged in communication. With the introduction of broadcast technologies people were able to enter, or to be drawn into, worlds of experience that may have no referent beyond the broadcast images themselves. Far more effectively than the book, the radio and television could make the viewer feel a part of the text. With the two-way communication made possible by computers and the Internet it became possible for individuals to interact virtually, through computer-mediated conversations, rather than face-to-face, and they are able to construct the virtual worlds that constitute 'cyberspace'. The material base for cyberspace is the computer technology, but cyberspaces are more completely detached from the form of this material base than any other form of space.

Surfaces and urban structures

Haggett has described the overall configurations of areas and territories that result from the movements of populations and the distribution of social activity as spatial 'surfaces', holding that these can be mapped with isometric contour lines to show their topographies. At its simplest, this has involved, for example, the mapping of rural and urban land use with shadings of different colours to represent the various activities and uses (von Thünen 1826; Stamp 1948). This has been extensively explored in studies of rural areas and the landscape of particular regions (Hoskins 1955). An early attempt to depict the class differentiation of urban spaces was Engels' (1845) study of Manchester. Addams (1895), Du Bois (1899), and Booth (1901–2) adopted similar procedures in their systematic mappings of the class, religious, and ethnic characteristics in the urban areas of Chicago, Philadelphia, and London. The classic works of the Chicago sociologists built on these ideas to map the distribution of suicide, lodging houses, gangs, and other 'social problems' (Thrasher 1927; Cavan 1928; Zorbaugh 1929). They used this work to chart the general social character of the various zones into which the city was organised.

The implications of economic processes for urban spatial surfaces were explored by Halbwachs (1909) in his study of the relationship between population and land use in Paris. Halbwachs saw land use as an expression of the mode of production, which produces a spatially organised division of labour and system of class inequalities. He followed Engels in showing that the economic differentiation of a society into classes generates distinct class spaces – and, hence, class milieux – within expanding cities. Industrial cities develop as class-divided spaces, each distinct locality characterised by uniform class conditions and experiences. Factories bring large numbers of workers together and require the construction of industrial districts and working-class housing estates. The owners of these factories and their professional employees, meanwhile, are housed in separate and distinct parts of the city (Halbwachs 1938: ch. 4).

This view of class differentiation was the basis of the work of the Chicago sociologists, who explored the dynamic features of the city as a system of zones. Where Thünen had proposed a simple 'ring' or gradient model of the land surface, Park and Burgess (1925) set out a morphological account of urban growth involving areal differentiation into a series of concentric circles. An urban area that grows through continuing waves of expansion from its nucleus tends to form a series of concentric zones. The dynamic mechanism behind this spatial structure is competition for land among the various business and residential users. These users compete for the most advantageous locations, within limits set by their resources, as determined by their class and ethnicity, and their struggles generate an ecological 'succession' in land use as occupants of each zone invade the next outer one. Inner zones become 'disorganised' as the 'organised' residential users move out to 'invade' more desirable locations. The typical spatial pattern for a mature city is a series of zones radiating out from a central business district that contains the 'downtown' retail and service units (McKenzie 1933). Further out from this central zone is a zone of working-class housing separated from it by a transitional zone of declining slum housing into which business and light manufacturing units move. Beyond the working-class zone is the affluent middle-class residential zone of superior apartments and family houses, while even further out is the commuter zone of suburban and satellite housing.

Applying this model to Chicago, Burgess identified a central 'loop' surrounded by a disorganised slum zone in which are the 'Hobohemia' of the homeless (Anderson 1923), the ethnic enclaves of 'Little Sicily', 'Chinatown', the Jewish Ghetto, and the black belt in which new migrants can find cheap housing (Drake and Cayton 1945). This decaying and declining slum zone also offers opportunities for artistic and creative workers who can find accommodation close to the clubs, bars, and cafés of the downtown district (Cressey 1932). Second-generation migrants were typically found in the working-class zone, where a degree of financial security allowed better-quality housing to be rented. It was the area to which those in the transitional zone aspired. The affluent and respectable workers, for their part, aspired to move into the outer residential zone of the so-called 'Gold Coast', with its apartments, family homes, and satellite shopping districts (Zorbaugh 1929). The most affluent Chicagoans were those who had escaped to the low-rise dwellings of the leafy suburbs and who travelled into work each day by car and train.

The concentric ring theory of the city is based on an assumption that land values decrease from centre to periphery as potential users of the space compete for the more accessible and desirable locations. Theories that take more seriously the income inequalities among households and businesses have suggested a 'sector' model in which the city comes to be divided into class, race, and commercial sectors or wedges, with each sector showing an internal gradient and ring zoning. Berry (1967; 1976) has extended this work to produce a powerful reconceptualisation of the zoning of Chicago (Berry *et al.* 1976).

On the basis of such arguments, Lefebvre (1974) developed a more general account of 'urban' phenomena. He defined an urban society as one that has been completely urbanised as a consequence of capitalist industrialism. Places of work, leisure, domesticity become connected through patterns of movement and interchange into villages, towns, cities, and larger regional administrative units. A similar conclusion was Dickinson's (1947) view that an increase in the size of the effective unit of social life led to a transition from the small rural community focused on the hamlet or village, to the larger region focused on the town as a trading centre for a number of rural communities, and the more extensive region focused on the city as an administrative and economic centre. An 'urban revolution' transforms agriculture into a form of industrial production and subjects it to the same constraints as other branches of capitalist production. As a result, the farming village, the rural countryside, and the mercantile structures with which they are involved are all transformed: 'The *urban fabric* grows, extends its borders, corrodes the residue of agrarian life' (Lefebvre 1970: 3). Population is concentrated into larger units with expanding labour markets, and smaller units become dependent on the larger ones. The larger units become true regions when social activities are no longer focused exclusively on the smaller units and integration is established at the higher level. Constituent units are dis-articulated as larger regional linkages are built (Stacey 1969). Regional entities such as the city region and extensive multi-city regions may also break up if activities are no longer integrated within them. The estab-lishment of national links, for example, may mean that the nation-state and its capital city becomes the focus rather than a particular city and so there would be a decline in regional integration alongside a correspond-ing increase in national integration. Similarly, the growth of transnational linkages may disarticulate the national economy and society, as activities become focused around networks of global cities (Sassen 1991; Scott 1997: ch. 8).

In this process of urbanisation, distinctively 'rural' activities are under-mined. Villages become commuter dormitories and locations for holiday homes, or they stagnate into decay. The depleted countryside – the loca-tion of industrial farming – becomes also a leisure 'environment' of farm parks, country parks, and theme parks for townspeople. Industrialisation and urbanisation completely transform nature into a mere simulacrum of itself (Lefebvre 1970: 26). Merchant cities, successors to the traditional 'political cities', are initially transformed into industrial cities dominated by the circuits of industrial capital. The development from industrial capital to finance capital was associated with a further morphological transformation of the city into a 'critical zone' (*ibid.*: 14) moving towards global urbanism.

The morphology of an urban society, Lefebvre argued, becomes the object of the rationalising urban practices of urban planners. Modernisation is a process in which spatial practices come to embody instrumental rationality to an ever greater degree and in which, there-fore, everyday life comes to take a more planned form. Oriented by a commitment to 'urbanism' as an ideological representation of the city, spatial structures are subject to state-regulated management and plan-ning that provides monumental architecture, large-scale projects of town planning, 'redevelopment', and new-town building.

Castells (1968; 1969) has questioned Lefebvre's use of the term 'urban', but recognises the importance of an ideology of 'urbanism' as the basis for managing spatial structures and processes of collective consumption in housing, transport, and leisure that can be provided only through their concentration in large centres of population. Such urbanism is the source of conflicts over collective consumption that give rise to the formation of urban social movements and distinctive urban conflicts.

It is important to note the assumption of economic rationality and their bracketing of non-economic considerations in many of these theor-ies. The specific spatial arrangements follow only to the extent that these conditions hold. Where other forms of motivation prevail, the morphological patterns will be modified. The actual surface of a city or area will also, of course, reflect the topography, as the presence of rivers and other water systems, of hills and valleys, etc., all affect the value and possible use of land (Aston and Bond 1976). Nevertheless, the hypothesised patterns have been found to correspond closely with actual morphological patterns, reflecting the centrality of strategic action and economic considerations and the power of material technology in modern societies.

Time

The idea of time as something real and substantial is central to everyday language.[4] It seems obvious that time is simply the medium within which things happen and that the passing of time can be measured with clocks and calendars, just as the distances between objects can be measured with rulers and meters. The inexorable movement of the hands around the face of a clock seems to mark out the equally relentless passage of time and makes it seem unproblematic to talk of 'taking' or 'using' time: people devise ways of 'spending' their 'free' time, and may feel their time has been 'wasted'. The idea that there is a past, a present, and a future is so commonplace that it barely seems to warrant further thought. People anticipate what might happen 'tomorrow' or remember what happened 'yesterday'. They recognise that they will live for a definite number of years and that other people and the things around them will change over time. Time, surely, is one of the most obviously real phenomena that humans experience.

To think this way would be a mistake. Time, like space, is not a substantial medium within which things exist. Neither is it an empty container through which things move. Time itself is not material and it cannot 'flow' or 'pass'. 'Time' at its simplest is the word used to describe the causal succession of happenings resulting from the movement of material objects.[5] It provides a frame of reference for understanding the sequential occurrences that happen as the properties of things in the world persist or change (Aminzade 1992: 459). If space can be considered as material *extension* – the arrangement of material objects – then time can be seen as the *duration* of those material states of arrangement. The duration of an object or spatial configuration is simply the persistence or change in their material relations. Persistence is the absence of change, while change itself is movement from one state of existence to another. Change is the process through which one material state becomes something different. An object or region of space that alters in respect of one or more of its properties has changed (Newton-Smith

1980: 15; see Jacques 1982: 41). The processual states of change comprise the 'flow' that is often attributed to time itself. Time is the dimension of reality in terms of which it is possible to talk about persistence and change.[6]

The duration of material objects as they move in space can further be described in terms of the pace or speed of motion and its rate of acceleration. The pace at which objects move is measured by the number of similar events that occur in any given measured length of time. A car, for example, might be said to move at a speed of 30 miles per hour. The acceleration of an object is the rate at which its speed of movement changes: a car may double its speed by accelerating from 30 to 60 miles per hour. Physicists have drawn up determinate mathematical models of the relations among measures of duration, pace, and acceleration. Thus, velocity (speed) is defined as a function of measured distance and time. A measured process of change can, finally, be described as having a particular trajectory or cadence, as being linear or progressive, cyclical or recurrent, continuous or episodic. These various patterns define the pulse, rhythm, or periodicity of change.

Contemporary scientific views of time are the result of a long series of cultural transformations through which people in the West have attempted to grasp the material reality of duration and change. Western science initially adopted an Aristotelian concept of time as a measurement of continuous motion, the earliest scientific writers seeing changes of state as movement from a 'past' to a 'future' state: past and future were seen as absolute and objective conditions such that things occur 'before' or 'after' each other.[7] Newton (1687) took this view to depict change as a process that could be measured on an invariant scale of infinitely divisible quantities. Happenings could be assigned to distinct and absolute locations in time, and so all occurrences could be fixed unambiguously in time in relation to other events. Any event can be unambiguously located in the past, present, or future of any other given event. Time was understood as if it were a continuous line running from the infinite past to the infinite future, and contemporary scientific observers have refined the use of calendars and clocks as objective standards for temporal measurement along this continuum.

Einstein assimilated time and space into a single scientific framework and saw material objects existing in a unified 'space-time'. According to Einstein, material reality exists in three dimensions of space and one dimension of time. Space-time is understood as the expanding four-dimensional configuration of material entities that move under the influence of the electro-magnetic, gravitational, and other physical forces they exert on each other. Changes in a spatial arrangement can be explored by examining successive three-dimensional spatial 'slices' along the fourth, time dimension (Barbour 1999).

Subsequent work in physics and cosmology has now suggested (though not without contention) that space-time is eleven-dimensional, rather than merely four-dimensional (Kaku 2004). According to this view, the primordial 'big bang' created a microscopically small eleven-dimensional universe that expanded exponentially along four of these dimensions as the other seven dimensions were compacted to the quantum level. As a result, macroscopic entities at the human scale and beyond can be understood in four-dimensional terms alone, and only those who study sub-atomic quantum occurrences need be directly concerned with the other seven dimensions (Rees 2001: chs. 10 and 11). For occurrences at the normal human scale of observation, then, the material world is a four-dimensional world.

Einstein's innovations went deeper than his recognition of a single multidimensional framework of space-time. His key insight was that there is no absolute time, only relative time (Einstein 1905; 1916). Measurements of time define the location of one object relative to all other objects in existence, and so all measures of time must be relative to a system of observation. Each object creates its own time, which varies with its speed of movement and the gravitational fields through which it moves. Measurements of time are necessarily made from the standpoint of a particular observer. This standpoint-dependence of time measurement holds for all material objects, though it is only human beings who can become conscious of it. Einstein's theory postulated that these relativistic features of space-time are, in principle, observable on the cosmological scale and at movement close to the speed of light. On a terrestrial scale and on the scale of the solar system, however, these effects are barely apparent. At the human scale, relativistic time differences are miniscule in relation to human perception and experience and so are almost completely unnoticeable. While the Newtonian view of absolute time has thus been superseded in physics by an Einsteinian view of the relativity of time, it remains a workable approximation to the human experience of material duration at the geographical scale. Nevertheless, time remains relativistic, even if human observers fail to notice this in their everyday physical experiences.

Material reality as a whole is comprehended as the concatenation of all relative, standpoint-dependent space-times, all occurrences happening within this complex configuration or manifold. For this reason, it is not possible to regard occurrences as being absolutely located in the 'past' or the 'future' as Newton had argued. The past of one object may be the 'future' of another. While each object may be characterised in terms of its own unique present and past, the universe as a whole has no such fixed points of reference. Andrew Abbott has expressed this well in his conclusion that the present is:

a moment in the conscious, personal experience of individuals. We denote by the word 'present' that period of time to which we as individuals have immediate cognitive and conative access and we distinguish it in relation to a past and a future. The present is neither the past, cognitively accessible only in memory and conatively forbidden by its irrevocability, nor yet the future, cognitively available only to the imagination and conatively dependent on chains of action yet undone. (Abbott 1994)

Many theorists have suggested that a spatially and temporally decentred universe is one in which movement should be possible back and forth in both space and time. If it is possible to move bi-directionally in measured space, then so, too, should it be possible in measured time. Time travel ought to be possible if only sufficient speeds of movement could be achieved. This implication has been denied by those who reject the parallel between movement in space and movement in time. The most influential such view was that of Bolzman, who proposed that the physical processes summarised in the famous 'second law' of thermodynamics indicate an overall direction and irreversibility in material change. According to this view, a physical system loses energy as it operates, and so there will always be a diminishing amount of available useful energy. Because the amount of useful energy held within a system dissipates over time, there is a tendency for structures in space-time to move towards greater entropy or disorder. Material processes in which energy is lost cannot, from their own internal resources, move back into states of lower entropy. Burning wood to produce heat, for example, produces ashes that cannot be reconverted into wood. A constant supply of new energy is required in order to maintain physical structure, and without such new energy a physical system becomes disorganised.

This irreversibility of causal processes in physical systems is most apparent at the cosmological level. Space-time began with a 'big bang' that produced a universe in a state of low entropy, and material structures have become ever more disorganised as this universe has expanded. Increasing entropy is an irreversible causal process and is the basis of a directionality in temporal change that makes it possible to use the terms 'before' and 'after' (Lucas 1973). The directionality of time is inherent in the structure of material objects, and time travel, as conventionally understood, is impossible.

Social time, temporalising practices, and objectified time

My discussion so far has concerned the temporality of the material world. There is, however, a distinctive temporality to the social world. Human beings, as material bodies, are elements in the material reality that exists as space-time. Cultural forms and social structures exist within the material world as memory traces, material artefacts, and social morphology. By virtue of their materiality, these social forms exist in physical space-time. However, their temporality is more than material, as the temporalising practices of human agents enable socially structured realities to transcend the material morphology of time. Temporalising practices are actions organised in relation to the experience and conceptualisation of time. They are the means through which the duration and sequencing of human activities can be rigidified or loosened, and involve processes of planning, project building, anticipating, deferring, habituation, ritualisation, and so on. These practices are constitutive of a 'social time' that expresses the change or movement of social phenomena relative to other social phenomena (Sorokin and Merton 1937: 618; Gurvitch 1963). Social events and situations are related to other social events that are rooted in their materiality but are not completely defined by their physical time.

The change, duration, pace, and acceleration of things are features of the external world that become significant only through the subjectivity of the people who experience them. Perception of occurrences as forming a temporal sequence is a product of the human ability to remember and recall occurrences and to relate them to each other. Humans relate observed persistence and change in objects to phenomena with which they are already familiar: to the duration of their own lifetimes, to recollections of salient events (such as the outbreak of a war), and so on. People organise their activities in relation to socially shared conceptions of time. They think of events as occurring 'after the war', 'before Christmas', 'during the winter', 'at the end of term', and so on. These ways of thinking about time are constitutive of social structures, shaping their persistence and change. At the same time, the experiences that people have of living within particular social structures, of occupying a particular standpoint, are elements in their conception of time. Conceptions of time and temporally organised social structures change through processes of mutual constitution. The experienced time of human beings, therefore, has properties quite distinct from those of the objects in the external world themselves. Experienced time is a cultural phenomenon, and cultural conceptions of time are the means through which the duration of occurrences in the overall succession of happenings is determined (Elias 1987: 3; Jacques 1982: 87):

the word 'time' ... is a symbol of the relationship that a human group, that is, a group of beings historically endowed with the capacity for memory and synthesis, establishes between two or more continua of changes, one of which is used by it as a frame of reference or standard of measurement for the other. (Elias 1987: 46)

Social time, as much as physical time, must be seen as relative to the standpoint of the observer: individuals located within distinct experiential standpoints within social structures will have varying perceptions of the overall temporality of their society.

Cultural conceptions of time are rooted in the developing awareness of natural processes. Internal bodily processes of hunger, digestion, sleep, etc., along with observations of birth, maturation, and death, provide people with an awareness of their own duration and of the rhythm or pattern of their life. The most fundamental basis for the experience of time is the human body itself and its biological conditions of existence. The idea of time as divisible into past, present, and future is, like the spatial ideas of 'here' and 'there', a feature of human experience in the world. The sense of a place that is here and is the focus of the present time ('now') derives from the experience an individual has of his or her bodily location in social and material space-time.

The bodies of human beings, like those of other animals, are organised through daily, monthly, and annual cycles that result from the interlocking of individual biology and environmental conditions (Hughes 1952). On a daily basis, the body operates according to circadian rhythms that regulate the processes of sleeping and metabolism. Human females, for much of their lives, experience a monthly cycle of hormone flow that regulates menstrual activity and affects mood states. Human beings also exist in 'geographical' time: a time formed by the physical and biological processes of the earth and of their own bodies.[8] Material or environmental time consists of such things as the rhythm of planetary movements and the consequent alternation of night and day (Ekirch 2006), the lunar phases, the rhythm of tidal movements, and the succession of seasons (Mauss 1904–5). Human daily and monthly cycles may become locked into larger annual cycles through human sensitivity to seasonal variations in sunlight. This interdependence of body and environment (Young 1988) occurs through the homeostatic mechanisms described by Cannon (1932).

The sense of time, therefore, begins in the unconscious, and a conscious awareness of time develops only dimly and partially as individuals reflect on their experiences (Jacques 1982: 63). A subjective sense of time develops alongside and in conjunction with the unconscious material time of the body. As a sense of self develops, so too does a sense of personal continuity in time. A conception of self rests on the belief that the experiencing subject continues through a sequence of experiences and is, to a greater or lesser extent, their agent. Memory and personal biography, as the sedimentation of experience, are the substance of the developing subjective sense of time. An awareness of the self's bodily continuity and transformation with age provides the raw material for intuition of a sense of duration (Whitrow 1988: 23). Human beings develop a subjective awareness of their own endurance and so tend to develop a more general sense of duration.

The subjective idea of time results from the reflexive awareness an agent has of his or her own duration, as generated by the rhythms and routines of biological and social existence that produce a subjective stream of consciousness and 'flow' of experiences. Agents draw upon shared frameworks for the assessment and measurement of the passage of time, which in contemporary societies includes the time of calendars and clocks. The subjective sense of duration alters as a person shifts from one sphere of social activity to another, with their particular, biologically specific sedimentations of experience, and with the particular conjunctions of occurrences they encounter. Movement from one social reality to another involves a shift in awareness and the calculation of time as the agent brings to consciousness his or her memories of the reality left behind and anticipations of the realities yet to be entered (Heidegger 1927: 39; Husserl 1928: 60, 79). The sense of time, therefore, rests upon the intentional aspects of human existence, on the human ability to anticipate and to plan the outcomes of actions and to adjust them accordingly as routines and projects or plans. Time is experienced as a directional flow because of the combined operation of the human capacities for perception, memory, and anticipation.

Kant saw time, like space, as a necessary category of human thought: as one of the innate and necessary logical devices hard-wired into the biology of the human brain and through which human beings are able to organise their experience of the world. For Kant, the relationship between the phenomena of experience and the noumenal reality of material duration was both unknown and unknowable. Durkheim (1912a) argued, however, that the categories of experience arise from social life. Built up through the reflexive grasping and interpretation of experience, they become the logical presuppositions of experience: they are logically but not biologically prior to experience. The shared conceptions of time held by individuals are products of their socialisation into a particular culture and, in particular, of their acquisition of a language through which it is possible to talk about and to calculate intervals of time (Whorf 1936; 1937). They arise within specific populations of associating individuals and they may also reflect the various differentiated fields of activity within which these individuals are involved. Time, therefore, takes an abstract, formal character as a collective representation. Public or official definitions of time become standards to which individuals must adapt, as they do to all social facts. The cultural matrix through which time is conceptualised is the basis on which the subjectively experienced sense of time is transformed into a fundamental category of human experience.

An individual's sense of time, therefore, becomes more 'objective' as individual experience is formed through culturally shared concepts. People acquire a 'temporal map' of their world – a cognitive schema of taken-for-granted expectations that allows observational cues to be related to known schedules and so allows time periods to be calculated. They can typically tell the time from observations of the state of the social world, just as much as they can from observing the regularities of the natural world, such as the succession of day and night. They know, for example, that it must be four o'clock because children are leaving school.

Time is most fundamentally marked and objectified by the giving of names to periods of time, allowing them to become the objects of reflection. Periods of time associated with particular occurrences or activities may be given names that mark and identify them, as with the identification of the season in which leaves die and drop from trees as 'the fall'. It is the occurrence of such periods that give rise to calendrical representations. Agricultural, climatic, and astronomical phases have been the most typical bases for this. Changes in daylight, the moon, and the seasons provide physical indicators that human duration is paralleled by patterned duration in the external world. The perception of the regular arrival of night-time, the changing phases of the moon, and of particular seasonal changes (weather, vegetation, animal migrations, etc.) have been the basis for conceptions of 'days', 'months', and 'years' in most societies. Zerubavel (1985) has shown that the development of formal time systems allows the introduction of measures of time that have no natural basis but follow only from the rules and principles according to which time has come to be calculated in a particular culture. The idea of a seven-day week, for example, is an arbitrary unit that originated in Mesopotamia and gradually spread to supplant and replace other cultural systems of measurement and to become the dominant form of representation in modern societies.

The prevailing conception of time in a society is embodied in its institutions and practices and is sustained, intentionally and unintentionally, by the activities of the group(s) that are central to those institutions. The adoption of such measures leads to a far more abstract and impersonal view of time and to the idea that lives should be organised in relation to schedules and abstract measurements (e.g., regular meal times) and to a reliance on technologies of measurement such as clocks, calendars, and personal organisers. The construction of clocks, calendars, and timetables allow people to mark out the temporality of particular spheres of activity, using these to organise their practices into routines and regularities of action.

Clocks and calendars have existed in many societies. The basis of the contemporary calendar now in global use is the Roman calendar and its elaboration in Christian Europe, where it was regulated and periodically modified by the ecclesiastical authorities. The so-called Julian calendar systematised a solar year of 365 days, together with a lunar month and a seven-day week. In the early medieval period the Dionysian (AD/BC) system of dating came into use, establishing a uniform linear framework of historical reckoning. The most significant changes to this calendar were the 1582 reforms of Pope Gregory, which brought the calendar year back into line with the solar (sideral) year by removing eleven days. The Gregorian reforms also introduced a new system of leap year calculation designed to keep the calendar and solar years in closer alignment. This Gregorian calendar was gradually adopted across the whole of Europe, and was finally taken up by Russia and the Orthodox Church in 1923.

The first systematic and disciplined schedule for a whole way of life was the Benedictine Horarium in which the annual and weekly cycles of the Christian Church were combined with rigorous daily routines. It was the need to schedule these daily activities that encouraged the mechanical innovations that produced the mechanical clock in the thirteenth century (Whitrow 1988: 103). Accurate mechanical timekeeping allowed the daily routines of the monasteries to be regulated through fixed and conventional units rather than more variable natural ones (Mumford 1934: 16; Zerubavel 1981: 33 ff). A uniform hour of sixty minutes became the basic unit in systems of measurement. This later made possible a tight regulation of the working day in the capitalist workshops and factories and allowed the precise calculation of labour inputs and rates of payment. The invention of accurate marine chronometers in the eighteenth century made possible the precise measurement of longitude and initiated a revolution in the understanding of space. Late in the following century a series of standardised time zones were established across the United States and the Greenwich meridian was established as the baseline for a global system of time zones. This spatial organisation of time became properly effective in 1913, when the regular telegraphic transmission of accurate time signals began from the Eifel Tower in Paris. Further precision was achieved when the length of a second was recalculated on a non-terrestrial standard with the introduction of the atomic clock in 1967. Various minor adjustments in the length of the day and the year have since been made through international agreements to increase the technical precision of time calculations.

This standardisation has led to a comprehensive measurement of day-to-day routines, the span of human lives, and the epochs of historical change as time, like money, became an abstract code of formal calculation and prediction. As Zerubavel argues:

> we are able to treat our time as standard quantities of duration mainly because we can measure them against a timepiece that is paced at a uniform rate. It is thus the clock, whose introduction to the West cannot be separated from the evolution of the schedule there, that allows the particular notion of temporality which has become so characteristic of Western civilization. It is *clock time* that is at the basis of the modern Western notion of duration and that allows the durational rigidity that is so typical of modern life. (Zerubavel 1981: 61)

Calendar and clock time has led to a great precision in the calculation of historical time, the time of the written and recorded events of human history. The Western conceptions of history and historical change that have increasingly spread across the globe have been transformed as these technical inventions developed and made more precise the temporal ideas that had emerged in medieval Europe. Independently of these transformations, however, a radical shift in scientific understanding with the development of evolutionary theories in the mid-nineteenth century helped to extend this historical vision into the pre-historic era. Although most scientists had come to reject a literal interpretation of the Bible and its chronology (which allowed a maximum of 6,000 years of world history), the timescale of earth history was still seen as quite short. An accumulation of fossil evidence, showing the periodic extinctions of whole species, encouraged the idea that earth history might run into millions of years. Not until the work of Charles Lyell (1830), however, did the real immensity of world history become apparent. Geologists had previously devised timescales from rock samples found in particular locations, but Lyell compared results from numerous different locations. Where fossil layers in the rock stratigraphy could be matched between two areas, he showed it was possible to combine the time estimates based on them into a single, and much longer, timescale. By comparing widely dispersed samples and placing them in a single stratigraphic series a massively long scale of geological time was produced, and one that showed the huge periods of time over which species had emerged or disappeared. Technical innovations since Lyell, such as dendrochronology (tree-ring dating) and radio-carbon dating, have made more precise a scale of time that many still find difficult to grasp.

Individual 'lived time' is generally synchronised with objective time, but may vary. The density or complexity of experience varies with the units of time established in a society. This is a major cause of the idiosyncratic experiences of the passage of time that constitute 'lived time' (Flaherty 1999: 5). In most circumstances, the subjective experience of time corresponds to established measures of time: periods of time feel as long as the periods measured by clocks and calendars. This is because the need to synchronise activities is an integral feature of social life. When the subjective experience of time is closely synchronised with the calendars and clocks through which everyday life is organised, lived duration goes unnoticed – it is a tacit feature of the experiential framework through which people organise their actions (Flaherty 1999: 33–4; Goffman 1974). The experience of time depends upon the intensity with which attentional resources are directed towards current activities. When the level of activity is unusually high or low and people must attend to the processing of a great deal of information, they become engrossed in their actions or are forced to become intensively concerned with themselves. Their minds are busy in extensive reflexive work and they become aware of time as a sense of 'protracted duration' that seems to pass very slowly. When actions are highly routinised, with low emotional involvement, and when people recall past episodes, there is less immediate information to process and they experience time as running more quickly, with a sense of 'compressed temporality' (Flaherty 1999: 107).

Levels of time and structures of time

Even when measured on the same temporal scale, social structures typically change at a different pace from the material artefacts that contain them. A family 'home', for example, may persist for less time than the 'house' in which it is contained: family bonds decay through migration, divorce, and death, and a 'family breakdown' following an amorous affair may be far more rapid than the crumbling of the bricks and mortar from which a house is built. Similarly, a structure of class relations that constitute positions of property ownership may persist for far longer than the paper from which currency notes are manufactured and may even outlast the particular machines that generate the material wealth of a dominant class.

As complex combinations of levels, social structures exhibit the multiple temporalities of family time, work time, religious time, and so on. Structures endure for greater or lesser periods and their rates of change may be more or less rapid, showing a distinct pace or rhythm of change. Thus, linguistic codes tend to change more slowly than dress codes, and governments may change more rapidly than state structures or property relations. Multiple temporalities typically exist in hierarchically organised structural relations, and any structure can be decomposed into its constitutive sequence of lower level happenings. The warfare of states can be translated into the policies of governments and the strategies of armies, which can be translated into the role relations of their members, and which can, in turn, be translated into the face-to-face relations of their incumbents. This move from the 'macro' to the 'micro', from historical epochs to everyday routines, does not involve a reductionism. It is a feature of the emergent properties of social phenomena that they can be redescribed at various levels.

It is in this sense that Gurvitch (1963) and Braudel (1986–7) saw some social structures as exhibiting a '*longue dureé*', an 'enduring time' of 'slowed down long duration'. This kind of temporality, they argued, is typical of kinship, locality groupings, and of rural activities and relations (Gurvitch 1963: 31, 40). High levels of long-term continuity and correspondingly slow rates of change occur when activities are closely dependent on a material environment that is itself relatively unchanging. Agrarian structures in climatically stable regions, for example, tend to persist for long periods. Such structures, Gurvitch argued, exhibit an 'ecological time', though this is not the time of the natural environment *per se* but the time of the humanly lived and transformed environment. Similarly, those aspects of social structure that are closely dependent on the relatively unchanging biological constitution of individuals will change slowly relative to other aspects of social structure. Family-based patterns of socialisation, rooted in the plasticity of human nature and the dependence of biologically immature individuals on adult carers, are examples of relatively long-lasting continuity in human society. In these circumstances, the long duration of social structures is likely to be reflected in particular customs, traditions, and collective memories that reinforce the conservative properties of the social process (Zerubavel 2003).

Other temporalities tend to show a greater rapidity of change. Formal social organisations, such as parties, states, and business enterprises, are more mobile than environmentally grounded social entities. Their organisation and technology gives them a greater autonomy from their environment and the temporal pattern of their development is one in which periodic innovations can transform the situation in which they and their members act (Virilio 1977). They may organise their internal time on a different basis from the external time in which they operate: they have daily, weekly, and other routines linked to their organisational requirements, rather than to diurnal or seasonal changes in the physical world, and that may contradict the schedules established by larger structures (Gurvitch 1963: 44).

Social processes, like physical processes, are irreversible, but this is not simply because of the thermodynamic properties of their material forms of containment. The irreversibility of social processes is a consequence of the transformation of the individuals whose actions constitute them by their experiences of living within them. Their memories of those experiences cannot be erased, especially when they form a part of a collective memory and are stored as a cultural heritage. Social actions always carry forward the residue of previous social experiences. Social structures cannot be 'undone' and there can be no reversion to an earlier state of existence. Historical change is an irreversible process that exhibits a necessary forward direction (Giddens 1984: 35).

The temporalities of organisations and other social groups depend upon their adoption of specific practices for organising their use and construction of time. Adapting the argument of Zerubavel, these internal temporalising practices can be referred to as sequencing, terminating, scheduling, and recurrence (Zerubavel 1981: 50–2; see also Sztompka 1993). Sequencing is a process through which a whole range of everyday activities are organised in relation to normatively defined temporal orderings with greater or lesser rigidity. Careers, for example, are the means through which a pattern of work life can be organised and controlled. Sequencing practices may be conditioned by a logical or technical necessity, as with socially defined stages of biological maturation or with the need to acquire building materials before constructing a house. Typically, however, sequencing practices also follow arbitrary cultural codes that give them a more conventional character. The balance between conditions and codings is quite variable, and such things as the sequence of courses that define a meal are purely conventional (Zerubavel 1981: 2–5). Terminating is a process through which culturally approved ways of demarcating the duration of an event are established. Appointments, holidays, terms of office, party invitations, and so on tend to involve specific and quite conventional durations for the events they regulate. Specific start and end times are set or indicated and there may be ritualised ways of marking beginnings and endings. Scheduling refers to the organisation of activities in relation to particular points in time. Lecture times, bed time, harvest time, and so on are all scheduled, often through a formal timetable. Recurrence is the practice through which a rhythm may be given to social life. Anniversaries, lectures, and meals, for example, all recur at particular conventional rates: they may be weekly, hourly, monthly, annual, and so on. Mauss (1904–5) showed that the way of life of the Eskimos of North America followed a recurrent pattern of seasonal transhumance. Practices that establish recurrence may involve particular cycles of activity, such as a business cycle, and may define standardised units of time such as the seven-day week.

It is through such practices that patterns of 'temporal symmetry' and 'temporal complementarity' mesh activities together and allow the activities of different people to be integrated and coordinated over time, and it is through these means that whole social systems may come to be integrated or equilibrated. Synchronisation through the symmetrical performance of simultaneous tasks contributes to the mechanical solidarity of a group. In more differentiated societies, integration can be achieved through the interlocking of a series of diverse schedules in a structure of organic solidarity.

The macro-micro hierarchy of temporality and temporalising practices constitutes a whole society as a complex and multilayered outcome of the multiple temporalities of its constituent structures. Within such a hierarchy, 'different manifestations of time meet, enter into conflict, are combined, and finally interpenetrate each other' (Gurvitch 1963: 52).

Space-time is fundamental to all reality, shaping natural and social processes and individual experiences of these. Reality exists as extended and enduring arrangements of material entities that also constitute the mental and social configurations that we refer to as societies and minds. Spatially, human phenomena exist as multilayered formations with distinct morphologies that comprise the complex articulations of zones, scenes, and surfaces that make up the social landscape. Temporally, human phenomena exist as multiple temporalities that comprise the complex patterning of duration into movements, phases, and recurrences that comprise the direction of change in these social landscapes. Human arrangements in space-time, as I will show, can be seen as the social structures produced through the actions of reflexive individuals.

Social systems emerge from human actions that are shaped by the interdependence of culture and nature. They exist in space and time as complex structures of human activity. Though used frequently in the chapters of this book, the idea of social structure has not yet been explicitly addressed. What exactly does it mean to describe social activity as 'structured'? This is not a straight-forward question to answer.

The word 'structure' appears frequently in the titles of sociology books, suggesting the centrality of the concept to sociological understanding. Examples are such classics as *The Structure of Social Action* (Parsons 1937), *Social Structure* (Murdock 1949), *The Theory of Social Structure* (Nadel 1957), *Social Theory and Social Structure* (Merton 1957b), and empirical reports such as *A Survey of the Social Structure of England and Wales* (Carr-Saunders and Caradog Jones 1927). Despite its frequent use, its theoretical value has been challenged by those who focus their attention on individual action. Such critics see action theories as requiring a repudiation of the concept of structure (Dawe 1970). Theories of structure, they argue, involve an outmoded attachment to deterministic models that echo the conservative, repressive, and totalitarian aspects of modernity. Theories of agency, on the other hand, stress freedom, creativity, and the abilities of human beings to act in ways other than those imposed on them in the name of 'society'. In the final quarter of the twentieth century these challenges led to persistent disputation over the relative importance of 'structure' and 'agency' and many concluded that sociologists must make a choice between theories of structure and theories of action.

This has not always been the case. Since Comte and Spencer set out their programmes for the development of sociology, the mainstream of the discipline has generally regarded social structure as its defining concept, as perhaps *the* central concept of the discipline. The concept was seen as an obvious and unchallengeable tool of sociological analysis. Just as the observable shape of a human body expresses its underlying skeletal structure, so the observable shape of a social group was held to reflect an underlying social structure. To talk of the 'structure' of a society is to refer to recurrent patterns of activity that endure over considerable periods of time, despite a continuous turnover in the particular people undertaking them. A social structure is the enduring pattern of arrangement among the individual members of a group; it is the 'anatomy' of a population considered as a social body.

This view of social structure was thought to follow from the emerging emphasis on cultural formation. Socialisation into a culture was seen as producing individuals endowed with the capacity and desire to act in specific culturally regulated ways. Social structure is the regulatory framework through which cultural meanings constrain people to act as 'social' individuals. It is a framework of social positions that tie and constrain individuals to act as members of social groups and in conformity with their ways of life. Individuals can be said to occupy 'positions' or places within a social structure, and so a social structure is a set of connections among positions rather than simply among the individuals who occupy them. Individuals are tied into structures such as families, sects, and classes that are the 'parts' or elements of larger structures. Families, comprising the positions of father, mother, son, daughter, brother, and sister, are the parts from which larger kinship structures are built. Kinship structures connect family members through such positions as cousin, aunt, uncle, nephew, and niece. Class structures, consisting of such positions as employer, employee, investor, and manager, are connected into economic and political structures through such positions as customer, lawyer, banker, legislator, and judge. A structural analysis explores the relations between social positions and the families, states, classes, ethnic groups, democratic institutions, churches, markets, schools, tribes, nations, and such other groups and institutions into which they are formed.

A fundamental question was left unanswered by many structural theorists: if social structures are frameworks of positions, then how can they exist apart from those individuals? Though referred to rather loosely as 'connections', 'patterns', or 'arrangements', the substance of these was rarely specified. This left theorists of social structure open to the objection that social structure has, in fact, no reality or substance and that all explanations must be cast in terms of individuals and their actions. In this chapter I will show that an adequate concept of social structure *was* adopted by these theorists and that it remains an essential aspect of sociological explanation. Explanations in terms of action and explanations in terms of social structure are not alternatives but are complementary to each other. A proper understanding of social structure certainly requires reference to the actions of individuals who produce,

oduce, and transform it, but social structure cannot be reduced to
e actions.

The facticity of social structures

Social structure was such a taken-for-granted idea that the earliest
detailed discussions of it concentrated on elucidating the formal properties of a structure rather than specifying what gave it substance as a
structure. Usage of structural concepts adopted analogies with the more
familiar properties of mathematical and architectural structures, using
the idea to describe the shape and relative fixity of social arrangements
over time. Structural thinking in sociology was also influenced by nineteenth-century biology, which had established that organisms have
skeletal and physiological structures of internally related or mutually
dependent organs. It was in this sense that Spencer (1873–93) argued
that societies, as 'social organisms', have structures of connected institutions, such as families, churches, markets, and states. Similarly, Marx saw
the members of a social class as defined by their relations to each other
and to members of other classes: the individual members of a class cannot be envisaged as separate and distinct objects collected together like a
mere 'sack of potatoes' (Marx 1852). The individual members of a class
act towards each other and towards those in other classes as the occupants of definite social positions and not as a mere aggregate of abstract
individuals. The internal relations among the parts of a whole are what
distinguish the structure of an organism or social organism from the
structure of a mechanical object.

Social structures as the distinctively social forms of human existence
were most clearly and rigorously discussed by Durkheim, for whom
they are the specifically 'social facts' that give sociology its *raison d'être*.
Sociologists must take account of phenomena at the level of individual
thought, feeling, and action, but must recognise that cultural formation
and structural regulation involve phenomena distinct from these psychological and biological facts. Social structures are the means through
which individual thought, feeling, and action is shaped and socialised
individuals are made to observe and accept the cultural demands placed
upon them.

In his discourse on *The Rules of the Sociological Method*, Durkheim
(1895) identified a very diverse list of social facts. He instanced the
duties that people have as the occupants of defined social positions such
as those of brother, husband, or citizen; the duties that are expected of
people in their professional and industrial working practices; the religious
beliefs and practices that people follow; the systems of money and credit

they use; the customs and conventions governing modes of dress, clean-liness, eating, drinking, and sleeping; the signs, symbols, and rules that comprise a language; the waves of collective enthusiasm, indignation, and panic that can sweep through crowds; movements of opinion; the distribution of population; patterns of communication; and the design of dwellings. Social facts vary considerably, ranging from purely morpho-logical conditions and social relations, through labile social currents, to formally established institutions.

Durkheim argued that behind the obvious diversity of these phenom-ena, there are a number of crucial characteristics that they have in com-mon as social facts. They are 'ways of acting, thinking and feeling which possess the remarkable property of existing outside the consciousness of the individual'. Social facts have a reality and an existence 'outside' of and distinct from – thus 'external to' – the individuals whose lives they regulate. They all comprise irreducibly collective phenomena 'endowed with a compelling and coercive power by virtue of which ... they impose themselves upon an individual' (*ibid.*: 51, translation corrected). Social facts can exert this pressure on individual agents because they originate outside any individual consciousness. This pressure, Durkheim argued, is a specifically *social* constraint, even if individuals may feel they are act-ing freely:

The authority to which an individual bows when he acts, thinks or feels socially dominates him to such a degree because it is a product of forces which tran-scend him and for which he consequently cannot account. It is not from within himself that can come the external pressure which he undergoes; it is there-fore not what is happening within himself which can explain it. (Durkheim 1895: 128)

This was later summarised by Mandelbaum in his claim that forms of social organisation have an irreducible autonomy and 'cannot be reduced without remainder to concepts which refer only to the thoughts and actions of specific individuals' (1955: 223). A description of what happens when a person withdraws money from a bank must necessarily make use of concepts that refer to the social positions of 'bank teller' and 'depos-itor'; it must describe the physical objects they manipulate as 'withdrawal slips' or 'cash'; and it must refer to the 'bank' and its particular 'opening hours'. Most fundamentally, such an account must invoke social institu-tions such as 'money', 'legal tender', and 'contract'. Individuals can write successfully on a piece of paper in return for cash only because they are positioned in specific ways as customers in a bank that operates within a monetary system. Any description that attempts to dispense with such social concepts, Mandelbaum argued, must be inadequate. An attempt to describe the actions of individuals in purely physical or psychological terms – as moving into buildings, making marks on paper, and receiving paper and metal in return – will miss all of the most important features of the *social* transaction, much as the adherents of the Melanesian cargo cults missed the significance of the political and economic structures of imperial administration that brought the cargo to their islands (Worsley 1957; Lawrence 1964).

Mandelbaum recognised, of course, that banks and monetary systems do not exist separately from individual human beings: social structures are instantiated only in and through individuals and their actions, and they 'do not exist unless there are aggregates of individuals who think and act in specific ways' and through whose thoughts and actions 'we can apprehend the nature of the societal organisation in which they live' (Mandelbaum 1955: 229). Nevertheless, an important distinction must be made between this *dependence* of 'societal facts' on the activities of human beings and their explanatory *reduction* to them. Descriptions of particular courses of action, Mandelbaum argues, must always refer to one or more societal facts that give them meaning.

Some of the early formulations of this idea of 'emergent' social properties made a stronger claim that social organisms have aims of their own and, like biological organisms, are activated by a 'vital spirit' (Bergson 1907). This vitalism has been the principal target of those who describe themselves as 'methodological individualists' (Watkins 1952; 1957). As I have shown in my discussion of culture as collective mentality, there is no implication that social structures have a separate substantial existence outside individual minds and courses of action. Social facts are real and have properties distinctive from their individual carriers, but they are immanent in particular events and actions and so have a virtual existence. They are not themselves either substantial or tangible. Social facts may be observed indirectly through their 'external manifestations', such as observed regularities of behaviour, but the social structures themselves are not directly observable. People are constrained by them and may conform to them, even when they have formed no conscious image of them. Many social facts are, of course, grasped in representations held in individual minds, and it is through the long repetition of actions that social facts come to be identified in consciousness and given a tangible shape in formulas, aphorisms, laws, moral prescriptions, articles of faith, and so on (Durkheim 1895: 55). Where they have been codified and crystallised in some external form, and especially when they have been written down, individuals may seek to clarify uncertainties about the social facts by consulting these codes and those who are their authorised interpreters (*ibid.*: 50).

Social facts pre-exist the particular individuals who 'internalise' them as ideas that become integral aspects of their individual mentality. Individuals may thus come to regard them as necessary, natural, and inevitable features of 'the way things are', or as matters of moral obligation. They may become so taken for granted that they are regarded as things to which they have an absolute personal commitment. When individuals feel that they are committed to a social fact, they are likely to form an emotional sentiment of attachment to it. In these circumstances, they conform to particular ways of acting, thinking, or feeling through their own free will and do not experience them as coercive. In the Preface to the Second Edition of *The Rules*, Durkheim held that:

the coercive power ... represents so small a part of its totality that it can equally well display the opposite characteristic. For, while institutions bear down upon us, we nevertheless cling to them; they impose obligations upon us, and yet we love them; they place constraint upon us and yet we find satisfaction in the way they function, and in that very constraint. (Durkheim 1901: 47 n. 4)

However, personal commitment is rarely sufficient to ensure the persistence of social facts. The constraining power of social facts is apparent in the reactions that occur whenever individuals attempt to resist them. Acts of resistance, whether deliberate or not, will result in a failure to realise an intention or in the direct sanctioning of the resistance by the others who are involved in the regulated activity. A person who ignores linguistic conventions, for example, may fail to be understood, and an individual who ignores monetary conventions may be arrested and punished as a thief.

The underlying principles of this view that social structures, as social facts, do not involve vitalism have been spelled out by Bhaskar (1975; 1979) on the basis of Althusser's (1962; 1963) idea of 'structural causality' (see also Keat and Urry 1975; Sayer 1984; Collier 1994; Somers 1998).[1] Bhaskar claims that the structure of any object comprises the properties that make up its powers to affect other objects. These properties constitute the generative or causal mechanisms of the structure. They define the ways in which an object must *necessarily* operate and so determine the effects that it would have in the absence of any interfering effects from other objects. Actual situations typically involve the operation of two or more structures whose causal mechanisms may influence and interfere with each other. Structures are 'complex objects, in virtue of which they possess an ensemble of tendencies, liabilities and powers' because their mechanisms 'combine to generate the actual flux of phenomena of the world' (Bhaskar 1975: 17, 47, 51). Faced with the contradictory expectations associated with being a mother and an employee, for example, a woman will be disposed to act in contradictory ways.

On the basis of his view of *how* social structures operate, Durkheim was able to begin to explore *what* social structures consist of and where sociologists should look for them. In his first major book (1893) he focused on the actual social relations and interdependencies that connect and constrain individuals in a social division of labour. His final work (1912a) was more concerned with the collective representations through which the social institutions of religion are formed. These exemplify, respectively, the relational and the institutional dimensions that Durkheim saw as constituting social structure (López and Scott 2000).

Durkheim's view of social institutions,[2] as 'ideal' factors, drew directly on Hegel, who distinguished the 'objective mind' or cultural spirit from mere external nature or 'matter'. Objective mind is externalised in historical, social forms as the rules, folkways, customs, and laws that, as 'alienated' spirit, make up the 'ethical substance' of human existence (Hegel 1807: sec. C). Culture crystallises as the obligations and expectations that define the institutions of the family, civil society, and the political constitution (Hegel 1845: 265; 1821: 174). Thus, the young Hegelians and the early Marx held that a normative order of institutions structures material activity (Alexander 1982–3: vol. 2, 16). Developed by Parsons from Durkheim's suggestions, this view established the idea that social structure can be seen as a socio-cultural lifeworld of institutions that constitute the cognitive and moral framework within which people live out their lives (see Bauman 1976).

Social structure also exists as a relational structure, which Durkheim found in the explorations of the political economists and which was also developed in Marxist theory. Through his critique of Hegel and political economy (Marx 1844a; and see 1843b; 1843a), Marx concluded that the ideal or institutional order – the 'ideological' level of social life – has its basis in 'material' social relations (Marx and Engels 1846: 42, 57; Marx 1859b).[3] He saw the social relations through which resources are distributed as differentiating social groups according to their capacity for domination and oppression.

Social structures, then, consist of institutionalised social relations. Some writers have given priority to uncovering the social institutions through which the relations among individuals are regulated. Others, however, have accorded priority to social relations, seeing institutional expectations as their secondary reflections. The key issue in structural analysis has been the relationship between institutional structure and relational structure in shaping the overall social structure of a society.

Institutional structure

Institutional structure, as the culturally constituted norms, rules, or principles through which actions are regulated, was really clarified only with the work of Parsons in the mid-twentieth century. It was Parsons who explored the construction, establishment, and function of norms as the building blocks of social institutions.

Parsons (1951) showed that people constitute each social encounter in which they are involved through a definition of the situation that comprises expectations about their own behaviour and that of the others with whom they engage. These expectations are acquired through socialisation: they are internalised as deep, taken-for-granted assumptions and commitments. Expectations are norms: assumptions about what will 'normally' happen in the situation. Norms are internalised cultural standards of conduct that specify the expected or approved ways of pursuing culturally defined goals and so regulate the ways in which people behave in relation to these goals (J. F. Scott 1971). They may not be explicit statements of principle. They are, rather, socialised or embodied dispositions to act in particular ways. Although dispositions may sometimes become conscious principles of action, and may even be codified as 'laws', this may be only partial or misleading as individuals are typically aware of their dispositions only vaguely and incompletely. It is essential, therefore, to distinguish between internalised normative dispositions and their external codifications as explicit maxims of conduct.

Norms take a number of forms. Predictive or descriptive norms comprise the factual expectations that allow anticipation of what is likely to happen as a normal, regular, or typical occurrence. They concern what is likely to occur 'as a rule' in particular social situations. Factual expectations are employed pragmatically and calculatively by agents as routine predictive devices. When agents also hold expectations about how they and others *should* or *ought* to behave, they can be said to hold prescriptive or proscriptive norms. These involve shared understandings of what each participant in a relationship ought to do and are likely to be associated with beliefs that non-conformity will be sanctioned. Agents feel a sense of moral obligation to conform and are committed to the norm and/or the value that underpins it. These commitments are likely to be expressed in feelings of shame or guilt over non-conformity and in anxiety about possible or anticipated non-conformity. Such morally sanctioned norms may become the basis of explicit ethical codes (Gross *et al.* 1958: 58–9).[4] Normative expectations provide a framework of predictability that allows individuals to act according to norms they feel to be appropriate or required.

Wherever there is a cultural consensus, socialisation is likely to result in a reciprocity of shared expectations and, therefore, an 'interlarding' or interlocking of behaviour into a stable pattern (Beccheria 2006: 11). The resulting pattern is, therefore, a normative pattern. Consensus is rarely complete and socialisation is rarely perfect, and so Parsons recognised a second mechanism that operates alongside socialisation to produce conformity to normative patterns. Those with whom a person interacts will sanction behaviour according to its perceived conformity or deviation from *their* expectations. Individuals who breach the expectations held by others are likely to be punished, while those who meet those expectations will be rewarded. Where people are motivated towards the approval of others and the avoidance of disapproval, there is both a commitment to a norm or principle of action (a value commitment) and a concern for the likely reaction of others (Wrong 1994: 44). The reactions of the others are, therefore, a means through which conformity can be produced.

Neil Gross and his colleagues have argued that prescriptive and proscriptive norms vary in intensity from the mandatory through the preferential to the permissive (Gross *et al.* 1958: 60; Dahrendorf 1958: 39–41; and see Parsons 1958a). Mandatory expectations are obligatory prescriptions or proscriptions that are likely to be systematically formulated, though they are rarely spelled out completely and always require interpretation and adjudication. They are supported by a machinery of social control, and compliance is likely to be enforced through sanctions applied by authorised office holders (Gibbs 1981). Preferential expectations concern those things that should or should not occur but are not regarded as compulsory. They rest on more informal sanctions of recognition or acceptance, such as inclusion or exclusion from participation in organisational activities. Finally, permissive expectations concern what can or may be done and what need not be done. These depend mainly on positive sanctions of esteem or praise.

When norms are enduring, standardised, and internalised, they can be seen as conventions or customs. These collective habits develop unintentionally and unplanned as ways of acting, thinking, and feeling that are adopted and repeated over time to become routinised and taken for granted. Following the terminology of Sumner (1906), Davis (1948) has argued that the customs of a society comprise its 'folkways' and its 'mores'. Folkways are taken-for-granted norms that can be enforced by purely informal social controls such as gossip, ridicule, or ostracism. Mores, on the other hand, are norms that are most strongly linked to the central values of a culture or subculture and are enforced through explicit moral approval and denigration (Davis 1948: 57 ff).

Folkways are likely to be found wherever expectations are widely shared within a society. Linguistic norms of grammar and usage, for example, are sanctioned, above all, through the comprehension or non-comprehension of others: if a person wishes to be understood by other speakers, he or she must observe the language rules (Durkheim 1895). Other folkways, such as the norms concerning conversations, interpersonal encounters, cooking and eating, family relations, and so on, are also widely shared, though rarely so widely as those of a language. It is important to recognise, however, that the degree of normative consensus is highly variable, both within and between societies (Young 1988).

Customary norms are rarely codified in an explicit form, and are often of obscure origin. *Legal* norms, on the other hand, originate in deliberate and formal enactments, are strictly codified, and have formal sanctions attached to them. Legal norms may be codified versions of folkways or mores, or they may be innovations of a legislative or deliberative body. The enactment and enforcement of legal norms often involves specialised bodies and agencies such as the police, the courts, and parliaments.[5]

Custom and law, then, are the two principal normative structures involved in defining a way of life. Durkheim recognised them as the principal social facts constraining individuals when he argued that the rational, calculative actions of economic agents presuppose a 'non-contractual element' (Durkheim 1893: 155) of custom and law to give them meaning. The social institution of contract – a cluster of laws and customs – is the basis on which individual transactions become binding on the participants.

Parsons argued that social institutions are clusters of interrelated norms, customary or legal, that are generalised across a society or social group as its common ways of acting, thinking, and feeling and that generate the recurrent social practices through which enduring social activities can be undertaken. While Parsons may sometimes have written as if institutions have a substantial and vital existence separate from that of the individuals who act on them, his symbolic interactionist critics firmly underlined the fact that they must be seen simply as the relatively stable patterns of meaning that are carried in the minds of individuals or written down in cultural artefacts. Institutions are elements in the loose organising framework of meanings through which people organise their collective activities. They provide the definitions of situations that allow people to identify the roles that may or should be adopted in their encounters. It was on this basis that Winch (1958), following Wittgenstein (1953), held that understanding a society involves understanding its institutions (see also Bloor 1997: 9–18).[6]

Examples of institutions include the normative patterns of private property, contract, democracy, professionalism, free speech, citizenship, sovereignty, medicine, motherhood, patriarchy, marriage, and such micro-level institutions as conversational turn-taking, bodily comportment, and gift giving. Institutions combine together to form larger institutional structures. States, for example, are systems of action in which participants organise their relations through such institutions as democracy, sovereignty, monarchy, and citizenship. Within the institution of medicine the social position of doctor is defined by norms of professionalism, technical expertise, and patient care, while the institution of professionalism itself comprises norms of trust, honesty, competence, and liability. Parsons classified institutions into economic, political, domestic, religious, and other categories, according to the primary social functions in which they are involved. Relating his argument to his system perspective, he held that such institutions form the various structural parts that are the poles of 'functional significance' around which social systems are organised. These structural parts include economies, political systems, kinship systems, and so on.

While Parsons and other structural-functionalist theorists have seen 'an effective consensus of the society' as central to the operation of institutions (Williams 1960: 30), they did not mean to suggest a complete consensus among all members of a society. As I have already shown, the assumption of perfect consensus was an idealised system state from which the operation of actual social structures could be analysed. Thus, Shils (1961: 6) saw norms as partially institutionalised whenever there is a consensus among the members of a 'ruling group' able to impose its norms on the rest of their society through the use of sanctions. Levy (1952) took a similar point of view, claiming that institutions vary in their degree of institutionalisation according to how generally an expectation of conformity is held and how strongly sanctioned it is.

Dahrendorf (1958) and Rex (1961) have argued even more strongly that complete consensus of values and norms is merely one extreme, limiting case and that institutional norms are more likely to be imposed and that the operation of institutions cannot be separated from power relations. The institutional regulation of social behaviour is a form of ideological control or hegemony. This was also the view of Foucault (1963; 1982), who saw the shared discursive knowledge through which people understand and define their social world as embodying power relations. Social order is a result of the combined application of knowledge and power and cannot be seen as a product of either in isolation.

Institutions organise particular positions or clusters of positions and the expected relationships among them (Nadel 1951: 107). The cultural knowledge embodied in social institutions defines the categories in terms of which people identify social positions. As unconscious, taken-for-granted knowledge, these 'typifications' constitute a framework or template of understanding that provides a sense of social structure that allows people to organise their encounters with each other (Cicourel 1972). With such a map of their society, individuals have an understanding of the positions they are likely to occupy or encounter. Such maps have been studied most comprehensively in investigations of kinship terminology and systems of kin classification (Morgan 1870; Murdock 1949; but see also the more general view in Klapp 1962). Occupying positions and enacting the expectations associated with them generates specific sets of relationships and forms of social organisation. Social theorists have long recognised this organisation of social expectations through the incorporation of cultural patterns into individual personalities by the use of such terms as character, mask, and persona. Not until the 1930s did the cultural anthropologist Ralph Linton's advocacy of the word 'role' lead to its adoption as the standard term. Linton's terminological innovation became the basis on which Parsons and others constructed the model of normative regulation that became the basis of mainstream sociology.

Linton held that positions (which he misleadingly called 'statuses') are associated with expected patterns of behaviour. There is a 'positional crystallisation' of norms into clusters of required or expected behavioural patterns for their occupants, and roles can be seen as 'bundles of expectations directed at the incumbents of positions in a given society' (Dahrendorf 1958: 36; Popitz 1967: 15). Roles are the organised expectations that relate to particular contexts of interaction and that shape the motivational orientations of individuals towards each other (Levy 1952: 158–60). They are the cultural patterns, blueprints, or templates for behaviour and through which people learn *who* they are in the eyes of others and *how* they should act towards them. Role behaviour is the enactment or performance of the expectations associated with a specific social position.

The role expectations associated with a particular position comprise a whole set of complementary expectations concerning specific others, to which Merton (1957a) gave the name 'role set'. A role set is based on a 'focal position' and two or more 'counter positions' with which occupants are regularly associated. Each counter position is understood as carrying a specific set of expectations that define a particular relationship as a 'role sector' (Gross *et al.* 1958: 52–62). A role sector comprises the expectations that define the relationship between a focal position and a particular counter position, and a role set comprises a cluster of role sectors. The ways in which a person in a focal position is expected to behave towards those in its various counter positions will generally be quite distinct from each other. A medical student, for example, is likely to have specific and distinct expectations concerning appropriate behaviour towards fellow students, teachers, doctors, nurses, and patients.[7]

'Intra-role conflict' exists when the expectations that a person faces within a role set are inconsistent, incompatible, or ambiguous. A teacher facing expectations that he or she both discipline and care for the personal welfare of students may experience a conflict between these demands. This subjective feeling of conflict may be compounded if it is also felt that the emphasis on these expectations varies from one role sector to another. The teacher may, for example, feel that the head teacher, parents, and pupils themselves have varying views on how these expectations should be balanced and reconciled. Faced with such intra-role conflict, people are likely to experience a pressure to choose between the contradictory demands, and the pressure of these demands will vary with the power that others can bring to the relationship.

This sense of conflicting expectations is reinforced whenever there is a lack of consensus among the partners in a role relationship. Even if there is a perfect congruence among the expectations that an individual knows to define his or her role, the other actors with whom the role is enacted may see things differently. A teacher may think that parents expect firm classroom discipline, but the parents themselves may expect the teacher to adopt a more relaxed approach. Such role dissensus magnifies any intra-role conflict.

Individuals rarely occupy just one social position, of course, and additional dilemmas of role behaviour occur because of contradictions that occur among the expectations attached to different positions. Someone may, for example, experience conflicting demands as child, student, and part-time employee. Thus, a woman may face especially deep conflicting demands placed on her in the positions of wife, mother, and employee. Once again, social constraints and social roles do not imply a complete consensus: 'the vexatious fact of society proves to be a conglomeration of more or less binding, more or less particular group norms' (Dahrendorf 1958: 52).

Symbolic interactionist writers have outlined further radical extensions to role theories, seeing them as overdeterministic in their implications (Blumer 1962). Roles and role expectations are not to be seen as fixed and given determinants of individual action. They are acquired as loose guidelines within which people must creatively improvise if they are to enact them at all (Turner 1962). Individuals do not simply enact roles automatically, but draw on shared and inherited ideas to guide and inform their behaviour. The scripts provided as cultural templates are mere outlines that define only the broad shape of a role and do not give detailed guidance on how actions should be carried out. In any particular situation, therefore, individuals must negotiate situational meanings and the applicability of specific role expectations. They tentatively interpret and reinterpret each other's actions and so recreate their roles from the blueprints provided. Inherited roles are, therefore, transformed through creative enactment and are made available to others in their transformed form. The social process involves a continuing reconstruction of social definitions and identities as a sense of order and stability is negotiated (Strauss *et al.* 1963; and see Strauss 1978).

People necessarily infer which roles are to be played in a particular situation. They make these inferences through observing cues or 'role signs' that indicate which roles should be considered to be 'in play'. Verbal cues signal the intentions of actors and help to trigger appropriate responses. They may also announce names or titles indicative of positions and expected behaviours. Non-verbal signs – insignia, decoration, clothing, and other material 'props' – may also signify the positions held by participants and the ways in which they are likely to behave. Non-verbal role signs are highly diverse and include such things as the clerical collar of a priest, the sleeve stripes of an army sergeant, the white coat of a medical technician, the leopard skin tunic of a tribal chief, the wig and gown of a barrister, the counter behind which a shop assistant stands, the lecturer's podium, and so on. While stature and pitch of voice may unintentionally indicate the age or sex of a person, they are not role signs in the strict sense as individuals have little or no control over them. Uniforms or badges of rank, on the other hand, are very clear markers of relative position that are specially adopted so as to ensure that role partners perform the appropriate actions. Such role signs may be more or less deliberately adopted and employed in interaction.[8]

Role signs are not absolutes, but, like roles themselves, are culturally and historically variable. For this reason, the nature and meaning of role signs in any particular society will be subject to change over time. Until the 1960s, for example, a waitress in an English restaurant would typically wear a white cap and apron and a black skirt. Today, only the black skirt and white blouse survive as a frequent, but not invariant, marker of the waitress role. The absence of an obvious role sign can lead to problems of interaction in many situations, as when a customer in a shop mistakes another customer for a shop assistant.

The implications of this view were taken further by Goffman in his account of the relationship between roles and the self. The private self – the 'I' – is the focus of autonomous agency and is distinct from the self displayed in any publicly enacted role. This autonomous agency is the basis of the choices and decisions made and is the means through which impressions are managed or calculatively manipulated in role performances. The autonomous agent, however, is not an asocial or pre-social entity. The materiality of the human body is subject to social construction (see Chapter 3). The social self is the precipitate or amalgam of roles enacted in the past and the actual or desired roles with which an actor currently identifies. It was on this basis that Goffman developed the concept of 'role distance', which exists where a person seeks to distance himself or herself from behaviour that is expected but that they have no desire to be identified with. A waiter in a restaurant, for example, may seek to maintain a degree of personal autonomy by engaging in the minimum of overtly expected deference or by acting in ways that exhibit a lack of complete identification and commitment to the role.

Institutional structure, then, comprises the clusters of normative expectations that form the skeletal organisation of a social system. Social institutions are sustained through a network of interlocking beliefs and rules of action held in individual minds as dispersed knowledge and reproduced or transformed through communication. While the contents of each individual mind may be unique (Turner 1994), they nevertheless cohere as institutions through the interlocking of individual definitions (Searle 1995; 2010). However, power, role conflict, role dissensus, role distance, and performative creativity all ensure that institutional structures are marked by incoherencies and contradictions. The perfect integration of institutions is unusual, and social structures are typically characterised by a greater or lesser degree of 'system contradiction' (Lockwood 1964; Parkin 1972; see also Gouldner 1959). The stresses and tensions inherent in institutional structures place conflicting pressures on individuals, resulting in psychic stresses and tensions.

The whole system of institutions can be said to exist, as a social structure, independently of each individual and to exist virtually and not substantively.[9] As the carriers or bearers of institutional structure, individual human beings ensure its reproduction and transformation over time. The institutional structure existed prior to any individual's birth, will continue to exist after their death, and will persist while they are asleep or unconscious because it is sustained by the complex interlocking beliefs of a very large number of individuals. If everyone were to simultaneously abandon a belief and cease to act on it, and if all intertwined beliefs were also disentangled and abandoned, then the institution would cease to exist (Jarvie 1972). Such a prospect is highly unlikely, and only situations of catastrophic decline in trust (Luhmann 1968; Misztal 1996) or the destruction of social life through warfare or natural catastrophe approximate to this. More typically, institutions are transformed through the gradual and unintended accumulation of changes in the myriad interlocking beliefs, and institutional change is likely to show much inertia and resistance to change.

Institutional structure is manifested in the actual relations in which people are involved as they enact their roles, yet this relational element is no mere derivative of the institutional structure. Parsons recognised the primacy and overriding importance of institutional structure, regarding the relational features of social life as mere 'residual' factors to be totally explained by the operation of institutions (see Lockwood 1992: 80). However, there is no one-to-one relationship between institutional structure and relational structure such that the autonomy of the latter can be ignored. The creativity and innovation with which people perform their roles and the material conditions that limit their ability to act as they intend combine to constrain individual actions independently of social institutions. Relational structure must, therefore, be considered in its own terms and not simply as a reflection of institutional structure.

Relational structure

The relational aspect of social structure comprises actual patterns of association and circulation among agents. Association is 'recurrent social interaction and communication' (Blau 1977: 1) through which messages are transmitted and attitudes conveyed. Circulation, or mobility, comprises 'all movements of persons between social positions' (*ibid.*: 5), and is the means through which people transfer from one group or social category to another. While association and circulation may be shaped by institutionalised expectations they are not exclusively shaped by it and must be considered in their own terms.

Theories of relational structure appeared initially in analyses of market exchange. The models of interweaving chains of action produced in classical political economy were generalised into theories of 'gravitational' attraction in which individuals were seen as attracted to or repulsed by each other as a result of the particular interests and preferences that led them to associate in 'economic' relations of exchange, competition, and cooperation. The earliest such account was that of Carey, who started from the assumption that the greatest need of human beings is that for association with others. This 'dependence' leads people to 'gravitate' towards each other (1858–9: vol. 1, 42). Association depends on difference and as 'Society consists in combinations resulting from the existence of differences' (*ibid.*: 198, 53), the range and extent of association must grow along with social differentiation. The more different that people are from each other, the more dependent they become and so the stronger is their need to associate. Carey saw this as the basis for the growth in the division of labour and exchange documented by Smith (1766) and Ricardo (1817).

Political economy and its view of micro-level relational structure became the basis on which the formal sociologies of Tönnies, Weber, and Simmel were constructed. They sought to ground social relations in subjective courses of action, arguing that individuals act on the basis of the social meanings acquired through socialisation and that actions cannot be understood without a knowledge of the norms that guide them. Nevertheless, the patterns of interaction formed through their actions have *sui generis* properties that shape the subsequent actions of the participants. The forms of social relations, therefore, comprise a distinct object of sociological analysis.

Simmel's essayistic writings were brought together for his comprehensive text on formal sociology (Simmel 1908a) and were elaborated into systematic accounts by Vierkandt (1923) and von Wiese (1924–9; 1931). Simmel's work was also a major source for the development of sociology in the United States, his essays being translated in early issues of the *American Journal of Sociology*. A formal, relational theme ran through American sociology in the early twentieth century to appear in the work of Giddings (1896: bk II, ch. 1) and Ross (1920), and in the Chicago sociologists of the city (Park and Burgess 1925). Around the same time, the Japanese sociologist Takata (1922) was taking a similar view. Ross's successor at Wisconsin, Howard P. Becker, worked on an expanded translation of Wiese's systematic sociology that became an important text on the relational structure of social forms (Wiese-Becker 1932). Mannheim, together with his assistant Elias, took the relational approach from Germany to Britain in the 1930s and 1940s (Mannheim 1934–5; Elias 1969), though their arguments had little influence until much later.

Simmel held that the key task for sociology was to explore the 'forms of sociation' (*Vergesellschaftung*) found in various cultural contexts. He saw social relations as motivated by positive and negative attitudes, and subsequent theorists added concepts referring to the direction and intensity of these attitudes and the distances involved (Park 1924; Bogardus 1925). Homans (1950), for example, conceptualised the frequency, duration, and direction of attitudes. Simmel saw positive attitudes motivating social relations of approach, reciprocity, and harmony, and negative attitudes motivating those of avoidance, hostility, and conflict. Thus, people may be involved in close intimate relations with each other or more distant and unconcerned ones. This allowed him to produce a systematic typology including advance, accordance, deference, gradation, favouritism, rivalry, schism, alliance, mutual aid, play, and other social relations (see the extension of this in Levine 1991: 198). In a similar vein, Giddings (1896) and Ross (1920) highlighted the aggregation and combination of people into social relations of antagonism, domination, opposition, exploitation, conflict, toleration, cooperation, alliance, mutual aid, play, gradation, and stratification. Durkheim's (1893) approach to relational structure had used similar ideas to depict the division of labour and social solidarity in terms of the density, volume, specialisation, dependence, control, struggle, conflict, cooperation, inequality, and reciprocity found in the association of individuals.

Simmel took particular account of the number of participants and the size of social groups, a view also taken by Carey, whose 'law of gravitation' held that the strength of attraction felt by a person towards a social group is directly proportional to the size of the group and inversely proportional to the distance maintained from others. His reasoning was that the chances of securing desired resources are greater in large groups than in smaller ones (1858–9: vol. 1, 43). Simmel recognised the importance of group size and used the number of participants in a social relation as the basis for a typology of social relations. Beginning with the individual as an isolate or outsider, he moved through the dyadic relations (or 'two-bonds') of intimacy to the triadic relations ('three-bonds') of secrecy, jealousy, mediation, and coalition formation. Further increases in the size of the pool of participants made more complex structures possible. Blau (1977) added ideas of exclusion, in-group/out-group relations, insulation, segregation, discrimination, minority/majority relations, mobility/immobility, closure, localism, and cosmopolitanism.

Durkheim held that an increase in the size of a society within a given territory tends to increase its 'dynamic density'. That is, it results in an increased intensity of association and communication, measured by their amount and speed, that allows an increased level of 'moral' interchange among the members of the population (Durkheim 1893: 201). An increase in the territorial scale or extent of a society – increasing its 'volume' – reinforces the effects of the increased density. Under these conditions, 'the struggle for existence becomes more strenuous' as people compete more intensively for resources: 'the closer functions are to one another, the more points of contact there are between them, and, as a result, the more they tend to conflict' (Durkheim 1893: 208, 210). If functions become specialised, however, the competition for resources can be limited, and Durkheim suggests that societies will be constrained to increase the amount of specialisation. A division of labour, then, is a direct consequence of these structural changes.

Formal sociology depicts patterns of social activity in terms of the quasi-geometrical properties that can be used to map the constraints operating on individual action and so shape the course of social development. Complex chains of interaction produced through the interweaving of individual actions are the means through which the mutual adjustment of actions results in a concatenation of 'reciprocal effects'. The interdependence of the individuals involved in such chains is the basis of persistent and regular patterns of behaviour, from small-scale interpersonal association to larger structures of relations referred to as 'social formations', 'social constructions' (*Gebilde*), or configurations.

These ongoing processes of social interaction form:

an apparently impenetrable network of lines between men [*sic*]. There is not only a line connecting A with B, and B with C, etc., but C is directly connected with A, and, moreover, A, B, and C are enclosed within a circle. Not only is there one line connecting A with B, and not only one circle in which both are enclosed, but there are many connecting lines. (von Wiese 1931)

The principles behind the network thinking required to investigate relational phenomena were first set out by Moreno (1934; 1941; Moreno and Jennings 1938; Jennings 1948; see also Bott 1928), who charted these configurations with novel 'sociometric' techniques. Sociometry, later referred to as social network analysis (Freeman 2004; Scott 2000: ch. 2), represents people as points and their relations as lines within 'sociograms' and shows that structures of interpersonal relations can be studied using precise and formal measures of the connectedness, density, centrality, and cohesion of the points and lines, the various points being formed into cliques, knots, circles, clusters, and components (Barnes 1954; Bott 1955; 1956; Mitchell 1969; and see Radcliffe-Brown 1940). Coser (1956) explored the idea that cross-cutting connections are central to patterns of conflict and solidarity. More recent work has shown how social positions can be modelled as categories of structurally equivalent or relationally substitutable points (White *et al.* 1976; Boorman and White 1976).

Small circles or clusters of relations concatenate into larger structures through processes of closure and mobility that establish patterns of community, domination, liberation, commercialisation, and democratisation (Sorokin 1927). These are the relations through which households, families, markets, classes, parties, churches, nations, and states are formed. For example, in a typology of religious forms, Troeltsch (1912) distinguished between church and sect, while Niebuhr (1929) added the 'denomination'. The Chicago sociologists developed a model of the city as a relational structure of zones, each of which has distinctive characteristics resulting from the competition of class and ethnic-based groups and the circuits and flows of resources claimed by the competitors (Park and Burgess 1925). Patterns of relations can be identified and described independently of the norms that may or may not define them: a political party, for example, may be organised around norms of democracy and equality yet be relationally structured as a tight oligarchy (Michels 1911). There may, therefore, be significant divergences between institutional structure and relational structure.

The relational ideas discussed so far have principally concerned micro-level relations among individuals. A properly macro-level approach, however, concerns the relations among social positions. Many positions are institutionally defined and can be objects of relational analysis, but a relational theory must also be concerned with positions that may not be explicitly labelled and recognised but may yet exist as purely relational phenomena. Blau has argued that 'Social positions are indicated by attributes and affiliations that distinguish people and that they themselves take into account in their social life and use as criteria for making social distinctions in their social intercourse' (Blau 1994: 9).[10] These are the structural 'places' resulting from affiliations and of which individuals may be only dimly aware, if they have any awareness of them at all (*ibid.*: 3). A relational structure is a multidimensional space of social positions or places among which the members of a population are distributed (Blau 1977: 4).

A relational structure constitutes a structure of opportunity. It 'circumscribes people's chances of occupying various positions and of establishing social relations with various other people. By circumscribing opportunities, the population structure supplies them and simultaneously limits them' (Blau 1994: 8). Echoing Giddens (1984), Blau sees social structure as both constraining and enabling – both restricting and opening up opportunities for action (Blau and Duncan 1967; see also Blau and Schwartz 1984).

Structural positions or places are connected into larger structures characterised by solidarity, cohesion, balance, and contradiction. These structural relations are defined by nominal and graduated parameters. Nominal parameters of group or category membership include measures of sex, religion, race, and occupation defined by category boundaries and that can be regarded as horizontal differentiations of 'heterogeneity'. Graduated parameters of order or inequality, on the other hand, include continuous measures of income, wealth, education, and power that form vertical differentiations of social inequality. The overall shape of a structure of inequality and its patterns of association can be examined through such measures as the Gini coefficient and its associated curve (Blau 1977: 69 ff).

The distribution of people and positions in terms of these two types of parameter creates barriers to association and circulation, and these barriers can be more or less permeable. For example, the sizes of the horizontal and vertical categories set certain mathematical limits, or constraints, to association and circulation, as Simmel had suggested for small groups. The upper limit to the frequency of class intermarriage or intergenerational class mobility depends on the relative sizes of the classes that figure in the analysis. The chance of upward mobility from class A to class B, for example, depends on the number of positions within class B that cannot be filled through self-reproduction – this is the question of the 'marginals' in mobility analysis. Such structural variables relate to the numbers and proportions of people and to amounts of time, and are measured by the salience, frequency, and intensity of association (Blau 1977: 27).

In the simplest societies only nominal parameters are relevant. These societies are structured through 'concentric circles' of connection that embed groups and categories in wider groupings that reinforce each other in the structure that Durkheim called mechanical solidarity. More complex societies are structured through 'intersecting circles' of association that cross-cut to create greater freedom of action for individuals and form a structure of organic solidarity. In these circumstances, people are held together largely through the division of labour itself. The differentiated parts of a society relate to each other in coordinated ways only on the basis of their mutual dependence within the structure of the whole (Durkheim 1893: 132). This coordination occurs through an adjustment of interests among interdependent individuals. Each interaction forms part of a larger chain of interactions that expresses the interdependence of distant parts of the same society. In Blau's words, 'Intersecting parameters generate structural complexity; consolidated parameters limit it' (Blau 1977: 102, 128; Blau and Schwartz 1984: chs. 4, 6).

Ekeh (1974: 52–4) has unpacked the idea of generalised exchange that he sees as the basis of organic solidarity. Beginning from the work of Lévi-Strauss, he showed how such structures can arise from individual transactions and without any overarching commitment to a norm of reciprocity. The simplest such structure is 'chain generalised exchange', taking the form A→B→C→D→E→A, with more complex structures comprising numerous overlapping chains. More complex than the chain is the 'net generalised exchange' structure where group activity benefits all individual members in turn (ABCD→E, ABCE→D, ABDE→C, ACDE→B, BCDE→A) or each individual gives in turn to the group

(A→BCDE, B→ACDE, C→ABDE, D→ABCE, E→ABCD). In all cases, individual transactions considered in isolation may be unbalanced, but the structure of the exchange relationships as a system is balanced. Ekeh notes that such relations can develop only if individuals are willing to grant 'extended credit' in their transactions, incurring costs in the short term in anticipation of receiving balancing rewards indirectly and over the long term. There must, therefore, be trust in the system rather than simply trust in each individual transaction. In such a situation, each individual believes that all others will observe an obligation to return, in some way, what they have received from others. This generalised trust allows the establishment of the 'credit mentality' that underpins generalised exchange (*ibid*.: 59). Where social differentiation occurs within a framework of systemic trust, exchange relationships are balanced through indirect chains and nets and this underpins social solidarity. This solidarity is itself a condition for widespread trust and extended credit (Ekeh 1974: 74–5; Gouldner 1960).

Durkheim's analysis of the division of labour showed that relational structure cannot be seen independently of institutional structure. Spencer, like Smith, had seen commercial societies as systems of contractual relations that link structurally placed individuals through their exchange relations. He therefore concluded that solidarity results from a spontaneous agreement among individual participants and an accommodation to each other's interests, and a social structure consists of nothing more than the contractual exchanges among self-interested individuals. Durkheim argued that such a contractual order, if it were ever to exist, could be only a very precarious and short-lived phenomenon. It would be subject to the continual disruption resulting from the ongoing clash of conflicting interests:

For where interest alone reigns, as nothing arises to check the egoisms confronting one another, each self finds itself in relation to the other on a war footing, and any truce in this perpetual antagonism cannot be of long duration. (Durkheim 1893: 152)

Durkheim concluded that stable and enduring contractual relations can exist only if they are entwined with 'non-contractual relationships' (*ibid*.: 155). That is, 'in a contract not everything is contractual' (*ibid*.: 158). Any contract rests upon regulatory structures of law and morality that define the conditions of their cooperation and the duties and rights of the contractors (*ibid*.: 160 ff). Thus, Durkheim recognised that institutional and relational structures had to be considered as the two facets of social structure. While one facet may be analysed independently of the other, and while each may vary independently, they are ultimately connected and must figure together in any comprehensive social theory.

Durkheim noted that integration through interdependence within relational structures is insufficient, in itself, to ensure the enduring social solidarity that occurs when the associated individuals are able to forge bonds of moral solidarity with each other. These institutional bonds develop only if individuals are aware of their difference and mutual dependence and can draw on subjective images of their complementarity that become integral elements in their sense of self. They feel emotionally tied to those from whom they differ and this sense of solidarity becomes a key element in the overall social cohesion or social integration of a society or social group (Durkheim 1893: 22–3). Contrary to the arguments of Spencer, then, coordination occurs only if contractual relations become grounded in non-contractual normative relations. This pattern of 'organic solidarity' does not rest upon a strong collective conscience but involves a regulation of exchange and cooperation through specialised institutions built from individual awareness of differences.[11]

The most rigorous discussion of macro-level relational structure has been pursued in Marxist considerations of the economic and class relations of a mode of production, first set out in the *Communist Manifesto* (Marx and Engels 1848). In this view, a mode of production comprises productive forces – people, land, machines, and raw materials – that are organised into specific social practices, such as technical divisions of labour and systems of distribution and consumption, through definite relations of production. Relations of production are the means of effective control and appropriation through which classes, or categories, of individuals become formed into distinct social locations or places that stand in relations of domination and exploitation (Cohen 1978). While legal and other norms are important elements in this social organisation of production, the relations themselves are not normative but 'factual' or 'real'. What Marx meant by this is that relations of dependence, access, exclusion, accumulation, and so forth, cannot be reduced to institutional clusters of norms but have, nevertheless, a constraining power over the individuals involved in them.

Marx (1867) explored the relational structure of class opposition in capitalist societies through an analysis of surplus value. Though aspects of his theory are much contested, this illustrates very clearly the nature of the relational method. Capitalist class relations, Marx argued, involve a separation between 'capitalists' having effective control of the means of production, and labourers or 'proletarians' with only their labour power and who have no alternative to working for capitalists. Labourers can secure subsistence only under terms set by the capitalists, who benefit from their ability to ensure that labourers work for longer than the time necessary to produce a marketable object. The 'surplus labour' performed in this time is realised as 'surplus value' when the products are marketed. Surplus value is the source of the profit that the owning class can make from the labour power of the labourers. The class relation is a relation of exploitation, with the rate of exploitation varying according to the balance between wages and surplus value.

Marx explored the connections between institutions and social relations in his analysis of a transition from personalised to credit-based relations of production in advanced forms of capitalism. Individual ownership of productive assets is regulated by the institution of private property as a legal relationship of control over productive assets that makes the individual owner the direct personal employer of the labour power of the propertyless. Exploitation follows from these legal relations. When production is organised through a joint stock company with share capital bought and sold through a credit system of corporate finance, the relations of production are transformed. They become more complex relations of *effective possession*, or control, that are a 'more concrete substratum' of the legal relations of property (Marx 1857: 98, 102, 109). Legal relations of property ownership are merely one element in the deeper relations of 'detention' or 'access' to social objects (Renner 1904: 81, 107, 117; Pashukanis 1929: 86). These are *de facto* relations of power over the forces of production. In a large corporation, legal rights to a share in the ownership of business assets, whether held directly by individuals or by trustees, are typically distributed in such a way that individual shareholders become merely small creditors divorced from any significant participation in effective control (Renner 1904: 142–3). The credit system concentrates control in ways that no longer correspond to the legal relations of property. As a result, there comes into being a capitalist class consisting of those involved in the ownership and manipulation of capital in its financial form of shares, bonds, and loans. The 'capitalist function', separated from personal shareholders, is exercised through the collective organisation of the business enterprise and its hierarchy of management. Control operates through structures of intercorporate relations with subsets of shareholders and other financial interests having powers over the productive use of assets that are disproportionate to their direct ownership stake (Scott 1997: 22 ff).

For Marx, the antagonistic structural relations between capitalists and proletarians constitute 'contradictions'. In idealist philosophy a contradictory proposition is one in which two or more constituent elements are mutually incompatible: the truth of one is negated by the other(s). Marx converted the idea of a contradictory proposition into that of a structural contradiction that exists when two or more entities are antagonistically opposed because their 'essences', or structures, necessarily work against or undermine each other (Marx 1843b). The constituent elements of a social structure are internally related: the relations among parts is a product of the structure of each element and their necessary relations to each other (Ollman 1971; see also Wilde 1989). The necessary consequences of each part, considered as a causal mechanism (Bhaskar 1975), may reinforce or interfere with each other. It is in this sense that the parts of a structure can be contradictory. Where the operations of elements are incompatible with each other, they comprise structural oppositions (*Gegensatzen*) or potential incompatibilities. As the structure develops, the structural oppositions become actual incompatibilities or contradictions (*Widerspruchen*). The development of a social structure with opposed elements will necessarily disclose the structural contradiction.

Marx held that the class relations of capitalism tend to develop as contradictions. The capital function and the labour function are each indispensable for the operation and reproduction of a capitalist mode of production, but they are incompatible because the expansion of capital can occur only at the expense of labour. The working out of this contradiction threatens the existence of the capitalist mode of production and can be resolved only if the mode of production itself is transformed. The agents placed in relation to these functions have structurally antagonistic interests and it is through their actions in pursuit of these interests that the contradiction can be overcome. Conflict occurs when the actions of individuals or groups are shaped by their position in relation to one of the opposed elements within a totality. They come into conflict with those in the opposed position and their conflict is the practical means through which the contradiction develops and, when they act on an accurate consciousness of their situation, is transformed.

Where Parsons and many 'normative functionalists' regarded relational structures as secondary, residual factors in sociological analysis, Durkheim and Marx treated them as primary and autonomous aspects of social structure, operating interdependently with institutional structures. Marx rejected what he saw as the overemphasis on cultural factors by idealist philosophers who saw human actions as expressions of legal, political, and religious ideas. Institutional structures of norms, Marx argued, are simply one of the factors that shape people's relations with each other and it is necessary to start out from 'real' relations rather than their 'ideological' expression in the 'phenomenal forms' of recognised and codified social institutions (Marx and Engels 1846: 47). This was the core of Marx's 'materialism', which held that relational structures, rooted in natural conditions, are the primary determinants of both individual action and institutional development.[12] While this led to a tendency for Marxists to minimise the importance of institutional factors and to posit a deterministic relationship of 'correspondence' between a relational 'base' and an institutional 'superstructure', it is clear that their conjoint operation was seen as fundamental (Lockwood 1956; 1992). There is a simultaneous and interdependent emergence and reciprocal shaping of social relations and institutional norms, each understood as an autonomous aspect of social structure. Relational and institutional structure can be explored separately as analytically distinct aspects of social structure, but they are integrally conjoined in concrete situations. The insights of institutional and relational sociologies are complementary. The specific analyses offered of kinship, religion, or class may be questioned, but the general principles behind these modes of analysis are essential elements in the study of social structure.

The relationship between institutional structure and relational structure has been famously illustrated in Merton's (1938) model of anomie. The institutional structure, referred to by Merton as the 'cultural structure', specifies expected goals or purposes as 'legitimate objectives' of action and sets a 'frame of aspiration' defining those things held to be worth striving for. Institutions also involve prescriptions, proscriptions, and preferences – norms – that define the acceptable or legitimate ways of pursuing these objectives (Merton 1938: 133). Where individuals pursue legitimate goals through approved means, they are acting in conformity with the cultural expectations attached to their social positions. Merton recognised, however, that the relational structure, which he referred to simply as the 'social structure', can constrain a person's ability to conform. The relational structure exerts pressure on individuals that enhances or limits their ability to conform. A state of anomie exists when a disjunction between institutional and relational structure detaches individuals from a taken-for-granted commitment to social norms and allows them to deviate in various ways. For example, the resources open to individuals in particular class positions may restrict their opportunities to pursue monetary success and social mobility and they may 'innovate', 'retreat' from, or 'rebel' against the institutional norms and goals (*ibid.*: 140, 145).

Structuration and causal power

Having clarified the appropriate view of the character and substance of social structure, it is possible to return to consider the challenges raised by those who have seen structural concerns as inimical to an appreciation of individual action and agency. Critics such as Watkins (1952; 1957) saw the 'holism' of structural analysts as requiring vitalist assumptions that imply a separate substantial existence for social structure and a complete structural determination of individual action: individual thoughts, feelings, and actions can have no independence and so there can be no such thing as voluntary action. Because he saw this rejection of creativity and innovation as self-evidently false, Watkins held that social structures must be regarded as illusory and with no reality apart from individuals and their actions. Harré (2002: 112) similarly argued against the idea of structural concepts, holding that 'such referents are not the kind of entities that could be causally efficacious': neither the following of an institutionalised rule nor the consequences of rule-following involve being causally affected by a rule.

Atkinson took an explicitly Weberian approach to this issue, seeing all social relations and social entities as the contingent products of individual action. Collectivities, he argued, are social 'fictions' and their effects on individuals are simply the result of the complex interplay of individual actions and their unintended consequences. This interplay, Atkinson argued, produces a 'disjointed and fractured' configuration or network of relations, not a substantial structure. Interaction networks are constantly shifting arrangements of individual actions. They are 'kaleidoscopes' that 'have no existence apart from the individuals whose ideals and activity create them' (Atkinson 1971: 261, 265). Social kaleidoscopes are simply 'the continuing and changing attempts which men [*sic*] make to control and shape their own social life and that of others' (*ibid.*: 266).

The principal response to these individualist critics has centred on the view that social structures are 'emergent' features of social interaction. In following the norms they have learned, people become subject to the constraint of social relations and social expectations that emerge, contingently, from their actions but are every bit as real as any other type of constraint. This was the view of Bhaskar (1979: 42 ff), who held that emergent structures have causal powers that are irreducible to those of the individual agents whose actions produce them. Social facts are, indeed, 'constructions', but not the direct and transparent creations of individual agents. Agents inherit social facts from their predecessors and so they pre-exist any particular individual act. Individual actions always encounter resistance from these inherited structures, while at the same time reproducing or transforming them through their actions. However creative they may be, actions always sustain or modify a pre-existing reality.

This argument answers many of the objections to structural analysis. Harré, for example, recognised that people follow norms because others sanction them, and Bhaskar's argument shows that it is the exercise of sanctions by the actor and the encountered others that constitutes the causal powers of social structures. The structural causality of institutional structures is exerted through this interpersonal constraint. Relational structures constrain actors because they set opportunities and limits for those in particular social positions. These positions involve, *inter alia*, a distribution of resources and of abilities to follow particular rules that cannot be reduced to discursive acts (Carter 2002). Structural constraints, as conditions, cannot be altered at will but are fixed and given limits on the possibilities open to individual agents.

This argument has been elaborated most forcefully in the 'structuration' theory of Giddens (1979; 1984) and the 'morphogenesis' theory of Archer (1995; 2003). Although their arguments differ on many points, they have thoroughly clarified a solution to the long-standing intellectual problem of the relationship between structure and agency. It is for this reason that Giddens sees his theory as *supplementing* theories of structure and agency, and not as an *alternative* to them (Giddens 1979: 80). He acknowledges the need for analyses of institutional and relational structures, but concentrates his own efforts on an agency-based theory of reproduction and transformation that elucidates the ways in which structural properties mediate between individual agency and system-level phenomena. Archer, however, feels that this focus on agents tends to reduce structures to the knowledgeability and habits of individual actors and so gives too much ground to methodological individualism. She takes the more radical view that structures and structural causality are not external top structuration but must themselves be incorporated into a theorisation of structure-building.

Giddens (1979) holds that structures are internalised as the dispositions and tendencies of action, so forming what López and Scott (2000) have called 'embodied structures'. This follows Chomsky's concept of linguistic competence as the rule-governed creativity of language users and parallels Bourdieu's (1972) introduction of the concept of 'habitus'. A habitus or embodied structure comprises 'the transposable dispositions embedded and embodied within an agent as a matrix of perceptual and linguistic schemas, competencies, appreciations, typifications, morals, sentiments, know-how and so on' (Stones 2005: 23, 88). The distinctively structural features of a social structure – 'structural principles' – are embodied in acquired habits and dispositions and so become inscribed in the minds and bodies of actors, generating their unconscious and habitual responses. Structural principles are, therefore, involved in the reproduction of the institutional and relational structures in which they are inscribed and from which they were acquired. Where actors are located in contradictory structures, their habituses will be equally contradictory and their routinised responses may reproduce incompatible or internally contradictory structures: the outcome will be structural transformation rather than structural reproduction.

Archer directs her attention to the ways in which social structures can constrain individual actions. Material factors can have direct causal effects on individuals, as in the case of the bodily changes that occur in response to diet or climate. Archer recognises that social structures cannot operate in this way. They operate, instead, through the 'social conditioning' of establishing fields of influences that set the range of opportunities open to agents, a process more akin to the selective effects of the material environment on gene distribution in a population. Agents exercise choice and creativity within these structural conditions, adapting to the logic of the situation as they define it. In their actions they may choose to defy or ignore the conditions under which they act, but these choices must always confront the consequences of any failure or ignorance. Social structures have their effects through the interpretations and experiences of agents. It is through their reception and realisation by human agents in their projects and actions that social structures are able to exercise their causal powers on human actions.

Archer argues, for example, that it is only when a person imagines or undertakes a project requiring a high level of financial investment that they will be directly frustrated by a limited availability of capital (Archer 1995: 198–9). A person who chooses to purchase a car, taking account of the available models and showrooms, their disposable income, etc., will be affected by the structural properties of the money and credit system, the system of retail distribution, the global system of automobile production, and numerous other structures of which they may be partially or perhaps totally unaware. In taking account of certain aspects of the circumstances under which they act, people endorse, evade, repudiate, or contravene the constraints inherent in the social structure.

The causal powers of social structures, then, are 'constraining or facilitating influences upon actors, which are not attributable or reducible to the practices of other agents' (*ibid.*: 90). Structural constraints are relatively enduring properties of social structures with a *potential* causal power that can become effective as an impediment or a facilitator only when taken into account in projects formulated by actors (Archer 2003: 7). People reflect on their perceived circumstances and concerns through the 'internal conversation' of reflective thought:

We survey constraints and enablements, under our own descriptions (which is the only way that we can know anything); we consult our projects which were deliberatively defined to realise our concerns; and we strategically adjust them into those practices which we conclude internally (and always fallibly) will enable us to do (and be) what we care most about in society. (Archer 2003: 133)

A satisfactory theory of structure and action must consider both how structures 'impinge' upon agents and how agents subjectively 'receive' them.

The embodiment of structure as habits and dispositions, on which Giddens concentrates, does not lead to the perfect reproduction of structures through individual actions: such a view would repeat the 'over-socialised' model of the actor sometimes attributed to Parsons (see Wrong 1961). The problem is not simply that structures may be contradictory rather than complementary. Rather, the causal powers of social structures are such that 'even the most stringent constraints never fundamentally determine the agent' (Archer 1995: 210). Knowledge of structures is imperfect and intentions are rarely realised in full. Because definitions of situations are only ever partial, actions will invariably have unintended and unanticipated consequences (Archer 2003: 140).

Archer also shows that an analysis of structure and agency must take account of their temporal separation. Each transformative act, she argues, is temporally separated from its antecedent and consequent acts by transformed structural conditions (Archer 1995: 157–8, 192–4; and see Stones 2005: 84–6). Archer has elaborated on this in a three-phase cycle involving successive phases of structural conditioning, social interaction, and structural elaboration. The overall social process, she argues, consists of overlapping and intersecting series of such sequences.

Structural conditioning is the process through which structures restrict and permit, constrain and enable, setting limits that provide agents with 'strategic directional guidance' by restricting the range of choices they are realistically able to make (Archer 1995: 90). Agents face a distribution of resources and a set of expectations, and they have access to socially distributed knowledge, all of which can facilitate or inhibit their projects. Structural conditions are inherited, not chosen, and actors must accommodate to their 'involuntary placement' in a social structure.

In a phase of social interaction, choices and decisions are made that reflect people's understandings of their given, and unchosen, structural conditions. While they may be able to confront or, in part, extricate themselves from these conditions, this will always involve costs and is likely to place them in a new context with other and different involuntary constraints and enablements. In such a phase, agents anticipate the consequences of acting in one way rather than another, estimating the opportunity costs involved. They weigh the rewards and costs they believe to be involved in various courses of action and they decide what sacrifices, if any, they are prepared to take. Actors always have variable 'degrees of interpretative freedom' in the choices they make: they may miscalculate or misunderstand the likely rewards and costs, their norms and sense of obligation may make them willing to pay higher costs, or they may simply choose to incur a loss or to sacrifice a potential gain (Archer 1995: 208).

It is in a final phase of structural elaboration that social structures are altered. Each participant acts in the light of their knowledge and their assessment of opportunity costs, but actions will invariably contradict or come into conflict with each other and no agent is likely to realise their intentions to the fullest extent possible. The effects of actions diverge from an actor's intentions, as all actions have unintended and unanticipated consequences (Merton 1936; Giddens 1976a). The resulting pattern of structural elaboration, then, is a largely unintended consequence of the simultaneous actions of myriad agents.

With the completion of this third phase of a cycle, there begins the first phase of a new one. The elaborated structure that results from the interactions of the various actors becomes the basis of the conditions under which actors must now construct their actions. It is in this sense, Archer holds, that conditioning structures pre-date the actions that transform them, and that structural elaboration post-dates those actions. It is in this way that Archer rounds out the theory of structuration and provides the solution to the issue of linking structure to action. The question can now be regarded as closed. Social structures have a reality as social facts and can be analysed in terms of the varying combination of their institutional and relational aspects. Structural integration and structural contradictions are responsible for the processes of reproduction and transformation through which structural elaboration – morphogenesis – takes place. This operates through structuration as agents knowingly, but imperfectly, produce the structural constraints on their own actions.

Social structures comprise the normatively patterned social relations that are produced, reproduced, and transformed through human activity and that set limits and opportunities that constrain those activities. The institutional and the relational aspects of social structure can vary independently, corresponding closely only in exceptional situations of social integration. Explanations of social action must attend to the interdependencies and contradictions that arise among the institutional norms of a society, as well as those that characterise the relational structuring of resources and opportunities. Processes of structuration and morphogenesis occur over time as activities are projected and undertaken, yet the resulting structural patterns cannot be reduced to those activities. Social structures are social facts *sui generis* and comprise an important focus of sociological work alongside those other aspects of sociological explanation that have been considered.

I have shown in the previous chapter that analyses of social structure are dependent upon, but not reducible to, analyses of social action. It is individuals and their socially organised actions that produce and transform, through a process of structuration, larger patterns of action and the structural properties that constrain and condition those very actions. The next step in my argument must therefore be to examine the concepts of action required to complete this understanding of structuration and morphogenesis.

The earliest action theories were those of political economists and culminated in the marginalist theories of Menger (1871; 1883) and Walras (1868; 1874). These theories concerned rational and self-interested, profit-seeking actions and depicted the concatenation of their largely unintended consequences into contingent and precarious macro-level patterns of market equilibration and of economic balance (Fisher 1926; Keynes 1936). Carried forward by von Mises (1949) and von Hayek (1942; 1962), these arguments were cast in a more generalised form in the strategic or transactional theories of Barth (1966) and Bailey (1969) and in theories of social exchange set out by Homans (1961) and Blau (1964). These arguments have been central to the development of a more general model of the rational choices involved in action.

These models of rational economic action were also taken up by Max Weber (1920), who placed them within a larger classification of action types that he based on the view that subjectively meaningful actions of all kinds were to be understood from the standpoint of the actor (see also Znaniecki 1935; 1919). Parsons (1937) elaborated on this in his action frame of reference, which stressed the importance of shared values and norms in the motivation of action. Parsons' action frame of reference became a widely accepted foundation for sociological analysis and was reworked in the 1960s and 1970s by more radical theorists such as Rex (1961), Dawe (1970; 1979), and Atkinson (1971), who connected his view of individual action with ideas of collective action.[1]

In parallel with Parsons' early work, Schütz (1932) had re-examined Weber's typology to uncover its phenomenological presuppositions. His work echoed some of the arguments through which Mead had begun to explore the interpretative processes involved in action (Mead 1910; 1927). Taken together, the ideas of Schütz and Mead produced a deepened appreciation of how agents give subjective meaning to their activities and define the situations in which they act. These arguments were developed by Hughes (1958), Becker (1963), and, most especially, Goffman (1959b; 1983) in his comments on the 'interaction order' of everyday life.

What these writers all alluded to was the need to recognise various 'non-rational' forms of action alongside the purely rational forms. Indeed, they showed that the frameworks of intersubjective meaning that inform the construction of rational acts are themselves the outcome of non-rational processes of action. Alongside rational actions must be recognised actions in which commitments to values and the communication of meanings are fundamental. These non-rational forms of action are especially involved in the construction of images of self and of collective identities and the forms of discourse through which narrative accounts of action are produced. These ideas were apparent in the work of Goffman and in the ethnomethodology of Garfinkel (1967), who used Schütz's ideas to reconstruct the Parsonian action scheme from a rigorously phenomenological basis. Garfinkel showed that agents negotiate the meanings of situations on the basis of reflexive interpretations and assessments, producing the accounts through which they make sense of their encounters. Mills (1940) similarly used ideas from Mead and Dewey to explore the 'vocabularies of motive' drawn on accounting for actions. These streams of theory merged into a larger understanding of accounts (Scott and Lyman 1968), cultural resources (Swidler 1986), and narratives of identity (Gergen 1991).

Many of these theories of action saw social structures and collective entities as constructed through the concatenation of actions and so as reducible to the observable acts of individual agents. They saw structural concerns as at best secondary and at worst mistaken. For some theorists concerned with class (Marx and Engels 1848), ethnic (Gumplowicz 1875; 1883), and elite relations (Mosca 1896; 1923), however, the reality of structures was taken seriously and it was held that specifically collective entities had a capacity for action in their own right. These ideas generated a powerful tradition of 'conflict theory'.

Action and social action

The foundations for almost all subsequent views of action were those laid down by Weber in his discussion of methodological principles. He saw 'action' (*Handeln*) as conduct (*Verhalten*) that is meaningful rather than merely reactive, holding that 'We shall speak of "action" insofar as the acting individual attaches a subjective meaning to his behaviour' (M. Weber 1920: 4–5; see also Parsons 1937: 46). Actions can be explained only to the extent that their meanings to the participating agents are understood. Involuntary responses triggered by physiological processes, such as breathing, sneezing, and reflex responses, involve no conscious deliberation. However, distinctively human forms of conduct are consciously and deliberately undertaken with a meaningful intention. Even emotional states of physiological arousal will typically depend upon an interpretation of the arousing stimulus. Thus, humans interpret their own feelings and 'assign meanings to situations and to the actions of others and react in terms of the interpretation suggested by these meanings' (Silverman 1970: 130). The degree of conscious, reflexive thought involved may vary, but human conduct can rarely be analysed without reference to its meaningful character. Through the mutual interpretation and assignment of meaning people construct courses of action that make sense in terms of some larger plan or project. It follows that a theory of action must consider things as they appear from the point of view of the person acting, as features of the world are relevant to human action principally in and through the ways in which they are perceived and interpreted. To understand an action the sociologist must place him or herself in the place of the acting individual and so see the world as it is seen by the participants. Understanding why an action was undertaken does not mean endorsing that action as right or morally acceptable, but it does require that the agent's assumptions, knowledge, and interests are seen as the basis on which it makes sense as a reasonable, or comprehensible, response.

Parsons (1937) showed that neither biological drives nor environmental conditions could be said to determine action as there is always a degree of subjective choice and initiative involved. Cultural socialisation provides the meanings through which they can – indeed, must – evaluate, consciously or otherwise, the alternatives available to them. Actions occur within situations that have been defined in relation to the pool of available and shared cultural meanings. This does not mean that action can be seen as a mere 'emanation' or automatic expression of cultural values. Human actors are active and creative agents of their own actions, acting voluntarily within the constraints of both their given physical circumstances and their inherited cultural values (Silverman 1970: 135). Actions are the outcomes of creative processes in which different individuals may interpret the same or similar situations in varying ways, and the same individual may arrive at varying interpretations on different occasions.

Cultural meanings depend on the social groups that sustain them, so all action is, in one sense, social (Barnes 1999). Weber argued, however, that some action can be regarded as social in the narrower sense of being oriented towards the actions of others (Campbell 1998). Thus, 'Action is "social" insofar as its subjective meaning takes account of the behaviour of others and is thereby oriented in its course'(M. Weber 1920: 4, 23). Action is social, in this sense, whenever there is a 'meaningful orientation to others' rather than mere contact or similarity of behaviour. Social action is oriented to the actual or expected behaviour of others and participants in a social relation must each interpret the actions, wants, and characteristics of the others, deciding on their course of action accordingly (M. Weber 1920: 22–3; see also Znaniecki 1935). This reciprocal social action or interpersonal action is 'interaction'.

Voluntarism is central to the action frame of reference that Parsons (1937: 44–5; see also Rex 1961) saw as the essential framework for a sociological description of actions.[2] This sees an 'act' – as the basic unit of complex systems of actions – having four analytical elements:

(1) an *agent* or actor who is the active centre of action;
(2) an *end* or goal towards which the action is oriented because the agent desires its realisation;
(3) a *situation* in which the action is initiated and comprising:
    (a) the *conditions* over which the agent has no control, and
    (b) the *means* the agent can use for attaining the ends;
(4) a *normative* or selective standard for choosing among means and ends.

Agents act in relation to ends that vary in the extent to which they are clearly specified and shared with others, and these are pursued within situations defined by the agents on the basis of their subjective experiences of circumstances. Desires are central motivational elements arising from the combination of cultural ideas with innate drives and instincts (Znaniecki 1935: 11). Agents typically pursue a plurality of ends, and must balance one against another in a calculus of alternatives and consequences when deciding on a particular course of action. Action also involves norm-governed choices concerning the appropriate means to adopt under the specific conditions treated as given.[3] Actors must choose reasonably and appropriately among their ends in terms of both their situational salience and feasibility and their relevance for the larger cultural values to which they subscribe (Cohen 1968: 72–3).

Weber's sociology centred on the 'motivational understanding' of action. This means that explanation of action involves identifying the complex of subjective meanings and affects (feelings) that an agent regards as adequate reasons for acting in a particular way. A motive is the whole complex of meanings and emotional drives that are drawn on, with varying degrees of consciousness, in choosing or accounting for actions. These aspects of motivation were referred to by Schütz (1953) as the 'in order to' and 'because' motives. Weber furthered his argument through a classification of typical motives in which the purely rational type of action, the easiest to understand, is the point of reference for the whole typology. Other types of action are seen as departures from pure rationality. The reflexive and deliberative character of rational action was contrasted with committed, routinised, and expressive forms of action where conscious deliberation and rationality are weak: 'For purposes of a typical scientific analysis it is convenient to treat all irrational, affectually determined elements of behaviour as factors of deviation from a conceptually pure type of rational action' (M. Weber 1920: 6).

Weber referred to the purely rational type as end-rational action (*Zweckrationalität*). This occurs where situational objects are defined by agents as either conditions or means and are calculatively assessed and instrumentally employed in order to pursue practical and well-defined ends (M. Weber 1920: 24):

This involves rational consideration of alternative means to the end, of the relations of the end to the secondary consequences, and finally of the relative importance of different possible ends. (M. Weber 1920: 26)

At the opposite pole Weber placed the 'affectual' type, in which activity is a direct and unmediated expression of inner feeling states, such as revenge, devotion, or sexual gratification (M. Weber 1920: 25). There is little or no conscious deliberation or calculation and agents respond automatically or unthinkingly through the reactive communication of emotional drives and impulses.

The other two ideal types fall between these extremes. In value-rational action (*Wertrationalität*), agents pursue a course of action because of an emotional commitment or allegiance to an absolute and overriding value. There is no calculation of means and alternative ends: action is planned in pursuit of a consciously held and formulated value and without regard for its practical efficacy. Prayer viewed as a means to eternal salvation, for example, is not evaluated against alternative means, and the absolute value of salvation is not weighed against alternative goals. End-rational action is pragmatic and calculative, but value-rational action is rational only in relation to fixed commitments to values and norms. In the final, 'traditional' type of action agents act purely through 'ingrained habituation' (M. Weber 1920: 25). Actions are routinised as habits, as recurrent and unreflective activity. In place of the explicit consideration of goals and means is simply an intention to act in the usual or customary way. Weber saw such unreflective action as typical of much everyday routine action. Where the repetition of past ways of acting itself becomes a value, traditional action shades over into value-rational action as 'traditionalism'.

Weber's typology conflated a number of separate distinctions and tends to be too restrictive in its view of rationality. Thus, Cohen (1968: 89–90) argued that commitments to norms and values, the availability of alternatives, and the degree of instrumentality, calculability, affectivity, creativity, and reflexivity can each vary independently, and they can combine in complex ways. Specifically, Cohen argued, the Weberian typology combined a distinction between rational and non-rational forms of action with conceptions of emotional expression and routinisation, each of these needing separate consideration. Atkinson (1971), for his part, held that the model of instrumental or technical rationality is too restrictive and has to be relaxed in favour of a looser idea of rationality. The model of end-rational action sees action following a situational logic based on perfect rationality and a complete practical knowledge (see Popper 1945; Jarvie 1964). Atkinson holds that actions may fall short of this technical or 'scientific' rationality yet nevertheless employ a 'commonsense' rationality (Atkinson 1971: 151). Non-rational forms of action are not 'irrational' *per se* but may be practically rational, relative to the information an agent has, the ends pursued, or the drives followed. Such actions are 'sensible' or reasonable responses according to the subjective rationality of the agent: 'There is a reason or a logic which any actor gives to his action in each situation even though that action be vague and unarticulated' (*ibid.*: 175). Action may be rational from the point of view of the actor, even if others may judge it differently: 'every situation, seen from the point of view of a particular type of actor or actors involved in it, has a particular logic which makes sense to that actor' (*ibid.*: 175). Thus:

All action, whilst not proceeding in accordance with the laws of classical logic, can be regarded as being within the bounds of reason and common sense when judged from the point of view of the actors involved. (Atkinson 1971: 175; and see Laing and Esterson 1964)

Parsons (1937) was among the first to reconstruct Weber's typology along alternative lines that anticipated some of these later criticisms. His view was that the basic typology could be simplified into a distinction between rational and 'ritual' forms of action, both of which could be contrasted with the affective or emotionally driven conduct that lies on the border-lines of action and mere behaviour. Similarly, rational and ritual actions may each be routinised as habits or customs.

Parsons underpinned this typology with a distinction between three bases of action orientation that he termed the cognitive, the cathectic, and the evaluative (Parsons 1951: 8). A cognitive orientation is based on concepts and existential beliefs that are the means through which perceptions of the external world and inner experience are built into a model of reality and a sense of order, providing the agent with a defin-ition of the situation. Agents can intervene and manipulate objects in order to achieve technical solutions to practical problems. A cathectic orientation is based on expressive or affective meanings through which wants and desires are formed into emotions. It concerns the 'consum-matory' aspects of the sentiments and feelings that drive actions. Finally, an evaluative orientation is based on values and preferences that allow choices and judgements to be made on the basis of desired states or purposes. These three modes of orientation allow agents to relate to the world through ideas that define or map their situation, feelings that grat-ify or deny their needs, and choices that order and select among alter-native ends. Action orientations are 'internalised' as integral elements of the personality in the form of, respectively, skills, tastes, and value commitments.[4]

Action is regulated by norms generated on the basis of specific action orientations. Cognitive orientations lie behind cognitive beliefs such as factual bodies of practical lore, magical formulae, and the more system-atic knowledge of philosophy, science, and technology. Cathectic orien-tations are found in aesthetic or appreciative standards of expressive symbolism that define proper or tasteful forms of expression, and evalu-ative orientations are systematised as the moral evaluation of behaviour as right or wrong. These three types of standard are analytical elements that figure in all actions, to a greater or lesser extent. In concrete situ-ations, agents factually interpret the objects and situations encountered, appreciate their aesthetic properties, and appraise their significance for moral criteria of goodness and badness (Parsons 1951: 7–8, 12–13), and particular courses of action will combine these in varying ways. In this way, action orientations become patterns or templates that guide and organise actions and set limits to them.[5]

These elements can be used to form a classification of action that reflects more closely the intentions behind Weber's own typology. Parsons' work undertook this task through a typology that used a set of

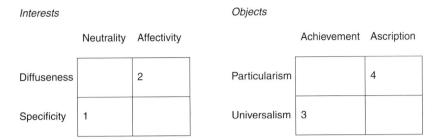

Figure 4 Action orientations
Source: adapted from Schluchter (1989: 67–8). Although cited as
Schluchter (1989), the book was put together from extracts from
three books published in 1980, 1985, and 1988.

variables to classify the orientations and normative standards involved in
patterns of action (Parsons *et al.* 1951b). These 'pattern variables' define
the 'dilemmas of choice' faced by agents in relating their interests to the
objects of their actions. An agent's subjective interest, Parsons argued,
is structured in relation to the two variables of affectivity/neutrality and
diffuseness/specificity. The objects towards which an action is oriented
are defined by the variables of achievement/ascription and particularism/
universalism. When agents act, their actions can be located in the conceptual space defined by the typologies of interests and objects shown in
Figure 4.

The scheme presents two polar types of action: the strategic and the
committed (or 'ritual'). Strategic action is instrumental and involves a
'technical' interest (box 1) towards useful objects (box 3). Committed
action, on the other hand, involves an emotionally engaged interest (box 2)
towards objects of identification (box 4). A strategic action is one in
which an emotionally neutral orientation is sustained through confining
an agent's subjective interest to the handling of interchangeable objects
as generalised resources for achieving highly specific goals. Strategic
actions involve 'orientation to the postponement of gratification, universal norms, individual achievement and active mastery, and specific
and analytical relationships' (Habermas 1965: 91). A committed action,
on the other hand, is one in which the agent's emotions are directed
towards a state of belongingness, of diffuse non-purposive solidarity or
sense of community, and objects are seen as having particular qualities
with which an agent can identify and can value. Other forms of action are
understood as departures from these two types along the various dimensions that define the typology, giving the whole scheme considerable

complexity and flexibility. The pattern variables define 36 possible types of action, though the principal use of the classification is not to produce such a system of boxes but to specify the dimensions along which concrete action patterns differ from the clearest analytically defined types of strategic and committed action. The polar types are ideal types in the Weberian sense: intellectually comprehensible abstractions that serve as yardsticks for comparison with real, concrete cases.

The polar types of action – the strategic and the committed – each have a rational structure in the broad sense emphasised by Atkinson. Strategic action has a formal, practical, and goal-oriented rationality that is 'outcome-oriented' or 'success-oriented' (Schluchter 1996: 247). Committed action is substantively rational in relation to an agent's absolute commitments to personal or shared values and norms (Elster 1989b: 113; 1989a: ch. 3). Each type is driven by emotional factors and cathectic orientations, but these are meaningfully elaborated in ways that distinguish them from mere expressive behavioural responses. In strategic action, emotional responses are suppressed to allow an emotionally neutral and 'objective' cognitive appraisal of situations. In committed action, emotions are expressed through appropriate aesthetic or moral standards, allowing identification, integration, and solidarity with others who subscribe to the same norms and values.

Habermas (1965: 91–2) made a similar distinction to this in his contrast between 'instrumental' and 'communicative' actions. Strategic or instrumental action involves choices made among the available means according to purely technical considerations. Agents act on predictions and expectations concerning objects, others, and conditions. Their knowledge is built and employed through pragmatic learning processes that subject expectations to critical assessment in the light of experience and establish skills and competences. Competent strategic action successfully achieves its ends; incompetent strategic action, as a result of a failure to fully observe the critical tests of rational, pragmatic appraisal, fails to realise the agent's intentions. Habermas' concept of communicative action tends to stress the purely discursive aspects of the action type over the emotional commitments. He sees participants establishing reciprocal expectations that define the obligations through which their actions are regulated. They act with respect to these recognised and accepted norms without regard for practical success or failure. Their actions are intended to realise a commitment to general values through conformity to the norms that express them. The learning processes involved build up commitments and motivations to act in 'legitimate' ways.

As Weber suggested, these reflexive forms of action can be contrasted with the unreflective habits through which much everyday behaviour is organised. Such action depends upon habitualised dispositions that generate recurrent practices as taken-for-granted routines in which any need for decision is minimised. The mental and physical habits of the body comprise a 'habitus', a bodily structure homologous with, or corresponding to, the structural conditions in which agents find themselves (Bourdieu 1972). The habitus arises from the common and recurrent experiences of living under particular social conditions, and the recurrent practices generated will tend to reproduce those structures. Archer has argued that:

When the context remains continuous over many generations, then very large tracts of everyday life come under the tutelage of routine action and remain there. Induction, initiation and imitation suffice for the transmission of this repertoire and for the conduct of most repetitive activities. (Archer 2007: 50)

Strategic action is understandable in terms of cognitive criteria that set standards for the accuracy and adequacy of the knowledge on which it is based and for assessing its practical consequences in relation to interests and goals. These standards define ideas of 'truth' and 'logic' in terms of which reason and 'intelligence' can be applied in the practical investigation and exploration of situations in the furtherance of interests (Parsons 1951: 328; Parsons *et al.* 1951b: 165; A. Weber 1920–1). Consciously and deliberately pursued, strategic actions are systematic acts of planning and technical adjustment of the kind found in much economic and political activity and in scientific investigation. They have been systematically explored by the rational action theorists who developed classical and marginalist accounts of economic action into more general models of action. Crystallised as habits, strategic actions become practical dispositions that comprise the skills and routines employed in elections (Downs 1957), educational choice (Boudon 1973), laboratory science (Latour and Woolgar 1979), etc. The prevalence of such habits underwrites the economist's view that conscious motivation is an unimportant element in scientific explanation: economic action can be explained 'as if' it were completely rational.

Committed actions have been given less attention by recent social theorists than have strategic actions, the most notable exception being discussions by Erving Goffman (1983) and Randall Collins (2004).[6] However, it was earlier theorists who set out its general characteristics. Committed action depends upon aesthetic standards of beauty, authenticity, loyalty, appropriateness, and similar canons of 'taste' (Parsons 1951: 402) or moral standards of 'right' and 'wrong' conduct that specify rights, duties, and obligations. Actions organised in relation to such norms express sentiments of commitment to shared values, sociability, and the solidarity of membership in a social group (Ross 1901: 17). Consciously and deliberately pursued, they comprise such acts as devotional religious and political commitment. Unreflectively pursued as habits, however, they comprise aesthetic and ethical dispositions of bodily habitus. By using particular styles of artistic expression, conforming to ethical proscriptions, recognising the authority and expertise of others, and similar acts and practices, the solidarity, cohesion, and legitimacy of group membership can be established and sustained. These actions are rooted in a systematic awareness of the needs and concerns of others, a need for gregarious association with others, and a desire to follow the prevailing rules (Ross 1901: 17). Agents engage in 'mutually focused' actions that maintain and sustain a shared sense of reality and a shared commitment to expected performances.

Desires and norms are typically internalised, but conformity is not automatic – though Parsons did tend to adopt what has been referred to as an 'oversocialised' model of the agent that saw committed actions as direct expressions of socialised routines (Wrong 1961). However, committed actions involve a creative, interpretative element (Turner 1962), often seen as 'freedom'. Habitualised as 'ritual action', however, it involves formulaic, stereotyped, and routinised conduct of the kind apparent in everyday conversations and gossip. The recounting of narratives, for example, dramatises events as part of the ongoing drama of everyday encounters and helps to build a sense of shared dramatic involvement and of social solidarity.

Weber and Parsons saw the analysis of action and social action as a prolegomenon to the analysis of patterns of social *interaction*, and Turner (1988) has gone so far as to claim that social interaction has to be the effective starting point for sociological analysis. In interaction, the participants orient themselves to each other as 'social objects'. They must each adjust their actions to the actual and anticipated reactions of others and so build up reciprocal and complementary expectations to guide their own actions by predicting the behaviour of others (M. Weber 1920: 26). As I have shown in the previous chapter, these expectations become the norms by which agents make their choices, defining what is 'normal' or expected to occur 'as a rule', whether as a *de facto* statistical expectation or a *de jure* sense of obligation (see Cohen 1968: 116). Parsons (1951) came to see the expectations through which people interpret their situations as inherent in the particular social positions they occupy. Through routinisation and long duration, they become 'given' facts in social interaction. However, I have argued that institutionalised expectations or typifications (Schütz 1953) provide a 'vocabulary' through which situations are defined but are not culturally expressed as fixed, deterministic definitions.

Parsons used the typology of strategic and committed actions to contrast 'the attitude of expediency', where action 'is a function of the instrumental interests of the actor', with the 'internalization of the standard' in such a way that conformity to normative expectations becomes a 'need-disposition' of the personality and drives people to act without regard for their interests (1951: 37). Social interaction based on expediency results in structures of action that are instrumentally coordinated through the mutual adjustment and 'interlacing' of interests (Ross 1901: 19). Examples are the economic and political interests involved in the 'associative' relations (Tönnies 1889) of the 'temporal' sphere (Comte 1851–4: vol. 2, ch. 5; Branford and Geddes 1919a), the sphere of 'steering interests' (Habermas 1968) and 'civilization' (A. Weber 1920–1). Social interaction grounded in internalised normative standards results in structures of interaction that integrate agents into solidaristic or 'communal' relations (Tönnies 1889). These are the religious and ethical orientations of the 'spiritual' sphere, the socio-cultural lifeworld of everyday life (Habermas 1981) and the larger structures of the institutional framework (Ross 1920: ch. 5).

Interactions are shaped both by normative expectations and by calculations of what is in the interest of the agents (Lockwood 1956: 256–7; Scott 1995). The two ideal types of action can be isolated only in abstract discussion. In real situations, the rational, interested calculations stressed by the utilitarians and economists are integrally related to the normative framework of committed actions that comprise the 'non-contractual' element in contract. Strategic actions occur under particular conditions and are always 'embedded' in a larger cultural and normative structure (Parsons 1958c; Granovetter 1986; Polanyi 1944).[7] Similarly, conformity to shared value commitments may be reinforced through sanctions (rewards and punishments) intended to ensure that normative expectations are aligned with strategic considerations. A pattern of action is fully institutionalised only when conformity follows from both an internal disposition to conform and a calculation of the advantages and disadvantages consequent on the sanctioning reactions of others (Parsons 1951: 38).

The action frame of reference is a basis for conceptualising action, social action, and interaction in ways that allow the building of more complex theories of action and the emergence of social structures from action processes. Action concepts are the building blocks for complex schemes of sociological analysis. This frame of reference also has an importance in its own right as a basis for developing descriptions and explanations of strategic and committed actions. The following sections look at the ways in which these two types of action have been explored in quite distinct theoretical traditions. Emotional expression will be discussed more fully in Chapter 8.

Strategic action and social exchange

Strategic action was systematically theorised by the political economists, who Parsons (1937: 51 ff) described as adopting a 'utilitarian theory of action'. Individuals are depicted as independent and autonomous centres of rational calculation, choosing among ends and means according to their utility or usefulness in strategic acts. They face situations with specific, fixed goals and are able to calculate how various alternative acts will affect these goals. Ends are seen as fixed elements given by the physical and biological conditions of individual heredity and the material environment, and individuals must choose the most appropriate means to these ends according to purely technical or scientific standards. Such action is 'rational' in the strongest sense of the word. Although some theorists hold that choice is exercised with full and complete information, the theory need assume only that agents calculate alternatives relative to their current state of knowledge.

Some later economic theorists took this in a more general direction to form a larger framework of rational choice or rational action theory (Downs 1957; Becker 1976). Rational action theorists recognise that an inherent scarcity of resources means that all action involves a choice among alternative goals and means. When this choice involves a rational calculation of the costs and benefits attached to various alternatives and agents choose the best or most efficient means towards a chosen goal, the action is strategic. Specific emotions (socially formed) drive the wants or desires that underpin the choice of goals, but strategic action is emotionally neutral with respect to the means, and rational calculation ensures optimal practical adaptation to given circumstances (Elster 1989b: 22, 25).

This model of rational choice sees agents having 'preferences' that allow them to rank the alternatives open to them according to their 'utility', their usefulness or overall 'value' to them. A course of action is chosen to maximise, or optimise, utility. This utility is manifest in the 'rewards' and 'costs' arising from actions, and utility maximisation involves a calculation aimed at maximising rewards relative to costs. Many economists posit an orientation towards utility as a useful fiction: human action occurs 'as if' it were subjectively motivated towards the attainment of utility. For others, however, real motivational processes are seen at work. Thus, Marshall (1890) saw the search for utility as rooted in socialised 'wants', and Blau (1964: 20) recognised deep psychological 'needs and dispositions'.

Agents organise the perceived utilities of varying quantities of available objects in an 'indifference function' or 'preference ordering'. This is a numerical mapping of the combinations of alternatives among which an individual is indifferent because they secure equivalent utility. An agent may, for example, be indifferent between obtaining two apples and one orange, on the one hand, and one apple and three oranges, on the other. The agent would, however, prefer six apples and two oranges to either of these alternatives. Thus, agents 'choose between alternative practical ... courses of action by evaluating the experiences or expected experiences with each in terms of a preference ranking and then selecting the best alternative' (Blau 1964: 18; Elster 1989b: 23). The scarcity of resources is such that an agent's choice among the indifferent alternatives must be made in relation to available resources: it costs more to buy six apples and two oranges than it does to buy two apples and one orange, and an agent with limited income may be more likely to choose the latter than the former. Rational agents are budgetary units.

Limits to this indifference ranking are inherent in the diminishing 'marginal utility' gained with each successive object. That is to say, 'the value of a single unit varies with the number of units received over a period of time' (Homans 1961: 40) because the increased utility gained from an additional object declines as the agent becomes progressively 'satiated'. The attractiveness of each additional apple, for example, declines as they are consumed and may decline very rapidly once the stomach is full.

A central assumption is that different objects can be compared with a common measure of utility. This is most clearly the case in economic activities, where monetary value serves as a measure of utility. The utility of an investment in capital goods, for example, can be measured by the profits anticipated from the sale of the commodities that can be produced with them. Similarly, the amount of time allocated to various activities can be compared in terms of the income gained or forgone in each. Any preference that can be expressed in monetary terms can be analysed by economic variants of rational choice theory.

The approach can, however, be extended beyond the economic case. Homans showed that 'social approval' is a utility analogous to money and that much non-economic behaviour can be explained by the motivation of agents to seek approval for their actions from others and to avoid 'rejection'. Blau added that 'Men [*sic*] are anxious to receive social approval for their decisions and actions, for their opinions and suggestions. The approving agreement of others helps to confirm their judgements, to justify their conduct, and to validate their beliefs' (Blau 1964: 62). Social approval is typically gained through conformity to group norms (Homans 1961: 46, 114 ff), and was seen as a fundamental drive by

Adler (1928) and Horney (1937). Other measures of utility have been suggested, though few have been analysed as systematically as money and social approval. For example, Parsons (1963b) suggested that power could be considered as a key source of rewards and costs and that the striving for power is analogous to the striving for money and approval.[8] Similarly, Foucault (1975–6; 1982), following Nietzsche (1886), stressed the striving for power as a critical human motive. Money, social approval, and power may, therefore, be the fundamental forms of utility.

The existence of multiple sources of utility, serving as 'general reinforcers' or 'generalised media of exchange', leaves many questions, as yet, unanswered. If agents can calculate differentials in anticipated social approval and power, as well as money, they can be seen to be acting in quasi-economic terms, but this cannot involve a reduction of all utilities to monetary terms. The generation and distribution of each source of utility must be explored independently, without reducing one to another. Similarly, the ways in which agents, in practical situations, are able to combine such diverse measures into a single comparison are unclear. For example, calculations of trade-offs in balancing monetary rewards against loss of social approval or enhanced power against increased social rejection are routine yet the mechanisms involved have yet to be established.

Even if a single source of utility is being considered, the calculation of utility is far from simple. Where the outcome of a course of action is indeterminate, it is impossible to produce a clear and coherent indifference function. One way of dealing with this is for agents to rank alternatives according to the probabilities – risks – of specific rewards and costs. Thus, a large improbable outcome, such as winning a national lottery, may be preferred to a small but certain outcome if the discrepancy between the returns is significantly great and the costs of the alternative actions are similar. If a lack of adequate information makes it impossible to assign probabilities, then agents are acting under conditions of 'uncertainty'. In a social encounter characterised by uncertainty, the expected outcomes for any one agent depend upon the actions of all others and utility cannot be maximised with any degree of certainty. They must, instead, seek to minimise possible loss of utility by comparing the worst possible outcomes and choosing the least worse of these. The implications of such uncertainty were noted by Arrow (1951), who showed that situational actions are decided on the basis of expectations about the future state of the macro-level structures reproduced and transformed through those actions.

The most advanced explorations of strategic action are the so-called agent-based computational models of decision-making. Originating in the strategic theories of Schelling (1960; 1978), these models were initially used to generate artificial societies for simulation studies (Epstein and Axelrod 1996) and were developed as theoretical schemes in work by Axelrod (1997) and Epstein (1999). Their arguments focus on the 'local' decisions made by agents following a set of simple and clearly defined rules of action. They trace the consequences of these decisions for the larger structures that emerge through interaction. Where many earlier rational choice theorists assumed a natural tendency for interaction to arrive at an equilibrium state, agent-based computational models are more open and aim to track the dynamics of evolving structures in all their complexity. Ormerod (1994) has shown that this requires the adoption of more realistic assumptions about economic motivation and the variety of sources of utility (see also Tong 1990).

Analyses of strategic action and social action are the means to understanding patterns of social interaction involving calculative agents. Interaction is seen as an exchange of rewards and costs (punishments) between agents and as resulting in forms of cooperation and conflict. Decisions taken by each participant in an exchange relationship depend on the actual and anticipated decisions taken by others and so there is a tendency towards mutually rewarding relationships. Individuals exchange with each other only if each believes this will secure greater gains than any realistic alternative. Blau (1964) showed that an office worker will offer help to a colleague if the esteem and praise secured in return for this help is more valuable than any income or satisfaction gained from simply carrying on with their own work. Similarly, a worker will ask for help only if the status lost by acknowledging incompetence is less valuable than the income or satisfaction lost through the failure to work effectively. Interaction is a result not only of the intrinsic value of sanctions but also of their frequency and duration. The more often an agent is rewarded, the longer the period over which rewards are received, and the more valuable is the reward, then the more likely is the relationship to continue (Homans 1961: 36–9, 54).

A voluntary exchange relationship can be modelled in simple supply and demand curves that intersect at the point of mutual benefit. Supply and demand curves derive from the indifference curves of the individuals involved, the particular point at which supply and demand are balanced depending on the bargaining power of the agents. Differentials of power in exchange relations were referred to by Weber as the differences of 'market situation' produced by a given distribution of resources. Each participant in an exchange relationship uses his or her resources to increase their utility, subject to the principle of diminishing marginal utility.

Power reflects the dependence of an agent on resources held by another, any imbalance in the distribution of resources being associated with a corresponding inequality of power (Thibaut and Kelley 1959: ch. 7; Emerson 1962; 1972a; 1972b). This 'reward power' is based on the manipulative inducement of activities through the use of resources (Molm 1997). Bargaining power varies with the availability of alternative sources of supply. Those who have no other way of securing desired objects have no bargaining power: there is no alternative and they must accept whatever is available under the terms offered, unless they are willing or able to completely forgo the object. Where the bargaining power of all the participants is equal, their activities will be exchanged at a unique 'price' set in a determinate rate of exchange between the objects and activities involved. Thus, agents in an exchange relationship are profit oriented. Each participant seeks to maximise the profit that can be gained through his or her activities, and an exchange relationship continues only so long as all participants are making a profit (Roemer 1982). Enduring relationships, therefore, depend on the state of the power relations among the agents.

Where participation in an exchange relationship is voluntary, participants are better off than they would be if they did not interact: if this were not the case, rational agents would refuse to enter into an exchange. In some situations, however, agents may be coerced into an exchange that disadvantages them. They calculate that the costs of disregarding the commands of a constraining agent are greater than the losses or reduced benefits secured through exchange. Being given the command 'Your money or your life' at the point of a gun may persuade an agent to exchange his or her wallet for the ability to walk away. Molm (1997) has defined this as 'coercive power', a form of power based on force and punishment that gives agents the ability to negatively affect the outcomes attained by others. Reward power and coercive power are the two forms of corrective influence in social relations (Scott 2001: 13).

Rational action theorists see social structures as emergent consequences of processes of social exchange. Direct bi-partisan exchange relationships concatenate into complex networks of relations, with stable and persistent exchange relationships being 'markets' or 'quasi-markets'. Because dyadic exchanges exhibit variations in their power-dependence balance, the overall network can show a greater or lesser degree of generalised reciprocity through circuits of exchange. Such an analysis shows the overall state of balance or equilibrium in the network conceived as a 'field' of influence (Ekeh 1974; Gouldner 1959; 1960).

Theories of rational choice have proved very valuable in explaining patterns of strategic action and interaction. In many real situations, however, assumptions of strategic orientation have to be relaxed and account must be taken of other dimensions of the overall action space. This is especially apparent when explanatory attempts move away from core economic activity. In Downs' (1957) model of the political process, for example, enfranchised citizens are seen as 'consumers' of policies offered by parties in the political 'market' of elections and public opinion. Deciding how to vote is a rational choice based on a calculation of the likely effect of a vote on the outcomes likely to result. Parties must maximise their vote if they are to secure election, and they seek to do this by offering policies that will appeal to the largest possible number of voters. In a two-party system, each party puts together a package of policies that it hopes will attract voters. They do this by promoting 'images' to which voters can respond, and electoral outcomes depend largely on the ways in which party images are presented and discussed in the mass media. In a political system where opinion runs along a left-right continuum, electoral competition tends to produce a convergence towards the centre as each party seeks to secure the support of the median voter.

There is, however, a fundamental problem with this argument. As Downs himself showed, a potential voter computes the personal advantages likely to result from the election of their preferred party and multiplies this by the probability that his or her vote will change the outcome of the election. The effect of any single vote in a large electorate is minute, and a rational choice would be to refrain from voting: the cost of voting outweighs any likely effect on the outcome. Convergence towards the centre can occur only if citizens do actually turn out and vote. Downs held that most people do, in fact, vote and so argued that there must be an additional reward attached to the act of voting: the vote affirms a commitment to the political system and expresses a valued citizenship right (see also Riker 1962). Barry (1970: 19–23) showed that this additional argument goes beyond rational choice theory. Willingness to vote results not merely from calculations of personal advantage but also from a sense of obligation and a commitment to an absolute value. Conversely, a declining electoral turnout may reflect a decay in the obligation to vote and a declining trust in the electoral mechanism.

Strategic action, then, cannot be separated from value commitments. What appears to be a purely instrumental act depends on a framework of norms and values that make it possible. This was recognised by institutional economists, who showed that the information, knowledge, and preferences on which economically rational actors act are cultural phenomena and are embedded in a social context of institutions (Commons 1924; Hodgson 1988; North 1990; and see Granovetter 1986). Rational action theory alone applies only where norms of emotional neutrality, objectivity, and calculability (universalism, specificity, neutrality, and achievement) are institutionalised. Embeddedness in an institutional structure means, furthermore, that tendencies towards strategic action may be countered by institutional elements that generate dispositions to act non-strategically in pursuit of value commitments.

Committed action and symbolic interaction

Committed action has been the central concern of theorists who drew on the social psychology of Mead (1910; 1927; and see the posthumous collection Mead 1938) to explore symbolic communication and the reciprocal interpretation of meaning. The leading theorist of committed action was Goffman, whose 'dramaturgical' model of the 'interaction order' explored the sphere of co-presence and face-to-face encounters. Goffman developed the view that each participant in interaction must interpret and anticipate the reactions of others, these expectations shaping their sense of self and their actions towards those others. Agents take on culturally defined roles and enact them to others as creative 'presentations' they hope will impress. People 'express' their sense of self and their intentions to audiences of others who are 'impressed' in some way and degree. Through the evidence intentionally and unintentionally presented, these others build an 'impression' of the agent and decide on their own actions in relation to the impression gained. Because all agents must interpret the presentations of others, interaction is a reciprocal process of impression formation.

Self-presentation and impression formation are emotionally driven by embarrassment and shame and the consequent anxiety concerning these. Agents are oriented towards the recognition, respect, prestige, or 'deference' they anticipate receiving from others and constantly compare what they feel they ought to receive with what they actually receive (Scheff 2006). For this reason, agents may engage in more or less deliberate techniques of 'impression management' (Goffman 1959b: ch. 1; 1969: 4–11), and Goffman recognised this strategic element as existing in all actual committed actions. Impressions gained in social encounters are the basis on which social identities are inferred from the evidence presented by agents in the 'sign-vehicles' intentionally given or unintentionally 'given off'. In face-to-face interaction, this information is typically 'embodied' in bodily comportment (Goffman 1963a: 14). Information flow is especially rich because of the variety of clues that come through sight, hearing, and other senses. Agents must exercise control over their bodies, ensuring that they do not give off the 'wrong' messages. For example, they must engage in 'face work' to control their facial expressions (Goffman 1955).

Agents in social encounters must convey an impression of their involvement and engagement through their attentiveness to others (Goffman 1957a: 114–17). Signs of non-involvement, such as yawning and dozing, must be shielded from vision lest the agent appear to be 'away' from what is going on (Goffman 1963a: 69 ff). Agents involved in focused interaction must therefore show appropriate 'face engagement' to convey their involvement to others: maintaining eye contact, nodding in agreement, and so on.

Interaction may also involve intentional misinformation through deceit and the feigning of unintended evidence. This typically occurs in relation to attributes likely to be perceived as undermining an apparent social identity. If others become aware of such an attribute they may regard it as a discrediting 'stigma': physical deformities, character weaknesses, 'racial' markers, and other social identifiers may all be seen in this way. Stigma is often the basis on which a wide range of other imperfections or forms of deviance are imputed (Goffman 1963b: 5). Anticipated stigmatisation leads agents to hide potentially discrediting characteristics through techniques of information control. They may attempt to 'pass' as normal, though a passing agent faces the ever-present possibility of being unmasked and so discredited (Goffman 1963b: 75). Where events or their own actions discredit the impression they hope to convey, agents will feel embarrassed (Goffman 1956).

Through communication people build a sense of the world in which they live. They construct a social space that clothes the inaccessible material space in which they live. Such space is an imaginary, having an unknown, and ultimately unknowable, correspondence with material space. It contains regions that may have no direct physical correlate yet are regarded and felt, nevertheless, as 'real'. Agents are, for example, concerned for their 'personal space' and that of others, negotiating the territorial structure of the situation in which they find themselves. Spatial claims are set out with 'markers' that stake out a territory through the use of objects and bodily movements to indicate boundaries (Goffman 1971: 51 ff). Intruders into defined territories may be seen as 'strangers' (Simmel 1908b; Wood 1934) or 'space invaders' (Puwar 2004).

Agents who come together must agree on a definition of the situation that specifies where they are and what they are doing. They construct this definition through a nested set of contextual framing devices (Goffman 1974; Scheff 2006: ch. 5). Through tentative presentations and inferences they negotiate meanings to govern their actions and so establish a 'negotiated order' (Strauss *et al.* 1963; Strauss 1993: 248–50). The structural order of everyday life is the outcome of a continual negotiation and renegotiation of meaning among participants in specific contexts of action. Participants draw on the available resources and so differ in terms of the power they can bring to bear on this negotiation of meaning. The agreements built up depend on shifting alliances and working arrangements that enable agents to cooperate and get things done.

Actions are performed to an audience of others, with each participant seeking to influence the definition of the situation constructed by all other participants (Goffman 1959b: 8–11). Agents may act together as a 'team' or troop of performers, the members of the team comprising the whole or a part of their own audience. Cooperation is essential if each individual performance is to come off as each participant is to play his or her own part (Goffman 1959b: 71–2). Typically, definitions of the situation 'projected' by the participants will be sufficiently aligned in a working consensus that avoids serious confusion or contradiction and provides a practical *modus vivendi*. Such a consensus may, however, conceal differences that remain as potential sources of disturbance. When contradictory or discrepant expressions occur, the definition of the situation is likely to be thrown into doubt and the impressions gained by participants may be recast. In such a situation, agents will engage in 'defensive practices' to save the definition of the situation and the impressions of self they are presenting. For this reason, agents tend to show loyalty to others in their team, overlooking slips and ineptness in performance so that all can collude in maintaining a shared definition of the situation and improve their chances of producing successful ongoing performances.

Actors infer from observable cues the nature of the situations in which they find themselves and, thereby, the norms that are relevant to them. They interpret the actions of others using available social categories and typifications (assessing, for example, the position they occupy) and so can produce a mental schema in the form of a screenplay or scenario of likely behaviour. They 'frame' the situation and are able to derive a 'script' for their own behaviour (Bicchieri 2006: 81; Gagnon and Simon 1973). Scenarios and scripts comprise the 'recipes' or 'cook-book knowledge' (Schütz 1943: 73) needed to produce everyday actions. This knowledge will often define 'auxiliary traits' of the age, sex, and race of those in a particular position. For example, people may expect a doctor to be male and white, a Catholic priest may be expected to be an Irish American, or a prominent and highly published academic may be expected to be middle-aged and grey-haired. These expectations may sometimes be contradicted by experience and those who do not display the expected auxiliary traits may not be taken seriously in their role or may find their technical expertise questioned (Hughes 1945).[9]

To be successful in their performances, agents must adopt appropriate means for establishing the definition of the situation in which they claim

to be acting. They must establish a 'front' or stage for their performance, this comprising the 'setting' of the action and the 'appearance' of
the agents. A setting comprises the scenery and props for performance
(furniture, decoration, lay-out) while appearance is conveyed by the cos-
tumes, posture, and speech patterns adopted (Goffman 1959b: 19–26).
Doctors and nurses, for example, may sustain a medical definition of
reality for their patients by wearing white coats and displaying medical
equipment in appropriately decorated and furnished rooms.

Scenery and props allow agents to produce effective performances: 'If
a performance is to come off, the witnesses by and large must be able
to believe that the performers are sincere' (Goffman 1959b: 62). A con-
vincing performance is one that is perceived to be authentic and sincere because of the impressions conveyed and the props and scenery
employed. A sincere agent wishing to have his or her sincerity recognised
by others is likely to manage performances in ways designed to emphasise this sincerity. This does not mean that agents deliberately mislead
their audiences, though this does of course occur. The point is that all
agents draw on repertoires of action through the socialised habits of
action they have built up through successful performances in the past.
In the same way that the rules of grammar are central to the socialised
linguistic ability that allows speakers to produce authentic utterances,
so the rules of everyday behaviour allow for the effective reproduction
of authentic performances. 'Performing' is an unavoidable feature of the
human condition.

A key feature of any performance is the regionalisation of its setting
by a division into distinct arenas of action. Particularly important is
the distinction between 'front region' and 'back region', frontstage and
backstage. Frontstage is where the focus of attention is to be and where
the agents are most directly in the view of their audience. Backstage is
the less visible area to which agents may withdraw and act in greater
privacy. They can relax and rehearse backstage, readying themselves for
their frontstage performances. There may be, for example, a distinction
between the public shop floor of a retail establishment and the storeroom
or staff-room, and there may be a distinction between the public rooms
of a hotel and its kitchen (which guests are not permitted to visit). For the
guests in a hotel, of course, their bedrooms may be the backstage region
to which they can withdraw from the public dining room and lounge
(Goffman 1959b: 97 ff). These are not sharply fixed divisions, and the
distinction often depends upon the presence or absence of particular
others. In the presence of a shop manager, for example, the storeroom
may become a frontstage area for the shop workers. Both front and back
regions are demarcated from 'outside', the place where outsiders are to

be found. A definition of the situation may be more difficult to sustain when outsiders intrude on front or back regions, and agents may develop specific routines for passing between the setting and its outside areas. Examples are routines of membership induction and ceremonial processions that enter through a particular door (Goffman 1959b: 116–17, 184). Many forms of regionalisation depend on the power relations that underpin definitions of situations. Inmates of prisons, mental hospitals, and other enclosed organisations, for example, find their activities limited by the power that the staff exercise over space: certain areas are 'off limits', some are subject to close supervision, and other areas may exist where control is more relaxed (Goffman 1957c).

The parts acted out by agents are the roles described by theorists of institutional structure and, as shown in Chapter 6, these are always 'made' rather than simply 'taken'. Roles may be played for a variety of reasons and agents may have varying degrees of commitment to them. Though they may drift into particular ways of acting (Matza 1964), they may gradually become more drawn in and build up interests and rewards that commit them to a particular way of behaving (Becker 1960). The committed actor begins to identify with the given role and may come to see it as an important aspect of their identity. Thus, roles enacted cynically may over time become sincerely embraced and may be given 'authentic' expression. Conversely, strong commitments to a role performance may become more attenuated and cynical over time as agents seek to distance themselves from the reactions of their audience. In 'role distance' agents may deny the identity and sense of self imputed by others through distancing themselves from the role being played. Agents subjectively draw back from commitment and may partially disengage from the expectations attached to a role. Through role distance they may convey a particular impression to their audience. The waiter who attempts to disengage himself from the obsequious subordination required by the role may come to be seen by customers as 'surly' or 'unhelpful' (Goffman 1961: 93 ff). Role distance also occurs where an agent is otherwise attached to the role and sees it as an important part of their identity. A relaxed, joking approach may be adopted by senior surgeons as a more effective way of maintaining the loyalty of other staff than is possible through the officious exercise of formal authority (Goffman 1961: 109).

Drift and role commitment are mechanisms through which 'careers' are built. A career is 'any social strand of any person's course through life' (Goffman 1959a: 127). More generally, it is a passage from one position to another in a socially structured sequence of stages that involves schemes of selection and training and shapes the ambitions and efforts of agents (Hughes 1937: 62–3; 1955: 127–30). Although a career is typically organised as a public or 'official' sequence of opportunities and restrictions on action, there is a parallel 'moral career' through which the private or internal images of self and sense of identity are reconstructed. There is a dialectic between the public and the private aspects of the career: as a person passes through each public stage, his or her sense of identity is reconsidered and reconstructed in the light of the reactions of others to their actions. The agent perceives the career subjectively and interprets his or her identity from their current standpoint. A patient admitted to a mental hospital, for example, comes to see him or herself as 'mentally ill' as he or she moves from ward to ward according to their diagnosis and their conformity to the expectations held by doctors and nurses. Goffman showed that mental hospitals, as 'total institutions', had the capacity to forcefully destroy the pre-existing identities of patients and subject them to continual redefinition (Goffman 1957b; and see Scheff 1966).

Central to this reconstruction of the self in the face of the power of others is the process that has come to be called 'labelling'. This was explored in the early 1960s by Erikson (1962) and by Cicourel and Kitsuse (1963), together with Becker's collected essays (1963) and a special issue of *Social Problems* (Becker 1964).[10] Individual agents are fundamentally affected by the reactions of others, and the specific labels applied to them – thief, delinquent, good girl, and so on – are highly fateful for their sense of identity, especially when imposed by those with the power to sanction their definitions and to close off possible courses of action (Matza 1969: 157–62). The power in labelling involves manipulative inducement through sanctions (corrective influence) but more specifically involves persuasive influence through the signification and legitimation of identities (Scott 2001).

This labelling of behaviour is one way in which non-conformity may be increased as 'deviant' identities are reinforced. The negative sanctioning of behaviour through labelling and punishment results in a stigmatisation of behaviour (Goffman 1963b). If combined with the closing-off of certain opportunities for action as a result of the reactions of others, people are constrained to act in terms of the negative label and may come to identify with it (Becker 1963; Lemert 1967). Their tendency to deviate is 'amplified' and the total amount of deviation observed may increase rather than decrease (Wilkins 1964; Young 1971a; 1971b).

Drawing on shared meanings in their performances, agents are engaged in 'an expressive rejuvenation and reaffirmation of the moral values of the community' (Goffman 1959b: 31). Their actions are rituals that sustain the integration and solidarity of their society through collective participation in a shared definition of reality. This is strongest when the consensus and the socialisation of agents is greatest: this is when action can properly be regarded as integrative or, in the words of Collins (2004), ritualistic (see also Goffman 1959b: 30–1). Ritual action is action in which norms are adhered to in formulaic, stereotyped, and routinised ways as expressions of an emotional commitment to underlying values and principles. Collins (2004: 7) sees such action involving 'mutually focused emotion and attention producing a momentarily shared reality' that supports an 'emotional entrainment' as the basis of social solidarity in everyday encounters. Through a shared commitment to standardised performances in everyday conversation and gossiping ('small talk') the rhythmic interdependence and turn-taking and the solidarity of listener and audience are often more important than the substantive content of talk and its instrumental significance. Agents enact or constitute the solidarity of the social order in their performances, the ongoing drama of everyday encounters sustaining a sense of 'we-ness'. Shared commitments and the mutuality that constitutes solidarity are maintained over the longer term when the emotions generated in action are embodied in symbols that allow people to recall and recapture these emotions in other situations (Collins 2004: 81 ff).

Analyses of interaction have been principally concerned with committed action in face-to-face encounters, but they are not limited to this. Social interaction may be direct (face to face) or mediated through some means of communication. All communication between minds is, of course, mediated in some sense. It is mediated by the human vocal and auditory apparatuses and by the medium of language itself: short of telepathy, there is no direct communication between minds. What is meant by mediation here, however, is the process through which linguistic communication itself depends upon some material medium for its ability to convey meanings from one person to another. At its simplest, mediation might involve the use of a megaphone while people remain in visual contact, but more typically people are separated by a distance or other physical barrier that makes visual contact impossible. Where this happens, linguistic communication occurs without the associated non-verbal communication that accompanies it in direct encounters.

Initially developed as a means of storing and recording information in societies that retained predominantly oral cultures, writing became the prototypical form of mediated communication (Goody 1986) and prepared the way for printing and for electronic forms of communication such as radio, telephony, television, and the Internet.[11] These forms of mediation have produced worlds into which people can move, or 'escape', when reading a book or watching a television programme. In societies with mass-circulation writings and media of mass communication, the various readers or viewers may come to share, to a greater or lesser extent, a world in which they may feel they are, to a greater or lesser extent, participants (McLuhan 1964). They come to 'know' the characters and places that appear in the media narratives and, reflexively, they come to know the actors and writers who produce them. They may produce books and magazines about these worlds in the same way they produce them about 'real' places. Such mediated realities are 'hyper-realities' (Baudrillard 1978). With the two-way communication made possible through computer technology, a more complex 'cyberspace' emerges as a computer-mediated reality within which people can 'meet', 'talk', 'tweet', and 'hang out' and through which they may 'surf' (Chayko 2002: 33–4). Cyberspace is a subuniverse of meaning and interaction from which further realities and identities may be constructed as 'simulations' (Baudrillard 1981).

Goffman's approach to committed action demonstrates many of the limitations of a purely rational choice approach. Even when engaged in the most instrumental and calculative acts, individuals will give off information that is unintended, and a model of instrumentally rational action cannot give a full picture of what is going on. The dynamics of impression management are such that non-rational considerations frequently outweigh the rational. Goffman explored rational, calculative orientations in his discussion of 'strategic interaction' (1969: 85 ff), arguing that for interaction to be strategic, agents must share a tightly structured definition of the situation and each must be aware that the other is 'likely to try to dope out his decision in advance' (1969: 101). Agents interpret evidence concerning the state of the other's awareness and knowledge and the normative restrictions that might apply. Where conditions are appropriate, they may act strategically. It is rational or reasonable to act strategically only if it is believed that the other will do so and that conditions make it likely that such actions will be successful.

This argument shows how strategic and committed actions are connected. Decisions on how to act are based upon subjective assessment of the situation. Marginalist and rational choice theories assume a deliberative model of choice in which agents systematically assess their situation and evaluate the alternatives identified in terms of their relative advantage or disadvantage in relation to their interests and purposes. A more realistic view is what Cristian Bicchieri (2006: 4–5) has termed a 'heuristic' model in which the agent relies on certain 'default rules' stored in memory and activated or felt to be appropriate on the basis of an interpretation of the situation. Such default rules comprise the agent's embodied skills and capacities (including social norms). While there may sometimes be a full, rational deliberation, actions are more typically routinised through a reliance on heuristic methods (see also Harré 1979).

This embedding of strategic action in structures of committed action was strongly emphasised by Malinowski (1922) in his account of Trobriand society. Malinowski showed that Trobrianders engage in far more labour on their gardens than is strictly necessary. Although they can produce a massive surplus, this is often allowed to rot and is not redirected to any alternative use. The tending of the gardens is surrounded by a mass of magic and ritual, overseen by a garden magician. The Trobriander 'works prompted by motives of a highly complex social and traditional nature and towards aims which are certainly not directed towards the satisfaction of present wants, or to the direct achievement of utilitarian purposes' (Malinowski 1922: 60). Trobrianders are not oriented towards want satisfaction but towards 'a very complex set of traditional forces, duties, and obligations, beliefs in magic, social ambitions and vanities' (*ibid.*: 62). Polanyi (1944) extended this argument to show that the stripping away of traditional value commitments and the focusing of commitments on emotionally neutral means is what allows a relatively free expression of strategic actions. Thus, actions must be seen as shaped by both normative commitments and interest-based calculations.

Agency, structure, and reflexivity

Social action and interaction combine, in varying degrees, strategic and committed orientations. Individuals act within distributions of resources, social relations, and institutional positions, culturally shaped as hierarchies and divisions of labour with their opportunity costs, vested interests, and value commitments. Many action theorists have taken a methodological individualist position that sees the competition of agents for resources as resulting in an inherent conflict that undermines any possibility of long-term stability. There is a Hobbesian 'war of all against all', with any social order being a precarious and tentative construction. Social structures, from this point of view, have no reality of their own. I have shown the general solution to this conundrum in Chapter 6, using the structuration and morphogenesis arguments of Giddens and Archer. These theorists show that the causal powers of structures are exercised only when agents adopt projects on which they impinge. There must, therefore, be some awareness or recognition of the constraining and enabling aspects of the situation and of how these relate to the projects in which agents are involved. Intentions and conceptions are an essential element in any explanation of the reproduction and transformation of social structures, and structural constraints operate through the reflexivity of agents.

Reflexivity and structural transformation are especially characteristic of modernity. Modern societies are characterised by structural differentiation and diversity. They are systems of 'shifting, temporary and precarious positions' in which social structures are 'too fluid to be consolidated into correlated dispositions which are inherited and shared by those similarly positioned' (Archer 2007: 38). As a result, the opportunities for reflexivity are enhanced, and in many respects required (Giddens 1991), and so modern societies exhibit a progressive 'detraditionalisation' and a greater 'individualisation'.

The reflexivity of action explored by Giddens and Archer has been usefully elaborated in relation to social structure by Emirbayer and Mische (1998). They recognise three moments of agency, which they call iteration, projectivity, and practical evaluation. All action, they argue, begins in iteration, or orientation to the past. There is a 'selective reactivation by actors of past patterns of thought and action' that are routinely incorporated into practical activities (Emirbayer and Mische 1998: 971). This is action with a habitual or 'traditional' form (see Camic 1986). It is largely unreflective, involving a schematisation of social experience as tacit, taken-for-granted knowledge that reproduces past patterns of action through the learned repertoires of the 'mutual tool box' of culture (Swidler 1986). Iteration is a process through which 'social actors develop a set of preconscious expectations about the future that are typically inarticulate, naturalized, and taken for granted but nevertheless strategically mobilized in accordance with the contingencies of particular empirical situations' (Emirbayer and Mische 1998: 978). As such, it is central to what has been termed embodied structure.

Action enters the moment of projectivity when a reflexive awareness of circumstances leads to an 'imaginative generation of possible future trajectories of action' through which courses of action are creatively reconfigured in relation to desires and interests (Emirbayer and Mische 1998: 971). This is the moment of creativity and inventiveness and involves a distancing from habit through the formulation of plans, projects, and objectives. A hypothetical comparison of alternatives occurs through a subjective construction of narratives of possible temporal and causal sequences in an 'internal conversation' (Archer 2003). The idea of the internal conversation is central to the very idea of reflexivity. Thought is internal talk in activities ranging from day-dreaming through the reliving of past events and the rehearsal of anticipated encounters, to the planning of projected activities. Such thought co-exists, in varying degrees, with external communication with others. It is properly reflexive when it is deliberative and turns back on the subject him or herself and so becomes an internal conversation. This reflexivity relies on 'techniques of the self' through which people can monitor and control their own experiences and actions in order to achieve an understanding of their own feelings and values (Foucault 1984). Foucault explored this in relation to sexuality as the basis of the modern view of the self, but Rose has recognised a broader emotional and cognitive basis to reflexivity (Rose 1990).

The reflexivity of the internal conversation gives people the capacity as active agents to exercise control over their own lives. Human beings have what is probably the unique ability to design and redesign their projects to realise particular goals in relation to the ongoing development of their situation as it is affected by their own actions (Archer 2007: 7). Structural conditions, like natural conditions, obstruct or facilitate actions, but humans are able to reflexively deliberate on actual or anticipated obstacles and facilities. They do so in terms of their particular definition of the situation and the descriptions and accounts involved. This allows them to resist or subvert obstacles and to take advantage of facilitations (Archer 2007: 8). It depends upon their knowledgeability and value commitments, and hence is creative and, potentially, innovative. There is no single response to given conditions: individuals always act 'voluntaristically' with what has sometimes misleadingly been described as 'free will'. What is actually involved is that each individual responds to given conditions in the light of their particular circumstances and their particular knowledge and values. If not unique, individual responses are highly variable and idiosyncratic. Responses are constructed through reflexive deliberations in an internal conversation. It is through projectivity that joint actions in relation to the transformation of institutionalised structures of relations can be pursued.

In the moment of practical evaluation or judgement, agents consider their practical capacities to pursue particular trajectories within the constraints they face. They reflect on their social context and conditions in an assessment of the resources available within the relational structure in relation to the demands and contingencies of the immediate situation. It is the moment of deliberation and decision (Arendt 1958) through which structures can be redesigned (Archer 2007: ch. 1).

Agents subjectively reflect on their objective circumstances as they are known to them, in relation to their particular concerns. They act in terms of their awareness of their own situations, in terms of their definitions of these situations and the descriptions that they apply to them. Structures condition actions in so far as these definitions grasp some aspects of the structures in which the agents are located. They do not typically have a full and comprehensive understanding of the generative mechanisms that structure their situation. Knowledge of the situation and dispositions can only ever be partial and structures are, in part, unacknowledged. Even strategic actions will have unintended and unanticipated consequences. Any person's definition of the situation grasps only a part of the total-ity of institutions and relations within which he or she acts. Actions based on that definition will, therefore, have unanticipated and unin-tended consequences and are likely to encounter unanticipated reactions from the other people who are affected by these consequences and may be unaware, or only partially aware, of the consequences of these reac-tions. Each person is in the same problematic situation and so the overall configuration is unlikely to be transparent to any of the actors involved (Atkinson 1971: 229 ff). A concern for the unintended consequences of action was drawn out in various, and somewhat diverse, 'amplification' models of social action produced by Parsons (1963b; 1963a), Scheff (1966), and Young (1971a; see also Wilkins 1964), and their general fea-tures were explored by Merton (1936) and Giddens (1976a; and see Elias 1969: ch. 3).

Collective action

Agents have, so far, been considered as persons, as embodied individ-ual agents involved in face-to-face or mediated encounters and who cooperate as participants in complex chains of action that, through their ramifying unintended consequences, acquire a solidity as social struc-tures with the power to constrain and condition subsequent individual-ual actions. However, a number of action theorists have taken agency beyond the individual level. They have recognised that forms of joint action can unite two or more individuals towards a shared end. In joint action, disparate individuals are coordinated in such a way that they become 'centred' on each other (Domingues 1995: 148) and are able to act collectively *as if* they were a single entity. In certain circumstances, then, complex structures of jointly acting individual agents are able to act as collectivities. These entities have been conceptualised in ways that do not make them subject to the methodological individualist's critique of vitalism.

The earliest systematic models of collective action were those of Marxist theorists who saw the occupants of structural positions, spe-cifically class positions, as provided with resources and constraints that predispose them towards forms of collective consciousness and to acting in common. Ratzenhofer's (1898) views extended this to ethnic con-flicts, while Small (1905) and Bentley (1908) generalised this to models of group conflict that entered into theories of urban conflict (Park and Burgess 1925), theories of ethnicity and class (Cox 1948), and a larger 'pluralist' approach to collective action in democratic political systems (Dahl 1958; 1961; Kornhauser 1959).

These ideas informed a variety of 'conflict' theories from the 1950s. Coser (1956), trained in the tradition of Simmel at Columbia University, made this the basis of a functionalist account of conflict and group formation. The German sociologist Dahrendorf (1957) returned to the ideas of Gumplowicz (1875; 1905) and Ratzenhofer (1898; 1923), using these and elements of organisation theory (see Etzioni 1961) to recast the Marxist theory of class conflict. Dahrendorf was influenced by a more or less orthodox Marxism he found at the London School of Economics, where he encountered the ideas that Lockwood (1956) had developed from Weber, Marx, and Parsons. Turk (1969) adapted Dahrendorf's theory to explain law-making in terms of conflict and power relations (see also Taylor et al. 1975). These arguments provided an alternative and complement to the structural functionalist theories that saw collective action simply as a consequence of the shared beliefs through which disparately placed actors can be mobilised.

Conflict theories were further developed in Mills's (1956) resurrection of Mosca's ideas in his analysis of 'power elites', echoing also Oppenheimer's (1914; 1922) conflict theory of state formation and Mannheim's (1935) elaboration of elite theory into a model of state policy and social reconstruction.[12] Rex (1961) used similar Weberian ideas in his theory of class conflict and later elaborated this into both a theory of ethnic conflict (1970) and a general theory of conflict (1981). From the late 1960s, theorists drawing on symbolic interactionism stressed the importance of recognising also the *construction* of the meanings through which collective actions are forged (Turner 1969; Turner and Killian 1957; Gusfield 1963). Quinney (1970) and Douglas (1971) drew on these ideas in radical variants of pluralism to explain the labelling of deviant behaviour as crime. Radical views of collective action were central to the historical sociology of Moore (1966) and Skocpol (1979) and were extended into a general theory of power by Mann (1986; 1993). The early work of Touraine (1964) developed this as a theory of social movements. These wide-ranging theories of conflict and power produced accounts of the conditions under which collective agencies arise as significant social forces. Theorists concerned with the analysis of conflict and the importance of relational structure saw those ideas in terms either of resource mobilisation (Zald and McCarthy 1979; see also Tilly 1978) or the constraints inherent in the political process (Gamson 1975; Tarrow 1994; Cloward and Piven 1977).

Collective entities capable of joint action are clusters of individuals who associate more frequently with each other than they do with anyone else and form a distinct network of association (Sprott 1958). The simplest collectivity is the 'primary group', a grouping in which the association of individuals is intimate and face-to-face and participants have a sense of mutual awareness and of their common 'membership' in the group. Members of a primary group are joined to each other through direct interpersonal intimacy in face-to-face contacts, these relations becoming emotionally charged forms of solidarity. The members of a primary group recognise their own existence as a social entity and can describe themselves as 'we' or 'us' (Cooley 1909: 23).

Primary groups are typically formed when people are brought into contact with each other as a result of commonalities in their ways of life. They may, for example, be born into particular kinship relations, live in a particular locality, or encounter fellow participants in a school, place of work, or place of leisure. In Homans' (1950) terms, involvement in an 'external system' of relations may lead people to form an 'internal system' of interpersonal associations. When their participation in these ascribed or given relations leads them to establish interpersonal bonds of friendship and personal intimacy, they solidify as families, friendship cliques, neighbourhoods, schoolmates, gangs, workmates, and so on.

The members of a family household, for example, live together in relations of connubium and commensality (Weber 1913–14: ch. 3). They are dependent on each other's work and domestic activities, providing a framework within which child socialisation and development takes place. The members of a family participate in numerous joint actions shaped by their shared identity as a family. Norms of behaviour that are more or less specific to the particular family emerge and enable its members to act in the name of or as representatives of the family (Berger and Kellner 1970). A shared situation may not, however, produce positive feelings. Family members may, for example, have some negative emotions towards each other, and family solidarity may be weakened to the point at which it is no longer possible to regard the family as a collectively acting primary group.

Primary groups tend to be small enough for members to have an intimate knowledge of each other. Where the groupings are larger, intimacy is less marked, solidarity is much weaker, and collective action becomes more difficult to sustain. People may comprise a 'mass' or a crowd that exhibits uniformities of action by virtue of the effects that each participant has on others, but has no unity of purpose or enduring sense of community. Ginsberg (1934) described certain large groupings as 'quasi-groups'. These are social categories with participants who have common interests, concerns, and experiences but are not involved in dense category-wide chains of intimate association. Examples might be territorial groupings such as villages, towns, cities, and nations, and non-territorial groupings such as social classes and ethnic minorities. While primary groups are capable of collective action, masses and quasi-groups are not. These larger groupings can become involved in collective action only in so far as their participants form 'secondary groups' united around particular interests or concerns and with definite decision-making and administrative mechanisms. These mechanisms make it possible for the group to act as a unified entity or collective agent.

The contrast between collective agencies and mere collections of individuals was drawn out by Weber (1913–14: 926 ff) in his discussion of political parties and forms of social stratification. Social classes, he argued, are collections of similarly situated individuals in relation to the material resources distributed through property and market institutions. The members of a social class occupy a similar structural position and so have similar experiences and life chances. They have a degree of solidarity as quasi-groups but do not act as a single entity (Dahrendorf 1957). Parties, on the other hand, recruit their membership from classes, ethnic categories, and other quasi-groups and are formally organised for action. Because of their capacity for collective action, they are able to 'represent' the interests and concerns of members of these quasi-groups within the political structure. This was the basis on which Weber rejected the Marxist view of class conflict and the claims of Gumplowicz (1905) on ethnic conflict (see also Mosca 1896; 1923). He did not deny the importance of class and ethnic divisions and the interests they generate, but held that they are politically relevant only when parties take up and articulate their interests in their collective agency.

Weber saw this view of the class-party relationship as a paradigm for the various other forms of relationship between structural positions and collective agents. This argument was generalised by Dahrendorf as an account of the formation of 'interest groups' as agencies of social conflict. An interest group is formed when a *cadre* of activists and intellectuals take the lead in promoting a programme of action aimed at influencing or altering state policies through the exercise of pressure, competition for votes, or other forms of support. If the interest group can establish forms of communication among the rank and file membership of social classes or other quasi-groups, they may build a common consciousness and outlook that encourages participation in the activities of the interest group (Dahrendorf 1957: 184–8). It is the interest group that is the focus of conflict, not a class or ethnic minority as such.

More generally, parties and interest groups are examples of the generic type of the 'organisation'. In the words of Simmel, organisations:

are nothing but immediate interactions that occur among men [*sic*] constantly, every minute, but that have become crystallised as permanent fields, as autonomous phenomena. (Simmel 1908a)[13]

It is these interactions that establish boundaries and give them solidity and reality as agents. Weber's crucial contribution was to see participants in an organisation (*Verband*) as coordinated through a structure of authority. An organisation is an authoritarian grouping (M. Weber 1920: 53; Coser 1956: 115). It is 'deliberately constructed and reconstructed to seek specific goals' formulated through its structure of leadership and administration (Etzioni 1964: 3). Its normative structure is regarded by participants as 'legitimate', as providing discursively defensible reasons for obedience to commands and technical advice from those in higher positions. The disposition to obey means 'there is a probability that certain persons will act in such a way as to carry out the order governing the organization' (M. Weber 1920: 49), so constituting its collective agency.

Examples of organisations include not only political parties but also religious sects, trades unions, business corporations, and medieval guilds. In pre-modern societies, Weber argued, organisations tend to be structured around traditionalism and forms of committed action. In the modern world, on the other hand, organisations tend mainly to be established in and through strategic action. The authoritarian structures of the modern organisation are those of formally rational authority and the organisation is, therefore, a 'formal organisation' capable of collective strategic action.

Central to the ability of formal organisations to act collectively are the structures of rational decision-making through which they formulate and pursue their ends. Simon (1945) argued that organisations can make complex but rational decisions if a formal apparatus combines the specialised rational actions of the members. In this way, organisational activities – the outcomes of myriad individual acts – are monitored in relation to standards of adequate, acceptable, or satisfactory performance relative to the costs and returns involved in alternative courses of action, and a formal organisation can pursue an optimum return on its activities through satisfactory, or 'satisficing' outcomes, of which economic maximisation is only one, highly unusual, variant (March and Simon 1958: 40–1).

Legal-rational authority operates through norms that have themselves been established on rational grounds and constitute a formally recognised framework of order sharply distinguished from the personal property and circumstances of the individual members. Rules are applied impersonally to particular cases on a purely instrumental basis and are implemented by a 'bureaucratic' administration. A bureaucracy comprises a hierarchy of functionally specialised tasks, with each level in the hierarchy having a specific rule-bound sphere of competence. Individual bureaucrats are recruited, promoted, and themselves act (*qua* members) only in terms of the rationally established rules of the organisation (Weber 1913–14: 956 ff).

The formal rules of an organisation establish the mechanisms of control through which individual actions are coordinated towards the attainment of collective goals. Etzioni (1961) has referred to these mechanisms of authoritarian control as the 'utilitarian' and 'coercive' controls that result, respectively, from powers of inducement and coercion. Coercive power involves the direct use or threat of physical force, while utilitarian power is based on the use of material rewards to induce people to act in one way or another (Scott 2001). Coercion tends to result in high levels of alienative involvement among the membership, while utilitarian power increases the level of calculative involvement. Utilitarian control combined with calculative involvement is characteristic of employing organisations, where salary systems are the basis of inducements. Organisations with voluntary membership, such as political parties, have fewer opportunities for inducement and tend to rely on legitimate authority alone.

The formal organisation is, in Weber's terms, an ideal type, and actual organisations combine strategic orientations with committed ones. This has been highlighted in discussions of *why* people join and become active members of voluntary organisations that generate benefits for both members and non-members. Olson (1965) and others have shown that purely calculative considerations cannot provide an answer to this 'free-rider' problem. Such organisations depend on the altruistic commitments of their members. More generally, it has been argued that an 'informal' structure tends to develop alongside formal rationality within actual organisations. This was first suggested by Mayo (1933) in his 'human relations' approach to organisation theory (Roethlisberger and Dickson 1939: 91–3; Blau and Scott 1961). The formal structure of an organisation is the basis on which members begin to build friendships and interpersonal relationships and so establish group solidarity, conceptions of status, and rules of behaviour that become integral elements in the overall structure of the organisation. The symbolic interactionist view of the negotiated order, discussed above, is central to understanding informal organisation. Informal organisation may lead people to new goals or to the displacement of some or all of the formally constituted goals. Thus, the formal and the informal aspects of an organisation may co-exist in varying degrees of tension. For example, the shop-floor employees of a business organisation may establish informally sanctioned norms concerning the appropriate level of effort to be expended in the course of the working day, and this may lead them to restrict their output to a level below that expected by the management (Roy 1952; Ackroyd 1974; 1976).[14] Similarly, the personal career interests of the leaders of a radical political party may lead them to accommodate themselves to the existing political system and so to connive in a limitation of internal democracy and a tempering of its radicalism. This tendency in left-wing parties has been described as the 'iron law' of oligarchy (Michels 1911; see also Etzioni 1964: 10–11).

Weber saw that a key question was that of the social base of an organisation and the extent to which it could be said to represent wider pools of actors. He recognised that parties recruiting from a particular class or ethnic group may represent their interests and concerns within a larger social movement, and subsequent writers have developed this as a distinct form of collective agency. Some have seen the social movement simply as an organisation, but it has more usefully been seen as a dispersed and fragmentary form of collective action without a unifying structure of formal authority. The roots of this view are in Marx's theory of class conflict, especially as developed by Plekhanov (1895) and then by Lenin (1902) and Lukács (1923a), where an attempt was made to explain the development of class consciousness and the class actions of a labour movement in terms of the leading role of a vanguard of party intellectuals. The analysis of social movements was taken forward in theories of the women's movement, black and civil rights movements, and the peace movement of the 1960s and 1970s that did not seem to be explicable in terms of a class vanguard.

According to these views, a social movement is not a unified organisation with a common leadership and administrative structure but is a loose and fragmentary form of collective action (Della Porta and Diani 1999). Movements are:

heterogeneous and fragmented phenomena, which internally contain a multitude of differentiated meanings, forms of action, and modes of organization, and which often consume a large part of their energies in the effort to bind such differences together. (Melucci 1996: 15)

They are more or less extensive networks of interaction that may include individuals, groups, and organisations loosely formed into a collective entity through joint action, coalitions, umbrella meetings, and so on (Della Porta and Diani 1999: 14–16; Diani 1992). The collective action of a movement is a product of 'multiform and heterogeneous' processes on a multitude of levels, expressed in a complex of rituals, practices, and cultural products. The key characteristic is the shared set of beliefs and sense of common involvement held by those who constitute it. Participants feel themselves to be part of a single movement with specific goals and shared means of action.

A social movement exists when individuals and groupings achieve a solidarity that unites them in a common purpose or set of purposes. The participants in a social movement must have established a 'we' sentiment by building a collective identity on the basis of their common experiences of the situations they encounter. Through social construction and negotiation, the individuals, groups, and organisations that articulate shared interests or concerns establish shared definitions concerning the field of constraints and opportunities within which they are located and the orientation of their actions in relation to these (Melucci 1996: 40, 67, 70). There is no monolithic consensus across the movement, but there may be a fragmentary one in which the various parts exist in tension with each other.

The key question is how this kind of solidarity and cohesion can be achieved without a unitary structure of authority: why are collective identities forged at certain times and places and not at others? Melucci (1996: 84, 382–4) has highlighted this as the question of how collective identities can be forged when the potential members of a movement have less narrowly structured conditions of action than in the class structures of the nineteenth and twentieth centuries. How, for example, did large numbers of diverse women come to constitute a cohesive movement during the 1960s and 1970s? The emerging view is that collective identities arise in and through the collective activity itself. There is a reciprocal relationship between collective action and collective identity such that the growth of one encourages the other. This is the view of Touraine (1965; 1978; and see Castells 1976), who argues that individual meanings must not be treated atomistically but must be recognised as social products, as the distributed outcomes of a larger process of collective formation. A collective subjectivity may be contained within 'individual' meanings, but is nonetheless real. Social movements emerge as collective actors when potential participants establish a reproducible identity for their involvement in a particular sphere of bounded activity. This may be further developed through collective learning processes that result in a constant redefinition and elaboration of identity and, therefore, of the boundaries, interests, and aims of a movement. The collective subject is a historical formation, and is, today, increasingly dependent on its constitution through new media of communication.

Social actions are the means through which social structures are reproduced and transformed and through which systemic processes are maintained. Culturally formed meanings shape emotional responses to constitute the motives that drive people to act strategically and in relation to socialised value commitments. Committed actions and the value commitments that underpin them sustain the possibilities that actors have to act reflexively and strategically in relation to their particular circumstances. While much action is interpersonal, occurring in face-to-face contexts, much is also collective and involved in macro-level social processes. The collective agency of groups, organisations, and social movements, shaped by the structural distribution of resources and opportunities and guided by values rooted in collective identities, drives historical change to shape the direction of social development.

8   Subjects: Socialised Minds

While many animals are conscious and some primates have rudimentary self-awareness, only human beings seem to possess the linguistic skills that make possible a fully reflexive self-awareness that allows them to act as the subjects of their actions. Through their cultural formation, they are able to develop a sense of self and forms of self identity that are integral to their embodied dispositions to act and to plan their actions. Socialised minds are, therefore, integral to the interplay of structure and action through which culture and nature are mediated. Sociology requires, as one of its strands, a social psychological point of view.

Explorations into the formation of socialised minds originated in Greek ideas of humans as 'rational' agents capable of conscious and purposive deliberation. This view of rational mentality was developed in Renaissance approaches to the cognitive and intellectual abilities of human agents. In the sixteenth century, and in reaction to this, theorists began to recognise also the importance of the feelings or emotions aroused through sensual, bodily existence in the world (Richards 1992). The emerging science of 'psychology' recognised cognitions and emotions as the principal elements in motivation. The mechanistic discourse of writers such as Hobbes (1651), Locke (1690), and Hume (1739–40) saw knowledge, understanding, and intelligence as 'theoretical reason' and feelings, passions, and appetites as 'practical reason'. Mind, however, was seen as disembodied, allowing them to incorporate highly gendered assumptions into their thought. While referring to the rational mind of the free and autonomous individual, this 'individual' was implicitly male. Constructed at a time of colonial encounters with those seen as 'savages', liberal thought was also racialised in seeing the individual as a 'civilised' European man. The emerging psychology thus bequeathed a considerable difficulty in conceptualising the mental characteristics of both women and ethnic minorities (Pateman 1988; Mills 1997). The most developed form of this psychology was the 'associationism' of Reid (1764), Bentham (1789), and James Mill (1829) in which the mind was seen as a largely passive receptacle for sense impressions that can be 'associated' or combined into concepts and complex ideas through the 'pleasure' and 'pain' experienced in behaviour. Innate faculties of 'instinct' and emotion (sex, hunger, imitation, sympathy, etc.) were seen as the means through which these mental associations could be combined.

John Mill (1843) developed his father's associationism into a more social form of psychology by taking account of the ways in which social context shapes character (see also Lewes 1874–9: vol. 2).[1] Following this, Bain (1855; 1859) took the first important step of seeing the mind in relation to the physiology of the organism, focusing on the flow of mental energies through a network of nerves. Not until the work of Darwin (1859; 1871), however, was the question of the embodiment of the mind raised and a more properly social psychology made possible. Spencer (1870–2), Carpenter (1874), and Sully (1884) began this task, recasting associationist psychology to take more account of the active adaptation of a mind to its containing body and its external environment, but this was taken much further in the startlingly innovative approach of James (1890). These novel ideas were developed in the classic individual psychologies of Stout (1896; 1898) and Ward (1918), while Wallas (1908) and McDougall (1908) took up James's recognition of the importance of the social environment and developed an account of the cultural context or social heritage in the shaping of cognitions and emotions (see also the earlier view of Bagehot 1872). Most importantly, Mead (1910) began to formalise James's view of the self as a social product, as a truly social self. Working from the philosophical assumptions of Kant and Leibnitz, German psychologists such as Herbart (1816), Brentano (1874), and Köhler (1917) produced complementary ideas that recognised the active role of the human mind in its engagements with the world and its reliance on innate categories of perception and understanding that made intentional consciousness possible. Similar concerns underpinned Wundt's (1912) move from a physiological to a social psychology.

Evolutionary ideas also stimulated a growing interest in developmental theories of the mind and the self. Influenced by Haeckel's (1879) idea of biological 'recapitulation' (discussed in Chapter 3) Romanes (1889), Baldwin (1893), and Hall (1904) saw mental development during infancy and childhood as repeating the mental stages reached during the various phases of social development. They saw a sequential structure to socialisation, which they related to biological maturation. Hall was the most influential advocate of this view of the concurrent development of biological and mental traits, influencing writers in Britain (Geddes 1904a; Branford 1913) and in the United States (Addams 1910). The somewhat later work of Piaget dispensed with the recapitulation framework but emphasised the ways in which infants and children develop their mental capacities as a result of their biological maturation and their actual engagement with the world around them. This view was developed in writings on language (Piaget 1923), judgement and representation (Piaget 1924; 1926), intelligence (Piaget 1936), and the formation of the ideas of number, time, and space (Piaget 1941; 1946; Piaget and Inhelder 1948). The importance of practical engagement with the social environment was central to the developmental psychology of Vygotsky (1934), which followed Marx in recognising the importance of actual social relations rather than culture alone.

Developmental ideas also underpinned the rather different perspective of the Viennese physician Freud, whose work with Breuer (Breuer and Freud 1895) on hysteria and the unconscious adopted emerging psychiatric ideas on the flow of nervous energy through the nervous system and saw this energy as saved or spent in mental behaviour. Freud initially saw a failure in the circulation of nervous energy as resulting in a 'nervous breakdown' or neurasthenia, but he moved this in the new direction of a 'psychoanalysis' in his early works on dreams and the unconscious (Freud 1900) and on pleasure-seeking instincts (Freud 1905). Taken up in Jung's (1906) investigations into schizophrenia and Adler's (1914) work on social recognition, this approach saw instincts as unconscious driving forces whose effects were magnified by the repression of unacceptable ideas back into the unconscious. They argued that while instincts have a biological basis, their modes of expression are shaped by cultural factors and by encounters with significant social objects. Jones (1912) and Rivers (1917) were early advocates of psychoanalysis in Britain (Richards 2000: 186–9), and specifically Adlerian ideas were influential for Faithfull (1927; 1933) and Mairet (1928). More orthodox Freudian theories were established when Freud and others of his school settled in Britain during the 1930s. This orthodox Freudianism was especially defended by Anna Freud (1936), while Klein (1932) opened up a greater concern for the effects of education. These ideas were developed by a number of rival British writers who abandoned deterministic biology in favour of a stronger emphasis on people's relations to the 'social objects' they encountered in their environment (see, especially, the later summaries in Fairbairn 1952; Bowlby 1969–80).

Much work on the socialisation of the mind has been predicated on an assumed dualism of mind and body. For some theorists, social processes are of greatest importance and personality is seen largely as a social construct: cultural meanings and interactional processes are seen as the central and constitutive factors in the formation of individual personality. Other theorists, however, see the natural conditions and constitution of the human body as more important and see social formation as simply the shaping of biologically given instincts, drives, and capacities. While there have been tendencies towards social determinism and biological determinism, most writers have recognised the interdependence of culture and nature in the formation of human mentality. The closest position to an exclusively social determinism is the view of enculturation developed by Boas and his followers, such as Benedict and Margaret Mead. In their accounts, socialisation tended to be seen simply as a process of becoming a cultural being through the absorption of cultural influences, an orientation developed by the 'culture and personality' theories that also drew on some elements of psychoanalysis.[2] Nevertheless, even these writers saw the need to acknowledge the potential effects of human biology and the material environment.

Mind and mentality

While there are many areas of contention among contemporary theorists of the mind and consciousness, philosophers of consciousness, evolutionary biologists, and neuroscientists have produced a workable model of mind and brain relationships and of the nature of conscious and unconscious activity. An appreciation of this model will allow the arguments of social psychologists to be better understood.

The contemporary view of consciousness has developed from the philosophies of Descartes and Locke, for whom consciousness comprised a person's knowledge of his or her own mental processes. These processes are, in large part, automatic, but humans have the ability to become aware of and to know them. To be conscious is to think or to have thought: in the words of Descartes, 'I think therefore I am'. Thought is the means through which humans become aware of their own mental processes, however partially, and so become 'sensible' of their own existence as thinking beings. The associationist psychologists stressed the ways in which thoughts and ideas influence each other, leading to a view of the mind as a 'spiritual' phenomenon separate from the physical structure of the brain and all purely mechanical processes. The mind became 'the ghost in the machine' (Ryle 1949; see the discussion in Crossley 2001).

Recent evolutionary theory and neuroscience has all but resolved this problematic dualism without resorting to either a materialistic or an idealistic reductionism. Contemporary approaches to mind and consciousness hold that the distinctive features of human behaviour must be explained by the distinctiveness of the (evolved) human mind. Human mentality is a product of evolution whereby increasingly complex brains and nervous systems have been transformed into systems characterised by consciousness. The mental systems found in mammals and primates were altered – through genetic variation and natural selection – into more coordinated systems capable of reflexive and sentient awareness.

Minds have been shaped by selective processes, operating more than one million years ago, that produced an organism capable of operating successfully in the specific environment it then faced. This adaptation is ad hoc and largely unplanned, with natural selection working on what already exists. Thus, biological changes are always modifications of existing structures. Of course, the mere existence of a trait or characteristic does not imply that it was ever adaptive for human behaviour: it may be a purely contingent outcome that survived simply because there were no pressures causing it to disappear and an organism may have non-adaptive traits as well as adaptive ones. So long as non-adaptive traits are not positively damaging or disabling in a particular environment, they are likely to be perpetuated along with successful adaptations.

As shown in Chapter 3, human beings exist as biological systems of functionally specialised organs or subsystems. Sensory organs, circulatory, respiratory, digestive, and nervous systems, all operate together through homeostatic mechanisms of control to form a single embodied system (Cannon 1932). The brain and nervous system, as one of these organic systems, is involved in the regulation of many other bodily systems and organs, but is also, and particularly, concerned with controlling overt behaviour through monitoring sensory stimuli and forming responses to them. A marked feature of human evolution was the development of brains that are very large relative to body size, but more important was that the brain developed as an internally complex structure with particular functions.

The human brain evolved from biological forms that had initially developed in reptilian animals and these early-evolved brain structures are largely responsible for 'instinctive' responses and for aggression and sexuality. With the evolution of mammals, systems developed that allowed greater sensory, emotional, and motivational capacities, and human evolution from its mammalian predecessors involved the development of a cerebral cortex. This gave the ability to process sensory inputs and to calculate, and it allowed the formation of memories, thoughts, and communications. Evolutionary psychologists have shown that human brains have the most advanced forms of cerebral functioning that have so far evolved, and that the more primitive structures of the brain have been integrated into a *sui generis* system in which a biological inheritance has been shaped into a number of specialised 'modules' or mental organs. Pinker holds that 'The mind is a system of organs of computation, designed by natural selection to solve the kinds of problems our ancestors faced' (1997: 21; 1994: 410, 413 ff).[3] Thus, the brain comprises a system of linked but distributed modules concerned with perception, memory, language, and other functions (Fodor 1983; and see Mithen 1996).[4] While such modular brains are found in other primates, human distinctiveness lies in the relative facility with which information can be conveyed from one module to another. This flow of information allows for higher levels of coordination than is possible in the more purely modular brains of early humans and primates. The system of flows among the modules of the nervous system comprise the mental activity that is now recognised as the distinctive feature of the 'mind' and is itself recognised as a crucial precondition for the existence of 'consciousness'.

Dennett has compellingly argued that consciousness must be seen as a product of brain states but not as something separate from those brain states. Nor is it located in any one place within the brain. Sensory processing in the various modules of the brain and nervous system produces successive representations of experiences in terms of their shape, texture, colour, and so on, and these rapidly repeated and interacting 'multiple drafts' produce the illusion of a stream of consciousness with a continuous narrative structure (Dennett 1991: 135; see also Rosenfield 1993). This is a mental process in which a 'movie' is constructed from the multiple still 'frames' and Searle (1997) has cogently argued that this emergent stream of mental activity, with its distinctive and irreducible properties, comprises the conscious mind. Consciousness, then, is a state of sentient awareness, an 'inner', subjective state of the brain. It is not, however, a separate entity from the brain – it is not a soul, spirit, or ghost in the machine. It is simply an emergent feature of the brain itself: 'Consciousness is caused by lower-level neuronal processes in the brain and is itself a feature of the brain' (Searle 1997: 17). Conscious life results from variable rates of neuron firings within the particular networks of neural pathways that comprise the various mental modules, these neural firings being triggered by stimuli received from the external world and the body itself.

Consciousness, then, is an awareness of or attention to perceived or otherwise experienced phenomena. A person's conscious relation to the world is mediated through the senses and is the means through which action orientations and courses of action are constructed. The exercise of attention, thought, and judgement allows a degree of conscious control over inherited instincts through the practical appraisal of means and the deferral of gratification. It is the capacity for consciousness that allows humans gradually to come to terms with an external reality and to adapt to it as a means of attaining their goals.

Noumenal things in the external world, including the body of the person him or herself, are experienced through the senses and represented as phenomena. Phenomenal knowledge, however, does not consist merely of discrete sensory impressions. Sense data are combined through a 'unity of apperception' (Kant 1781) in which the neural processes of the brain 'bind' perceptual impressions into objects of awareness. This binding is a result of the flow of neural signals between different areas and modules within the brain. It occurs 'behind the scenes' and is not itself, at its simplest, a conscious process. Objects of consciousness are experienced holistically and without conscious and deliberate effort.

Visual perceptions, for example, are organised through the categories of shape, colour, and movement into unified visual images of the objects encountered. These representations may then enter conscious awareness and affect consciously constructed courses of action. As objects of thought, they may be given names or labels ('cats', 'cars', 'bananas', etc.) and can be mentally manipulated through logical reasoning and inference. In this way, conscious processing enters into the binding process, and subsequent neural processing can eventually produce complex verbal representations and narratives.

Memory is central to representation, and Dennett argues that the stream of consciousness is a 'rolling consciousness with swift memory loss' (1991: 137; Blakemore 1988: 308). Unless it has been stored in a longer-term memory, an object that has been formed in thought cannot be recalled on other occasions. Initial experiences are held in a buffer memory that is overwritten with each successive experience, and the contents of the buffer memory must be transferred to short-term memory if they are to persist. Short-term memory is the 'working memory' in which information is stored and made available for actual use. Such memories persist as long as the particular nerve pathways in the brain that hold them are reinforced and strengthened by periodic refreshing (Hebb 1949). This refreshing of the neural pathways through the use and recall of the memories builds up the persisting 'traces' in the brain that James (1890) saw as central to mental activity. 'Forgetting' occurs whenever a trace is weakened or fades with the passage of time. Thus, short-term memory is the means through which a meaning or idea can be 'kept in mind' as a more or less transient memory trace. Research has shown that the nerve pathways in the short-term memory area of the brain can hold information for around 15–30 seconds, though this can be lengthened through the repetition of the items to be remembered.

The contents of short-term memory will be lost unless they are transferred to long-term memory. This is an area of the brain where the nerve pathways can hold information for much longer periods – perhaps permanently – as repeated neural activity results in structural changes in the pathways that allow memories to endure. This 'rewiring' of the pathways produces patterns that necessarily reproduce the original meaning or experience when they fire. Transfer of information from short-term to long-term memory involves a scanning of short-term memory contents for items that match the templates already held in the long-term memory, and those items that match a particular template can be transferred to the appropriate part of long-term memory. The templates through which long-term memory is organised are the categories and coding schemes built up as the memory is itself built up. The categories (*Gestalten*) and general concepts employed in conscious thought are not the purely innate devices that Kant believed, but are shaped through reflection on the objects of consciousness. Their specific forms, however, are necessary consequences of the ways in which the brain processes the information that it receives from the senses. They allow experience to be coded in semantic and visual form and to be retained for future recall. Within long-term memory, however, memory traces may sometimes 'interfere' with each other, resulting in the decay or confusion of memories or making them more difficult to recall with accuracy.

It seems, however, that objects are not stored in memory as single representations. The constituent perceptual and experiential elements from which an object was constructed in the first place are stored separately in memory, and objects are reconstructed on the fly from these distributed elements. Memories, then, are distributed in fragments that can be rebuilt, with greater or lesser accuracy, into representations as and when required (Edelman 1989).

Long-term memory forms what Freud referred to as the 'preconscious'. This comprises all those memories that are not held in immediate consciousness but that can become conscious through recall. Its contents are 'latent' and are available for access when required. Though established as a term in psychoanalysis, it is somewhat misleading to imply that it is literally 'pre' conscious, as it is that part of the mind that holds all currently non-conscious but recallable mental processes and memories. For Freud, however, it is differentiated from the purely 'unconscious' elements that are normally beyond conscious recall. The unconscious part of the mind comprises the purely physiological aspects of the brain and the body itself, together with those memories that have been 'repressed' and held inaccessibly behind 'defensive' barriers. Unconscious elements may force themselves into awareness as feelings, desires, and vague impressions, but they are not typically open to conscious recall or reflection.

The unconscious part of the mind, then, is the most 'primitive' level of mentality in evolutionary terms. It is:

> a vast and complicated structure of memory, of which only a working minimum is accessible to conscious recall. Much the greater part of memory continues to play its part in the individual's life in a transmitted form, not as recollection, but as feeling – as emotional reaction to things and persons. In that way it continually exercises more or less suggestive power, but it is difficult, and perhaps sometimes impossible, to recall it to consciousness in the form of the original impressions. (Mairet 1928: 15)

Instincts and emotions

This summary account of consciousness and mind makes it possible now to consider the ways in which the more specifically social theories of mind can be brought together. A key area of discussion and debate has been the formation of emotional responses and their relationship to, on the one hand, instinctive drives and, on the other, socialisation.

Instincts (broadly understood as the bodily needs, capacities, and reflex reactions that are the basis of animal behaviour) have often been seen in highly deterministic terms as fixed and given elements that generate automatic and stereotyped responses (K. Lorenz 1963). From this point of view, different forms of behaviour are to be explained by identifying the generative instincts behind them. Within sociology, however, it has more typically been recognised that instincts are culturally conditioned and socially constrained. This view of instinct and emotion has its roots in the work of Darwin, who saw each species as having evolved with innate needs and impulses that drive the behaviour of its individual members. By 1890, when James published his *Principles of Psychology*, the idea of instinct had become established as a central psychological mechanism and the human nervous system was seen as comprising a complex system of instinctive reactions. One of the first fruits of the Darwinian orientation in Britain was Bagehot's (1872) political psychology, but it was also systematically applied in Westermarck's (1894) investigation of marriage patterns. This emerging view was further explored in the closely connected physiological work of Lloyd Morgan (1894; 1896; 1905) and the more sociological accounts of Hobhouse (1901), Wallas (1908), and McDougall (1908; 1912).[5] All these writers saw instincts as inherited and stereotyped patterns of behaviour that have culturally variable forms of expression. As a result of the work of Bateson (1902), these biological mechanisms came to be seen as the results of inherited variations at the genetic level.

The early social psychologists, then, saw the interplay between genetic inheritance and conscious social experience as shaping instincts and their forms of emotional expression. Emotional states, as crucial components in the 'bio-regulatory devices with which we come equipped to survive' (Damaisio 1999: 53), produce a state of preparedness for action by altering blood flow, breathing rate, the flow of endocrines, and other bodily changes. This view of the emotional basis of instinctive responses was first formulated in the so-called James-Lange theory of emotions, according to which an emotion comprises a subjective 'feeling' or experience associated with the primary bodily responses that are aroused by a stimulus (James 1894; Le Doux 1998). Purely physiological responses such as sweating, blushing, and changes in the rate of breathing are initiated by flows of hormones that are, themselves, triggered by brain activity. The physiological changes constitute the charged 'emotional states' that arouse subjective states of feeling and, in many cases, a conscious awareness of these feelings (Damaisio 1999: 37). Drever (1917; see also Ginsberg 1931; 1932) showed that the emotional aspect of an instinct is highly variable and that it may be quite weak in many instincts of a mere reflex character.

James's particular contribution had been to emphasise the role of will and choice. He argued that human action involves the subduing and overcoming of emotional impulses. People are driven in various ways to define the particular goals that they believe will secure their wants and they will choose what they believe will be the most effective and appropriate means to these ends. In this way, purposive conduct can direct and often suppress emotional drives. James argued that inherited responses could be subjected to far greater control than could purely reflex actions and that the learning processes involved in the channelling of behaviour through social interaction can transform instincts into socially variable habits (Dewey 1922). When behaviour becomes more reflexively directed by will and choice, habit is transformed into purposive action (Hobhouse 1901; Hetherington and Muirhead 1918: 55–61).[6]

Instincts have been seen as adaptive responses that result from the natural selection of the spontaneous variations in biological endowment that occur through sexual reproduction. Turner holds that it was the move onto the savannah that led to the anatomical changes that underpin human instinctive and emotional structure. Many inherited traits were unsuited to life on the open plains, and the successful savannah species were those that developed upright posture and greater cortical control over their emotions: automatic emotional responses, such as vocal warnings, were not effective in an open environment, and successful species were those that evolved a rewiring of instincts and emotions to bring about greater conscious control over their expression. Similarly, the tighter forms of social organisation that proved helpful in adaptation to the new way of life and had been made possible by the development of linguistic communication and culture were also made possible by the more elaborated emotional capacities. There was:

a reorganization and elaboration of subcortical limbic structures, and their rewiring to neocortical and brain-stem systems, so as to produce an animal that could use and read a wide variety of emotional cues for enhanced social bonding. (Turner 2000: 20)

Selective processes on the African savannah, Turner argues, would favour a quiet primate able to control its own emotional expressions and able to visually interpret the emotions of others. These abilities enhanced survival chances in the open countryside and made possible the further selection of the forms of emotional expression that made a degree of social solidarity possible. In particular, their visual and gestural language was the basis on which auditory and spoken language would later develop. A complex system of emotions was built up, making possible the construction, learning, and sanctioning of moral rules of behaviour.

Each instinctive response is called into play by a specific stimulus, though an instinct may often consist of a chain of connected behaviours leading to a single goal. A fully developed instinct consists of processes in the nervous system that drive mechanical bodily responses, together with associated mental processes of cognition (knowing), affect (feeling), and conation (striving). An instinctive response occurs when a sense impression excites the nervous system and triggers a complex of meanings, feelings, and desires or aversions and so generates a tendency to act in certain specific ways towards the object causing the sense impression (McDougall 1908: 25; see also Mead 1910: 3–4, 11–13).[7] While instincts in many species may be expressed purely automatically, most animal instincts are shaped by learning processes and may be exercised with a degree of intelligent purpose.

Because they are capable of conscious thought, humans are able to know that they have feelings and can reason about the objects of their emotional responses. In conscious and intelligent beings, furthermore, emotional and instinctive reactions can be initiated by ideas as well as by sense impressions, and the link between nervous stimulation and a final course of action may be considerably modified through learning experiences. It is through learning that emotions may become attached to a whole range of objects, events, and memories, and the only invariant aspect of a human instinct is the 'emotional excitement' and associated nervous activity that it produces. The cognitive and the motor aspects, on the other hand, are highly plastic (McDougall 1908: 29). Humans are behaviourally incomplete without the knowledge they learn from each other. This means that both the ends and the means of action are organised by learning processes into socialised dispositions to act in particular ways. Repetition of an action builds up the meanings and expectations that comprise learned changes in instinctive response. Mental processes of sympathy, suggestion, and imitation shape the emotionally disposed responses into definite habits of action that are more or less uniform within particular circles of interaction (McDougall 1908: 283 ff). Instincts, therefore, become expressed as habits of action and dispositions towards particular types of action:

the instincts [are] … of the nature of innate promptings, cravings, or determining tendencies, which are specific in themselves but which do not comprise fixed inherited motive-patterns of behaviour. The actual overt pattern of behaviour which is manifested in efforts to satisfy these promptings is not automatically given, to the same degree as in the lower animal species, but depends largely upon the experiences and intelligent control of the individual and also upon the complex influences of the social tradition into which he [sic] is born and within which he lives. (Fletcher 1957: 46)

Understood in this way, instincts underlie the motivation of action. In human individuals, and in certain other animals, instinctive responses involve a cognitive appraisal of the significance of a stimulus in relation to emotional desires. The responses reflect the *meaning* or significance that objects of perception have in relation to the needs of the person acting. Cognition and emotion operate together to give human action its 'conative' or purposive character. This was expressed by Ward as a combination of thought and feeling, where feeling is a property of awareness of the actor and his or her needs. It therefore involves a rudimentary sense of self, rooted in an emotional recognition of 'wanting' something, of having 'passions' that comprise the affective or dynamic aspect of behaviour. Behaviour becomes properly purposive, or 'telic', when passions and affects are given direction by thought, a specific property of higher animals that allows a concern for means rather than simply for ends. People are motivated towards particular goals by their desires (their wants, volitions, and aspirations) as their will passes into effort. Particular combinations of feeling and thought – of the dynamic and the directive – constitute the various 'social forces' that interest, motivate, and 'propel' people (Ward 1903: 97, 101 ff; Dealey and Ward 1905: 56–8, 61 ff):

Man is thus a theatre of desires, positive, negative, or suppressed, all of which cause some form of action, and which together constitute the dynamic agent. (Dealey and Ward 1905: 65; see also Patten 1896; Ross 1920: 42–3)

This kind of argument lay behind Weber's conception of action as the meaningful behaviour of self-conscious and rational agents, and his view that behaviour is distinguished from mere mechanical movement by the fact that it is purposive or oriented towards specific ends through the selection of appropriate means (see also McDougall 1912: 307–9; 1923: 43 ff). Human conduct is marked by the ability (not always exercised) to employ a high degree of self-consciousness in the choice of ends and means. Instinctual responses may, therefore, be shaped by conscious judgements about how behaviour should be modified, and they may be reinforced or deferred according to the actual or anticipated social reactions of others. Instincts are 'favoured or checked' in their expression by the culture or social tradition under which an individual lives, and it is this varying mix of biological and cultural determinants that produces variations in human motivation (McDougall 1908: 17).

Instincts and their associated emotions have a physiological basis in the flow of hormones and a number of determinate links between hormones and emotions have been established: the flow of adrenaline is responsible for 'fight/flight' responses, corticosterone triggers stress, and oestrogen and testosterone lead to sexual responses. The links between hormones and feelings, however, are complex because of the key part played by culture, and it has proved difficult to arrive at any universal classification of instincts, emotions, and feelings. There is a wide agreement, however, that the variety of human emotional response is rooted in a more limited number of basic biological drives.

One of the most influential contributions to the classification and understanding of instincts was that of Freud, whose early work emphasised the instinct to satisfy a need for genital sex. He was particularly concerned with the consequences of the expression and inhibition of this need for the development of 'hysteria' (Breuer and Freud 1895). This was the basis for his later reconceptualising of sex in broader terms as a drive for bodily, sensual pleasure, together with various 'sublimated' tender emotions of love and affection and the drives associated with these (Freud 1905; 1925).[8] 'Sexual needs' are specific 'object cathexes': urges or desires for particular objects that would fulfil those needs. Their basis is the drive to achieve pleasure through orgasm, which had been selected through evolution because of its connection with reproduction. This drive creates an 'excitation' that builds up as 'tension' when not released through gratification. The genital pleasures of sex were seen as simply one element, albeit a crucial one, in what Freud later (1915) came to call the 'libidinal' instinct. Freud saw libido most broadly as the 'pleasure principle', regarding this as the central and overriding human instinct. Somewhat later, Reich (1933; 1942) took the opposite step and narrowed down libido to orgasmic, penetrative sexuality. Henceforth, 'sexuality' came to be used confusingly in psychoanalysis in both its broad sense of libido and its narrow sense of genital sex.

The libidinal instinct co-exists, Freud argued, with lesser 'ego drives' such as the instinct for self-preservation, but he saw these as theoretically uninteresting and as having much less importance in the motivation of action. In his later work, however, he began to take more account of hostility and of the destructive and aggressive impulses that result from the organism's drive to die 'in its own way'. This organic drive to survive means that people seek to avoid things that threaten their own survival and express aggressive attitudes such as hatred, disgust, hostility, and envy towards things that threaten them. Klein (1957) advanced this view and saw the aggressive drive as rooted in an infant's feelings of anxiety concerning undesired and threatening objects and experiences that are 'projected' outwards as aggression against those objects. Through the First World War, Freud began to construct a theory of the whole mental structure and to recognise (thanks to his reflections on the dreams of battle-shocked soldiers) that the aggressive instinct might also figure as an important component in people's emotional life and may be subject to similar processes of repression as the libidinal instinct. This formed part of a wider reconstruction of his theory that saw human behaviour as driven by two especially powerful instincts: the life instinct ('Eros'), which combines libido with the instinct for self-preservation, and the death instinct ('Thanatos'), which involves self-aggression and self-destruction. The death instinct is typically handled by directing it outwards, either on its own or in combination with libido (as in the case of sadism).

Freud's work was initially developed in Britain as an extension of the established instinct psychology (Rivers 1920; McDougall 1936; and see the discussions in Fletcher 1957: 309–15; Fine 1979: ch. 8). Rivers, for example, classified instincts into three basic categories: instincts of self-preservation (thirst, hunger, disgust, sucking, and protective instincts), instincts serving the continuation of the race (sexuality and the parental instinct), and instincts that maintain the cohesiveness of the group (gregariousness, including suggestion, sympathy, imitation, and intuition). Rivers' work on war-time 'shell shock' sufferers emphasised the instincts concerned with protection from danger, leading to his concern for such reactions as flight, aggression, manipulative activity, immobility, and collapse (see also Miller 1930). An alternative classification of instincts is that of McDougall, who began with a distinction between 'primary instincts' and 'lesser instincts'. The primary instincts, he held, are rooted in the most fundamental emotional and motor responses of flight, repulsion, curiosity, pugnacity, self-abasement, self-assertion, and tenderness. The so-called lesser instincts are those of sexuality, feeding, sociability, acquisition, and creativity. He saw these various instincts as combining in complex ways. Flight, for example, is a response rooted in feelings of fear. It is, however, linked with the 'fight' response of the pugnacity instinct and is stimulated by feelings of anger (McDougall 1923: 352; 1914: 338; see also Dealey and Ward 1905: 79).

Complex emotional states – 'sentiments' – result from the simultaneous experiencing of two or more feeling states and of the socialised responses to them. Sentiments are systems of emotional dispositions organised in relation to particular objects and types of objects. They are enduring tendencies to experience particular combinations of emotions whenever a specific object is called to mind (McDougall 1908; see also Shand 1896). Thus, the sentiment of love (affection or attachment) is rooted in a combination of tenderness and sexuality, while hate (dislike or aversion) combines anger and fear. The experiencing of a sentiment triggers other complexes of feeling in relation to having or losing an object. The most complex emotions are those that are 'compounded' or constructed into complex states, pleasurable or painful, and typically recognised by distinct names in everyday speech (McDougall 1908: ch. 5; 1919). Thus, anxiety is seen as anger and tenderness towards a loved object that is combined with a fear of its loss. Turner (2000) sees shame and guilt as being particularly important complex emotions and draws on the work of Lewis (1971) and Scheff (1990) to depict them as rooted in disappointment and sadness concerning behavioural failure (see also Craib 1994). Shame and guilt differ according to whether this is expressed mainly as aversion-fear for the consequences of this failure (shame) or as assertion-anger for having failed (guilt). In similar terms, Damaisio (1999: 50–1) has referred to 'moods' as the sustained emotional states that colour people's responses to a range of situations, seeing depression as enduring sadness and 'mania' as sustained elation.

The analysis of complex emotions has been taken furthest in psychoanalysis. Adler (1914) had already begun to broaden the Freudian view of instinct in a different direction and his main concern, and the source of his break with Freud in 1911, was to examine 'life plans' and the subjective consequences of instinctive drives rather than the drives themselves. He saw humans as having, to varying degrees, feelings of inferiority. Inferiority feelings are rooted in an innate need for recognition and acceptance by others and a drive to achieve superiority. The need for recognition leads people to compare themselves with others and to assess perceived differences and inequalities. An individual's character, he argued, is a sedimented result of the strategies adopted for dealing with his or her sensed inferiority and of the reactions of others to these strategies. Adler held that feelings of inferiority, or superiority, are universal and, therefore, normal. Individuals exhibit pathological or neurotic behaviour when their attempts to overcome feelings of inferiority are expressed in such things as an aggressive striving for superiority and a reliance on inferiority claims to justify abandonment of desired goals; that is, when felt inferiority itself becomes the overriding motive in action.

This approach to instincts was taken further by Horney after her arrival in the United States in the early 1930s, when she engaged more directly with the ideas of Adler. She stressed the part played by interpersonal and cultural factors in shaping individual motivation, seeing the emerging personality of the child as a product of parental behaviour in particular cultural contexts (Horney 1937; 1939). With Kardiner (1939), Linton (1936), Margaret Mead, and the 'culture and personality' school, she held that it is possible to identify a basic personality type as 'normal' for a specific culture. Thus, high levels of anxiety are normal for contemporary Western societies. Horney's explanation of the differences between normal and neurotic behaviour relied on her view that people were driven by an underlying need for security. Pathological personality traits emerge, she argued, when socialisation has produced a deep-rooted 'basic anxiety' as a result of a lack of demonstrated parental love to meet this need. A child with exaggerated basic anxiety feels small and insignificant in the face of an external world that is perceived as dangerous and threatening. The result is low self-esteem and the sense of inferiority recognised by Adler. It is expressed in such behaviour as a compulsive striving for affection, a striving for power, emotional withdrawal, or over-conformity and submissiveness. This aspect has recently been taken up by Giddens (1991).

It is through socialisation that combinations of emotions and responses to them are organised into dispositions to exhibit particular thoughts, feelings, and actions to others (McDougall 1908: ch. 4). Hochschild (1979; and see 1983) has shown that emotional expressions are normatively regulated and consciously 'managed'. People must engage in 'emotion work' if they are to display – and so induce – the appropriate emotions for the social situations in which they find themselves. Subjective feelings produced through this emotion work will reflect the particular repertoire of cultural narratives available for describing emotional responses.

Emotions depend, then, on cultural socialisation and interactional encounters in social relations. The importance of interaction has been pursued by Turner (2000), who has drawn on theories of the language instinct (Pinker 1994) to develop a theory of emotional expression. Language is rooted in a need to communicate and an in-built linguistic competence, and it is the need to communicate that drives an infant to exercise this innate competence. However, linguistic ability develops only if the infant encounters communicative interaction partners from whom the grammar of a specific language can be learned. According to Turner, there is a similar innate capacity for emotional response that develops through an infant's emotional encounters with others. The growing child builds expectations concerning its encounters with others, and conformity with or departure from these expectations leads to positive or negative emotional arousal. It is only if emotional competence has been properly activated in childhood that the full range of adult emotional expression is possible. The particular emotions aroused depend upon the particular 'need states' that underlie the child's (and later the adult's) expectations (Turner 2007). Turner identifies needs for 'verification of self' through self-presentation and the reactions of others, distributive justice in exchange relations, group inclusion through recognition and acceptance, a sense of trust, and a sense of the facticity and reality of the encountered world.

The mind, then, must be seen as fully embodied. It is not simply located in the brain but depends also on the senses, the flow of hormones, and the manipulative abilities of human hands. Thinking and feeling are whole-body processes, coordinated through the brain. They are also, however, social processes. Thinking and feeling within an individual mind depends upon the linguistic communication of ideas from one individual to another and so mental capacities depend upon the particular pattern of social life in which an individual is embedded.

Personality structure and the unconscious

The core of the unconscious, in the narrower sense of the mental system that excludes the 'pre-conscious', comprises the systems of instincts and emotions that generate cognitive and cathectic orientations that are beyond the level of consciousness but have a conative significance. The various systems of the unconscious work in parallel, though not necessarily in cooperation. They are, in Freud's terms, governed by drives towards satisfactions that will avoid frustration and the build-up of excitation or tension. They are not externally oriented, but self-referential, simply aiming at their own immediate realisation or satisfaction. Operating on their separate principles, which are subsymbolic, or non-logical, and cannot be deciphered in consciousness, they are uncoordinated. The unconscious also includes, however, all those thwarted emotions that have been discarded, denied, or repressed during childhood or adult mental development and so are held inaccessibly, below the level of consciousness but within long-term memory. The contents of this repressed unconscious result from experiences that are 'not capable of being brought into the field of consciousness by any of the ordinary processes of memory or association' (Rivers 1920: 9; and see his 1917).

Experiences become unconscious through processes of suppression and repression. Where suppression is a conscious attempt to redirect attention away from a threatening or painful thought or feeling, repression involves pushing and holding the threatening thoughts and feelings within the unconscious. Successful repression involves the 'sublimation' of instinctive energies: the energy attached to a threatening object becomes attached to a more acceptable one and so is redirected into 'safer' channels.[9] The repressed contents of the unconscious are, therefore, memories of experiences with especially painful or distressing connotations, together with associated memories that may not themselves have had any painful implications but are strongly associated with those that do: the latter are repressed because the affective and conative states associated with them have been repressed. The unconscious, therefore, is 'a storehouse of instinctive reactions and tendencies, together with the experiences associated with them, when they are out of harmony with the prevailing constituents of consciousness so that, when present, they produce pain and discomfort' (Rivers 1920: 38; Ross 1920: 42–4).

Conscious reflection cannot easily access the unconscious, as defences have been built up precisely in order to prevent its contents re-emerging into consciousness. Reflective consciousness is oriented towards adaptation to the external world, responding to the tensions generated in the unconscious through the 'reality principle'. Deliberate deferral of satisfaction or temporary toleration of dissatisfaction allows an accommodation to be made to the demands and requirements of the external world. Agents' responses to the unconscious, however, may themselves be partly unconscious, and human attitudes to the world typically combine conscious and unconscious responses.

Conscious control is, in contemporary societies, advanced through growth in the rationality that Weber saw as the central feature of modernity (Marcuse 1964; 1956). Inclinations, emotions, and appetites are disciplined and regulated through rationalised processes that are internalised as forms of self-discipline (Foucault 1976a). Mental defences establish a system of 'censorship' that filters unconscious ideas and impulses according to the likelihood that they will disturb attempts to relate to the world (Rivers 1918). Censorship ensures that threatening feelings and memories are held in long-term memory in a form in which it is very difficult to recreate them in consciousness through any voluntary act of will. Repressed memories and their emotional connotations can, however, break through into consciousness in distorted form, as they often do in dreams, slips of the tongue, and neurotic disorders.

Psychoanalysis places great emphasis on the significance of memories and experiences that have been repressed during infancy and childhood. Painful experiences from early life, before conscious reflection and appraisal have fully developed, are likely to have been repressed before their meanings have been properly explored or understood, and they may be so deeply buried beneath later repressions that they become associated with inappropriate emotional responses. They may be remembered, if at all, in crude and unsophisticated form as distorted or fragmented memories.

Unconscious memories are consciously experienced as sources of stress and tension, their origin or true significance remaining unknown. People tend to produce narrative 'rationalisations' of their reactions to these sources of discomfort and may construct 'false memories' of their past. Their accounts of and justifications for actions neither question nor uncover and understand the true reasons behind the emotional responses they feel. Rationalisations 'explain away' emotional responses or cast them as 'rational' responses to experiences. The true meaning and significance of unconscious processes, psychoanalysts argue, are accessible only with great difficulty through hypnosis or 'free association' under expert guidance. The aim of psychoanalytic therapy is to bring deeply rooted memories and emotional responses out of their 'coagulated emotional state into clearness and objectivity' (Mairet 1928: 20).

Human personality and character develop through the interplay of conscious reflection with unconscious experiences, especially as people become more aware of themselves as both agents and bodies. A sense of the body and its representation in consciousness establishes the basis for a sense of mental agency, of a body that actively thinks (Searle 1997: 185). This occurs when children have learned to separate perception from action so that they can reflect on what they perceive and so construct a meaningful response to it. Transforming an immediate perception into a free-standing image – an object of reflection – allows the image to acquire emotional content and so become meaningful. Through the gradual accretion of emotional significance, an image is transformed into a meaningful symbol (Greenspan and Shanker 2004: 26–7). It is in this way that a sense of self or identity is developed as a representation of the person as separate from and acting in relation to the external world and its objects.

Recent work in neuroscience has demonstrated the basis for this sense of self in the brain, converging with some of the work of Jung on the origin and function of 'archetypes'. Jung held that much human mental activity is driven by innate neural structures that are inherited genetically as a 'collective unconscious' or a universal invariant of the evolved human mind. They are, nevertheless, formed into psychic 'complexes' – clusters of ideas, images, and affects – through interaction with the external world and, in particular, with the social objects encountered. The resulting archetypes are templates or blueprints for the organisation of experience, comprising 'active living dispositions ... that perform and continually influence our thoughts and feelings and actions' (Jung 1931: 154; 1934; 1936).[10]

Damaisio has suggested that the conscious sense of self originates in one such archetype. This 'proto-self' consists of a collection of neural patterns that map the state of the organism as it encounters its environment (1999: 153–4). The proto-self is built up as an infant engages with the world and becomes the template for a rudimentary non-verbal representation of the self in the conscious stream of thought. As the capacity for memory grows, so the transient image of the self can be formed into what Damaisio calls an 'autobiographical self': a representation constructed verbally through narrative devices and personal descriptors (Damaisio 1999: 17–18, 173).[11] The basis for this is the growing ability of the child to name objects in the world. Objects experienced are identified and categorised in relation to the paradigms or templates that have been built up in memory and in this way they can be labelled – named and located in relation to other objects – and so can become objects of thought and communication (Moscovici 1984: 44–6). The human capacity for language and complex memory allows people to reconstruct their autobiographical self as an image of themselves as a 'person' with an 'identity'. Indeed, people continually reconstruct their autobiographies and may construct a number of autobiographical selves corresponding to the variety of situations in which they are involved (Goffman 1959b). The various constructions and reconstructions of self are constrained only by their relationship to the neurological proto-self, the biologically fixed 'home base' to which all representations of self relate (Damaisio 1999: 225–6).[12]

Freud saw the self in relation to what he called the *Ich* or 'ego', an idea that he developed relatively late in his career (Freud 1920; 1923). He used this term to refer both to the subject of action and the sense of self formed by that subject. The capacity for agency as a subject of action develops from an infant's attempts to cope with both its internal, instinctive demands and the external conditions and constraints imposed on them. The developing ego judges its responses against the external environment rather than allowing the direct expression of its unconscious responses. In developing as a conscious agent – an active reflective subject – the infant also develops a sense of itself and its own agency: it begins to think in terms of 'I'. The Freudian concept of the ego, therefore, comprises the conscious and the pre-conscious and refers somewhat ambiguously to both the agent and its representation of agency. Recognising a distinction between the self as representation and the self as subject or agent allows aspects of Freud's ideas to be reconciled more easily with those of Mead, as was initially attempted in the work of Harry Sullivan (1939; amongst many others see also Giddens 1984).

Mead had argued that while 'the body can be there and can operate in a very intelligent fashion without there being a self' (Mead 1927: 136), the formation of a sense of self allows the subject to take itself as its object, to take its own cognitive and emotional states as objects of reflection and so to plan and monitor courses of action (see also McDougall 1908: 283 ff). Mead showed that children develop a sense of 'I', of themselves as agents. Through their actions they become aware of the reactions and attitudes of others and these become an object of consciousness – a sense of 'me' – that forms an integral element in the self. The me – myself – exists as the set of attitudes perceived to be held by others, it is what 'they' think of me. Mead held that the me is equivalent to the Freudian censor (Mead 1927: 210). This sense of 'me' arises in interaction as others label and define people through the meanings given to their acts. These definitions become objects of thought and so the way an actor defines him or herself depends on how actions have been 'reflected' in the eyes of others. A person reflecting on his or her own actions can capture and objectify their agency as a self only as the me (Mead 1913). The self, in Cooley's (1902) words, is a 'looking glass self': the others with whom we interact are the mirrors in which we see ourselves reflected. It is initially the attitudes of the parents that are most salient in the formation of the me, but a wider circle of others becomes relevant as the growing child begins to interact beyond the family. The self is, therefore, continually created and recreated in the ever-shifting flow of interaction (Mead 1927: 175; see also Blumer 1987: 61).[13]

Freud saw the 'me' as encompassing a 'superego'. This is an aspect of the self representation that reflects the idealised expectations of the parents or intimate carers with whom the infant identifies. These expectations are conveyed through instructions, rewards, and punishments and are 'introjected' to become a partly conscious sense of moral proscriptions and prescriptions. As such, the superego becomes an important source of guilt and anxiety. The superego, like the self, is partly unconscious and can influence conscious deliberations in the same way as any other unconscious structures and impulses.

Mead developed the idea of the superego as the generalised other. Representations of the generalised other that have been built up comprise a sense of how 'people in general' are likely to react to our actions. Mead saw this developing initially through children's play activities in games. It is through play that they begin to explore the attitudes and expectations of people other than their parents. They play at the roles taken on by adult others and begin to build an idea of how 'they' generally act (Mead 1927: 154, 160; McDougall 1908: 154, 160; and see Blumer 1987: 61). The generalised other shapes their sense of 'me'. It is in taking on the attitudes of a generalised social group or category that a person becomes a socialised member of that group and is able to participate effectively in it. In societies that are undifferentiated, behaviour is controlled by the generalised other as a collective expression of the views of society as a whole. In differentiated societies where people participate in numerous different groups, they learn that they may act differently in the various situations that they encounter and are likely to build representations of generalised others appropriate to each of these groups and, perhaps, a complex and differentiated representation of an overarching generalised other that recognises the diversity of attitudes held (Shibutani 1955). In such a society, as Durkheim (1893) argued, the overall 'collective conscience' is relatively weak. The diversity of the groups in which people are involved in modern societies is the basis for the autonomy of judgement that they are able to exercise. As they become aware of the relativity of group norms, so they also realise the need to choose among them as an act of will (McDougall 1908: 3).

Ego and superego co-exist with a subjective representation of bodily drives and impulses, seen as an impersonal and anonymous structure disconnected from the consciously acting self. Freud termed this mental structure the *Es* or 'id', comprising the instinctual drives and impulses together with their repressed effects. Constructed as a representation of something operating against 'me' and beyond conscious control, 'it' – the dark and unknown noumenal thing that is known only through its effects – is the 'chaotic power house' of energy (Craib 2001: 34) that drives behaviour by pushing us to act in particular ways. The demands of the id are appraised in conscious reflection against our sense of self. Those demands that are regarded as inappropriate or unacceptable are likely to be repressed into the unconscious and held there through the 'ego defences' of repression (A. Freud 1936) or through processes of sublimation, redirection, and reaction formation. In this way, the superego, as the source of the standards by which the subject appraises the self and the id, is the origin of the inhibitions that a subject feels in relation to his or her unconscious impulses.

Cognitive and emotional integrity

Human minds, I have argued, are integrated systems of dispersed mental modules, pushed by conflicting emotional drives as they respond to an uncertain external world. Faced with such internal conflict and environmental uncertainty, it is striking that any degree of integration into a single system is typically achieved. How is it that conflicting representations and emotions can be brought into some kind of unity within an integrated sense of self?

The earliest attempt to answer this question originated in the *Gestalt* theories of Köhler (1917) and its offshoots in the field theory of Lewin (1936). This led to the view that responses to emotional tensions are oriented to the establishing of an equilibrium in the mental system. Conflict between two or more emotions held towards an object representation creates an experienced 'imbalance' or 'dissonance', a source of tension that leads people to respond by altering their attitudes toward the object in an attempt to restore balance (Heider 1958; Festinger 1957).

Festinger showed that dissonance may be reduced in a number of ways: by changing one or more cognitions, by searching for additional evidence that will strengthen one or other cognitions, or by derogating the source of one or other cognition. It has also been suggested that people may attempt to reduce dissonance through selective attention or exposure to knowledge and situations they feel will increase the level of dissonance. Cigarette smokers, for example, may attempt to avoid situations in which they are likely to be exposed to information about the health risks of smoking. The most important suggestion in this research, however, is that many individuals will reduce feelings of dissonance by changing their own views to reflect the perceived views of significant others.

When the emotions aroused are low in intensity, these mechanisms usually resolve the dissonance, but when emotions are stronger it is likely that mechanisms of defence will come into operation. Festinger pointed to many such mechanisms: the selective interpretation of evidence and information, disavowal of performances and responses as unimportant or misinformed, withdrawal from a situation, and so on. These ad hoc rationalisations evade rather than resolve the imbalance. Where the causes of the imbalance persist and/or emotional arousal are particularly intense, the attempt to achieve balance is likely to involve repressing the emotions, which can result in new or deepened states of imbalance (Turner 2007: 91 ff).

Pressures to establish or re-establish mental balance may have their origin in the desire to avoid discomfort and an instinct to imitate (Tarde

1890; Giddings 1896), but they also result from the dynamics of interactions with others. The early 'crowd psychology' of Dunlop (1840),
Hamerton (1885), and, above all, Sighele (1891) and Le Bon (1895a;
see also Tayler 1921), suggested that people's attitudes are strongly influenced by the number of others with whom they interact and the consensus among them.[14] Crowd theorists showed that the sheer physical
presence of others leads people to think, feel, and act differently from
the ways they would in isolation. The 'interpersonal influence of physically proximate individuals independently of their membership of social
groups' (Greenwood 2004: 162) result in an enhanced suggestibility. All
individuals are susceptible to the attitudes and opinions of others and
may tend to emulate them, but when they join a large group with a common spirit and feeling they tend to feel a particularly strong desire to
conform to perceived group behaviour and may be especially open to the
persuasive efforts of dominant members (Moscovici 1981: 289 ff).

Le Bon drew on Charcot's pioneering work on mental suggestion
through hypnosis or mesmerism, holding that 'submergence' in an
anonymous crowd produces a state of diminished personal responsibil-
ity in which unconscious and unsocialised instincts and drives are more
likely to be expressed. Individuals who are in a state of high suggestibility
are subject to a 'magnetic attraction' that weakens individual rationality
and intelligence and makes them more susceptible to the emotions and
'irrationality' of the group. All group members face a similar situation,
and so each individual is influenced by the increased emotional volatility
of all others. Ideas and sentiments cascade through the group in a wave
of contagion (Le Bon 1895a: 32). These collective effects can be amplified wherever ritual, rhetoric, and theatricality are able to emphasise the
collective spirit and purpose of the group.

Freud himself took up these ideas and sought to give collective influences a base in psychoanalytic theory (Freud 1921: 119–21). He held
that group membership can lead to a loss of inhibition (a weakening of
the psychic censor) and a willingness to abandon individual judgement
in favour of group opinions and preferences, so allowing the 'release'
of instinctual energy. This rests on a process of 'identification' in which
another is regarded as an ideal or model to emulate (Parsons *et al.* 1951b).
Initially, a child identifies with its parent and then generalises this identification to those who have some of the same characteristics as the parent
and so are placed in a similar position. Within a group, Freud believed,
participants identify with each other and so build up emotional ties of
solidarity. Where individuals are members of numerous groups, their sol-
idarities and commitments may criss-cross, but when the group forms a
large crowd these group differences are submerged and anonymised and

people are influenced at a 'mass' level. The relaxing of censorship may be seen as reflecting a weakening of the superego in the face of a strong but anonymous generalised other.

This tendency for individuals to adopt or express the opinions of others has been confirmed in a number of laboratory and ethnographic studies. A key experimenter was Asch (1951), who showed that individuals tend to adjust their own cognitive judgements to reflect their perceptions of group opinion. Where a majority of group members express a definite view, individuals whose views differ tend to experience cognitive dissonance. Those who are less self-confident, who fear disapproval, or are more anxious about the opinions of others experience self-doubt and uncertainty that they attempt to resolve by changing their view to match that of the majority. They may convince themselves that their own perceptions were wrong, or they may simply accept the group view so as not to appear different. The extent of conformity found in the Asch studies was far lower if individuals were able to keep their judgements private, showing that it is concern over public perception and reaction that is the crucial factor. Thus, perceptions of the generalised other are the important influences on individual attitudes. These conclusions were supported in studies undertaken by Milgram (1974) and Zimbardo (2007) on obedience to social expectations and the exercise of authority. They showed that the existence of an authority structure within a group strengthens the influence that a group can exercise over an individual: conveying an opinion or a command carries weight over and above the effects of group size.

Sleep, dreams, and neuroses

The resolution of dissonance, then, involves both conscious and unconscious processes, and a full account of mental functioning must rest on an understanding of the mechanisms through which the unconscious processes operate. Freud examined these as they affect the parapraxes of everyday life, the making of jokes, dreaming, and the causation of physical neurotic symptoms and obsessional actions. I will look at them through his analysis of dreams and neuroses.

Freud saw dreams as having an adaptive function. Relaxation of the psychic censor during sleep allows the partial release of repressed desires from the unconscious, meaning that dreams can be considered as forms of 'wish fulfilment': in a dream the individual is able to express wishes and desires that are normally suppressed or repressed. However, they can be expressed only in a disguised form that draws on unconscious symbolism. Because the censor remains partially active, a dream must encode the repressed ideas and feelings, disguising them from conscious awareness. Memories of objects experienced in everyday life that have, for some reason, become associated with repressed feelings can become the means through which those feelings and their associated ideas can be partially expressed. An interpretation of dream contents, therefore, allows a psychoanalyst to discover and understand the contents of the unconscious: dreams are 'the royal road to the unconscious'.

This view of dreams has been criticised for its exaggerated view of the symbolic and narrative structure of dreams, a criticism supported by contemporary understandings of sleep. Sleep is now recognised to be a by-product of the evolved consciousness. However, experiences during sleep have no direct adaptive function themselves but occur simply because of the human capacity for conscious mental activity. Dreaming is, therefore, the particular form of conscious thought that takes place during sleep (Flanagan 2000: 4–5).

The understanding of sleep was revolutionised during the 1950s, when it was discovered that sleep is not a uniform state but follows a cyclical course of alternating periods of rapid and slow eye movement, with dreaming occurring principally, but not exclusively, during rapid eye movement (REM) phases of heightened brain activity (Aserinsky and Kleitman 1953; cited in Williams 2005: 16). REM sleep allows the building and strengthening of neural brain connections, especially those that consolidate recent memories, those that process visual images, and those that rest the mental systems involved in attention, memory, and learning. Non-REM (NREM) sleep allows restorative, conservatory, and body-building processes to take place and during this phase many bodily functions are shut down; some are simply relaxed, and others may be completely paralysed.

Mental activity during sleep comprises a chaotic jumble of images, memories, and emotions, structured only by 'residual activations', which are differentially experienced during NREM and REM sleep. The sleeping brain remains open to stimulation from a range of ideas, feelings, and processes. These include the contents and state of mind at the time of entering and changing a state of sleep and the residual awareness of external stimuli, such as the auditory and tactile stimuli that impinge on sleeping consciousness. The brain is also excited by the random activation of memories, images, and feelings aroused by the relatively unregulated brain activity. When unconscious memories and drives are associated by the sleeping consciousness with contingent, external, and random stimuli, they may be given conscious expression as the censor is less likely to suppress the associations made by the sleeping mind (Flanagan 2000: 51–3). During NREM sleep, mental activity is circular and rut-like, the mind going over and over again the ideas, images, and feelings associated with waking anxieties and worries. In REM sleep, on the other hand, mental activity tends to flow as discontinuous and incongruous images marked by little or no logical connection.

NREM and REM mental activities provide the raw materials for the conscious experiences that are recalled as 'dreams'. The conscious mind attempts to make sense of the mental chaos experienced while sleeping, much as it would try to make sense of wakeful mental activity. There may well be a momentum or dynamic to this mental activity as sleep continues: each phase of sleep inheriting, as its starting point, the mental contents of the previous phase. Thus, the sleeping mind will often attempt to make the stream of mental experience meaningful and plausible in the light of what is already known and has already been experienced. Such sleep work may have an effect on waking knowledge, through the reorganisation of neural connections, even if the actual dreams are not remembered on waking. The sleeper may also be aware, especially at the actual point of waking, of a sequence of dream experiences that can be captured and reported. Wakeful reflection on these recalled experiences may give them a more logical form than was the case in the original dreams. They may, for example, be given an episodic or thematic structure and may even be constituted as chronological narratives or fragments of narratives (Flanagan 2000: 123, 158).

This understanding of dreaming provides a basis for assessing the significance of Freud's account of dreams and the unconscious. The recall and reconstruction of dream material in a wakeful state involves what Freud called 'secondary revision'. Because the censor is more active in this state, the narratives constructed in secondary revision are likely to involve a heavier disguising of memories and feelings than was the case during the actual dream. The reconstructed dream narrative, which the dreamer may believe to be an accurate report on the actual dream, may have more in common with other wakeful accounts and narratives. Such reflection may give the person a degree of self-understanding, though the inevitable misremembering and misinterpretation that occurs in secondary revision will colour and shape this. The task of a psychoanalytic investigation is to take the dream narratives, perhaps as later embellished by the dreamer in full consciousness, as the means through which the actual dream experiences can be recovered and decoded in order to uncover whatever repressed ideas and feelings they may contain.

Contrary to what Freud often implied, it is the individual's sense-making activities, rather than the experiences themselves, that are of critical significance. The attempts that people make, in a wakeful state, to deny and suppress their unconscious desires in the reconstructions and reports on their dream experiences are the evidence used to uncover both the fact that suppression and repression take place and the unconscious desires themselves. The interpretation of a dream in analysis, therefore, is the result of a complex negotiation between analyst and dreamer as the analyst seeks to uncover the actual dream and the wishes that inform it, and the dreamer seeks to retain or reconstruct the defences built up.

Freud saw the encoding of repressed ideas and feelings as taking place through processes of 'condensation' and 'displacement' that together constitute 'dream work'. While he saw these as integral to actual dreaming, they are more particularly relevant to the interpretation of secondary revisions. Numerous ideas may be associated with each other and condensed into a single (if complex) symbol. This may be an image of a place, person, or event that stands for or connotes a whole range of other images. Ideas may also be displaced through metaphorical and other forms of symbolisation. The dreamer displaces ideas and feelings using both idiosyncratic and shared symbols and meanings. Some Freudians hold that there is a universal dream symbolism, a view sometimes implied by Freud himself. This has more generally been seen as altogether too strong a claim to make. The symbols that appear in dream work are those common to the particular social groups of which the dreamer is a member and that have acquired some personal significance to them through their own lived experience.

Freud's psychoanalysis also led to a novel approach to neurotic forms of mental illness. The so-called neuroses were seen as resulting from the repression of unbearable and unacceptable ideas and desires. The ego may be able to channel the 'sublimated' instinctual energy into artistic, scientific, or other 'civilised' pursuits. Indeed, the whole of everyday social life depends upon this 'renunciation' of libidinal energy in acts of deferred gratification (Freud 1927; 1930). Thus, the framework of everyday life and larger 'civilised' structures become possible only because instinctive urges are repressed and their energy put to other uses. However, this may not always be possible. Energy that is unattached to acceptable ideas or objects remains as a source of 'free floating anxiety' and the build up of large amounts of such anxiety can predispose a person to transfer it to ideas or objects felt consciously to be inappropriate or unacceptable. Where particularly strong impulses have been repressed, their partial release in dreams may be insufficient to alleviate the psychic tensions they produce and the repressed impulses may seek expression in ways that by-pass ego controls. When sublimated energy has been attached to objects that the ego judges to be inappropriate, its expression will tend to be disguised in a 'hysterical' or neurotic form as physical disorders and compulsive behaviours. The neurotic is a person who has transferred the energy associated with things that they find unacceptable to behaviour that others find unacceptable or problematic. Freud further argued that if the intensity of the original desire is particularly great, then even the socially acceptable behaviour into which it has been channelled may be expressed neurotically. Examples are a compulsive engagement in scientific work and an obsessive attachment to another person. What counts as neurotic behaviour depends upon changing conceptions of acceptability and normality and so is, in important respects, dependent on historically specific social standards.

Freud paid particular attention to the neuroses he saw as having a sexual origin. His earliest work had seen physical symptoms with no immediate physical causes as neurotic or hysterical consequences of psychic problems that resulted from early sexual experiences. He initially saw these as resulting from actual child abuse ('childhood seduction') that makes itself felt when the sexual changes of puberty are experienced and memories of the abuse are denied or repressed. Hysterical symptoms result from symbolic associations unconsciously made between the abuse and current life experiences. In his essays on sexuality, Freud (1905) announced the abandonment of his theory of actual abuse in favour of a theory of imagined sexual abuse. From this new point of view, hysterical symptoms result from the projection back into childhood of fantasies that themselves result from a failure to progress through the normal stages of infant libidinal development. Thus, people may become 'fixated' at an infantile stage of development and their adult sexual development will be distorted by the tensions and anxieties generated through the repression of their false memories of abuse. Freud's account of the unconscious, dreaming, and mental illness rested on an understanding of personality development.

Personality development

Early accounts of the development of personality and the sense of self relied on ideas of 'recapitulation' to justify their focus on developmental stages (Hall 1904). Though this idea was subsequently abandoned, the idea that mental development occurred through the interdependence of biological maturation and social interaction had been firmly established. Forms of interaction and association within specific cultural contexts result in contingencies that can be experienced and engaged with only if appropriate biological capacities have matured. This view of personality formation has been developed in psychoanalytic theories of sexuality and in theories of cognition, moral judgement, and language.

Freud saw sexuality as developing in two phases of life – the infantile and the adolescent – separated by a period of 'latency'. He initially thought that the differences in sexuality between men and women emerged at puberty, but came to realise that sexual differentiation was also important at earlier stages of psychological development. The sequence of stages that Freud arrived at was based on the biological maturation of human individuals as they pass from the generalised focus on bodily functions in infancy to a pubertal stage of adult sexuality. Through this fixed sequence of stages, the biological capacities of the infant are channelled through cultural formation and social encounters. It is through this social construction that sexual drives are formed in a subjectively oriented search for alternative sources of pleasure and Freud later employed a more flexible scheme of successive 'strategies' for securing pleasure (Lacan 1966a: 24; Mitchell 1974: 26–7). In Klein's terms, these are a series of successively adopted psychic 'positions'. Psychoanalytic work on the development of sexuality and emotional attachments has been complemented by parallel work on the development of cognitive and linguistic skills. Piaget set out a framework of developmental psychology that, like Freud's, focused on the interplay between biological maturation and interactional encounters with the physical and social world.

The period of infantile sexuality, Freud argued, lasts from birth to the age of four or five. The focus of this infantile sexuality alters developmentally around various zones of the body, the infant moving through oral, anal, and phallic stages of sexuality. At the same time, libido is gradually transformed from 'narcissistic' auto-erotic concerns with bodily functions into an erotic orientation towards others. The infant initially encounters and tests the world through its mouth, seeking oral experiences and pleasures. The infant is indiscriminate – 'polymorphously perverse' – but is especially oriented to objects such as a mother who can provide food and care. Sensual sucking, thanks to the sucking reflex, is a source of food that depends on the availability of the mother's breast and leaves the infant with little control over its own sources of pleasure. Any failure to secure satisfaction becomes a source of great anxiety. Towards the end of its first year the infant acquires the ability to control its anal and sphincter muscles, and the anus becomes an additional source of pleasure through the retention and expulsion of faecal material. The development of the muscular system gives the infant the capacity for greater control over its environment and its sources of pleasure. The anal stage results in struggles through which the parents attempt to establish a regime of toilet training and deferred gratification. As the infant loses control over its pleasure it begins to acquire a new biological capacity for self-directed pleasure through the genitals. In this phallic stage, beginning around the end of its third year, rubbing of the penis or clitoris becomes a source of pleasure until this, too, is suppressed by the parents. Parental suppression of phallic pleasure initiates a latency period in which few biological changes other than physical growth occur and the infant 'gives up' the search for self-directed pleasure and accepts parental control over the sources of its pleasures.

The stages of childhood development that Piaget identified parallel closely those of Freud. Corresponding closely to the oral and anal stages Piaget recognised what he called a 'sensorimotor' stage of cognitive development, while the phallic stage corresponds to what Piaget called the 'pre-operational' stage. The sensorimotor stage of development, lasting roughly for the first two years of life, is a period in which the child's exploration of the world occurs through the senses and the motor activities generated by sensory perceptions. Sucking, touching, and seeing are the means through which the infant builds up a picture of the world and comes to realise that he or she is separate from the external world. Only in the pre-operational stage, from the age of two up to six or seven, does the child acquire the ability to form images of objects that are not currently present to the senses. The child acquires the idea of 'object permanence' – the idea that things can continue to exist when not seen or touched – and becomes more curious in active explorations of the world. Among the objects encountered are other people, and the child is able to build ideas about parents and others as objects separate from themselves and having a continuing existence apart from them.

These first two stages in Piaget's scheme were seen as central to language acquisition by Chomsky (1980: 33, 44–5), who saw language developing as an innate linguistic competence that is nurtured through social interaction. Early in the first two years of life, Chomsky argues, children begin to produce noises that express biological states of hunger, excretion, and pain, and later they begin to 'coo' with contentment when their needs have been satisfied. As the mother or close carer talks to the infant, so these focused and rhythmic noises develop into a babbling that imitates the parental speech patterns. By the end of the first year of life, infants begin to recognise certain discrete words in parental speech and may themselves begin to use these words to signal intentions and desires. By the end of their second year they may have a vocabulary of 200 words and are forming two-word sentences. As the child enters the pre-operational stage and parents become more salient as enduring objects, so the child begins to produce sentences of three or four words with grammatical constructions that allow them to form questions and commands.

There is a clear link between cognitive and emotional development and the emergence of a sense of self. The acquisition of language allows the infant to form images with emotional content, including an image of itself as separate from others. Infants use their ability to engage in 'emotional signalling' in interaction with care givers and begin to respond to intentions rather than merely to overt actions. An infant learns that a parent can be made to do things through signalling and that outcomes can be achieved through cooperation (Greenspan and Shanker 2004: 37). Communication through gestures and significant symbols was recognised by Mead (1927) as advancing rapidly during the period beginning from around age three.

The child's new linguistic abilities allow it to identify and name the various objects in its environment, to define its situation, and, in particular, to recognise its parents as significant others. It is in this way, Mead argued, that children are able to develop a true sense of self and, therefore, a capacity for self-consciousness and symbolic communication with others. Vygotsky (1930–4) saw the social aspects of speech at this age as the basis on which a child begins to use words to talk to itself. The infant comments on its own activities in the world and instructs itself, just as adults comment and instruct it. The young child, then, develops the ability to handle simple conversations in which it acts in terms of meanings shared with others who are important to it. Over the years up to age seven, Chomsky argues, the child's grammatical structures become more complex as the child acquires the ability to use clauses and complex tenses and is eventually able to identify and correct most errors of syntax and morphology. Vygotsky held that children gradually acquire the ability to internalise their conversations as 'inner speech' or thought. Conscious thought, therefore, develops as a consequence of learning a language. It is not a pre-existing 'mentalese' that is subsequently translated into external speech, as argued by Pinker (1994). Very young infants are driven by unconscious emotional drives that orientate them to the world, and it is only when they have learned a language that they begin to think about the objects in the world and their actions towards them.

Chomsky argues that it is the possession of an innate capacity to construct a grammar – one mental module alongside others – that combines with a growing sense of self and an increased social interaction to produce a simple grammatical system that is related to, but not identical with, that spoken by their parents and the others children encounter. They recognise and decode parental linguistic forms and are able to reconstruct these into their own simplified grammatical structures. To know a language, for Chomsky, is to have a practical ability to speak it. It is 'to have a certain mental structure consisting of a system of rules and principles that generate and relate mental representations of various types' (Pinker 1994: 82). These linguistic structures are inferred from heard speech. Once the rules have been inferred, they are built into the mind and brain as dispositions and are not remembered or recalled as codified rules. Speech is therefore produced dispositionally rather than through the considered application of rules (Caws 1988: 195; Calvin 1996).

Piaget saw language acquisition somewhat differently and did not accept Chomsky's idea of an innate capacity to create (as opposed to learn) a language. He held that through operating, or acting, in the world, a child gradually assimilates objects into experience and forms them into a scheme of interpretation that can be applied to subsequent experiences. As a child begins to reflect upon his or her experiences, it modifies the scheme and stable mental structures are built that correspond to its range of encounters with the world. Piaget termed these 'equilibrated structures'. He held that children's linguistic operations are the experimental means through which they formulate equilibrated grammatical structures. This is supported by the view of Sampson (1997) that trial and error learning is of far more significance than any innate structures. While this issue remains unresolved, it seems clear that some kind of innate capacity is involved in language acquisition.

The mechanism responsible for initiating a latency phase in boys was called by Freud the Oedipus complex, while a parallel mechanism in girls he called the Electra complex. The Oedipus complex is the means through which a boy develops a strong love for his mother and, therefore, strong feelings of jealousy and resentment towards his father, who is seen as a threat to his source of pleasure. When he 'gives up' his mother (through fear of castration) and represses his sexual desires, he comes to identify with his father and so acquires a masculine identity. Freud understood this transition in a male-centred and highly schematic way as a virtual enactment of the Oedipus myth and his views have been heavily criticised, but his key point was that the establishment of a stable sexual attachment to a member of the opposite sex is linked to the internalisation of parental controls as a 'superego' and the expectation to perform masculine behaviour. Identification with the parent of the opposite sex is based on an inhibition of sexuality, a conversion of libidinal energy into affection, and the intensification of internalised parental attitudes as the superego, all of which trigger the entry into sexual latency. Girls, Freud argued, experience a 'castration complex': they feel that they must have been castrated and so cannot have the mother sexually. The girl's resulting 'penis envy' is the basis of a deep feeling of inferiority that leads to an acceptance that she must find a man in order to achieve satisfaction and to an acceptance of the authority of her father. The girl identifies with the mother as someone oriented to the father (Mitchell 1974).

Freud's view of the formation of the superego and of gender identities is over-schematic, especially in the case of girls.[15] Not only does Freud presume the conventional nuclear family of the West as the universal form of childrearing, but, despite the valiant efforts of writers such as Craib (2001: 54–5), the ideas of castration fears and penis envy are problematic. There is, nevertheless, truth in his view that the development of a genital orientation is linked to the search for potential sexual partners and that this search becomes fixated, initially, on the mother. It is also likely that jealousy of the father plays a part in the dynamics of this search and the eventual establishment of sexual identity and entry into the latency phase. It is also likely that there is something particular about the mother-daughter link in socialisation (Chodorow 1978). However, it remains an area of great theoretical uncertainty.

Piaget identified the years from age seven to around eleven (Freud's latency period) as that of the concrete operational stage of cognitive development. It is in this period that children learn to reason logically about the objects they encounter. They can imagine the alternative arrangements of these objects that would result from varying their own position and altering their actions. They are able to imagine the world as others see it and so are able to take the part or role of the other. In this stage of cognitive development, according to Chomsky, language use also becomes more sophisticated in both grammar and semantic knowledge. By the age of eleven, the adolescent mind possesses a more or less fully developed grammatical ability and correct adult language can be produced. After the age of eleven the child is able to make the transition to more abstract thinking and enters the formal-operational stage. It is the acquisition of complex linguistic structures that allows the formation of these abstract concepts and the ability to manipulate them mentally. The adolescent and the adult operate in the world on the basis of formally defined abstract concepts and can easily handle issues of number, time, and space without having to relate them directly to concrete physical objects.

Thought, however, is not merely silent or unvoiced speech (Vygotsky 1930–4). Once the capacity to think has been formed, people can think with half-formed sentences, hints, and allusions rather than precise and elaborate grammatical structures. They can use a simplified and condensed syntax and phonetics and have no need to put everything into words. A stream of conscious thought involves images, unvoiced representations and meanings, and allusions, and is quite distinct from a flow of external speech.[16] It is for this reason that the solution to an apparently intractable logical problem may 'come to us' in a sudden mental leap rather than through the silent mental construction of a logical argument.

Piaget (1932) attempted to show that similar processes are involved in the development of moral reasoning and judgement. He suggested that an awareness of moral rules develops only during the pre-operational stage. The child begins to see rules of behaviour as externally fixed and given as part of a coercive order to whose authority they must submit. This is the phallic period, in which, according to Freud, the child is struggling with the Oedipus or Electra complex and is internalising parental authority as a punitive superego. When they enter adolescence, Piaget argued, they begin to recognise the consensual, constituted nature of moral rules and adopt a more rational attitude towards them. Rules are seen as 'conventional', as results of an agreement, and so can be the objects of autonomous judgements that might lead to their change (Kohlberg 1981).[17] The key to moral development, Piaget argued, is to be found in play activities. It is in their play with others that children learn about rules and, eventually, come to understand them as the results of cooperative activity (Mead 1927: 154; and see Caldwell Cook 1917; Bott 1928).

When a child matures into the biological stage of puberty, sexual concerns are reactivated in a genital form and the adolescent begins to build an adult pattern of sexuality. There are new possibilities of pleasure and for the transition to mature sexual expression. This can occur, however, only on the basis of the conflicts and tensions that have been suppressed (and often repressed) during the latency period. The nature of adult sexuality depends on how the anxieties associated with each of the childhood stages have been dealt with. If the Oedipus complex has not been adequately resolved, then the adolescent boy is likely to develop neurotic responses to the re-emergence of his libidinal desires. He may 'regress' to an earlier stage and engage in acts that are 'perversions' of normal adult sexuality. Libido that is frustrated flows back to a sensual orientation that was more successful and to which it had been partially fixated at an earlier stage. Freud saw hysteria in women as a detachment of the idea of genital pleasure from the genital organs that blocks the flow of libido to them and diverts it to 'infantile' zones. Objects of sexual attachment are not, therefore, fixed in biology but are significantly shaped through socialisation.

Freud regarded the pattern of sexuality as being largely fixed by the end of adolescence, but Erikson (1950) has shown that this does not mark the end of all psychological development. Largely accepting Freud's account of psychosexual development, he saw this as linked to an over-arching concern for personal identity that continues into adult-hood. Where early sexual development is strongly conditioned by bio-logical maturation, however, Erikson saw adult personal development as culturally variable and as reflecting the particular patterns of social rela-tions in which an individual is involved as he or she ages. The period of adolescence in contemporary societies is marked by a growing separation from the family of origin as the adolescent searches for an independent role in life. Youths are engaged in a search for inspiration in life choices that they must make and they must cope with the tensions inherent in the uncertainty and confusion of identity (Erikson 1968: 128–35; 1958). Middle adulthood begins with the process of family building and the associated establishment of a career. Work and parenthood are the over-riding concerns and the adult must cope with the potential problems of stagnation and boredom as adolescent dreams are scaled down to the requirements of supporting a family.

The final stage of 'maturity' or old age (beginning, Erikson argued, in the fifties) is that in which the person must come to terms with chil-dren who are entering independent adulthood and the fact that their own careers are approaching retirement. Maturity is a period in which people must face their own declining health, their mortality, and the 'des-pair' that life may be too short to achieve their adolescent goals. Jacques (1965) suggested that this characterises a 'mid-life' stage of crisis that anticipates old age proper, when the inevitability of imminent death has been accepted. The important point in this discussion, however, is that while the construction of identity is related to individual biological mat-uration and ageing, it is also related to the development of the individual and family life course. The precise age at which 'crises' are encountered and attempts are made to resolve or repress their anxieties will vary with an individual's contingent life circumstances and with the cultural and social structural context in which these occur.

Consciousness and a sense of self are central to what it is to be human, and social existence is both a condition for and a consequence of the reflexive search for and expression of identity and individuality. However, much human mental activity is unconscious, driving people to act in ways of which they are partly or completely unaware and leading them to express or repress their emotional reactions to the world around them. These unreflective habits of thought, feeling, and action form a substan-tial part of human activity and are the bases of dreams and neuroses and the socialised routines of everyday life. Purposive activity must con-front unconscious routines, and social action results from a constant and shifting interplay between conscious reflection and unreflective habit. All human mental traits are the results of psychological development in which biological maturation establishes the physical conditions under which socialisation can shape individual personality. Crucial to the conversion of infantile pleasure seeking into socially acceptable motivations to act is the linguistic representation and appropriation of the world, and this linguistic ability, too, is a combined product of biological maturation and socialisation.

9   Social Development: Differentiation and Change

I have shown that the relations of social structure to social action must be seen as a process occurring over time, with the reproduction and transformation of social structure understood as a process of temporal change. Social systems, therefore, are characterised by continual social change, sometimes small-scale and transient and sometimes large-scale and enduring. Where change is enduring and exhibits a direction, it is usual to speak of development rather than merely of change. Change and development are temporal processes, as discussed in Chapter 5, and the history of any social situation or social system requires a description and explanation of their changing patterns over time.

Much historical writing has seen change simply as a temporal succession of events linked to each other through discrete causal connections. Descriptive narratives have presented historical events as the contingent outcomes of causal chains of connection. This focus on the constant flux of occurrences through an incremental movement from one set of circumstances to another has led many to see history, in the words attributed to Henry Ford, as merely 'one damned thing after another'. Historical change is simply a kaleidoscopic succession of happenings.

The structural ideas established in the formative period of sociology posed a first challenge to this view. It was argued that the individualistic focus of many historians on the actions of individual monarchs, statesmen, and political leaders had to be complemented by an awareness of the structural conditions under which they acted and an understanding of historical change itself as a structured process. The eighteenth-century enlightenment theorists had glimpsed the need for a structural explanation of historical change, but it was Comte, Spencer, and their contemporaries who set out a theoretical rationale for a generalising account of history. Their view was that historical change had to be seen as a process of development within which the discrete events studied by narrative historians could be seen as the outcomes of the internal or endogenous mechanisms at work in social systems (Sewell 2005: 84). These ideas laid the foundations for a developmental approach to sociology that dominated the field for many years and provided a first approximation to a comprehensive theory of social change.

Generally described as 'evolutionism', this developmental perspective highlighted the ways in which the internal processes of a system could generate stable patterns of structural change. Central to this argument was a contrast between the study of social structure ('statics') and the study of social dynamics. As I have shown in Chapters 4 and 6, a static, structural, analysis uncovers the anatomy of a system by investigating the arrangement of its 'parts': the organs, bones, and tissues of a biological organism and the roles, classes, and institutions of a social system. A static analysis is 'synchronic' in the sense defined by Radcliffe-Brown and is aimed at uncovering the 'laws of co-existence' that describe the relations among the parts of the system. Social dynamics, on the other hand, is concerned with the internal functioning of a structure, with the respective contributions of the parts to its maintenance or change. A dynamic or functional analysis uncovers the physiology of the system and its laws of succession. It investigates the internal processes of metabolism, circulation, and exchange that sustain the growth or development of a system. In such an analysis the structure is taken as given and the flows that make up the functional connections between the various parts of the social structure are explored. The functional interdependence of parts within a system generates the processes that reproduce the structure and bring about its patterned development over time according to an immanent 'logic' of social change.

In this chapter I will set out the basis of an evolutionary account of structural change and I will show that this can be refined and transformed into a more adequate account of historical change and development that is sensitive to variations in the environmental conditions faced by human populations and the openness and flexibility inherent in the cultural creativity of social action.

Growth, development, and differentiation

Many of the nineteenth-century social theorists relied on a biological analogy, using a metaphor of growth and development taken from the observation of plants and other organisms, and in terms of which 'social organisms' change over the course of their lifetimes in the same way as biological organisms. System change was understood as occurring through ontogenetic ideas of internal potential rather than Darwinian ones of environmental adaptation. Thus, social development was seen as analogous to the biological maturation of individual organs or the growth of a seed into a plant. This metaphor had, in fact, first been employed in Greek thought, most notably in the works of Heraclitus and Aristotle. Their understanding of growth in plants, achieved in a society based upon agriculture and the systematic formulation of the techniques of farming, led them to study the origins and structures of all things in order to uncover the mechanisms responsible for growth. The original, primitive form of a thing was seen as a seed or embryo state that already contains the potentialities of the fully developed form. The development of this primitive, embryonic form is a process of 'becoming', a process that moves towards some pre-ordained goal or final state. From this point of view, the inscription of the mature form of a plant within the genetic code of the seed is a model for the inscription of the mature form of a social system in its initial social conditions. More generally, endogenous processes cause a system to move towards a state in which one or more of its properties exhibit an enhanced or more advanced expression.

Growth in an organism was seen as an increase in size, with consequent alteration of structure, as a result of the incorporation of environmental materials as nourishment or sustenance. A seed, for example, requires planting and watering if it is to grow into a plant. Development through growth consists in the 'unfolding' or actualisation of a potential fed by environmental resources. While this involves activation or nourishment from outside, the actual course of development is a necessary consequence of the internal structure of the entity itself and so is both inexorable and irreversible. The growth course taken as an entity develops is a cumulative outcome of the prior changes undergone. This growth may be smooth and continuous but it may also sometimes show a sequence of more or less distinct stages, with each new step in its development being the outcome of processes immanent to the preceding stage (Nisbet 1969). The direction of change in an entity, then, is one of maturation, of an endogenously generated advance towards a final state.

If development is the unfolding or realisation of a potential encoded in the initial conditions of the system, history becomes the necessary and inexorable unfolding of tendencies contained in the structure or constitution of a society. Spencer stressed parallels with cellular division in biological organisms. Structural differentiation in social systems, he argued, results in an increasing 'heterogeneity' as processes of ontogenesis generate a movement from a condition of 'incoherent homogeneity', characteristic of primitive forms, to one of 'coherent heterogeneity' (Spencer 1862: 321). This is the means through which he saw functionally specialised 'organs' – states, churches, families – as formed. Though he paid less attention to developmental processes, Durkheim (1893) proposed a similar view of the differentiation of specialised structures. He saw the growth in size of a society and the consequent increase in the 'dynamic density' of human association as introducing a tendential increase in task specialisation such that an increasingly complex division of labour was produced. Occupational and other social roles become progressively more specialised and each individual becomes correspondingly more dependent on the activities of others.

Social theory after Durkheim, especially the functional and structural-functional approaches, focused more particularly on statics rather than dynamics, leading to a declining interest in the study of social change. In the second half of the twentieth century, however, these evolutionary ideas of development were rediscovered and developed by Parsons and other theorists of living systems. Incorporating a more strictly Darwinian mechanism, the imperative for environmental adaptation was seen as setting a direction to social development. Development is adaptive change, and surviving societies are those that have followed a pattern of adaptive upgrading. From this point of view, societies move towards what Parsons (1966: 22) referred to as greater 'generalised adaptive capacity'. Parsons and Smelser (1956) agreed with Spencer and Durkheim that adaptive upgrading occurs through differentiation, seeing this as resulting from the attempts made by people to adapt their social structures to their changing environments. If a society is to survive in a changing environment, its structures must be transformed through a division of tasks that enhances its adaptive capacity. They argued that functionally specialised tasks, other things being equal, are more likely to prove effective and so there is an inevitability to increases in social differentiation wherever environmental conditions require adaptation.

Differentiation may, however, also lead to social disintegration in the short term. For example, a growing specialisation of activities will tend to undermine existing social norms and practices, and a society can persist in stable form only if new norms can be established that can integrate the now-differentiated tasks. Unless processes of integration operate effectively, anomie and social breakdown are likely to result and may persist as a chronic feature of a system. Smelser (1959) saw this as an almost inevitable consequence of the conflict and protest engendered by the strains inherent in social differentiation. Such processes are not, of course, inevitable, any more than the process of differentiation itself is inevitable. Although the system models described in Chapter 4 provide some basis for anticipating a tendency to equilibrium and reintegration through cybernetic and autopoetic mechanisms, their actual occurrence will always depend upon a variety of contingent factors that have not figured as central variables in evolutionist accounts.

While Durkheim had seen increasing differentiation as an inherent tendency of social organisation, he gave little attention to the causal mechanisms responsible for this. His concern was, rather, with the *functions* of the division of labour. Spencer, however, had wanted to *explain* differentiation. He wanted to see *why* it was that development occurred in the same way in physical, biological, and social systems. The explanation he gave was in terms of three fundamental principles. The first of these was 'the instability of the homogeneous'. What he meant by this was that, universally, the component parts of a homogeneous system cannot maintain their arrangement unaltered. The various parts are exposed to different forces, however slight, because of their position in relation to the environment. As a result, they will change in different ways. Thus, no matter how homogeneous the system, it will tend to become more heterogeneous over time. Once any such heterogeneity is introduced, it will be magnified through exactly the same processes. The second principle is 'the multiplication of effects'. By this Spencer meant that all changes will have reverberating consequences through a system, bringing about differential changes at its various points (Spencer 1862: chs. 19 and 20). The heterogeneity that results from these two processes is not chaotic, argued Spencer, but tends to be organised through the *segregation* of similar units into a subgroup or subsystem, separate from other parts: the system becomes differentiated and the parts become specialised. In an attempt to adapt to their environment, systems move towards equilibrium through processes of instability, multiplication, and segregation. Environmental changes and internal processes mean that this equilibrium is constantly being undermined and re-established. A system will, therefore, always exhibit a 'moving equilibrium'.

The view of causation adopted in these models of change is what Althusser (1962) has termed 'structural causality'. The various levels of the overall structure have their distinctive temporalities, and the overall pattern of change is a consequence of the concatenation of their structural times. Historical occurrences are not, therefore, contingent events but are 'conjunctures' – completely determined outcomes of the structure of the system. Local-level happenings are manifestations of system-level dynamics.

An important rider to these theories of endogenous development was the claim that many patterns of change are cyclical rather than linear. If biological and social organisms have a natural life span of growth that runs through stages of birth, maturation, decay, and death, then the developmental potential inherent in any social system will eventually be exhausted and the system must break down or give birth to a new germinal system (Nisbet 1969). Greek philosophical thought on social life had identified a sequence of such cycles, each catastrophic termination being followed by the birth of a new system. In this view, no long-term development can be discerned from one system to the next. There is only the continuing repetition of cycles of development. Phases of growth are followed by phases of decline and 'death' and these are, in turn, followed by renewed phases of growth and decline. Thus, the development of the universe as a whole consists of the numerous and varied intersecting cycles followed by its constituent systems. Such an account breaks with any idea of the inexorability of continual progress, though some cyclical theories postulated a 'ratchet' mechanism through which each successive cycle could show an upward trend from the stage reached by its predecessor.

Cyclical theories typically emphasised the importance of cultural creativity and exhaustion in defining the trajectory of social change. Danilevsky (1869) and Spengler (1918–22), for example, held that the cultural spirits of particular civilisations and cultures contain the potential for their rise and decline in world prominence. Sorokin (1937–41) took a similar view and explored the ways in which systemic contradictions and failures of integration at the cultural level could give rise to cultural expansion and exhaustion. In a different vein, Marxist theory saw successive modes of production as contradictory structures that arrive at a point of revolutionary transformation to a new system when the structural limits of a particular mode of production are reached. A new mode of production resolves the contradictions of its predecessor and can move on to higher phases of development until its contradictions, too, result in system breakdown and transformation.

Unilinear and multilinear development

Developmental theorists have often tried to identify a primary causal factor in social change, typically casting economic factors, and more particularly technology, in this role. Marx and Engels were among the first to emphasise the key role of the productive forces within the economic structure, making this the basic tenet of 'historical materialism' (Marx and Engels 1846: 42–3). Lloyd Morgan's (1877) argument that the social organisation of material production sets the conditions under which all other social activities take place and drives the development of societies from primitive 'savagery' into more 'civilised' forms was taken up by Engels (1884) as supporting evidence for the Marxian claim. Beyond orthodox Marxism, Morgan's argument had a wider impact within comparative social anthropology (for example, White 1949; and see also the summary statements in Lenski 1966; Lenski and Lenski 1974).

Other theorists looked to human consciousness and intellectual creativity as the critical factor responsible for technological innovation and so for all other forms of social change. Lester Ward (1883), like Comte before him, had seen the power inherent in scientific knowledge as attaining a critical significance once social conditions were such that humans could exercise purposive control over the direction of their own social development. Ward saw this knowledge as central to the 'sociogenesis' through which structural transformations occur as consciously implemented processes of socially planned reconstruction. In a different vein, Benjamin Kidd (1894) saw religious beliefs and meanings as the key determinant of social change.

Materialist and idealist arguments were brought together by those who held that technology itself develops as a result of the application of scientific knowledge to material production. In theories of industrialism (Kerr *et al.* 1960; Rostow 1960) and in the theories of Herbert Marcuse (1964) and Jürgen Habermas (1965), the rational complex of science and technology is accorded primacy in driving social change. For these theorists, social development occurs increasingly as a result of the application of natural and social science in technologies of production and political intervention.

However, the adoption of a developmental theory does not require that a particular social factor be accorded causal primacy under all circumstances. Developmental theories rely on adaptation as the mechanism driving social change, and the adaptive significance of particular social factors is likely to vary as the environment is altered. The relative importance of natural and cultural factors may vary from one society to another and from one phase of social development to another. A general account of social development must focus on the process of adaptation itself. Social structures change as they adapt to pressures imposed by the natural environment, in the state into which it has already been transformed through prior processes of adaptation. Societies that fail to adapt will collapse and, eventually, disappear. For this reason, the history of surviving societies is a history of progressively improved adaptation.

This generic requirement to adapt has led some theorists to see social development as both inexorable and irreversible. According to Parsons, for example, it is the need to adapt through differentiation and integration that provides a direction to social change in a social system. It is on this basis that societies, if they survive, grow towards ever-improved effectivity in relation to their environments. This is the basis on which evolutionary social theories took a 'unilinear' form, a form in which development moved in one direction under all social circumstances.

'Multilinear' theories of development have highlighted the variations in structure that can enable a system to adapt to its environment. This argument takes up Merton's (1949) idea of 'functional alternatives' and draws out its implications for theories of social evolution. Such theories recognise a number of variant paths of development (Steward 1955; and see Smith 1976). Societies may move in parallel, they may diverge, and if a particularly strong causal factor or set of factors is operating there may be an asymptotic convergence of the variant structures towards a common state (Kerr *et al.* 1960). While there may be general adaptive upgrading at the global scale for humanity as a whole (termed 'general evolution', see the chapters in Sahlins and Service 1960: chs. 2, 3; see also Sanderson 1990), the specific pattern of development followed by particular societies within this broad overall trend will reflect their cultural and structural diversity (see Feldman and Moore 1962).

Thus, increasing adaptive capacity may be apparent only at a global level. Particular societies can decay, collapse, or regress. Like individual plants, some societies may experience terminal pathologies and die before they achieve maturity. Societies grow to achieve their full potential only if they are actually able to adapt. Contact and continuity between societies, however, is likely to ensure that, in the long run, humanity as a whole continues to develop in an adaptive direction.

Evolutionary theories have typically claimed that the development of whole societies can be seen as a movement through a definite sequence of stages. A remarkably consistent sequence has dominated social thought since at least the eighteenth century. The early evolutionists saw this as a single sequence followed by all human societies and that, therefore, constitutes a series of developmental stages for humanity as a whole. They assumed a uniformity in the 'primitive' forms of society, analogous to the similarities in particular types of seed or embryo, and anticipated that each society would follow a similar path as it grew. For this reason, human history would follow a sequence of definable stages.

Western self-understanding since the Enlightenment had identified these as the three ages of ancient (classical), medieval, and modern times, understood largely as stages of intellectual development. The Biblical narrative continued to offer a chronology of the development of the known world until the European discovery of the Americas and other distant lands posed the problem of how the histories of these societies were to be interpolated with that of the 'old world'. The perception of modern, Western society as a specifically commercial society meant that constructing technologically and economically defined stages seemed a way of building a more general, and perhaps universal, history. Adam Smith was among the first writers to posit a passage from the primitive 'savagery' of non-literate and kinship-based hunter-gathering societies through 'barbarian' herding and pastoralism to 'civilised' agrarian and urban societies. Savagery, barbarism, civilisation, and commerce became a commonly recognised sequence that could be modified by a division of the savage and barbarian stages into lower, middle, and upper states and through a mapping of the economic sequence onto a technological sequence that defined three ages of stone, bronze, and iron technology (Morgan 1877; Lubbock 1865). This was partly paralleled in Comte's reformulation of the Enlightenment typology into the theological (savage and barbarian), metaphysical (civilised), and positive or industrial (commercial) stages. Spencer saw the sexual division of labour, found in 'barbarous' tribes, evolving into the more complex class and political divisions that allowed other specialised social institutions to develop. Later approaches recast the distinction between savage and barbarian societies in more neutral terms as that between 'band' and 'tribal' societies. Parsons (1966) saw primitive band societies as developing into 'intermediate' (civilised) societies in which differentiated political tasks emerge, forms of stratification appear, and a move towards a differentiation of economic activities begins. Hobhouse (1924) had seen a transition from early 'civilised' societies and empires with 'authoritarian' states to modern societies with more egalitarian 'civic' states. In a similar vein, Lenski (1966) set out a four-stage account in which hunting and gathering societies are seen as developing into horticultural societies, agrarian societies, and then industrial societies. Spencer combined his own account of social development with a more refined but more abstract typology of structural forms. The differentiation of social institutions, he argued, followed a sequence from simple, through compound and doubly compound, to trebly compound societies. The trebly compound societies were the most complex yet achieved, and included the 'militant' empires of Mexico, Egypt, and Rome as well as the modern 'industrial' societies.

The various types of human society, then, have been seen as forming a historical sequence rather than a mere classification. The historical sequence is seen as one of higher or lower stages of development, as measured by particular structural criteria: societies are advanced or less developed, simple or complex, and so on. This assumption makes social change cumulative and, therefore, directional. Human societies develop through a succession of societal types in which their structural properties alter progressively. Thus, a social system, or one of its parts, can become larger, more differentiated, more complex, more individualised, and so forth.

The most contentious aspect of many developmental theories has been the application of a moral judgement to this structural alteration from lower to higher states. This led to the equating of change with 'progress'. Thus, changes in a system property may be equated with increases in human happiness or welfare. Conversely, a move from a higher to a lower state may be seen as moral decline or 'degeneration'. The strongest forms of such theories are those that take a 'teleological' form by assigning primary causal significance to internal mechanisms directed towards the future, the strongest of these teleological theories positing an ultimate 'goal' or end-state towards which the social process must inexorably move. Classical theories of progress saw development as an inexorable teleological movement towards moral improvement. However, both the teleology and the moral judgements are highly contestable, and the idea of development is not tied to such strong ideas of the inevitability of moral progress.

Evolutionary and cyclical theories have largely worked with endogenous models of change. Their strength has been a recognition of the ways in which endogenous processes within a system are able, via adaptation, to generate structured processes of directional change. While many theories of evolution have been unilinear, deterministic, and progressive, a growing awareness of the logical and moral problems of these theories has led to a reformulation of some of the key assumptions of evolutionism to produce more refined theories of development.

Evolutionary theorising established the view that human history exhibits recognisable phases of directional change in the structural parameters and modes of action characterising social systems. These phases are not fixed 'stages' but periods of linear advance and reversal, punctuated by perturbations, cyclical movements, and periodic disruptions operating over greater or lesser lengths of time and unevenly spread across the social system. It is these myriad movements that give the history of any particular society its shape and direction. Taken together, the directional movements of each society comprise the overall directional movement of human society as a whole. The widely recognised movement from 'primitive' to 'modern' (and 'post-modern') societies at a global scale is the outcome of such processes operating over many millennia. It is clear from the various refinements made to evolutionary theory that these can no longer be seen as fixed stages in a continuous and inexorable global movement of growth or advance – no more can it be seen as a sign of continuous moral progress. If history is not mere contingency, then nor can it be a simple expression of the necessary unfolding of endogenous mechanisms. It is in the work of those who have stressed exogenous factors that there can be found a way to refine the evolutionary account into a more adequate developmental theory.

Conflict, diffusion, and path dependence

Critics of evolutionism have held that while each society occupies a specific environment to which it must adapt, there is no unique way in which this adaptation must occur and so variant forms are to be anticipated. In technologically advanced societies there is likely to be considerable autonomy from the natural, ecological environment that makes possible a huge variety of cultural forms. Discussion of the limitations inherent in any explanation concerned solely with endogenous mechanisms of change has highlighted two sets of causal factors as necessary for any more comprehensive theory. Some theorists have highlighted the importance of the conscious and deliberate action of collective agencies and their struggles as the means through which endogenous conditions make themselves felt and have their effects. Other theorists have emphasised the importance of the exogenous factors of conquest, migration, and cultural diffusion and have often also depicted collective agencies as central to these processes (Ogburn 1922: 88–9).

The importance of cultural diffusion and the migration of populations was recognised by Perry (1924) in Britain and Danilevsky (1869) in Russia and was central to a number of popular accounts of social development (e.g., Peake and Fleure 1927–56). They have remained a central feature of contemporary studies (e.g., Renfrew 1987). That the migration of populations shades over into inter-societal conflict and conquest was recognised by those such as Gumplowicz (1883), Oppenheimer (1914), and Toynbee (1934–9). These arguments, too, have been carried forward in a number of contemporary forms (Rüstow 1950–7; Mann 1986; 1993; Huntington 1996). In these theories, individuals and the groups of which they are members are seen as the carriers of ideas from one population to another, so introducing innovative and alien practices that may prove adaptive or cause a society to move in a direction other than that implied by its endogenous conditions – though these conditions will, nevertheless, set limits to the possibilities for change. Such change may, therefore, be the result of a gradual and peaceful 'infiltration' of a society that comes to accept, absorb, or modify the cultural innovations. It may also, however, result from conflict and conquest, especially where large-scale migration encounters opposition. The forcible incorporation of new groups or the replacement of one dominant group by another may result in more radical, and more sudden, structural transformations.

Under these circumstances, cultural variations, inherited structures and practices, and pressures posed by neighbouring societies are able to have a relatively much greater influence on the direction of social development. Parsons (1966; 1971) himself held that general tendencies towards increasing 'adaptive capacity' result from the interplay between environmental conditions and cultural influences. On this basis, Parsons had argued that modern societies developed only in the West because of the specific cultural context provided by Christianity and, in particular, the Protestant reformation. Parsons allied this argument with a recognition of the importance of diffusion, conquest, and domination. Indeed, he argued that key innovations and preconditions for overall developmental change originate in specific 'seedbed' societies and then diffuse directly and through their consequences across other societies that therefore acquire the potential to modernise. For Western societies, Greece and Rome provided such seedbed conditions (Parsons 1971: ch. 3). The decline and fall of the Roman Empire did not result in the complete disappearance of all the achievements of Graeco-Roman civilisation, as these were rediscovered by the Renaissance and Enlightenment thinkers whose influence on European societies renewed long-term cultural development. Transmission and learning from one society to another, whether peaceful or forceful, allows later societies to build on the achievements of earlier ones.

This recognition of the importance of exogenous influences was strongly furthered by the work of the Annales school of historical writers and their growing influence. Formed by Lucien Febvre (1922) and Marc Bloch (1923) to build on the historical ideas of François Simiand and the environmental theories of Vidal de la Blache (1922), the key substantive works of the Annales theorists were those of Fernand Braudel (1949; 1967) on the development of the capitalist world in the Mediterranean, and Immanuel Wallerstein (1974; 1980; 1989) on the formation of the modern world system. Rejecting the unilinear accounts of modernisation found in both evolutionary theories and orthodox Marxism, Wallerstein saw the world system as a complex articulation of often contradictory structural levels that generate the dynamic processes moving individual states and economies within the world system towards modernity. Thus, the dynamics of the structural relations defining core, peripheral, and semi-peripheral locations drive the system towards global capitalist expansion. The modern world system has developed in this specific direction as a result of a particular combination of elements. Conflict among states and other units in a multicentric political structure generated a unique logic of development and precluded the development of the system into a unified political empire.

The recognition of exogenous factors alongside endogenous processes in social development has allowed the construction of more powerful explanatory studies. An adequate view of historical change, however, must combine a recognition of endogenous and exogenous influences with a greater recognition of the role of collective agency set out in Chapter 7. While traditional history has focused almost exclusively on individual agency, much sociology has focused on collective agency as the means through which systemic tendencies of change and external influences may lead to fundamental structural transformations.

The historical sociology derived from certain interpretations of Marx and Weber has, in particular, examined the interplay of individual and collective action with social structure as the basis for explaining long-term developmental processes. While orthodox Marxism relied on a deterministic view of historical change that shared many ideas with evolutionism, academic historians and social scientists have tended to place much greater emphasis on Marx's view of class conflict as the driving force in social change. They have produced more open, voluntaristic accounts in which collective agencies are able to transform social structures from within the given social constraints that define their social locations and standpoints. Starting from Marx's argument that history is made by people under structural conditions that are 'directly encountered, given and transmitted from the past' (Marx 1852: 15), they have showed how the self-conscious and collectively organised agency of those in subordinate class positions has the capacity to transform those structures. This was the means through which Marx thought the contradictions inherent in a particular mode of production and wider social formation could be transformed into a new and radically different mode of production. These themes were elaborated in the works of Moore (1966; see also 1958), Anderson (1974; 1975), and Mann (1986; 1993), all strongly influenced by the Marxist-inspired social history of Edward Thompson (1963) and Moses Finley (1973) and the debates they promoted in the pages of the *New Left Review* and *Past and Present* (e.g., Hilton 1976; Aston and Philpin 1985; Wood 1986).

Weber's starting point in individual action was very different, yet his historical work shared a similar concern for the collective agency of a variety of classes, status groups, and parties. Rejecting evolutionism and deterministic Marxism, he saw such collective entities as the carriers of the religious and political ideas and interests that inform their actions. Some of the most sophisticated writers within the functionalist tradition abandoned Parsons' strong evolutionism and produced accounts of historical change that drew on Weber's historical and comparative sociology to recognise the critical role of conflict and collective agency (Lipset 1963; Eisenstadt 1963; Bendix 1964). Eisenstadt, in particular, has continued to develop powerful studies in historical sociology (see especially Eisenstadt 1987; 1997; 2006). This work echoes earlier ideas in Elias

(1939) and Polanyi (1944) and recognises also the contributions that many Annales school writers made to the analysis of social conflict (see, e.g., Bloch 1938).

These writers take seriously the contingency of events, but within a framework that recognises the causal constraints inherent in systemic processes. Past action choices and their consequences constrain present action alternatives and their consequences in such a way that the knowledge that results from socially structured experiences and that is stored in memories, institutions, and technologies results in specific capacities and dispositions that, in the context of historically derived structures of opportunities, generate patterns of development that are continuous with the trajectory of past development.

This leads to what Sewell has called an 'eventful' model of change (Sewell 2005). While the actions of agents may typically reproduce or slowly transform structures, there are crucial points at which structural change can be initiated. These 'turning points' (the 'catastrophic' states of a system, Thom 1972) are conditions for the occurrence of historical 'events' rather than mere routine 'happenings': they allow actions to make a significant difference to the overall development of a society. Historical transformations are possible when structural temporalities combine in such a way as to bring together the times and rhythms of social and natural processes, as focused through the agency of individuals and, in particular, groups. As Mann shows, the contradictory development of systems of power, combined with the exogenous effects of conquest and transnational economic linkages, generates the space within which agency can make a difference. Explanatory theories are attempts to uncover the salience of the different temporalities in constraining actions.

There is no necessary homology among the various structures of a society and the habituses they produce. Complex and perhaps contradictory combinations of structures and their associated temporal heterogeneity make historically significant events possible. Radical events can occur when contingent factors tip the system into a state in which structural transformation becomes a possibility. Whatever endogenous processes may be at work (and these will invariably be contradictory), historical outcomes are shaped additionally by such contingent events. Developmental outcomes, therefore, are not completely determined, though they are path dependent (Liebowitz and Margolis 1990). Events are the outcomes of the exercise of agency within structural conditions that are themselves the outcome of prior events.

The basis of this reformulation of the idea of development was explored by Elias (1969), who explicitly rejected the view that directional development involves 'inevitability' or historical necessity. His argument was that there can be no grounds for any view that long-term developmental trends will necessarily or automatically continue into the future. A sequence may be predicted to continue, and may actually continue, but there are no causal mechanisms in the social world that could make that continuation a *necessary* consequence of its past pattern. The retrospective examination of a trend may suggest that one set of circumstances, or system 'figuration', was a necessary condition for the development of a subsequent set of circumstances, but a prospective examination cannot show that a future figuration is a necessary consequence of the present one. A future figuration can only ever be *one* of the possible consequences of a previous system state:

From the viewpoint of the earlier figuration, the later is – in most if not all circumstances – only one of several possibilities for change. From the viewpoint of the later figuration, the earlier one is usually a necessary condition for the formation of the later. (Elias 1969: 160)

While any figuration has a potential for change, and for varying kinds of change, figurations that are not completely fixed and rigid (where socialisation is not 'perfect') will exhibit an indeterminacy in the outcome of their processes of change. The purposive actions of agents enter into this as contingent factors, but these actions have unanticipated consequences that vary according to the state of the figuration. Any process of change is a cumulative, incremental process in which the initially open range of possibilities is gradually narrowed down to a single outcome. This is why:

a retrospective developmental investigation can often demonstrate with a high degree of certainty that a figuration had to arise out of a certain earlier figuration or even out of a particular type of sequential series of figurations, but does not assert that the earlier figurations had necessarily to change into the later ones. (Elias 1969: 161, emphasis omitted)

Thus, it is better to talk about varying degrees of probability than of 'inevitability', of stronger or weaker *tendencies* of development that are inherent in the path dependence of social processes.

Social change is a developmental process that exhibits certain structured properties but is always the outcome of human agency occurring under definite and given conditions. Early evolutionary theorists focused their attention on the inherited conditions and their effects on the internal processes of social systems and tended to see development as occurring in a unilinear trajectory. Later evolutionists opened up the idea of development to recognise the multilinearity of social change as a result of historically specific conditions that allow alternative patterns of development within an overall process of adaptation. The potential of this argument was not fully realised, however, until it was recognised that theorists of collective agency had pointed to the crucial mechanism through which structural constraints and environmental conditions are mediated. It is the combination of these ideas that makes possible a comprehensive understanding of social development as an ongoing process of change within systems of action that shape historical trajectories.

10 Conclusion

My argument in this book has been that the diversity in forms of social theorising is a sign of intellectual strength rather than disciplinary failure, and that it can be nurtured and pursued through a cooperative division of labour rather than a contentious struggle for theoretical exclusivity. The diverse principles of sociological analysis highlight distinct and equally significant mechanisms through which descriptions and explanations of social phenomena can be constructed, and any attempt to limit socio- logical attention to just one of these principles can only ever produce a limited and very partial account. Such accounts are, of course, useful and important and are the principal ways in which specialised theories and disciplinary concerns can be pursued. Indeed, some of the most important theoretical advances in sociological understanding have been achieved through such specialisation. To limit ourselves to such one- sided views, however, would be to impoverish the discipline. Analyses based on different principles can complement each other by highlighting important social processes that have been neglected or marginalised and by suggesting a larger context within which specialised accounts can be placed. A social science that excludes certain principles of analysis is unlikely to prosper in the long term. A social science that is inclusive and cooperative is richer and is likely to prove more productive and to garner wider respect for its work.

Not all of the principles of analysis proposed by sociologists are worthy of perpetuation. Some have proved to be intellectual dead-ends or have been shown to be without foundation. The attempt to base sociological analysis on the biology of racial difference, for example, has foundered on its misunderstanding and misrepresentation of biological difference and on its failure to assign any explanatory significance to non-biological factors. Some principles are highly specific and have a greater relevance to some phenomena than to others, and their generality may, indeed, be questioned. Ideas of stigmatisation, maximisation, exploitation, citizen- ship, and patriarchy are examples of principles that are too specific to form major foci of intellectual cooperation at a disciplinary level. They find their place, rather, within the intellectual space created by broader principles and within the specific theories constructed through their use. It is the broad principles of sociological analysis on which I have focused my attention and that I claim to be able to sustain a cohesive disciplinary conspectus and foundation for social science.

The eight principles that I have identified are culture, nature, system, space-time, structure, action, mind, and development, and a strong case can be made for seeing these as having been the principal foci of sociological work and the best bases for a cooperative division of labour.

Humans are formed into specifically social beings through a process of cultivation or enculturation. Human populations sustain a pool of shared meanings, held in and reproduced through linguistic and other signs, and each individual must learn to use these meanings if he or she is to act socially as a participant in that population. Individuals are not born social but must be socialised. Cultures differ from one population to another and it is through socialisation into a particular culture, and its constituent subcultures, that people are socially constructed as members of particular societies or social groups. Cultures tend to be internally diverse, their fluid boundaries marked by gender, class, regional, and other differences. Cultural meanings interpenetrate to form intersecting spheres of meaning along inter-class, transnational, and similar frontiers of intercommunication. Such cultural spheres are more or less focused around core concerns or cross-cutting values, and the degree of integration among its relatively autonomous elements is an important determinant of the social constructions that characterise any particular society.

If individuals must be socialised, this is because they are born as biological organisms without in-built cultural knowledge. Such individuals must not only learn their culture, however, they must continue to relate biologically to the physical and chemical environment in which they live. Culture, then, co-exists with nature – with the materiality of the body and the environment – the interplay of the two producing socialised beings. Human beings are born with specific biological properties and capacities that both constrain and enable their participation in social groups. As biological organisms, they must eat, sleep, and shelter, and so must engage with an environment that conditions their ability to do so and brings about an adaptation of all surviving populations to their environments. The cultural formation of human beings as social agents is conditioned by these biological requirements. The geological distribution of the minerals that humans use as resources, the botanical distribution of the plants and animals that are used for food and as sources of energy, and the global pattern of climate and its associated weather systems underpin the habitats that people are able to form into places in which to live. Technologies of production, defence, communication, etc., are culturally formed objects that extend individual capacities and enhance the collective powers of human populations. They may allow people to adapt to a wide range of environments and may even develop to the point at which they seem to liberate people from their own nature. Technologies may, however, have paradoxical effects if their mastery of the environment and the body overextends human influence and generates climate change, genetic disruption, resource depletion, and other 'natural' disasters. If environmental adaptation depends on cultural knowledge and the technologies it nurtures, then it is equally the case that cultural liberation from nature cannot persist if environmental conditions and bodily requirements are disregarded by the technologies used by socialised agents. Cultural control through the social organisation of information cannot be understood in isolation from the natural conditions that underpin the energies and capacities of human populations.

Culturally formed human populations under definite material conditions must be understood in system terms: as geo-systems, organic systems, and human systems. Human systems have many characteristics in common with the systems of nature and similar principles of interdependence, function, and self-regulation are in operation. Cultural spheres of meaning, for example, comprise interdependent systems of signs and representations that allow human communication to channel a flow of information through which social relations and social groups are able to function in particular ways and so to produce the positive and negative feedback that results in social reproduction and transformation. Such cybernetic processes depend upon the cultural characteristics of human populations and allow human agents to build socially organised systems of action and to develop their mental capacities as the psychological systems of the personality. Human systems, therefore, include cultural, social, and personality systems.

The systemic processes through which culture and nature are mediated occur in space and time. Space-time is a fundamental feature of all human existence and experience. Space and time are connected categories of understanding through which human existence in the world is organised. Knowledge of the material world and of human phenomena is to be understood as the extension and duration of systems that can, therefore, be characterised by their spatial form and temporal change. Social phenomena exist only as spatio-temporal phenomena and no analysis of the human world can ignore the multiple and intersecting levels of space and time that organise human existence.

Social structures are spatially extended and temporally enduring systems of institutions and relations. The institutional aspect of social structure comprises the established and enduring normative expectations through which individuals organise their own actions and seek to control the actions of others. Through a reciprocity and complementarity of expectations, anticipated courses of action are institutionalised as sanctioned forms of behaviour imputed to specific positions and as defining the roles expected of their occupants. In creatively enacting their roles, people produce the more or less stable and enduring practices that comprise the relational aspect of social structure. Individuals come to be related in patterns of interdependence and causal influence. In some situations there is a close correspondence between institutional and relational structure, but the creative interpretation of the cultural scripts attached to roles ensures that the two aspects of social structure are able to vary independently and there may be various forms of incompatibility or contradiction between institutional and relational structures. Each aspect of social structure is, in turn, subject to processes that can produce varying degrees of integration, structural autonomy, and contradiction. Social structures are complex combinations of institutions and relations that exhibit the particular spatial and temporal regularities that constitute them as enduring systems.

Social structures are produced and transformed in and through social action. They have properties distinct from those of individual agents, but they cannot be understood apart from the actions of those agents. Actions are purposive in relation to the desires and circumstances of the individual agents, taking a means-ends form. They can, therefore, be seen as comprising a strategic choice of means relative to given commitments. Concrete courses of action necessarily combine strategic and committed aspects, but strategic and committed actions can be considered as two polar types of action that systematise these aspects of action. Strategic action involves an instrumental orientation towards the means and resources required in order to pursue specific goals. Such 'rational' choices are embedded within a broader pattern of cultural value commitments that inform those patterns of committed action in which general commitments are directly expressed without specific regard for their strategic significance. It is through individual actions that social structures and collective agencies are built, often as unintended consequences of actions that, nevertheless, contribute to equilibrium and change in the structural features of a system. The collective agency of groups, organisations, and social movements is especially important in driving change in their social and cultural systems and in exerting pressures to change in those other systems on which they impinge.

The subjectivity of socialised agents is a crucial factor in the patterning of social actions. The human mind is culturally formed and is the means through which cultural meanings are stored for communication to other minds as a process of cultural transmission. The instinctual drives and dispositions of individuals, considered as organisms, are constructed and channelled into subjectivity through a transformation of the nerve connections and memory receptors brought about through recurring experiences and reinforced behaviour. As unconscious forces they influence the conscious reflection and deliberation that informs purposive action and can have a direct – but often unacknowledged – effect on individual behaviour. Reflexivity and conscious, strategic planning enter into the temporal articulation of action with structure, though structures also depend upon the unconscious dispositions produced and expressed in committed actions. Conscious and unconscious mentality develops over the course of the individual life from infancy to old age, though crucial developmental phases are those of infancy and childhood when biological maturation produces the conditions under which particular forms of socialisation can be effective. The subjective sense of self and social identity and the ability to use language as a mechanism of socialisation and cultural transmission result from the interplay of culture and nature in individual bodies.

The development of personality systems is paralleled by the development of social and cultural systems. These systems undergo structured processes of change when endogenous mechanisms produce strains and tensions that predispose individuals and groups to change the way they behave in order to resolve these strains and tensions. Tendencies towards structural change are furthered by externally induced forces of cultural diffusion, migration, and conquest. As a result of the interplay of endogenous and exogenous forces, social change exhibits a direction of change, though not the inexorable unfolding of pre-given tendencies that figured in classical evolutionism. Development can be uneven and irregular, showing reversals and stoppages as well as ongoing 'progressive' movement. While the direction of change appears in retrospect to be a necessary outcome of pre-existing social forces, the creativity of individual and collective actions will always ensure that its outcome is, to a greater or lesser degree, contingent on the particular circumstances, natural and cultural, facing human agents.

Culture, nature, system, space-time, structure, action, mind, and development are the core ideas that I see as comprising the principles of sociological analysis and as the basis of an intellectual division of labour that defines sociology as a discipline. At this disciplinary level they are all equally important, though their actual explanatory significance will vary from one situation to another. Thus, the question of whether the spirit of capitalism is better explained by a Protestant ethic or a structure of economic relations is an empirical question and not one that can be resolved on the basis of purely theoretical considerations. If sociology is to develop – as I believe it should – as a coordinated and cooperative intellectual venture, then those who see themselves as adherents of one perspective must recognise and respect the work of those who ally themselves with other theoretical perspectives. This does not mean that all their arguments must be accepted as equally valid. The mere fact that, say, cultural factors prove to be especially important in the explanation of one situation or for one particular explanatory purpose tells us nothing directly about its relative importance in other situations or for other purposes. Acceptance of the coordinated pursuit of all eight principles in a disciplinary division of labour is quite separate from the assessment of specific descriptions and explanations for their empirical validity.

The division of labour that I propose goes beyond sociology to the wider social sciences. While sociology as a discipline must be concerned with all eight principles, various other disciplines concerned with social matters have contributed to the developing framework of social theory and have been drawn on within this book. Some social science disciplines have developed around specific principles or aspects of these that are seen as especially relevant for their objects of analysis: economics has focused on strategic action, cultural studies and linguistics on culture, geography on environment and space, history on time and development, and social psychology on mind. Economics has tended to concern itself with strategic actions, especially in so far as these are concerned with adaptation to the material environment through processes of production, distribution, and consumption. These are, of course, oversimplifications. There is no neat and coherent intellectual mapping of intellectual issues onto disciplinary concerns. Economists have generalised these concerns into theories of rational choice that have been seen as having a general significance and, in many cases, an exclusive validity in social affairs. Their theories have been exported to other disciplines and have been taken up with great enthusiasm. This has particularly been the case in political science, but rational choice theories have also found a welcome reception in criminology and in a number of subdivisions within sociology. Disciplinary boundaries are historically contingent processes of professional and political conflict.

In an absolute sense, I would argue, there is no real distinction to be made between, for example, economics, political science, the sociology of religion, and the sociology of the mass media in terms of intellectual logic. Their substantive objects differ, but in so far as they are concerned with social phenomena they must all draw on the eight principles that I have outlined here. Each may, nevertheless, maintain a degree of distinctiveness. What has distinguished economics, for example, is the narrowing of its disciplinary concerns to theories of rational choice and system equilibrium, leaving the use of most other principles in the understanding of economic phenomena to economic sociology and to business and management studies. This narrowing of disciplinary concerns, however, has led to many advances in the understanding of strategic action, and these must figure in any general account of social theory. What must also be recognised, however, is that economics has also been limited by its narrowed focus and could benefit considerably from greater cooperation with other social scientists.

The relationship between sociology and geography is complex. For much of their early history they competed for the status of the general social science, though the close links between human geography and physical geography meant that the natural environment provided a dominant explanatory principle in geography for much of its history. It developed specialisms that paralleled those in sociology (economic, political, medical, urban, and so forth), treating each of these from the standpoint of the naturally grounded habitats or regions within which they could be located. From the middle of the twentieth century, this focus on the natural environment was virtually replaced by a concern for space and especially for the formal properties of the spatial distribution of human phenomena. Geography has subsequently come to draw more widely on the theories of structure and action produced by sociologists and economists and it has become increasingly difficult to distinguish studies in sociology from those in geography. This has ensured that both geographers and sociologists have been able to contribute to the development of the social theory that I have outlined here.

A final case to consider is history. This is a discipline concerned with social change and with the development of societies over time. However, its practitioners have often pursued these concerns in a less theoretical way than have sociologists. The differences between history and sociology in their approaches to the past have often been exaggerated – and by those on both sides of the disciplinary divide – yet they have much to offer to each other. History has, indeed, taken a more theoretical direction in recent work and has borrowed theoretical ideas from both sociology and geography. As a result, the work of historians has contributed to the clarification of issues in social theory and they should be seen as participants (reluctant participants still in some cases) in the intellectual division of labour that I have advocated.

Sociology does, however, have a special place within the social sciences. It is the only discipline that has consistently sought to maintain a concern for the social as its broad disciplinary focus. The social has been variously understood, as I have shown in this book, but a discipline that takes seriously the principles of sociological analysis and seeks to maintain them through a division of labour and through interdisciplinary collaboration with other social sciences is crucial for the survival of all specialised social sciences and humanities that draw upon one or more of the eight principles. Their interdependence can be recognised and furthered only by a discipline that makes this theoretical work its central concern. This aspiration was central to the founding statements of sociology and I have sought to show that we can and must continue to sustain it as a precondition for theoretical advance and for fruitful theoretical innovation and diversity.

Notes

NOTES TO CHAPTER 1

1 The most notable and systematic example of this view remains that of Marsland (1988).
2 This is often seen, incorrectly, as being justified by the arguments of Becker (1967).

NOTES TO CHAPTER 2

1 On the history of the concept see Williams (1958; 1976).
2 This echoed earlier Greek ideas of *paideia*.
3 Contemporary British writers such as Buckle (1857–61) and Lubbock (1870) used the word 'civilised' in the same sense.
4 At more or less the same time, the Turkish nationalist Gökalp was formulating a similar idea as the basis of the 'spirit of the nation' (Gökalp 1913: 91).
5 As late as the 1920s Freyer (1924) was using the Hegelian terms 'objective spirit' or 'objective mind' as synonyms for culture. Spengler (1918–22), Oppenheimer (1922), and Alfred Weber (1920–1) preferred the word culture, though all contrasted the 'spiritual' aspects of culture with the practical and technical aspects of 'civilisation' (see also Elias 1939: I, ch. 1).
6 White's book consists of essays published between 1938 and 1948.
7 Archer tends to see the established logical principles as 'invariant' aspects of human thought and consciousness, but this is not essential to her more general argument.
8 This is central to the view of Kuhn (1962) on the role of scientific frameworks and paradigms in scientific discovery.
9 This point is further considered in Chapter 8.
10 Vygotsky (1934) showed that thought develops in children only because of their prior internalisation of speech. This point is developed in Chapter 8.
11 This distinction between the diachronic and the synchronic is a direct echo of Comte's division of social theory into 'dynamics' and 'statics'.
12 Saussure used the word 'language' (*langage*) to refer to both synchronic tongue and diachronic speech, though translators have generally confused this distinction by translating both *langage* and *langue* as 'language'.

13 The term *masse parlante* has normally been translated as 'community of speakers', but this implies a greater degree of social solidarity than may generally be the case.

14 In the terminology that Morris (1964) derives from Peirce, the signified is termed the 'significatum'.

15 As Leach (1970: 60) pointed out, this strategy resembles that of Frazer (1890) in *The Golden Bough*.

16 This view of coding is paralleled in Goffman's (1974) frame analysis.

17 Goldmann's (1956) term is 'potential consciousness'.

18 There are, of course, wider epistemological questions about the ultimate 'truth' contained in particular worldviews, but these need not be considered here. Some discussion will be found in Scott (1998) and Letherby *et al.* (2011).

NOTES TO CHAPTER 3

1 The world, also, of course, reflects the activities of other animals and, to the extent that they are sentient, it will reflect their mental activity too.

2 The effects of variation in light and heat were taken up in physiological psychology and especially in the industrial psychology of Myers (see Rose 1975) where explorations into the effects of artificial modifications of natural light formed the first stage of the Hawthorne experiments (Roethlisberger and Dickson 1939).

3 Cohen has argued that, in a strict sense, the productive forces do not comprise a part of the 'economy' (Cohen 1978: 28–9) on the grounds that the economy comprises 'relations' and so the productive forces must lie outside the economy. The forces are the conditions on which the economy stands, but they are not themselves part of the economy.

4 The Affluent Worker study (Goldthorpe *et al.* 1969), for example, was an investigation of Luton.

5 Real name Charles-Edouard Jeanneret-Gris.

6 This summary discussion draws on Jones (1993) and Dawkins (1986).

7 Genetic technologies have now begun to develop techniques for the direct implantation of genetic variants in host organisms but this has not yet reached the point at which the overwhelming importance of sexual reproduction must be questioned.

8 Marx's somewhat chaotic emphases (by underlining) have been ignored in this quotation.

9 A version of this argument was adopted in the work of Herder (1770).

10 This is the reason why Down and others depicted certain forms of learning disability as 'Mongolism'.

11 These are discussed in Chapter 8.

12 This argument was initially developed in his papers of the 1890s and republished in 1903.

13 The discussion in this paragraph draws on Maryanski and Turner (1992: 13, 16–22).

14 For many people there is considerable moral significance about the point at which 'life' begins, and there is hot debate over whether this occurs at the

moment of conception or some weeks later. However morally important this question may be, it is not of direct relevance to the issues discussed here. The existence of the debate, however, highlights the socially constructed nature of 'life'.

NOTES TO CHAPTER 4

1 See the general critical discussion in Sorokin (1928).
2 Engels' *Dialectics of Nature* was written in 1873–6 but published only in 1925. Some parts were used in his *Anti-Dühring* of 1878, where they were modified to recognise certain changes in his views.
3 Helmholtz clarified a conventional distinction between attraction, understood as a 'force', and repulsion, as 'energy'.
4 See the discussion of these ideas in Mirowski (1989: ch. 2).
5 Podolinsky sent his paper to Marx, though the latter did not take up the parallels with his own work.
6 The ideas of Ostwald, along with those of Solvay (1904), were critically considered in M. Weber (1909). See the general discussion of this approach in Martinez-Alier (1987) and Rosa and Machlis (2007).
7 General equilibrium analysis was formalised for use beyond the economic context by James Coleman (1990), who presented economic theories as a special case of his account. See also the overview of economic equilibrium models in Ingrao and Israel (1990).
8 Linear equations take the form $ax = b$ and are distinguished from quadratic and cubic equations. A quadratic equation takes the form $ax^2 + bx + c = 0$, while a cubic equation takes the form $ax^3 + bx^2 + cx = 0$.
9 Pareto himself used the language of 'system' only lightly.
10 A similar method was followed by George Catlin in his equilibrium model of politics in which the supply and demands for government restrictions and the rule of law are balanced (Catlin 1930).
11 See also the later work of Tolman.
12 Buckley (1967: 58) terms this 'morphostasis'.
13 Cannon (1932: 314 ff) gave a fairly crude outline of a sociology.
14 The fundamental elements, termed 'analytical elements', are the variables, described as the 'dynamically variable elements' of the system (Parsons 1945: 217).
15 In terms of the argument developed later, functions and dysfunctions are, respectively, the negative and positive effects of feedback.
16 The general logic of this form of cybernetic explanation has been explored through various applications in the work of Buckley (1967). See also Collins (2004).
17 Parsons' own recognition of the importance of strains in actual systems can be found in his paradigm for social change (Parsons 1961b: 196).
18 His most systematic discussion of the effects of other societies was in relation to the cultural system, where he recognised the trans-societal influence of Graeco-Roman and Hebrew cultural ideas as 'seedbed' influences on European cultural development.

NOTES TO CHAPTER 5

1 See the review of changing conceptions of time and space in Kern (1983).
2 See the arguments in Barabási (2002) on this point.
3 Such arrangements can be mapped through the construction of input-output tables.
4 I am grateful to Ewa Morawska for comments on an earlier draft of this chapter.
5 This is, I think, the nub of the definition of time given by Gurvitch (1963): the 'convergent and divergent movements which persist in a discontinuous succession and change in a continuity of heterogenous movements' (*ibid.*: 18).
6 McTaggart (1908) referred to this as the 'B-series' concept of time.
7 This is what McTaggart (1908) referred to as 'A-series' time.
8 As noted in Chapter 3, the term 'geographical' must be used with some reservations as humans exist, strictly, at an astronomical level.

NOTES TO CHAPTER 6

1 The primary influence on Bhaskar's transcendental or 'critical realism', however, is the realism of Harré (1961; 1964; Harré and Madden 1975), though Harré himself remains a resolute methodological individualist.
2 In the Preface to the Second Edition of *The Rules*, Durkheim misleadingly adopts the term 'institution' as an equivalent to social fact, understanding this to refer to 'all beliefs and modes of behaviour instituted by the collectivity' (Durkheim 1901: 45).
3 Marx was influenced by work undertaken by von Stein in the 1840s and consolidated into von Stein's later book on the social movement (von Stein 1850). Marx identified parallels with the insights of Feuerbach (1841).
4 For a recent general discussion of norms see the contributions in Hechter and Opps (2001).
5 Davis (1948) distinguishes 'enacted law' from customary law, where formal sanctions are attached to folkways and mores.
6 Gellner (1962) argued that this is insufficient: in order to understand a society, he argues, it is also necessary to understand the working of the concepts that form its institutions.
7 White (1992) has introduced the term 'netdom' to emphasise that the networks of expectations defining a role set must also be considered as a domain of narrative meanings through which people account for behaviour.
8 This topic is more fully discussed in Chapter 7.
9 Somewhat misleadingly, Nadel (1951: 107) makes the point that social structure exists in 'the non-spatial and in a sense timeless validity of concepts', using space and time in their exclusively material sense.
10 Blau, like Coser, studied for his doctorate at Columbia University, where Giddings had pioneered the use of relational ideas.
11 Spencer, disregarding the moral element in social solidarity, referred to the integration achieved through contractual interdependence as 'industrial solidarity'.

12 The naturalistic aspects of this argument are considered in Chapter 3, and I am here concerned with his particular arguments about the relative autonomy of relational structures from institutional structures.

NOTES TO CHAPTER 7

1 Rex was the key figure through his influence on Dawe, who worked closely with Atkinson at the LSE from 1963.
2 Useful, sometimes critical, discussions of the action frame of reference are those of Bierstedt (1938) and Hinckle (1963).
3 As shown in Chapter 2, these norms are shared with other agents but 'can be conceived of as "existing" only in the mind of the actor' (Parsons 1937: 733).
4 Parsons was here reflecting a long tradition in social psychology in which Brentano (1874: ch. 5) had distinguished between ideas, feelings, and desires, and Wundt (1912) had distinguished the cognitive, feeling or drive, and will or valuation aspects of action (see also Jahoda 1992: ch. 11).
5 Compare the views of Kuhn (1962) on scientific paradigms and the analyses of Simmel (1916) and Lukàcs (1910) on artistic forms.
6 Collins's discussion of committed action concentrates on its routinised, habitual forms, which he describes as 'ritual action'.
7 Though Granovetter's view of embeddedness was presented as a critique of the Parsonian view of action, it is compatible with Parsons' view in so far as it focuses on the varying degrees of differentiation of rational action from the environing communal structures.
8 Parsons' (1963a; 1968a) discussions of influence and commitment can, perhaps, be seen as elaborations of ideas concerning forms of social approval, as can Luhmann's (1982) discussion of love.
9 At the 1971 BSA conference Howard Becker gave a plenary address (Becker 1972), his first in the United Kingdom. Those in the audience who knew him from his published work were surprised by his youthful appearance: long hair, beard, denim jeans, and tall boots. They had expected to see a grey, balding, and bespectacled professor. One prominent criminologist joked to another: 'Perhaps he sent his son to deliver the paper' (personal observation).
10 See also Erikson (1966), Scheff (1966), and Cicourel (1967).
11 An interesting discussion is that of Chayko (2002), though she restricts the term 'sociomental connections' to mediated communications and underplays the fact that direct relations are also sociomental.
12 See also Rüstow (1950–7).
13 As translated in Wolff (1950: 10).
14 And see the general argument on economic interest and the effort bargain in Baldamus (1961).

NOTES TO CHAPTER 8

1 See the discussion in Rylance (2000).

2 This is found in Parsons, too, but Parsons' theory of socialisation did try to take account of Freudian arguments (see Parsons 1964a).

3 It is, of course, highly misleading to use the term 'designed', as no conscious designer is required (Dawkins 1986).

4 Rose (2005: 115) makes the important point that modules need not be purely innate but can develop as specialised systems through experience.

5 See the discussion in Jones (1980: ch. 7).

6 This view underwrites the view of strategic action set out in Chapter 7.

7 McDougall argued that instincts vary in strength with the sexual and racial constitution of the individual and, in common with many of his contemporaries, he adopted a biological definition of race that went beyond skin colour and other superficial characteristics and that would now be rejected.

8 Freud based his account of instinctive drives on a model of the flow of psychical energy, where mainstream instinct theory stressed the evolutionary origins of instincts. Bowlby (1969–80: vol. 1) has attempted to reconcile these two arguments with a recognition of the evolutionary origins of instinctive energy. Where Freud saw social bonds as direct expressions of physiological needs, Bowlby stressed that needs can have such effects only through the formation of behavioural systems oriented to their satisfaction.

9 Branford (1913) referred to this as 'conversion'.

10 See also Fordham (1953: 23–4) and Stevens (2002).

11 Kagan (1981) holds that a sense of the autobiographical self emerges from around the age of eighteen months.

12 The role of autobiographical memory in the construction of the self is discussed in Draaisma (2001) and Conway (1990).

13 Blumer's book (1987) was left unpublished at the time of his death. Charon (2001) has argued that Mead, like Freud, conflated the 'I' as the actor with the 'I' as an aspect of the self, leading him to restrict the 'I' to the idea of agency. The position that I have set out here would seem to resolve that problem.

14 A critical discussion on these ideas can be followed through Lefebvre (1934), Rudé (1959; 1964), and Canetti (1960).

15 Not the least problem is his assumption that young girls all have an accurate knowledge of male anatomy, something that is least likely in precisely the kinds of middle-class families with which he was mainly concerned.

16 This underlines the points made above about dream experiences and their subsequent waking reconstruction as narratives.

17 See Gilligan (1982) for an elaboration on this point in relation to the specific features of moral development in girls.

References

Abbott, Andrew 1994. 'Temporality and Process in Social Life' in A. Abbott (ed.), *Time Matters: On Theory and Method*. Chicago: University of Chicago Press, 2001

Aberle, David F., Cohen, Albert K., Davis, Alison K., Levy, Marion J., and Sutton, Francis X. 1950. 'The Functional Prerequisites of a Society'. *Ethics* 60: 100–11

Ackroyd, Stephen C. 1974. 'Economic Rationality and the Relevance of Weberian Sociology to Industrial Relations'. *British Journal of Industrial Relations* 12: 236–48

1976. 'Sociological Theory and the Human Relations School'. *Sociology of Work and Occupations* 3, 4: 379–410

Addams, Jane 1895. *Hull-House Maps and Papers*. New York: Thomas Y. Crowell

1910. *The Spirit of Youth and the City Streets*. London: Macmillan

Adler, Alfred 1914. 'Individual Psychology, its Assumptions and its Results' in A. Adler (ed.), *The Practice and Theory of Individual Psychology*. London: Routledge and Kegan Paul, 1923

1928. *Understanding Human Nature*. London: George Allen and Unwin

Agassiz, Louis 1869. *Essay on Classification*. Cambridge: Cambridge University Press, 1962

Alexander, Jeffrey 1982–3. *Theoretical Logic in Sociology*. Berkeley: University of California Press

1988. *Action and its Environments*. New York: Columbia University Press

Alexander, Jeffrey (ed.) 1985. *Neofunctionalism*. Beverley Hills: Sage

Althusser, Louis 1962. 'Contradiction and Overdetermination' in L. Althusser (ed.), *For Marx*. Harmondsworth: Allen Lane

1963. 'On the Materialist Dialectic' in L. Althusser (ed.), *For Marx*. Harmondsworth: Allen Lane

1971. *Lenin and Philosophy and Other Essays*. London: New Left Books

Aminzade, Ronald 1992. 'Historical Sociology and Time'. *Sociological Methods and Research* 20, 4: 456–80

Ammon, Otto 1895. *Die Gesellschaftsordnung und Ihr Natürlichen Grundlagen*. Jena: Gustav Fischer

Anderson, Benedict 1983. *Imagined Communities*. London: Verso

Anderson, Nils 1923. *The Hobo: The Sociology of the Homeless Man*. Chicago: University of Chicago Press

Anderson, Perry 1974. *Lineages of the Absolutist State*. London: New Left Books

281

1975. *Passages from Antiquity to Feudalism*. London: New Left Books

Anthony, David W. 2006. *The Horse, the Wheel, and Language: How Bronze-Age Riders from the Eurasian Steppes Shaped the Modern World*. Princeton: Princeton University Press

Arber, Sara, Davidson, Kate, and Ginn, Jay (eds.) 2003. *Gender and Ageing: Changing Roles and Relationships*. Maidenhead: Open University Press

Archer, Margaret S. 1988. *Culture and Agency*. Cambridge: Cambridge University Press

   1995. *Realist Social Theory: The Morphogenetic Approach*. Cambridge: Cambridge University Press

   2003. *Structure, Agency and the Internal Conversation*. Cambridge: Cambridge University Press

   2007. *Making Our Way Through the World: Human Reflexivity and Social Mobility*. Cambridge: Cambridge University Press

Ardrey, Robert 1961. *African Genesis*. London: Collins

   1967. *The Territorial Imperative*. London: Collins

   1970. *The Social Contract*. London: Collins

Arendt, Hannah 1958. *The Human Condition*. Chicago: University of Chicago Press

Ariès, Philippe 1963. *Centuries of Childhood*. New York: Random House, 1965

   1977. *The Hour of Our Death*. New York: Alfred A. Knopf, 1981

Arrow, Kenneth 1951. *Social Choice and Individual Values*. New Haven: Yale University Press

Asch, Solomon E. 1951. 'Effects of Group Pressure upon the Modification and Distortion of Judgement' in H. Guetzkow (ed.), *Groups, Leadership and Men*. Pittsburgh: Carnegie Press

Aserinsky, E. and Kleitman, N. 1953. 'Regularly Occurring Periods of Eye Motility, and Concomitant Phenomena'. *Science* 118: 273–4

Aston, Michael and Bond, James 1976. *The Landscape of Towns*. London: Allen Sutton, 1987

Aston, Trevor H. and Philpin, C. H. E. (eds.) 1985. *The Brenner Debate: Agrarian Class Structure and Economic Development in Pre-industrial Europe*. Cambridge: Cambridge University Press

Atkinson, Dick 1971. *Orthodox Consensus and Radical Alternative*. London: Heinemann

Augé, Marc 1992. *Non-places: Introduction to an Anthropology of Supermodernity*. London: Verso, 1995

Axelrod, Robert 1997. *The Complexity of Cooperation: Agent-Based Models of Competition and Collaboration*. Princeton: Princeton University Press

Bagehot, Walter 1872. *Physics and Politics*. London: Kegan Paul, Trench, Trübner, 1905

Bailey, Frederick George 1969. *Strategems and Spoils*. Boulder: Westview Press

Bain, Alexander 1855. *Treatise on the Mind: The Senses and the Intellect*. Bristol: Thoemmes Press, 1998

   1859. *Treatise on the Mind: The Emotions and the Will*. Bristol: Thoemmes Press, 1998

Baldamus, W. G. 1961. *Efficiency and Effort*. London: Tavistock

Baldwin, James Mark 1893. *The Mental Development of the Child and the Race*. New York: Macmillan

Balkin, Jack M. 1998. *Cultural Software: A Theory of Ideology*. New Haven: Yale University Press

Banton, Michael 1977. *The Idea of Race*. London: Tavistock

1987. *Racial Theories*. Oxford: Oxford University Press

Barabási, Albert-László 2002. *Linked: The New Science of Networks*. Cambridge: Perseus

Barberis, Daniela S. 2003. 'In Search of an Object: Organicist Sociology and the Reality of Society in Fin-de-Siecle France'. *History of the Human Sciences* 16, 3: 51–72

Barbour, Julian 1999. *The End of Time*. London: Weidenfeld and Nicolson

Barnes, Barry 1999. *Understanding Agency: Social Theory and Responsible Action*. London: Sage

Barnes, John A. 1954. 'Class and Committee in a Norwegian Island Parish'. *Human Relations* 7: 39–58

1998. 'Physical and Social Kinship'. *Philosophy of the Social Sciences* 28: 296–9

Barrett, Michele 1980. *Women's Oppression Today*. London: Verso

Barry, Brian 1970. *Sociologists, Economists and Democracy*. London: Collier-Macmillan

Barth, Fredrik 1966. *Models of Social Organization*. London: RAI

Barthes, Roland 1957. *Mythologies*. London: Paladin, 1973

1964. 'Elements of Semiology' in R. Barthes (ed.), *Writing Degree Zero and Elements of Semiology*. Boston: Beacon Press, 1968

Bastian, Adolf 1860. *Der Mensch in Geschichte*. Leipzig.

Bateson, William 1902. *Mendel's Principles of Heredity*. Cambridge: Cambridge University Press

Baudrillard, Jean 1978. *In the Shadow of the Silent Majorities*. New York: Semiotext(e), 1983

1981. *Simulations*. New York: Semiotext(e), 1983

Bauman, Zygmunt 1973. *Culture as Praxis*. London: Routledge and Kegan Paul

1976. *Towards a Critical Sociology*. London: Routledge and Kegan Paul

Beccheria, Cristina 2006. *The Grammar of Society: The Nature and Dynamics of Social Norms*. New York: Cambridge University Press

Beck, Ulrich 1986. *Risk Society: Towards a New Modernity*. London: Sage, 1992

1988. *Ecological Politics in an Age of Risk*. Cambridge: Polity Press, 1995

2006. *Cosmopolitan Vision*. London: Polity Press

Becker, Gary S. 1976. *The Economic Approach to Human Behaviour*. Chicago: University of Chicago Press

Becker, Howard S. 1953. 'Becoming a Marihuana User' in H. S. Becker (ed.), *Outsiders: Studies in the Sociology of Deviance*. Glencoe: Free Press, 1963

1960. 'Notes on the Concept of Commitment' in H. S. Becker (ed.), *Sociological Work*. Chicago: University of Chicago Press, 1970

1963. *Outsiders: Studies in the Sociology of Deviance*. New York: Free Press

1964. *The Other Side: Perspectives on Deviance*. New York: Free Press of Glencoe

1967. 'Whose Side are We On?' in H. S. Becker (ed.), *Sociological Work*. Chicago: Aldine, 1970

1972. 'Labelling Theory Reconsidered' in P. S. Rock and M. McIntosh (eds.), *Deviance and Social Control*. London: Tavistock

Beddoe, John 1862. *The Races of Britain*. London: Renshaw

Bell, Colin and Newby, Howard 1976. *Community Studies*. London: George Allen and Unwin

Bendix, Reinhard 1964. *Nation Building and Citizenship: Studies of Our Changing Social Order*. Berkeley: University of California Press

Benedict, Ruth 1934. *Patterns of Culture*. London: Routledge, 1965

1946. *The Chrysanthemum and the Sword*. London: Routledge and Kegan Paul, 1967

Benjamin, Walter 1940. *Charles Baudelaire: A Lyric Poet in the Era of High Capitalism*. New York: Verso, 1997

Bentham, Jeremy 1789. 'Introduction to the Principles of Morals and Legislation' in W. Harrison (ed.), *A Fragment on Government and an Introduction to the Principles of Morals and Legislation*. Oxford: Basil Blackwell, 1948

Bentley, Arthur F. 1908. *The Process of Government: A Study of Social Pressure*. New Brunswick: Transaction Publishers

Benton, E. 1991. 'Biology and Social Science: Why the Return of the Repressed Should be Given a (Cautious) Welcome'. *Sociology* 26: 225–32

Berger, Peter L. and Kellner, Hansfried 1970. 'Marriage and the Construction of Reality' in H.-P. Dreitzel (ed.), *Recent Sociology, Number 2*. New York: Macmillan

Berger, Peter L. and Luckmann, Thomas 1966. *The Social Construction of Reality*. Harmondsworth: Allen Lane, 1971

Bergson, Henri 1907. *Creative Evolution*. New York: Henry Holt and Co., 1911

Bernard, Claude 1865. *An Introduction to the Study of Experimental Medicine*. London: Macmillan, 1927

Bernard, Louis L. 1925. 'A Classification of Environments'. *American Journal of Sociology* 31, 3: 318–32

Bernstein, Basil 1962. 'Linguistic Codes, Hesitation Phenomena and Intelligence' in B. Bernstein (ed.), *Classes, Codes, and Control, vol. I*. London: Routledge and Kegan Paul, 1971

1971. 'On the Classification and Framing of Educational Knowledge' in B. Bernstein (ed.), *Class, Codes and Control, vol. I*. London: Routledge and Kegan Paul

1996. *Pedagogy, Symbolic Control and Identity*. London: Taylor and Francis

Berry, Brian 1967. *Geography of Market Centres and Retail Distribution*. New Jersey: Prentice-Hall

1976. *Urbanisation and Counter-Urbanisation*. London: Sage

Berry, Brian, Cutler, Irving, Draine, Edwin H., Kiang, Ying-Cheng, Tocalis, Thomas R., and de Vise, Pierre 1976. *Chicago: Transformations of an Urban System*. Cambridge: Ballinger

Bhaskar, Roy 1975. *The Realist Theory of Science*. Leeds: Leeds Books

1979. *The Possibility of Naturalism*. Brighton: Harvester

Bicchieri, Cristian 2006. *The Grammar of Society: The Nature and Dynamics of Social Norms*. New York: Cambridge University Press

Bierstedt, Robert 1938. 'The Means-Ends Scheme in Sociological Theory'. *American Sociological Review* 3: 665–71

Billig, Michael 1995. *Banal Nationalism*. London: Sage

Blackmore, Susan 1999. *The Meme Machine*. Oxford: Oxford University Press

Blakemore, Colin 1988. *The Mind Machine*. London: BBC Publications

Blau, Peter M. 1964. *Exchange and Power in Social LIfe*. New York: John Wiley

1977. *Inequality and Heterogeneity: A Primitive Theory of Social Structure*. New York: Free Press

1994. *Structural Contexts of Opportunities*. Chicago: University of Chicago Press

Blau, Peter M. and Duncan, Otis D. 1967. *The American Occupational Structure*. New York: Wiley

Blau, Peter M. and Schwartz, Joseph E. 1984. *Crosscutting Social Circles: Testing a Macrostructural Theory of Intergroup Relations*. Orlando: Academic Press

Blau, Peter M. and Scott, William R. 1961. *Formal Organizations: A Comparative Approach*. San Francisco: Chandler Publishing

Bloch, Marc 1923. *The Royal Touch: Sacred Monarchy and Scrofula in England and France*. London: Routledge and Kegan Paul

Bloch, Maurice 1938. *Feudal Society*. London: Routledge and Kegan Paul, 1961

Bloor, David 1997. *Wittgenstein, Rules and Institutions*. London: Routledge

Blum, Ken 1992. *Alcohol and the Addictive Brain*. New York: Free Press

Blumenbach, Johann Friedrich 1795. 'On the Natural Variety of Mankind' in T. Bendyshe (ed.), *The Anthropological Treatises of Johann Friedrich Blumenbach*. London: Longman, Green

Blumer, Herbert 1962. 'Society as Symbolic Interaction' in H. Blumer (ed.), *Symbolic Interactionism*. Englewood Cliffs: Prentice-Hall, 1969

1987. *G. H. Mead and Human Conduct*. Walnut Creek: AltaMira Press, 2004

Boas, Franz 1911. *The Mind of Modern Man*. New York: Macmillan

Bogardus, Emory S. 1925. 'Measuring Social Distance'. *Journal of Applied Sociology* 9: 219–308

Bogdanov, Aleksandr 1913–22. 'Tektologia' in P. Dudley (ed.), *Bogdanov's Tektology*. Hull: University of Hull, Centre for System Studies, 1996

Boltanski, Luc and Thévenot, Laurent 1991. *De la justification. Les économies de la grandeur*. Paris: Gallimard

Boorman, Scott A. and White, Harrison C. 1976. 'Social Structure from Multiple Networks: II'. *American Journal of Sociology* 81: 1384–1446

Booth, Charles 1901–2. *Life and Labour of the People of London*. London: Macmillan

Bosanquet, Bernard 1899. *The Philosophical Theory of the State*. London: Macmillan

Bott, Elizabeth 1955. 'Urban Families: Conjugal Roles and Social Networks'. *Human Relations* 8: 345–84

1956. 'Urban Families: The Norms of Conjugal Roles'. *Human Relations* 9: 325–41

Bott, Helen 1928. 'Observation of Play Activities in a Nursery School'. *Genetic Psychology Monographs* 4: 44–8

Boudon, Raymond 1973. *Education, Opportunity and Social Inequality*. New York: Wiley

Bourdieu, Pierre 1972. *Outline of a Theory of Practice*. Cambridge: Cambridge University Press, 1977

  1979. *Distinction: A Social Critique of the Judgment of Taste*. London: Routledge, 1984

  1989. *The State Nobility*. Cambridge: Polity Press, 1998

Bowlby, John 1969–80. *Attachment and Loss*. London: Hogarth Press

Bradley, Francis Herbert 1876. 'My Station and its Duties' in F. H. Bradley (ed.), *Ethical Studies*. New York: Bobbs-Merrill, 1951

  1893. *Appearance and Reality*. London: Macmillan

Branford, Benchara 1916. *Janus and Vesta: A Study of the World Crisis and After*. London: Chatto and Windus

Branford, Victor Verasis 1901. 'On the Calculation of National Resources'. *Journal of the Royal Statistical Society* 64, 3: 380–414

  1913. *St. Columba: A Study of Social Inheritance and Spiritual Development*. Edinburgh: Patrick Geddes and Colleagues

Branford, Victor Verasis and Geddes, Patrick 1919a. *The Coming Polity*. Revised edn. London: Williams and Norgate

  1919b. *Our Social Inheritance*. London: Williams and Norgate

Braudel, Fernand 1949. *The Mediterranean and the Mediterranean World in the Age of Philip II*. London: Collins, 1972–3

  1967. *Capitalism and Material Life, 1400–1800*. London: Weidenfeld and Nicolson, 1973

  1986–7. *The Identity of France*. London: Collins, 1988 and 1990

Brentano, Franz 1874. *Psychology from an Empirical Standpoint*. London: Routledge and Kegan Paul, 1974

Breuer, Josef and Freud, Sigmund 1895. *Studies in Hysteria*. Harmondsworth: Penguin, 1974

Buchanan, Colin 1963. *Traffic in Towns*. London: HMSO

Buckle, H. T. 1857–61. *History of Civilization in England, vol. I*. London: Watts and Co., 1930

Buckley, Walter 1967. *Sociology and Modern Systems Theory*. Englewood Cliffs: Prentice-Hall

Bukharin, Nikolai Ivanovich 1921. *Historical Materialism: A System of Sociology*. New York: International Publishers, 1925

Burckhardt, Jacob 1860. *The Civilisation of the Renaissance in Europe*. Oxford: Phaidon Press, 1944

Burnett, James (Lord Monboddo) 1779. *Ancient Metaphysics, vol. I*. Bristol: Thoemmes Press, 2001

Butler, Josephine 1993. *Bodies That Matter: On the Discursive Limits of 'Sex'*. London: Routledge

Butler, Judith 1990. *Gender Trouble: Feminism and the Subversion of Identity*. London: Routledge

Byrne, David 1998. *Complexity Theory and the Social Sciences*. London: Routledge

Caldwell Cook, Henry 1917. *The Play Way*. London: William Heinemann

Calvin, W. H. 1996. *How Brains Think: Evolving Intelligence, Then and Now.* London: Weidenfeld and Nicolson

Camic, Charles 1986. 'The Matter of Habit'. *American Journal of Sociology* 91: 1039–87

Campbell, Colin 1998. *The Myth of Social Action.* Cambridge: Cambridge University Press

Canetti, Elias 1960. *Crowds and Power.* Harmondsworth: Penguin, 1973

Cannon, Walter Bradford 1932. *The Wisdom of the Body.* New York: W. W. Norton

Carey, Henry C. 1858–9. *The Principles of Social Science.* New York: Augustus M. Kelley, 1963

 1872. *The Unity of Law: As Exhibited in the Relation of Physical, Social, Mental, and Moral Science.* New York: Augustus M. Kelley, 1967

Carpenter, W. B. 1874. *Principles of Mental Physiology.* New York: D. Appleton

Carr-Saunders, Alexander and Caradog Jones, D. 1927. *A Survey of the Social Structure of England and Wales.* Oxford: Oxford University Press

Carter, Bob 2002. 'People Power: Harré and the Myth of Social Structure'. *European Journal of Social Theory* 5, 1: 134–42

Cartwright, D. and Zander, A. (eds.) 1953. *Group Dynamics.* London: Tavistock

Casati, R. and Varzi, A. C. 1999. *Parts and Places: The Structure of Spatial Representation.* Cambridge: MIT Press

Casey, Edward S. 1993. *Getting Back into Place: Toward a Renewed Understanding of the Place World.* Bloomington: Indiana University Press

 1997. *The Fate of Place: A Philosophical History.* Berkeley: University of California Press

Castells, Manuel 1968. 'Is There an Urban Sociology?' in C. G. Pickvance (ed.), *Urban Sociology.* London: Methuen, 1976

 1969. 'Theory and Ideology in Urban Sociology' in C. G. Pickvance (ed.), *Urban Sociology.* London: Methuen, 1976

 1976. 'On the Study of Urban Social Movements' in C. G. Pickvance (ed.), *Urban Sociology.* London: Methuen

Catlin, George E. G. 1930. *A Study of the Principles of Politics.* London: George Allen and Unwin

Catton, W. R. J. and Dunlop, R. E. 1978. 'Environmental Sociology: A New Paradigm'. *American Sociologist* 13, 41–9

Cavan, Ruth Shonle 1928. *Suicide.* Chicago: University of Chicago Press

Caws, P. 1988. *Structuralism.* New Jersey: Humanities Press International

Charon, Joel M. 2001. *Symbolic Interactionism: An Introduction, an Interpretation, an Argument.* 9th edn (1st edn 1979). New Jersey: Prentice-Hall

Chase, Ivan D. 1991. 'Vacancy Chains'. *Annual Review of Sociology* 17: 133–54

Chayko, Mary 2002. *Connections.* Albany: SUNY Press

Chernin, K. 1985. *The Hungry Self: Women, Eating and Identity.* New York: Harper and Row

Chodorow, Nancy 1978. *The Reproduction of Mothering: Psychoanalysis and the Sociology of Gender.* Berkeley: University of California Press

Chomsky, Noam 1980. *Rules and Representations.* New York: Columbia University Press

Christaller, W. 1933. *Central Places in Southern Germany*. New Jersey: Prentice-Hall, 1966

Cicourel, Aaron V. 1967. *The Social Organisation of Juvenile Justice*. New York: Wiley

　1972. 'Interpretive Procedures and Normative Rules in the Negotiation of Status and Role' in A. V. Cicourel (ed.), *Cognitive Sociology*. Harmondsworth: Penguin, 1973

Cicourel, Aaron V. and Kitsuse, John I. 1963. *The Educational Decisionmakers*. New York: Bobbs-Merrill

Clarke, Jon, Hall, Stuart, Jefferson, Tony, and Roberts, B. 1976. 'Subcultures, Cultures and Class' in S. Hall and T. Jefferson (eds.), *Resistance Through Rituals: Youth Subcultures in Post-War Britain*. London: Hutchinson

Clausius, Rudolf 1885. *Über die Energievorräthe der Natur und ihre Verwerthung zum Nutzen des Menschen*. Bonn: Verlag von Max Cohen & Sohn

Clout, Hugh 2003. 'Place Description, Regional Geography and Area Studies' in R. Johnston and M. Williams (eds.), *A Century of British Geography*. Oxford: Oxford University Press

Cloward, R. and Ohlin, Lloyd E. 1960. *Delinquency and Opportunity: A Theory of Delinquent Gangs*. Glencoe: Free Press

Cloward, Richard A. and Piven, Frances Fox 1977. *Poor People's Movements: Why They Succeed, How They Fail*. New York: Pantheon Books

Cohen, Albert K. 1955. *Delinquent Boys: The Culture of the Gang*. London: Routledge and Kegan Paul

Cohen, Anthony P. 1985. *The Symbolic Construction of Community*. London: Taylor and Francis

Cohen, Gerry A. 1978. *Karl Marx's Theory of History*. Oxford: Oxford University Press

Cohen, Percy S. 1968. *Modern Social Theory*. London: Heinemann

Cole, T. 1992. *The Journey of Life: A Cultural History of Ageing*. Cambridge: Cambridge University Press

Coleman, James S. 1990. *Foundations of Social Theory*. Cambridge: Belknap

Coleman, James S., Katz, E., and Menzel, H. 1966. *Medical Innovation: A Diffusion Study*. New York: Bobbs-Merrill

Collier, Andrew 1994. *Critical Realism: An Introduction to Roy Bhaskar's Philosophy*. London: Verso

Collins, Randall 2004. *Interaction Ritual Chains*. Princeton: Princeton University Press

Commons, John R. 1924. *The Legal Foundations of Capitalism*. London: Macmillan

Comte, Auguste 1851–4. *System of Positive Polity*. Bristol: Thoemmes Press, 2001

Conway, M. A. 1990. *Autobiographical Memory*. Milton Keynes: Open University Press

Cooley, Charles Horton 1894. 'The Theory of Transportation'. *American Economic Association Publications* 9, 3: 17–118

　1902. *Human Nature and the Social Order*. New York: Scribner's

　1909. *Social Organisation*. New York: Schocken

Coser, Lewis 1956. *The Functions of Social Conflict*. London: Routledge and Kegan Paul

Cosgrove, Denis 1984. *Social Formation and Symbolic Landscape*. London: Croom Helm

1993. *The Paladian Landscape*. University Park: Penn State University Press

2001. *Apollo's Eye: A Cartographic Genealogy of the Earth in Western Imagination*. Baltimore: Johns Hopkins University Press

Cox, Oliver Cromwell 1948. *Caste, Class, and Race: A Study in Social Dynamics*. New York: Doubleday and Co.

Craib, Ian 1994. *The Importance of Disappointment*. London: Routledge

2001. *Psychoanalysis: A Critical Introduction*. Cambridge: Polity Press

Cressey, Paul G. 1932. *The Taxi-Dance Hall: A Sociological Study in Commercialized Recreation and City Life*. Chicago: University of Chicago Press

Crossley, Nick 2001. *The Social Body: Habit, Identity and Desire*. London: Sage

Cuvier, Georges 1834. *The Animal Kingdom, Arranged in Conformity with its Organization*. London: Whittaker and Co.

Dahl, Robert A. 1958. 'A Critique of the Ruling Elite Model' in J. Scott (ed.), *The Sociology of Elites, vol. I*. Aldershot: Edward Elgar, 1990

1961. *Who Governs?* New Haven: Yale University Press

Dahrendorf, Ralf 1957. *Class and Class Conflict in an Industrial Society*. London: Routledge and Kegan Paul, 1959

1958. 'Homo Sociologicus: On the History, Significance, and Limits of the Category of Social Role' in R. Dahrendorf (ed.), *Essays in the Theory of Society*. London: Routledge and Kegan Paul, 1968

Damaisio, António 1999. *The Feeling of What Happens: Body, Emotion and the Making of Consciousness*. London: Vintage, 2000

Danilevsky, Nikolai 1869. *Rossiya i Evropa*. Moscow: Kniga, 1991

Darby, Clifford 1951. 'The Changing English Landscape'. *Geographical Journal* 117: 377–98

Darwin, Charles 1859. *On the Origin of Species*. Harmondsworth: Penguin, 1968

1871. *The Descent of Man, and Selection in Relation to Sex*. London: John Murray

Davis, Kingsley 1948. *Human Society*. New York: Macmillan

Dawe, Alan 1970. 'The Two Sociologies'. *British Journal of Sociology* 21, 2: 207–18

1979. 'The Sociology of Action' in T. B. Bottomore and R. A. Nisbet (eds.), *The History of Sociological Analysis*. London: Heinemann

Dawkins, Richard 1976. *The Selfish Gene*. Oxford: Oxford University Press

1986. *The Blind Watchmaker*. Harmondsworth: Penguin, 1990

de Beauvoir, Simone 1949. *The Second Sex*. London: Jonathan Cape, 1953

de Gobineau, Arthur 1853. *The Moral and Intellectual Diversity of Races*. New York: Garland, 1984

de Greef, Guillaume 1886–9. *Introduction à la sociologie*. Brussels: G. Mayolez

de Landa, Manuel 1997. *A Thousand Years of Non-Linear History*. New York: Zone Books

2006. *A New Philosophy of Society: Assemblage Theory and Social Complexity.* London: Continuum

de Roberty, Evgeniy Valentinovich 1904. *Nouveau programme de sociologie.* Paris: F. Alcan

Dealey, James Q. and Ward, Lester 1905. *Textbook of Sociology.* New York: Macmillan

Deleuze, Gilles and Gattari, Felix 1972. *Anti-Oedipus: Capitalism and Schizophrenia.* New York: Viking, 1977

Della Porta, Donatella and Diani, Mario 1999. *Social Movements: An Introduction.* Oxford: Blackwell

Demolins, Edmond 1901–3. *Comment la route Crée le type sociale.* Paris: Firmin-Didot

Dennett, D. 1991. *Consciousness Explained.* Harmondsworth: Penguin, 1997

Dennis, Norman, Henriques, Ferdinand, and Slaughter, Clifford 1956. *Coal is Our Life.* London: Eyre and Spottiswoode

Derrida, Jacques 1967. *Writing and Difference.* London: Routledge, 1978

Dewey, John 1922. *Human Nature and Conduct.* New York: The Modern Library, 1929

Dexter, Edwin 1904. *Weather Influences.* New York

Diani, Mario 1992. 'The Concept of Social Movement'. *Sociological Review* 40, 1: 1–25

Dickens, Peter 2000a. 'Linking the Social and Natural Sciences: How Capital Modifies Human Biology in its Own Image'. *Sociology*: 93–110

2000b. *Social Darwinism.* Milton Keynes: Open University Press

Dickens, Peter and Ormerod, James 2007. *Cosmic Society: Towards a Sociology of the Universe.* London: Routledge

Dickinson, Robert E. 1947. *City, Region and Regionalism: A Geographical Contribution to Human Ecology.* London: Kegan Paul, Trench, Trubner and Co.

1964. *City and Region: A Geographical Interpretation.* London: Routledge and Kegan Paul

Dilthey, Wilhelm 1883. *Introduction to the Human Sciences.* Princeton: Princeton University Press, 1989

Dodd, Stuart Carter 1942. *Dimensions of Society.* New York: Macmillan

Domingues, José M. 1995. *Sociological Theory and Collective Subjectivity.* London: Macmillan

Douglas, Jack 1971. *American Social Order.* New York: Free Press

Downes, David 1966. *The Delinquent Solution: A Study in Subcultural Theory.* London: Routledge and Kegan Paul

Downs, Anthony 1957. *An Economic Theory of Democracy.* New York: Harper and Brothers

Draaisma, Douwe 2001. *Why Life Speeds Up as You Get Older: How Memory Shapes Our Past.* Cambridge: Cambridge University Press, 2004

Drake, St. Clair and Cayton, Horace B. 1945. *Black Metropolis.* New York: Harcourt Brace

Draper, John W. 1867–70. *History of the American Civil War.* New York: Harper and Brothers

Drever, J. 1917. *Instinct in Man.* Cambridge: Cambridge University Press

Du Bois, William Edward B. 1899. *The Philadelphia Negro.* Philadelphia: University of Pennsylvania Press, 1996

1903. 'The Souls of Black Folk' in *W. E. B. Du Bois: Writings.* New York: Viking Press, 1986

Dühring, Eugen 1873. *Kursus der National- und Sozialökonomie.* Leipzig: O. R. Reisland, 1925

Dunlop, John 1840. *The Universal Tendency to Association in Mankind.* London: Houlston and Stoneman

Dunn, L. C. 1951. 'Race and Biology' in UNESCO (ed.), *Race and Science.* New York: Columbia University Press, 1969

Durkheim, Emile 1883–4. 'Philosophy Lectures' in N. Gross and R. A. Jones (eds.), *Durkheim's Philosophy Lectures: Notes from the Lycee de Sens Course, 1883–4.*

1887. *Ethics and the Sociology of Morals.* Buffalo: Prometheus Books, 1993

1892. 'Montesquieu's Contribution to the Rise of Social Science' in H. Peyre (ed.), *Emile Durkheim: Montesquieu and Rousseau.* Ann Arbor: University of Michigan Press, 1965

1893. *The Division of Labour in Society.* London: Macmillan, 1984

1895. *The Rules of the Sociological Method.* London: Macmillan, 1982

1897. *Suicide: A Study in Sociology.* London: Routledge and Kegan Paul, 1952

1898. 'Individual and Collective Representations' in D. F. Pocock and J. G. Peristiany (eds.), *Sociology and Philosophy.* London: Cohen and West, 1965

1899. 'Morphologie sociale'. *Année Sociologique* 2: 521–2

1901. 'Preface to the Second Edition' in 1895, *The Rules of the Sociological Method*

1912a. *Elementary Forms of the Religious Life.* London: George Allen and Unwin, 1915

1912b. *Moral Education.* New York: Free Press, 1961

Durkheim, Emile and Mauss, Marcel 1903. *Primitive Classification.* London: Cohen and West, 1963

Dury, George H. 1959. *The Face of the Earth.* Harmondsworth: Penguin

Edelman, G. 1989. *The Remembered Present: A Biological Theory of Consciousness.* New York: Basic Books

Einstein, Albert 1905. 'On the Electrodynamics of Moving Bodies' in A. Einstein *et al.* (eds.), *The Principle of Relativity.* New York: Dover

1916. 'The Foundation of the General Theory of Relativity' in A. Einstein *et al.* (eds.), *The Principle of Relativity.* New York: Dover

Eisenstadt, Shmuel N. 1963. *The Political Systems of Empires.* New York: Free Press

1965. 'The Study of Processes of Institutionalisation, Institutional Change, and Comparative Institutions' in *Essays on Comparative Institutions.* New York: John Wiley and Sons

1987. *European Civilization in a Comparative Perspective.* Oxford: Oxford University Press

1997. *Japanese Civilization: A Comparative View.* Chicago: University of Chicago Press

2006. *The Great Revolutions and the Civilizations of Modernity*: Brill: Leiden

Ekeh, Peter 1974. *Social Exchange Theory*. London: Heinemann

Ekirch, A. Roger 2006. *At Day's Close: Night in Times Past*. New York: W. W. Norton

Elias, Norbert 1939. *The Civilizing Process: Sociogenetic and Psychogenetic Investigations*. Oxford: Basil Blackwell, 2000

1969. *What is Sociology*. London: Hutchinson, 1978

1987. *Time: An Essay*. Oxford: Basil Blackwell, 1992

Ellis, Havelock 1894. *Man and Woman: A Study of Secondary and Tertiary Sexual Characteristics*. London: Walter Scott

Elster, Jon 1989a. *The Cement of Society*. Cambridge: Cambridge University Press

1989b. *Nuts and Bolts for the Social Sciences*. Cambridge: Cambridge University Press

Emerson, Richard M. 1962. 'Power-Dependence Relations' in J. Scott (ed.), *Power, vol. I*. London: Routledge, 1994

1972a. 'Exchange Theory, Part I: A Psychological Basis for Social Exchange' in J. Berger, M. Zelditch, and B. Anderson (eds.), *Sociological Theories in Progress, vol. II*. Boston: Houghton Mifflin Company

1972b. 'Exchange Theory, Part II: Exchange Relations and Network Structures' in J. Berger, M. Zelditch, and B. Anderson (eds.), *Sociological Theories in Progress, vol. II*. Boston: Houghton Mifflin Company

Emirbayer, Mustafa and Mische, Anne 1998. 'What is Agency?'. *American Journal of Sociology* 103, 4: 962–1023

Engels, Friedrich 1845. *The Condition of the Working Class in England in 1844*. Oxford: Basil Blackwell, 1958

1876a. *Anti-Dühring*. Moscow: Foreign Languages Publishing House, 1954

1876b. *The Part Played by Labour in the Transition from Ape to Man*. Peking: Foreign Languages Press, 1975

1884. *The Origin of the Family, Private Property, and the State*. New York: International Publishers, 1942

1886. *Dialectics of Nature*. Moscow: Progress Publishers, 1964

1890. 'Engels to Conrad Schmidt' in F. Engels (ed.), *Marx and Engels: Correspondence*. London: Lawrence and Wishart, 1968

1894. 'Engels to Starkenburg' in F. Engels (ed.), *Marx and Engels: Correspondence*. London: Lawrence and Wishart, 1968

Epstein, Joshua 1999. 'Agent-based Computational Models and Generative Social Science'. *Complexity* 4: 41–60.

Epstein, Joshua and Axelrod, Robert 1996. *Growing Artificial Societies: Social Science from the Bottom Up*. Cambridge: MIT Press

Erikson, Eric 1950. *Childhood and society*. New York: W. W. Norton

1958. *Young Man Luther*. London: Faber and Faber, 1959

1968. *Identity, Youth and Crisis*. New York: W. W. Norton

Erikson, Kai T. 1962. 'Notes on the Sociology of Deviance'. *Social Problems* 9, Spring: 307–14

1966. *Wayward Puritans: A Study in the Sociology of Deviance*. New York: John Wiley

Etzioni, Amitai 1961. *A Comparative Analysis of Complex Organizations: On Power, Involvement, and their Correlates.* New York: Free Press

1964. *Modern Organizations.* Englewood Cliffs: Prentice-Hall

Eve, Raymond, Hirsfall, Sara, and Lee, Mary 1997. *Chaos, Complexity and Sociology.* London: Sage

Fairbairn, W. Ronald D. 1952. *Psycho-Analytic Studies of the Personality.* London: Tavistock

Faithfull, Theodore 1927. *Bisexuality.* London: John Bale, Sons and Danielsson

1933. *Psychological Foundations.* London: John Bale, Sons and Danielsson

Fararo, Thomas J. 1988. *The Meaning of General Theoretical Sociology.* Cambridge: Cambridge University Press

1993. 'General Social Equilibrium: Toward Theoretical Synthesis'. *Sociological Theory* 11, 3: 291–313

Fawcett, Charles Bungay 1918. *Frontiers: A Study in Political Geography.* Oxford: Clarendon Press

1919. *The Provinces of England.* London: Hutchinson, 1960

Febvre, Lucien 1922. *A Geographical Introduction to History.* Westport: Greenwood Press, 1974

Feldman, Arnold S. and Moore, Wilbert E. 1962. 'Industrialism and Industrialization: Converence and Differentiation' in *Transactions of the Fifth World Congress of Sociology.* Washington, DC: International Sociological Association

Festinger, Leon 1957. *A Theory of Cognitive Dissonance.* Stanford: Stanford University Press

Feuerbach, Ludwig 1841. *The Essence of Christianity.* New York: Harper and Row, 1957

Fine, Reuben 1979. *A History of Psychoanalysis.* New York: Columbia University Press

Finley, Moses 1973. *The Ancient Economy.* Berkeley: University of California Press

Firestone, Shulamith 1970. *The Dialectic of Sex.* London: Jonathan Cape, 1971

Fisher, Irving 1911. *The Purchasing Power of Money.* New York: Augustus M. Kelley, 1985

1926. 'A Statistical Relation Between Unemployment and Price Changes'. *International Labour Review* 13, 6: 785–92

Fitzhugh, George 1854. 'Sociology for the South' in H. Wish (ed.), *Ante-Bellum.* New York: G. P. Putnam's Sons, 1960

Flaherty, Michael G. 1999. *A Watched Pot: How We Experience Time.* New York: New York University Press

Flanagan, Owen 2000. *Dreaming Souls: Sleep, Dreams and the Evolution of the Conscious Mind.* Oxford: Oxford University Press

Fletcher, Ronald 1957. *Instinct in Man, in the Light of Recent Work in Comparative Psychology.* London: George Allen and Unwin

Fleure, Herbert J. 1918. *Human Geography in Western Europe: A Study in Appreciation.* London: Williams and Norgate

1919. 'Human Regions'. *Scottish Geographical Magazine* 35: 94–105

Fodor, Jerry 1983. *The Modularity of Mind.* Cambridge: MIT Press

Forde, Daryll 1934. *Habitat, Economy, and Society*. London: Methuen, 1963

Fordham, Frieda 1953. *An Introduction to Jung's Psychology*. Harmondsworth: Penguin

Foucault, Michel 1963. *The Birth of the Clinic*. New York: Vintage Books, 1975

    1971. *The Archaeology of Knowledge*. New York: Pantheon, 1972

    1975. *Discipline and Punish*. London: Allen Lane, 1977

    1975–6. *Society Must be Defended*. Harmondsworth: Penguin, 2003

    1976a. *The History of Sexuality, vol. I, An Introduction*. New York: Vintage Books, 1980

    1976b. 'Questions on Geography' in M. Foucault (ed.), *Power/Knowledge*. Brighton: Harvester Press, 1980

    1982. 'The Subject and Power' in J. Scott (ed.), *Power: Critical Concepts, vol. I*. London: Routledge, 1994

    1984. *The History of Sexuality, vol. III, The Care of the Self*. New York: Vintage Books, 1988

Frankenberg, Ronald 1967. *Communities in Britain*. Harmondsworth: Penguin

Frazer, James 1890. *The Golden Bough*. London: Macmillan

Freeman, Derek 1996. *Margaret Mead and the Heretic: The Making and Unmaking of an Anthropological Myth*. Harmondsworth: Penguin

Freeman, Linton C. 2004. *The Development of Social Network Analysis: A Study in the Sociology of Science*. Vancouver: Empirical Press

Freud, Anna 1936. *The Ego and the Mechanisms of Defence*. London: The Hogarth Press, 1937

Freud, Sigmund 1900. *The Interpretation of Dreams*. London: George Allen and Unwin, 1954

    1905. 'Three Essays on Sexuality' in J. Strachey (ed.), *The Complete Psychological Works of Sigmund Freud, vol. VII*. Harmondsworth: Penguin, 2001

    1915. 'Instincts and their Vicissitudes' in J. Strachey (ed.), *On Meta-psychology: The Theory of Psychoanalysis, Penguin Freud Library, vol. XI*. Harmondsworth: Penguin, 1984

    1920. 'Beyond the Pleasure Principle' in A. Phillips (ed.), *Sigmund Freud: Beyond the Pleasure Principle and Other Writings*. Harmondsworth: Penguin, 2003

    1921. 'Group Psychology and the Analysis of the Ego' in S. Freud (ed.), *Civilisation, Society and Religion*. Harmondsworth: Penguin, 1985

    1923. 'The Ego and the Id' in A. Phillips (ed.), *Sigmund Freud: Beyond the Pleasure Principle and Other Writings*. Harmondsworth: Penguin, 2003

    1925. 'An Autobiographical Study' in J. Strachey (ed.), *The Complete Psychological Works of Sigmund Freud, vol. XX*. Harmondsworth: Penguin, 2001

    1927. 'The Future of an Illusion' in S. Freud (ed.), *Civilisation, Science and Religion*. Harmondsworth: Penguin, 1985

    1930. 'Civilization and its Discontents' in J. Strachey (ed.), *The Complete Psychological Works of Sigmund Freud, vol. XXI*. Harmondsworth: Penguin, 2001

Freyer, Hans 1924. *Theory of Objective Mind: An Introduction to the Philosophy of Culture*. Athens: Ohio University Press

Friedrich, C. J. 1929. 'Introduction' in *Alfred Weber's Theory of the Location of Industries*. Chicago: University of Chicago Press

Gagnon, John H. and Simon, William 1973. *Sexual Conduct: The Social Sources of Human Sexuality*. Chicago: Aldine

Galton, Francis 1881. *Natural Inheritance*. London: Macmillan

Gamson, William A. 1975. *The Strategy of Protest*. Homewood: Dorsey Press

Garfinkel, Harold 1967. *Studies in Ethnomethodology*. New Jersey: Prentice-Hall

Geddes, Patrick 1884. *An Analysis of the Principles of Economics*. London: Williams and Norgate (Reprint of the Proceedings of the Royal Society of Edinburgh)

    1904a. 'Adolescence'. *Saint George*, 7 October: 303–27

    1904b. 'Civics as Applied Sociology, Part 1' in H. Meller (ed.), *The Ideal City*. Leicester: Leicester University Press, 1979

    1905. 'Civics as Applied Sociology, Part 2' in H. Meller (ed.), *The Ideal City*. Leicester: Leicester University Press, 1979

    1915. *Cities in Evolution*. London: Williams and Norgate

Gellner, Ernest 1962. 'Concepts and Society' in E. Gellner (ed.), *The Concept of Kinship and Other Essays on Anthropological Method and Explanation* (originally: *Cause and Meaning in the Social Sciences*). Oxford: Basil Blackwell

    1973. *The Concept of Kinship*. London: Routledge and Kegan Paul

Gergen, Kenneth J. 1991. *The Saturated Self: Dilemmas of Identity in Contemporary Life*. New York: Basic Books

Gibbs, Jack P. 1981. *Norms, Deviance, and Social Control: Conceptual Matters*. New York: Elsevier

Giddens, Anthony 1976a. 'Functionalism: après la lutte' in A. Giddens (ed.), *Studies in Social and Political Theory*. London: Hutchinson, 1977

    1976b. *New Rules of Sociological Method*. London: Hutchinson

    1979. *Central Problems in Social Theory*. London: Macmillan

    1984. *The Constitution of Society*. Cambridge: Polity Press

    1990. *The Consequences of Modernity*. Cambridge: Polity Press

    1991. *Modernity and Self-Identity*. Cambridge: Polity Press

Giddings, Franklin Henry 1896. *Principles of Sociology*. New York: Johnson Reprint, 1970

Gilligan, Carol 1982. *In a Different Voice*. Cambridge: Harvard University Press

Gilman, Charlotte Perkins 1898. *Women and Economics: A Study of the Economic Relations Between Women and Men as a Factor in Social Evolution*. London: Prometheus Books, 1994

    1911. *The Man-Made World, or Our Androcentric Culture*. New York: Humanity Books, 2001

Ginsberg, Maurice 1929. 'The Contribution of Professor Hobhouse to Sociology and Philosophy' in M. Ginsberg (ed.), *Essays in Sociology and Social Philosophy, II: Reason and Unreason in Society*. London: William Heinemann, 1947

    1931. 'The Place of Instinct in Social Theory'. *Economica* 31, 1: 25–44

    1932. 'Emotion and Instinct' in M. Ginsberg (ed.), *Studies in Sociology*. London: Methuen

    1934. *Sociology*. Oxford: Oxford University Press

Glaser, Barney G. and Strauss, Anselm L. 1965. *Awareness of Dying*. Chicago: Aldine

1968. *Time for Dying*. Chicago: Aldine

Goffman, Erving 1955. 'On Face Work' in E. Goffman (ed.), *Interaction Ritual*. Harmondsworth: Penguin Press, 1972 (1st edn 1967)

1956. 'Embarrassment and Social Order' in E. Goffman (ed.), *Interaction Ritual*. Harmondsworth: Penguin Press, 1969 (1st edn 1967)

1957a. 'Alienation from Interaction' in E. Goffman (ed.), *Interaction Ritual*. Harmondsworth: Penguin Press, 1972 (1st edn 1967)

1957b. 'On the Characteristics of Total Institutions' in E. Goffman (ed.), *Asylums: Essays on the Social Situation of Mental Patients and Other Inmates*. New York: Doubleday, 1961

1957c. 'The Underlife of a Public Institution' in E. Goffman (ed.), *Asylums: Essays on the Social Situation of Mental Patients and Other Inmates*. New York: Doubleday, 1961

1959a. 'The Moral Career of the Mental Patient' in E. Goffman (ed.), *Asylums: Essays on the Social Situation of Mental Patients and Other Inmates*. New York: Doubleday, 1961

1959b. *The Presentation of Self in Everyday Life*. Harmondsworth: Penguin Press, 1969

1961. *Encounters*. Harmondsworth: Penguin Press, 1972

1963a. *Behaviour in Public Places*. New York: Free Press

1963b. *Stigma*. Englewood Cliffs: Prentice-Hall

1969. *Strategic Interaction*. Oxford: Basil Blackwell, 1970

1971. *Relations in Public*. Harmondsworth: Penguin Press

1974. *Frame Analysis*. New York: Harper and Row

1983. 'The Interaction Order'. *American Sociological Review* 48: 1–17

Gökalp, Ziya 1913. 'Civilization of the People' in Z. Gökalp (ed.), *Turkish Nationalism and Western Civilization*. Westport: Greenport Press, 1959

Goldmann, Lucien 1956. *The Hidden God*. London: Routledge and Kegan Paul, 1964

Goldthorpe, John H., Lockwood, David, Bechhofer, Frank, and Platt, Jennifer 1969. *The Affluent Worker in the Class Structure*. Cambridge: Cambridge University Press

Golledge, Reginald G. and Stimson, R. J. 1987. *Analytical Behavioural Geography*. London: Croom Helm

Goody, Jack 1986. *The Logic of Writing and the Organization of Society*. Cambridge: Cambridge University Press

2000. *The Power of the Written Tradition*. Cambridge: Cambridge University Press

Gordon, Milton 1947. 'The Concept of Subculture and its Application'. *Social Forces* 26: 40–2

Gossen, Hermann 1853. *The Laws of Human Relations*. Cambridge: MIT Press

Gould, Peter and White, Rodney 1974. *Mental Maps*. Harmondsworth: Penguin

Gouldner, Alvin W. 1959. 'Reciprocity and Autonomy in Functional Theory' in A. W. Gouldner (ed.), *For Sociology*. Harmondsworth: Penguin, 1973

1960. 'The Norm of Reciprocity: A Preliminary Statement'. *American Sociological Review* 25, 2: 161–78

Gramsci, Antonio 1929–35. *The Prison Notebooks (Selections From)*. London: Lawrence and Wishart, 1971

Granovetter, Mark 1986. 'Economic Action and Social Structure: The Problem of Embeddedness'. *American Journal of Sociology* 81: 481–510

Greenspan, Stanley I. and Shanker, Stuart G. 2004. *The First Idea: How Symbols, Language, and Intelligence Evolved from our Primate Ancestors to Modern Humans*. Cambridge: Da Capo Press

Greenwood, John D. 2004. *The Disappearance of the Social in American Social Psychology*. New York: Cambridge University Press

Gregory, Derek 1994. *Geographical Imaginations*. Oxford: Basil Blackwell

Gross, Neal, Mason, Ward S., and McEachern, Alexander W. 1958. *Explorations in Role Analysis: Studies of the School Superintendency Role*. New York: John Wiley and Sons

Guha, Ranajit 1982. 'On Some Aspects of the Historiography of Colonial India' in V. Chaturvedi (ed.), *Mapping Subaltern Studies and the Postcolonial*. London: Verso, 2000

1983. *Elementary Aspects of Peasant Insurgency in Colonial India*. Delhi: Oxford University Press

Gumplowicz, Ludwig 1875. *Rasse und Staat*. Wien: Manz

1883. *Der Rassenkampf*. Innsbruck: Wagner'sche Univ. Buchhandlung

1905. *Outlines of Sociology*. 2nd edn. New Brunswick: Transaction, 1980

Gurvitch, Georges 1963. *The Spectrum of Social Time*. Dordrecht: D. Reidel, 1964

Gusfield, Joseph 1963. *Symbolic Crusade*. Illinois: University of Illinois Press

Habermas, Jürgen 1965. 'Technology and Science as "Ideology"' in J. Habermas (ed.), *Towards a Rational Society*. London: Heinemann, 1971

1968. *Knowledge and Human Interests*. London: Heinemann, 1972

1973. *Legitimation Crisis*. London: Heinemann, 1976

1981. *The Theory of Communicative Action, vol. II, The Critique of Functionalist Reason*. London: Heinemann, 1987

Haeckel, Ernst 1879. *The Evolution of Man*. London: Watts, 1910

Hägerstrand, T. 1953. *Innovation Diffusion as a Spatial Process*. Chicago: University of Chicago Press, 1976

Haggett, Peter 1965. *Locational Analysis in Human Geography*. London: Edward Arnold

Haggett, Peter and Chorley, Richard John 1969. *Network Analysis in Geography*. London: Edward Arnold

Halbwachs, Maurice 1909. *Les expropriations et le prix des terrains à Paris*. Paris: Cornély

1925a. *Les cadres sociaux de la mémoire*. Paris: Alcan

1925b. 'The Social Framework of Memory' in *Maurice Halbwachs: On Collective Memory*. Chicago: University of Chicago Press, 1992

1938. *Population and Society: Introduction to Social Morphology*. Glencoe: Free Press, 1960

1950. *The Collective Memory*. Posthumous. New York: Harper-Colophon

Hall, G. Stanley 1904. *Adolescence: Its Psychology and its Relation to Psychology, Anthropology, Sociology, Sex, Crime, Religion*. New York: D. Appleton

Hall, Stuart 1973. 'Encoding/Decoding' in S. Hall, D. Hobson, A. Lowe, and P. Willis (eds.), *Culture, Media, Language: Working Papers in Cultural Studies*. London: Hutchinson, 1980

Hamer, D. H., Hu, S., and Magnuson, V. L. 1993. 'A Linkage Between DNA Markers on the X-Chromosome and Male Sexual Orientation'. *Science* 258: 1784–7

Hamerton, Philip G. 1884. *Human Intercourse*. London: Macmillan

Haret, Spirou 1910. *Mécanique Sociale*. Bucharest: C. Göbl

Harré, Rom 1961. *Theories and Things*. London: Sheed and Ward
    1964. *Matter and Method*. London: Macmillan
    1979. *Social Being*. Oxford: Basil Blackwell
    2002. 'Social Reality and the Myth of Social Structure'. *European Journal of Social Theory* 5, 1: 112

Harré, Rom and Madden, E. H. 1975. *Causal Powers*. Oxford: Oxford University Press

Harris, Christopher C. 1990. *Kinship*. Buckingham: Open University Press

Hartshorne, Richard 1939. *The Nature of Geography*. Lancaster: Association of American Geographers

Hartsock, Nancy 1983a. 'The Feminist Standpoint: Developing the Ground for a Specifically Feminist Historical Materialism' in S. Harding and M. Hintikka (eds.), *Discovering Reality: Feminist Perspectives on Epistemology, Metaphysics, Methodology and Philosophy of Science*. Dordrecht: D. D. Reidel
    1983b. *Money, Sex and Power: Toward a Feminist Historical Materialism*. Boston: Northeastern University Press

Hebb, Donald O. 1949. *The Organization of Behaviour*. New York: Wiley

Hebdidge, Dick 1979. *Subculture: The Meaning of Style*. London: Routledge

Hechter, Michael and Opps, Karl-Dieter (eds.) 2001. *Social Norms*. New York: Russel Sage Foundation

Hegel, Georg W. F. 1807. *The Phenomenology of Spirit*. Oxford: Oxford University Press, 1977
    1812–16. *Science of Logic*. London: George Allen and Unwin, 1929
    1821. *Hegel's Philosophy of Right (Naturrecht und Staatswissenschaft im Grundrisse/Grundlinien der Philosophie des Rechts)*. London: Oxford University Press, 1952
    1845. *Hegel's Philosophy of Mind (Die Philosophie des Geistes)*. Oxford: Oxford University Press, 1971

Heidegger, Martin 1927. *Being and Time*. London: SCM Press, 1962

Heider, Fritz 1958. *The Psychology of Interpersonal Relations*. New York: Wiley

Helm, Georg 1887. *Die Lehre von der Energie*. Leipzig: Felix

Henderson, Lawrence J. 1935. *Pareto's General Sociology: A Physiologist's Interpretation*. Cambridge: Harvard University Press
    1938–42. 'Sociology 23 Lectures' in B. Barber (ed.), *L. J. Henderson on the Social System*. Chicago: University of Chicago Press, 1970

Herbart, Johann F. 1816. *Textbook in Psychology*. New York: D. Appleton, 1891

Herbertson, Andrew John 1905. 'The Major Natural Regions'. *Geographical Journal* 25: 300–12

Herbertson, Andrew John and Herbertson, F. D. 1920. *Man and His Work: An Introduction to Human Geography*. London: A. and C. Black

Herder, Johann Gottfried 1770. *On the Origin of Language*. Chicago: University of Chicago Press, 1986

1784–91. 'Reflections on the Philosophy of the History of Man' in H. Adler and E. A. Menze (eds.), *On World History*. New York: M. E. Sharpe, 1997

Hervieu-Léger, Danièle 2000. *Religion as a Chain of Memory*. Cambridge: Polity Press

Hesse, Mary 1962. *Forces and Fields: The Concept of Action at a Distance in the History of Physics*. London: Thomas Nelson

Hetherington, H. J. W. and Muirhead, John H. 1918. *Social Purpose: A Contribution to a Philosophy of Civic Purpose*. London: George Allen and Unwin

Hill Collins, Patricia 1990. *Black Feminist Thought: Knowledge, Consciousness and the Politics of Empowerment*. London: HarperCollins

Hillier, Bill and Hanson, Julienne 1984. *The Social Logic of Space*. Cambridge: Cambridge University Press

Hilton, Rodney (ed.) 1976. *The Transition from Feudalism to Capitalism*. London: New Left Books

Hinckle, Roscoe C. 1963. 'Antecedents of the Action Orientation in American Sociology Before 1935'. *American Sociological Review* 28: 705–15

Hirst, Paul Q. 1975. *Durkheim, Bernard and Epistemology*. London: Routledge and Kegan Paul

Hjelmslev, Louis H. 1943. *Prolegomena to a Theory of Language*. Madison: University of Wisconsin Press, 1963

Hobbes, Thomas 1651. *Leviathan*. Harmondsworth: Penguin, 1977

Hobhouse, Leonard Trelawny 1901. *Mind in Evolution*. London: Macmillan

1911. 'Liberalism' in L. T. Hobhouse (ed.), *Liberalism and Other Writings*. Cambridge: Cambridge University Press, 1994

1913. *Development and Purpose: An Essay Towards a Philosophy of Evolution*. London: Macmillan

1924. *Social Development: Its Nature and Conditions*. London: George Allen and Unwin, 1966

Hobsbawm, Eric 1983. 'Introduction: Inventing Tradition' in E. Hobsbawm and T. Ranger (eds.), *The Invention of Tradition*. Cambridge: Cambridge University Press

Hochschild, Arlie Russell 1979. 'Emotion Work, Feeling Rules and Social Structure'. *American Journal of Sociology* 84: 551–73

1983. *The Managed Heart: Commercialization of Human Feeling*. Berkeley: University of California Press

Hodgson, Geoffrey M. 1988. *Economics and Institutions: A Manifesto for a Modern Institutional Economics*. Cambridge: Polity Press

Holmes, Arthur 1944. *Principles of Physical Geology*. London: Thomas Nelson

Homans, George 1941. *English Villagers of the Thirteenth Century*. Cambridge: Harvard University Press

1950. *The Human Group*. London: Routledge and Kegan Paul, 1951

1961. *Social Behaviour: Its Elementary Forms*. London: Routledge and Kegan Paul

Homans, George C. and Curtis, Charles P. 1934. *An Introduction to Pareto: His Sociology*. New York: Alfred A. Knopf

Horney, Karen 1937. *The Neurotic Personality of Our Time*. New York: W. W. Norton

1939. *New Ways in Psychoanalysis*. London: Routledge and Kegan Paul

Hoskins, William G. 1955. *The Making of the English Landscape*. London: Hodder and Stoughton

Hotelling, H. 1929. 'Stability in Competition'. *Economic Journal* 39: 41–57

Hudson, Ray 1986. 'Producing an Industrial Wasteland: Capital, Labour and the State in North-east England' in R. Martin and B. Rowthorn (eds.), *The Geography of Deindustrialisation*. Basingstoke: Macmillan

2001. *Producing Places*. New York: Guilford Press

Hughes, Everett Cherrington 1937. 'Institutional Office and the Person' in E. C. Hughes (ed.), *Men and Their Work*. Glencoe: Free Press, 1958

1945. 'Dilemmas and Contradictions of Status' in E. C. Hughes (ed.), *Men and Their Work*. Glencoe: Free Press, 1958

1952. 'Cycles, Turning Points, and Careers' in E. C. Hughes (ed.), *The Sociological Eye*. Chicago: Aldine, 1971

1955. 'The Making of a Physician' in E. C. Hughes (ed.), *Men and Their Work*. Glencoe: Free Press, 1958

1958. *Men and Their Work*. Glencoe: Free Press

Hughes, Henry 1854. *Treatise of Sociology: Theoretical and Practical*. New York: Negro Universities Press, 1968

Hume, David 1739–40. *Treatise of Human Nature*. London and Glasgow: J. M. Dent, 1911 (Book One); Fontana, 1972 (Books Two and Three)

Huntington, Ellsworth 1915. *Civilization and Climate*. New Haven: Yale University Press

1924. *Civilization and Climate*. 3rd edn. Hamden: Archon Books, 1971

1940. *Principles of Human Geography*. 5th edn. New York: John Wiley

1945. *Mainsprings of Civilization*. New York: Mentor Books, 1959

Huntington, Samuel P. 1996. *The Clash of Civilizations and the Remaking of World Order*. New York: Simon and Schuster

Husserl, Edmund 1905. 'Zur phänomenologie der intersubjectivität' in *Husserliana 13*. The Hague: Nijhoff, 1973

1907. 'Ding und raum' in *Husserliana 16*. The Hague: Nijhoff, 1973

1928. *The Phenomenology of Internal Time-Consciousness*. Bloomington: Indiana University Press, 1965

Illich, Ivan 1977. *Limits to Medicine: Medical Nemesis – The Expropriation of Health*. Harmondsworth: Penguin

Ingold, Tim 1986. *Evolution and Social Life*. Cambridge: Cambridge University Press

Ingrao, Bruna and Israel, Georgio 1990. *The Invisible Hand: Economic Equilibrium in the History of Science*. Cambridge: MIT Press

Jacques, Elliott 1965. 'Death and the Mid-life Crisis'. *International Journal of Psycho Analysis* 46: 502–14

1982. *The Form of Time*. London: Heinemann

Jahoda, Gustav 1992. *Crossroads Between Culture and Mind*. Cambridge: Harvard University Press

James, William 1890. *The Principles of Psychology*. New York: Dover Publications, 1950

1894. 'The Physical Basis of Emotions'. *Psychological Review* 1: 516–29

Jarvie, Ian C. 1964. *The Revolution in Anthropology*. London: Routledge and Kegan Paul

1972. *Concepts and Society*. London: Routledge and Kegan Paul

Jennings, Helen Hall 1948. *Sociometry in Group Relations*. Washington, DC: American Council on Education

Jones, Ernest 1912. *Papers on Psycho-Analysis*. London: Bailliere, Tindall and Cox

Jones, Greta 1980. *Social Darwinism and English Thought*. Brighton: Harvester Press

Jones, Henry 1883. 'The Social Organism' in D. Boucher (ed.), *The British Idealists*. Cambridge: Cambridge University Press, 1997

Jones, Steve 1993. *The Language of the Genes*. London: Flamingo

Jung, Carl Gustav 1906. *Studies in Word Association*. London: Routledge and Kegan Paul, 1969

1931. 'The Structure of the Psyche' in C. G. Jung (ed.), *The Structure and Dynamics of the Psyche*. London: Routledge and Kegan Paul, 1960

1934. 'Archetypes of the Collective Unconscious' in C. G. Jung (ed.), *Collected Works, vol. IX, Part 1*. London: Routledge, 1959

1936. 'The Concept of the Collective Unconscious' in C. G. Jung (ed.), *Collected Works, vol. IX, Part 1*. London: Routledge, 1959

Kagan, Jerome 1981. *The Second Year: The Emergence of Self-Awareness*. Cambridge: Harvard University Press

Kaku, Michio 2004. *Parallel Worlds: The Science of Alternative Universes and Our Future in the Cosmos*. London: Allen Lane

Kant, Immanuel 1768. 'Concerning the Ultimate Ground of Differentiation of Regions in Space' in G. B. Kerford and D. E. Walford (eds.), *Kant: Selected Pre-Critical Writings*. Manchester: Manchester University Press, 1968

1781. *Critique of Pure Reason*. London: J. M. Dent, 1934 (a translation of the 2nd edn of 1787)

1790. *Critique of the Power of Judgement*. Cambridge: Cambridge University Press, 2001

Kardiner, Abram 1939. *The Individual and His Society*. New York: Columbia University Press

Keat, Russell and Urry, John 1975. *Social Theory as Science*. London: Routledge and Kegan Paul

Keller, Albert Galloway 1915. *Societal Evolution*. New York: Macmillan

Kern, Stephen 1983. *The Culture of Time and Space*. Cambridge: Harvard University Press

Kerr, Clerk, Dunlop, John T., Harbison, Frederick, and Myers, C. A. 1960. *Industrialism and Industrial Man*. Cambridge: Harvard University Press

Keynes, John Maynard 1936. *General Theory of Employment, Interest and Money*. London: Macmillan, 1970

Khaldun, Ibn 1377. *The Muqaddimah: An Introduction to History*. Princeton: Princeton University Press, 1967

Kidd, Benjamin 1894. *Social Evolution*. London: Macmillan

1898. *The Control of The Tropics*. London: Macmillan

Kirkwood, T. B. L. 1999. *Time of Our Lives: The Science of Human Ageing*. London: Weidenfeld and Nicolson

Kitchin, Robert M. and Blades, M. 2001. *The Cognition of Geographic Space*. London: I. B. Taurus

Klapp, Orrin E. 1962. *Heroes, Villains and Fools: The Changing American Character*. Englewood Cliffs: Prentice-Hall

Klein, Melanie 1932. *The Psychoanalysis of Children*. London: The Hogarth Press

1957. *Envy and Gratitude: A Study of Unconscious Sources*. London: Tavistock

Klemm, Gustav 1843. *Allgemeine Cultur-Geschichte der Menschheit*. Leipzig: Teubner

Kluckhohn, Clyde 1949. *A Mirror for Man*. New York: McGraw-Hill

Knox, Robert 1850. *The Races of Men*. London: Henry Renshaw

Kohlberg, Lawrence 1981. *Essays on Moral Development, vol. I*. San Francisco: Jossey Bass

Köhler, Wolfgang 1917. *The Mentality of Apes*. London: Routledge and Kegan Paul, 1924

Komarovsky, Mira and Sargent, S. Stansfeld 1949. 'Research into Subcultural Influences upon Personality' in S. S. Sargent and M. W. Smith (eds.), *Culture and Personality*. New York: The Viking Fund

Köppen, Wladimir and Geiger, Rudolph 1928. *Klimukarte der Erde*. Gotha: Perthes

Kornhauser, William 1959. *The Politics of Mass Society*. New York: Free Press

Kroeber, Alfred 1917. 'The Superorganic'. *American Anthropologist* 19: 163–213

1923. *Anthropology*. New York: Harcourt Brace

1948. *Anthropology*. Revised edn. New York: Harcourt Brace

Kropotkin, Pyotr 1902. *Mutual Aid*. London: William Heinemann

Kuhn, Thomas S. 1962. *The Structure of Scientific Revolutions*. 2nd edn 1970. Chicago: University of Chicago Press

Lacan, Jacques 1966a. *The Language of the Self*. Baltimore: Johns Hopkins Press, 1968

1966b. *Ecrits*. Paris: Seuil

Laing, Ronald D. and Esterson, Aaron V. 1964. *Sanity, Madness, and the Family*. Harmondsworth: Penguin

Lamarck, Jean-Baptiste 1809. *Zoological Philosophy: An Exposition with Regard to the Natural History of Animals, with introductory essays by David L. Hull and Richard W. Burkhardt Jr*. Chicago: University of Chicago Press, 1984

Lamb, H. H. 1982. *Climate, History and the Modern World*. London: Methuen

Lash, Scott and Urry, John 1994. *Economies of Signs and Space*. London: Sage

Latour, Bruno and Woolgar, Steve 1979. *Laboratory Life*. London: Sage

Lawrence, Peter 1964. *Road Belong Cargo: A Study of the Cargo Movement in the Southern Madang District, New Guinea*. Manchester: Manchester University Press

Lazarus, Morits and Steinthal, Heymann 1860. 'Einleitende Gedanken über Völkerpsychologie'. *Zeitschrift für Völkerpsychologie und Sprachwissenschaft* 1: 1–73.

Le Bon, Gustave 1895a. *The Crowd*. London: Ernest Benn, 1896
1895b. *The Psychology of Peoples*. New York: Macmillan, 1898
Le Doux, Joseph 1998. *The Emotional Brain*. London: Weidenfeld and Nicolson
Le Goff, Jacques 1988. *History and Memory*. New York: Columbia University Press, 1992
Le Play, Frédéric 1855. 'Les ouvriers Européens' in C. C. Zimmerman and M. Frampton (eds.), *Family and Society*. Condensed translation. New York: D. van Nostrand, 1935
Leach, Edmund R. 1970. *Lévi-Strauss*. Glasgow: Fontana
LeCorbusier 1925. *The City of Tomorrow and its Planning*. New York: Dover, 2000
Lee, Alfred McClung 1945. 'Levels of Culture as Levels of Social Generalization'. *American Sociological Review*: 485–95
Lefebvre, Georges 1934. *La Foule*. Paris: Centre international desynthèse
Lefebvre, Henri 1970. *The Urban Revolution*. Minneapolis: University of Minnesota Press, 2003
1974. *The Production of Space*. Oxford: Basil Blackwell, 1991
Leffingwell, Albert 1892. *Illegitimacy and the Influence of Seasons on Conduct*. London: Swan and Sonnenschein
Lemert, Edwin (ed.) 1967. *Human Deviance, Social Problems and Social Control*. Englewood Cliffs: Prentice-Hall
Lenin, Vladimir Ilyich 1902. *What is to be Done?* Harmondsworth: Penguin, 1988
Lenski, Gerhard 1966. *Power and Privilege*. New York: McGraw-Hill
Lenski, Gerhard and Lenski, Jean 1974. *Human Societies: An Introduction to Macrosociology*. New York: McGraw-Hill
Letherby, Gayle and Reynolds, Gillian 2005. *Train Tracks: Work, Play and Politics on the Railways*. Oxford: Berg
Letherby, Gayle, Scott, John, and Williams, Malcolm 2011. *Objectivity*. London: Sage
Lévi-Strauss, Claude 1945. 'Structural Analysis in Linguistics and Anthropology' in C. Lévi-Strauss (ed.), *Structural Anthropology, vol. I*. London: Penguin Press, 1968
1958. *Structural Anthropology, vol. I*. London: Penguin Press, 1968
1960. 'The Myth of Asdiwal' in E. R. Leach (ed.), *The Structural Study of Myth and Totemism*. London: Tavistock, 1967
1964. *The Raw and the Cooked (Mythologiques, vol. I)*. London: Cape, 1969
Levine, D. 1991. 'Simmel Reappraised: Old Images, New Scholarship' in C. Camic (ed.), *Reclaiming the Sociological Classics*. Oxford: Basil Blackwell, 1997
Levy, M. J. 1952. *The Structure of Society*. Princeton: Princeton University Press
Lévy-Bruhl, Lucien 1921. *Primitive Mentality*. Boston: Beacon Press, 1966
Lewes, George H. 1874–9. *Problems of Life and Mind*. London: Kegan Paul
Lewin, Kurt 1936. *Principles of Topological Psychology*. New York: Harper and Row
Lewis, Helen 1971. *Shame and Guilt in Neurosis*. New York: International Universities Press

Liebowitz, Stanley J. and Margolis, Stephen E. 1990. 'The Fable of the Keys'. *Journal of Law and Economics* 22: 1–26

Lilienfeld, Pavel Feodorovich 1898. *Zur Verteidigung der Organischen Methode in der Soziologie*. Berlin: Georg Reimer

Linton, Ralph 1936. *The Study of Man*. New York: D. Appleton Century

Lipset, S. Martin 1963. *The First New Nation*. New York: Basic Books

Littlejohn, James 1963. *Westrigg: The Sociology of a Cheviot Parish*. London: Routledge and Kegan Paul

Locke, John 1690. *Essay Concerning Human Understanding*. Harmondsworth: Penguin, 1998

Lockwood, David 1956. 'Some Remarks on the Social System'. *British Journal of Sociology* 7, 2: 134–46

  1964. 'Social Integration and System Integration' in G. K. Zollschan and W. Hirsch (eds.), *Explorations in Social Change*. London: Routledge and Kegan Paul

  1992. *Solidarity and Schism*. Oxford: Clarendon Press

López, José and Scott, John 2000. *Social Structure*. Buckingham: Open University Press

Lorenz, Edward Norton 1963. 'Deterministic Nonperiodic Flow'. *Journal of the Atmospheric Sciences* 20, 2: 130–41

Lorenz, Konrad 1963. *On Aggression*. New York: Harcourt Brace

Lösch, A. 1940. *The Economics of Location*. New Haven: Yale University Press, 1954

Lowe, Marion 1983. 'The Dialectic of Biology and Culture' in M. Lowe and R. Hubbard (eds.), *Women's Nature*. New York: Pergamon Press

Lubbock, John 1865. *Prehistoric Times*. London: Williams and Norgate

  1870. *The Origin of Civilization and the Primitive Condition of Man*. Chicago: University of Chicago Press, 1978

Lucas, J. R. 1973. *A Treatise on Time and Space*. London: Methuen

Luhmann, Niklas 1965. *A Sociological Theory of Law*. London: Routledge and Kegan Paul, 1985

  1968. 'Trust' in N. Luhmann (ed.), *Trust and Power*. New York: Wiley, 1979

  1970. 'The Economy as a Social System' in N. Luhmann (ed.), *The Differentiation of Society*. New York: Columbia University Press, 1982

  1975. 'Power' in N. Luhmann (ed.), *Trust and Power*. New York: Wiley, 1979

  1977. 'Systems Theory, Evolution Theory and Communication Theory' in N. Luhmann (ed.), *The Differentiation of Society*. New York: Columbia University Press, 1982

  1982. *Love as Passion*. Stanford: Stanford University Press

  1996. *The Reality of the Mass Media*. Cambridge: Polity Press, 2000

Lukács, Gyorgy 1910. *The Soul and the Forms*. London: Merlin Press, 1974

  1919. 'What is Orthodox Marxism?' in G. Lukács (ed.), *History and Class Consciousness*. London: Merlin Press, 1971

  1923a. *History and Class Consciousness*. London: Merlin Press, 1971

  1923b. 'Reification and the Consciousness of the Proletariat' in G. Lukács, (ed.), *History and Class Consciousness*. London: Merlin Press, 1971

Lundberg, George 1939. *Foundations of Sociology*. New York: Macmillan

Lyell, Charles 1830. *Principles of Geology*. Harmondsworth: Penguin

Lynd, Robert S. and Lynd, Helen M. 1929. *Middletown*. New York: Harcourt Brace
  1937. *Middletown in Transition*. New York: Harcourt Brace
MacAndrew, Craig and Edgerton, Robert B. 1969. *Drunken Comportment*. Chicago: Aldine
Macdonald, John S. and Macdonald, Leatrice D. 1964. 'Chain Migration, Ethnic Neighbourhood Formaton, and Social Networks'. *Millbank Memorial Fund Quarterly* 42, 1: 82–97
MacIver, Robert M. and Page, Charles H. 1949. *Society*. London: Macmillan
Mackenzie, John S. 1895. *An Introduction to Social Philosophy*. Glasgow: James Maclehose
Mairet, Philip 1928. *ABC of Adler's Psychology*. London: Kegan Paul, Trench, Trubner and Co.
Malinowski, Bronislaw 1922. *Argonauts of the Western Pacific*. London: G. Routledge
  1926. 'Anthropology' in *Encyclopaedia Britannica*. 13th edn, vol. I, 131–40
  1939. 'The Functional Theory' in B. Malinowski (ed.), *A Scientific Theory of Culture and Other Essays*. Chapel Hill: University of North Carolina Press, 1944
  1941. 'A Scientific Theory of Culture' in B. Malinowski (ed.), *A Scientific Theory of Culture and Other Essays*. Chapel Hill: University of North Carolina Press, 1944
  1944. *A Scientific Theory of Culture and Other Essays*. Chapel Hill: University of North Carolina Press
Mallory, J. P. 1991. *In Search of the Indo-Europeans*. London: Thames and Hudson
Mandelbaum, Maurice 1955. 'Societal Facts' in J. O'Neill (ed.), *Modes of Individualism and Collectivism*. London: Heinemann, 1973
Mann, Michael 1986. *The Sources of Social Power, vol. I, A History of Power from the Beginning to AD 1760*. Cambridge: Cambridge University Press
  1993. *The Sources of Social Power, vol. II, The Rise of Classes and Nation States, 1760–1914*. Cambridge: Cambridge University Press
Mannheim, Karl 1925. 'The Problem of a Sociology of Knowledge' in K. Mannheim (ed.), *Essays on the Sociology of Knowledge*. London: Routledge and Kegan Paul, 1952
  1927. 'The Problem of Generations' in K. Mannheim (ed.), *Essays on the Sociology of Knowledge*. London: Routledge and Kegan Paul, 1952
  1929. 'Ideology and Utopia' in K. Mannheim (ed.), *Ideology and Utopia*, chs. 2–4. London: Routledge and Kegan Paul, 1936
  1932. 'The Sociology of Intellectuals'. *Theory, Culture, and Society* 10, 3, 1993: 69–80
  1934–5. 'Systematic Sociology' in K. Mannheim (ed.), *Systematic Sociology*. London: Routledge and Kegan Paul, 1957
  1935. *Man and Society in an Age of Reconstruction*. London: Routledge and Kegan Paul, 1940
March, J. G. and Simon, Herbert 1958. *Organizations*. New York: Wiley
Marcuse, Herbert 1956. *Eros and Civilization*. London: Routledge and Kegan Paul

1964. 'Industrialization and Capitalism in the Work of Max Weber' in H. Marcuse (ed.), *Negations*. New York: Beacon Press, 1968

Marshall, Alfred 1890. *Principles of Economics*. London: Macmillan

Marsland, David 1988. *Seeds of Bankruptcy: Sociological Bias Against Business and Freedom*. London: Claridge Press

Martin, John L. 2003. 'What is Field Theory?'. *American Journal of Sociology* 109, 1: 1–49

Martinez-Alier, Juan 1987. *Ecological Economics: Energy, Environment and Society*. Oxford: Basil Blackwell

Marx, Karl 1843a. 'A Contribution to the Critique of Hegel's "Philosophy of Right": Introduction' in K. Marx (ed.), *Critique of Hegel's 'Philosophy of Right'*. Cambridge: Cambridge University Press, 1970

  1843b. *Critique of Hegel's 'Philosophy of Right'*. Cambridge: Cambridge University Press, 1970

  1844a. *Economic and Philosophical Manuscripts*. London: Lawrence and Wishart, 1959

  1844b. 'Theses on Feuerbach' in C. J. Arthur (ed.), *The German Ideology*. London: Lawrence and Wishart, 1970

  1852. *The Eighteenth Brumaire of Louis Bonaparte*. Moscow: Foreign Languages Publishing House, no date

  1857. 'Introduction' in K. Marx (ed.), *Grundrisse*. Harmondsworth: Penguin, 1973

  1859a. *Contribution to the Critique of Political Economy*. London: Lawrence and Wishart

  1859b. 'Preface to a Contribution to the Critique of Political Economy' in K. Marx and F. Engels (eds.), *Werke, vol. XIII*. Berlin: Dietz Verlag, 1964

  1864–5. *Capital, vol. III*. Harmondsworth: Penguin, 1981

  1867. *Capital, vol. I*. Harmondsworth: Penguin, 1976

Marx, Karl and Engels, Friedrich 1846. *The German Ideology*. London: Lawrence and Wishart, 1970

  1848. *The Communist Manifesto*. Harmondsworth: Penguin, 1967

Maryanski, Alexandra and Turner, Jonathan H. 1992. *The Social Cage*. Stanford: Stanford University Press

Massey, Doreen 1978. 'Regionalism: A Review'. *Capital and Class* 6: 106–25

  1984. *Spatial Divisions of Labour*. Basingstoke: Macmillan

Massey, Doreen and Thrift, Nigel 2003. 'The Passion of Place' in R. Johnston and M. Williams (eds.), *A Century of British Geography*. Oxford: Oxford University Press for the British Academy

Maturana, Humberto and Varela, Francisco 1972. *Autopoesis and Cognition: The Realization of the Living*. The Hague: D. Reidel, 1980

Matza, David 1964. *Delinquency and Drift*. New York: John Wiley and Sons

  1969. *Becoming Deviant*. New Jersey: Prentice-Hall

Matza, David and Sykes, Gresham 1961. 'Subterranean Traditions of Youth'. *Annals of the American Academy of Political and Social Science*, 338: 102–8

Mauss, Marcel 1904–5. *Seasonal Variations of the Eskimo*. London: Routledge and Kegan Paul, 1979

1934. 'Techniques of the Body'. *Economy and Society* 2, 1, 1973: 70–87

Maxwell, James Clerk 1865. *A Dynamical Theory of the Electromagnetic Field.* Edinburgh: Scottish Academic Press, 1982

1877. *Matter and Motion.* London: Routledge, 1996

Mayo, Elton 1933. *The Human Problems of an Industrial Civilization.* London: Macmillan

McDougall, William 1908. *An Introduction to Social Psychology.* London: Methuen, 1923

1912. 'Theories of Action' in W. McDougall (ed.), *An Introduction to Social Psychology.* 20th edn. London: Methuen, 1926

1914. 'The Sex Instinct' in W. McDougall (ed.), *An Introduction to Social Psychology.* 20th edn. London: Methuen, 1926

1919. 'The Derived Emotions' in W. McDougall (ed.), *An Introduction to Social Psychology.* 20th edn. London: Methuen, 1926

1920. *The Group Mind.* Cambridge: Cambridge University Press, 1939

1923. *An Outline of Psychology.* London: Methuen

1936. *Psychoanalysis and Social Psychology.* London: Methuen

McKenzie, Roderick D. 1933. *The Metropolitan Community.* New York: McGraw-Hill

McLuhan, Marshall 1964. *Understanding Media: The Extensions of Man.* New York: McGraw-Hill

McTaggart, John M. E. 1908. 'The Unreality of Time'. *Mind* 17: 457–74

Mead, George Herbert 1910. *Essays in Social Psychology.* New Brunswick: Transaction Publishers, 2001

1913. 'The Social Self' in A. J. Reck (ed.), *Selected Writings: G. H. Mead.* Chicago: University of Chicago Press, 1964

1927. *Mind, Self and Society from the Standpoint of Social Behaviourism.* Chicago: University of Chicago Press, 1934

Mead, George H. (ed.) 1938. *Philosophy of the Act.* Chicago: University of Chicago Press

Mead, Margaret 1935. *Sex and Temperament in Three Primitive Societies.* London: Routledge and Kegan Paul, 1977

1950. *Male and Female.* London: Gollancz

Meillet, Antoine 1903. *Introduction à l'étude comparative des langues Indo-Européenes.* Paris: Librairie Hachette

Melucci, Alberto 1996. *Challenging Codes: Collective Action in the Information Age.* Cambridge: Cambridge University Press

Menger, Carl 1871. *Grundsätze der Volkwirtschaftslehre.* Aalen: Scientia Verlag, 1968

1883. *Investigations into the Methods of the Social Sciences.* New York: New York University Press, 1985

Merleau-Ponty, Maurice 1945. *The Phenomenology of Perception.* London: Routledge, 2002

Merton, Robert K. 1936. 'The Unanticipated Consequences of Purposive Social Action'. *American Sociological Review* 1, 6: 894–904

1938. 'Social Structure and Anomie' in R. K. Merton (ed.), *Social Theory and Social Structure.* Revised edn. Toronto: Free Press of Glencoe, 1957

1949. 'Manifest and Latent Function' in R. K. Merton (ed.), *Social Theory and Social Structure*. New York: Harper and Row

1957a. 'The Role Set: Problems in Sociological Theory'. *British Journal of Sociology* 8, 2.

1957b. *Social Theory and Social Structure*. Toronto: Free Press of Glencoe

Merton, Robert K. and Barber, Elinor G. 1958. *The Travels and Adventures of Serendipity: A Study in Sociological Semantics and the Sociology of Science*. Princeton: Princeton University Press, 2004

Meszaros, I. 1970. *Marx's Concept of Alienation*. London: Merlin Press

Michels, Roberto 1911. *Political Parties*. New York: Herst's International Library, 1915

Milgram, Stanley 1974. *Obedience to Authority*. London: Pinter and Martin, 1997

Mill, James 1829. *Analysis of the Phenomenon of the Human Mind*. London: Continuum, 2001

Mill, John Stuart 1843. *The Logic of the Moral Sciences*. London: Duckworth, 1987

Miller, Emanuel 1930. *Modern Psychotherapy*. London: Jonathan Cape

Miller, Walter B. 1958. 'Lower Class Culture as a Generating Milieu of Gang Delinquency'. *Journal of Social Issues*, 14: 5–20

Mills, Charles 1997. *The Racial Contract*. Ithaca: Cornell University Press

Mills, C. Wright 1940. 'Situated Actions and Vocabularies of Motive' in C. W. Mills (ed.), *Power, Politics, and People*. New York: Oxford University Press, 1963

1956. *The Power Elite*. New York: Oxford University Press

Mirowski, Philip 1989. *More Heat than Light*. Cambridge: Cambridge University Press

Misztal, Barbara A. 1996. *Trust in Modern Societies: The Search for the Bases of Social Order*. Cambridge: Polity Press.

2003. *Theories of Social Remembering*. Buckingham: Open University Press

Mitchell, J. Clyde 1969. 'The Concept and Use of Social Networks' in J. C. Mitchell (ed.), *Social Networks in Urban Situations*. Manchester: Manchester University Press

Mitchell, Juliet 1974. *Psychoanalysis and Feminism*. London: Allen Lane

Mithen, S. 1996. *The Prehistory of the Mind*. London: Thames and Hudson

Molm, Linda 1997. *Coercive Power in Social Exchange*. Cambridge: Cambridge University Press

Monkhouse, Francis J. 1954. *Principles of Physical Geography*. London: University of London Press

Montesquieu, Baron de 1748. *The Spirit of Laws*. Cambridge: Cambridge University Press, 1989

Moore, Barrington 1958. *Political Power and Social Theory*. Cambridge: Harvard University Press

1966. *The Social Origins of Dictatorship and Democracy*. Harmondsworth: Pelican

Moore, P. D., Chaloner, B., and Stott, P. 1996. *Global Environmental Change*. Oxford: Basil Blackwell

Moore, Wilbert E. 1974. *Social Change*. Englewood Cliffs: Prentice-Hall

Moreno, Jacob L. 1934. *Who Shall Survive?* New York: Beacon Press

1941. 'Foundations of Sociometry: An Introduction'. *Sociometry* 4, 1: 15–35

Moreno, Jacob L. and Jennings, Helen Hall 1938. 'Statistics of Social Configurations'. *Sociometry* 1, 3/4: 342–74

Morgan, C. Lloyd 1894. *Introduction to Comparative Psychology*. London: Walter Scott

1896. *Habit and Instinct*. London: Edward Arnold

1905. *The Interpretation of Nature*. Whitefish: Kessinger Publishing, 2005

Morgan, Lewis Henry 1870. *Systems of Consanguinity and Affinity of the Human Family*. Lincoln: University of Nebraska Press, 1997

1877. *Ancient Society*. Chicago: Charles H. Kerr

Morrill, Richard 1970. *The Spatial Organisation of Society*. Belmont: Wadsworth

Morrill, Richard, Gaile, Gary L., and Thrall, Grant 1988. *Spatial Diffusion*. Beverley Hills: Sage

Morris, Charles W. 1964. *Signs, Language and Behaviour*. New York: Prentice-Hall

Mosca, Gaetano 1896. 'Elementi di Scienza Politica, vol. I' in G. Mosca (ed.), *The Ruling Class*, chs. 1–11. New York: McGraw-Hill, 1939

1923. 'Elementi di Scienza Politica, vol. II' in G. Mosca (ed.), *The Ruling Class*, chs. 11–17. New York: McGraw-Hill, 1939

Moscovici, Serge 1981. *The Age of the Crowd*. Cambridge: Cambridge University Press

1984. 'The Phenomena of Social Representations' in S. Moscovici (ed.), *Social Representations: Explorations in Social Psychology*. New York: New York University Press, 2001

Mouzelis, Nicos 1991. *Back to Sociological Theory: The Construction of Social Orders*. London: Macmillan

Müller-Lyer, Franz 1908. *The History of Social Development (Phasen der Kultur und Richtungslinien des Fortschritts)*. London: George Allen and Unwin, 1920

Mumford, Lewis 1934. *Technics and Civilization*. New York: Harcourt Brace

1938. *The Culture of Cities*. New York: Harcourt Brace

Münch, Richard 1982a. *Theory of Action: Towards a New Synthesis Going Beyond Parsons*. Part translation of *Theorie des Handelns*. London: Routledge and Kegan Paul, 1987

1982b. *Understanding Modernity: Towards a New Perspective Going Beyond Durkheim and Weber*. Part translation of *Theorie des Handelns*. London: Routledge and Kegan Paul, 1988

Murdock, George P. 1949. *Social Structure*. New York: Free Press

Murdock, Graham and McCron, Robin 1976. 'Consciousness of Class and Consciousness of Generation' in S. Hall and T. Jefferson (eds.), *Resistance Through Rituals*. London: Hutchinson

Nadel, Siegfried Frederick 1951. *Foundations of Social Anthropology*. London: Cohen and West

1957. *The Theory of Social Structure*. Glencoe: Free Press

Nagel, Ernest 1956. 'A Formalization of Functionalism' in G. K. Zollschan and W. Hirsch (eds.), *Explorations in Social Change*. New York: Houghton Mifflin, 1964

Nettl, Peter and Robertson, Roland 1968. *International Systems and the Modernization of Societies: The Formation of National Goals and Attitudes.* New York: Basic Books

Newton, Isaac 1687. *Mathematical Principles of Natural Philosophy.* London: Dawsons, 1969

Newton-Smith, W. H. 1980. *The Structure of Time.* London: Routledge and Kegan Paul

Nicolis, G. and Prigogine, I. 1977. *Self-Organisation in Nonequilibrium Systems.* New York: John Wiley

1989. *Exploring Complexity: An Introduction.* New York: W. H. Freeman

Niebuhr, H. Richard 1929. *The Social Sources of Denominationalism.* New York: Holt

Nietzsche, Friedrich 1886. *Beyond Good and Evil.* Oxford: Oxford University Press, 1998

Nisbet, Robert A. 1969. *Social Change and History: Aspects of the Western Theory of Development.* Oxford: Oxford University Press

North, Douglas C. 1990. *Institutions, Institutional Change, and Economic Performance.* Cambridge: Cambridge University Press

O'Brien, Mary 1981. *The Politics of Reproduction.* London: Routledge

Oakley, Ann 1972. *Sex, Gender and Society.* London: Temple Smith

Odum, Howard Washington and Moore, Harry Estil 1938. *American Regionalism.* New York: H. Holt and Co.

Ogburn, William Fielding 1922. *Social Change, with Respect to Culture and Original Nature.* New York: Viking Press

Ollman, Bertell 1971. *Alienation: Marx's Conception of Man in Capitalist Society.* Cambridge: Cambridge University Press

Olson, Mancur 1965. *The Logic of Collective Action.* Cambridge: Harvard University Press

Oppenheimer, Franz 1914. *The State.* Montreal: Black Rose Books, 1975

1922. *System der Soziologie.* Jena: G. Fischer

Orans, Martin 1996. *Not Even Wrong: Margaret Mead, Derek Freeman, and the Samoans.* Novata: Chandler and Sharp

Orbach, Susie 1978. *Fat is a Feminist Issue.* London: Arrow, 1988

Ormerod, Paul 1994. *The Death of Economics.* London: Faber and Faber

Ostwald, Wilhelm 1892. 'Studien zur Energetik'. *Zeitschrift für physikalische Chemie* 9: 563–78

1909. *Energetische Grundlagen der Kulturwissenschaften.* Leipzig: Duncker

1912. *Der Energetische Imperativ.* Leipzig: Akademische Verlagsgesselschaft

Pareto, Vilfredo 1896–7. *Course d'economie politique.* Lausanne: Rouge

1916. *A Treatise on General Sociology.* New York: Dover, 1963

Park, Robert E. 1924. 'The Concept of Social Distance'. *Journal of Applied Sociology* 8, 6: 339–44

Park, Robert E. and Burgess, Ernest W. 1925. *The City.* Chicago: University of Chicago Press, 1967

Parkin, Frank 1972. 'System Contradiction and Political Transformation'. *European Journal of Sociology* 13, 1: 45–62

Parsons, Talcott 1937. *The Structure of Social Action.* New York: McGraw-Hill

1945. 'The Present Position and Prospects of Systematic Theory in Sociology' in T. Parsons (ed.), *Essays in Sociological Theory*. Revised edn. New York: Free Press, 1954

1951. *The Social System*. New York: Free Press

1953. 'The Theory of Symbolism in Relation to Action' in T. Parsons, R. F. Bales, and E. A. Shils (eds.), *Working Papers in the Theory of Action*. New York: Free Press

1958a. 'Authority, Legitimacy and Political Action' in T. Parsons (ed.), *Structure and Process in Modern Society*. New York: Free Press, 1960

1958b. 'Definitions of Health and Illness in the Light of American Values and Social Structure' in T. Parsons (ed.), *Social Structure and Personality*. New York: Free Press, 1964

1958c. 'The Institutional Framework of Economic Development' in T. Parsons (ed.), *Structure and Process in Modern Societies*. New York: Free Press, 1960

1959. '"Voting" and the Equilibrium of the American Political System' in T. Parsons (ed.), *Politics and Social Structure*. New York: Free Press, 1969

1961a. 'An Outline of the Social System' in T. Parsons, E. A. Shils, K. D. Naegele, and J. R. Pitts (eds.), *Theories of Society, vol. I*. New York: Free Press

1961b. 'A Paradigm for the Analysis of Social Systems and Social Change' in N. J. Demerath and R. A. Peterson (eds.), *System, Change and Conflict*. New York: Free Press, 1967

1963a. 'On the Concept of Influence' in T. Parsons (ed.), *Politics and Social Structure*. New York: Free Press, 1969

1963b. 'On the Concept of Political Power'. *Proceedings of the American Philosophical Society* 107: 232–62

1964a. 'Some Reflections on the Place of Force in Social Process' in T. Parsons (ed.), *Sociological Theory and Modern Society*. New York: Free Press, 1967

1964b. *Social Structure and Personality*. New York: Free Press

1966. *Societies: Evolutionary and Comparative Perspectives*. Englewood Cliffs: Prentice-Hall

1968a. 'On the Concept of Value Commitments' in T. Parsons (ed.), *Politics and Social Structure*. New York: Free Press, 1969

1968b. 'Social Systems' in T. Parsons (ed.), *Social Systems and the Evolution of Action Theory*. New York: Free Press, 1977

1970a. 'Some Problems of General Theory' in T. Parsons (ed.), *Social Systems and the Evolution of Action Theory*. New York: Free Press, 1977

1970b. 'On Building Social Systems Theory' in T. Parsons (ed.), *Social Systems and the Evolution of Action Theory*. New York: Free Press, 1977

1971. *The System of Modern Societies*. Englewood Cliffs: Prentice-Hall

1975. 'Social Structure and the Symbolic Media of Interchange' in T. Parsons (ed.), *Social Structure and the Evolution of Action Theory*. New York: Free Press, 1977

1978. 'A Paradigm of the Human Condition' in T. Parsons (ed.), *Action Theory and the Human Condition*. New York: Free Press

Parsons, Talcott and Bales, Robert F. 1953. 'The Dimensions of Action Space' in T. Parsons, R. F. Bales, and E. A. Shils (eds.), *Working Papers in the Theory of Action*. New York: Free Press

    1956. *Family, Socialization and Interaction Process*. London: Routledge and Kegan Paul

Parsons, Talcott, Bales, Robert F., and Shils, Edward A. 1953. *Working Papers in the Theory of Action*. New York: Free Press

Parsons, Talcott and Shils, Edward A. (eds.) 1951. *Towards a General Theory of Action*. Cambridge: Harvard University Press

Parsons, Talcott, Shils, Edward A., Allport, Gordon W., Kluckhohn, Clyde, Murray, A., Sears, Robert F., Sheldon, Richard C., Stoufer, Samuel A., and Tolman, Edward C. 1951a. 'Some Fundamental Categories of the Theory of Action' in T. Parsons, R. F. Bales, and E. A. Shils (eds.), *Towards a General Theory of Action*. Cambridge: Harvard University Press

Parsons, Talcott, Shils, Edward A., and Olds, James 1951b. 'Values, Motives and Systems of Action' in T. Parsons, R. F. Bales, and E. A. Shils (eds.), *Towards a General Theory of Action*. Cambridge: Harvard University Press

Parsons, Talcott and Smelser, Neil J. 1956. *Economy and Society*. New York: Free Press

Pashukanis, Evgeny 1929. *Law and Marxism: A General Theory*. London: Pluto Press, 1978

Pateman, Carole 1988. *The Sexual Contract*. Stanford: Stanford University Press

Patten, Simon 1896. *The Theory of Social Forces*. Philadelphia: American Academy of Political and Social Science

Peake, Harold and Fleure, Herbert J. 1927–56. *The Corridors of Time*. Oxford: Clarendon Press

Pearson, Karl 1909. *The Groundwork of Eugenics*. London: Dulaou

Peirce, C. S. 1877. 'The Fixation of Belief'. *Popular Science Monthly*, 12: 1–15

    1878. 'How to Make Our Ideas Clear'. *Popular Science Monthly*, 12: 286–302

Peristiany, J. G. 1965. 'Introduction' in J. G. Peristiany (ed.), *Emile Durkheim: Sociology and Philosophy*. London: Cohen and West

Perry, William J. 1924. *The Growth of Civilization*. Harmondsworth: Penguin, 1937

Peschel, Oscar 1875. *The Races of Man*. New York: D. Appleton

Peterson, Richard A. and Bennett, Andy 2004. 'Introducing Musical Scenes' in A. Bennett and R. A. Peterson (eds.), *Music Scenes: Local, Translocal, and Virtual*. Nashville: Vanderbilt University Press

Piaget, Jean 1923. *The Language and Thought of the Child*. London: Routledge, 2001

    1924. *Judgment and Reasoning in the Child*. London: Routledge and Kegan Paul, 1928

    1926. *The Child's Conception of the World*. New York: Harcourt Brace, 1929

    1932. *The Moral Judgement of the Child*. London: Routledge and Kegan Paul, 1975

    1936. *The Origins of Intelligence in the Child*. London: Routledge and Kegan Paul, 1953

1941. *The Child's Conception of Number*. New York: Humanities Press, 1952
1946. *The Child's Conception of Time*. London: Routledge, 2006
Piaget, Jean and Inhelder, Bärbel 1948. *The Child's Conception of Space*. London: Routledge and Kegan Paul, 1956
Pickering, W. S. F. (ed.) 2000. *Durkheim and Representations*. London: Routledge
Pigou, Arthur Cecil 1927. *Industrial Fluctuations*. London: Routledge and Kegan Paul, 1968
Pinker, Steve 1994. *The Language Instinct*. London: Allen Lane
1997. *How the Mind Works*. London: Allen Lane
2002. *The Blank Slate*. Harmondsworth: Allen Lane
Plekhanov, Georgy 1895. 'On the Development of the Monist Conception of History' in A. Rothstein (ed.), *G. V. Plekhanov: In Defence of Marxism*. London: Lawrence and Wishart, 1947
1897. 'The Materialist Conception of History' in G. Plekhanov (ed.), *Fundamental Problems of Marxism*. London: Lawrence and Wishart, 1969
1908. *Fundamental Problems of Marxism*. London: Lawrence and Wishart, 1969
Podolinsky, Sergei 1881. 'Socialism and the Unity of Physical Forces'. *Organization and Environment* 17, 1: 61–75
1883. 'Human Labour and Unity of Force'. *Historical Materialism* 16, 1: 163–83
Polanyi, Karl 1944. *The Great Transformation*. Boston: Beacon Press
Popitz, Heinrich 1967. 'The Concept of Social Role as an Element of Sociological Theory' in J. A. Jackson (ed.), *Role*. Cambridge: Cambridge University Press, 1972
Popper, Karl R. 1945. *The Open Society and Its Enemies*. London: Routledge and Kegan Paul
1968. 'On the Theory of the Objective Mind' in K. R. Popper (ed.), *Objective Knowledge*. Oxford: Oxford University Press, 1972
Pred, Alan 1986. *Place, Practice and Structure*. Totowa: Barnes and Noble
Price, J. and Shildrick, M. 1999. *Feminist Theory and the Body*. Edinburgh: Edinburgh University Press
Puwar, Nirmal 2004. *Space Invaders: Race, Gender and Bodies Out of Place*. Oxford: Berg
Quesnay, Francois 1758. *Tableau economique*. London: Macmillan, 1972
Quetelet, Lambert Adolphe Jacques 1848. *Du système sociale et des lois qui le régissent*. Paris: Guillaumin
Quinney, Richard 1970. *The Social Reality of Crime*. Boston: Little, Brown
Radcliffe-Brown, Alfred Reginald 1937. *A Natural Science of Society*. Glencoe: Free Press, 1957
1940. 'On Social Structure' in A. R. Radcliffe-Brown (ed.), *Structure and Function in Primitive Society*. London: Cohen and West, 1952
Ratzel, Friedrich 1887-8. *History of Mankind*. London: Macmillan, 1896-8
Ratzenhofer, Gustav 1898. *Die Soziologische Erkenntnis*. Leipzig: F. A. Brockhaus
Rawls, Annje Warfield 2004. *Epistemology and Practice: Durkheim's The Elementary Forms of the Religious Life*. Cambridge: Cambridge University Press

Reclus, Elisée 1868. *The Earth: A Descriptive History of the Life of the Globe.* New York: Harper and Brothers, 1872
    1869. *The Ocean.* London: Chapman and Hall, 1873
    1905–8. *L'homme et la terre.* Paris: Librairie Universelle
Rees, Alwyn D. 1961. *Life in a Welsh Countryside.* London: Thames and Hudson
Rees, Martin 2001. *Our Cosmic Habitat.* Princeton: Princeton University Press
Reich, Wilhelm 1933. *Character Analysis.* New York: Farrar, Straus, and Giroux, 1972
    1942. *The Function of the Orgasm.* London: Panther Books, 1968
Reid, Thomas 1764. *An Inquiry into the Human Mind.* London: T. Cadell
Renfrew, Colin 1987. *Archaeology and Language: The Puzzle of Indo-European Origins.* London: Jonathan Cape
Renner, Karl 1904. *The Institutions of Private Law and their Social Function.* London: Routledge and Kegan Paul
Rex, John A. 1961. *Key Problems of Sociological Theory.* London: Routledge and Kegan Paul
    1970. *Race Relations in Sociological Theory.* London: Weidenfeld and Nicolson
    1981. *Social Conflict.* Harlow: Longman
Ricardo, David 1817. *Principles of Political Economy and Taxation.* London: J. M. Dent, 1911
Richards, Graham 1992. *Mental Machinery: The Origins and Consequences of Psychological Ideas, 1600–1850.* Baltimore: Johns Hopkins University Press
    2000. 'Britain on the Couch: The Popularization of Psychoanalysis in Britain 1918–1940'. *Science in Context* 13, 2: 183–220
Rickert, Heinrich 1910. *Science and History: A Critique of Positivist Epistemology.* Princeton: Van Nostrand
Ridley, Matt 1999. *Genome.* London: HarperCollins
Riker, W. H. 1962. *The Theory of Political Coalitions.* New Haven: Yale University Press
Riley, Matilda W. 1987. 'On the Significance of Age in Sociology'. *American Sociological Review* 52, 1: 1–14
Ripley, William Z. 1899. *The Races of Europe: A Sociological Study.* London: Kegan Paul, 1900
Rivers, William H. R. 1917. 'Freud's Psychology of the Unconscious' in W. H. R. Rivers (ed.), *Instinct and the Unconscious.* Cambridge: Cambridge University Press, 1920
    1918. 'Freud's Conception of the "Censorship"' in W. H. R. Rivers (ed.), *Instinct and the Unconscious.* Cambridge: Cambridge University Press, 1920
    1920. *Instinct and the Unconscious.* Cambridge: Cambridge University Press
Robertson, John M. 1897. *The Saxon and the Celt: A Study in Sociology.* London: University Press
    1911. 'The Sociology of Race'. *Sociological Review* 4: 124–30
    1912. *The Evolution of States.* London: Watts and Co.

Robertson, Roland 1992. *Globalisation: Social Theory and Global Culture.* London: Sage

Rodman, Hyman 1965. 'The Lower-Class Value Stretch' in L. Ferman (ed.), *Poverty in America.* Ann Arbor: University of Michigan Press

Roemer, John 1982. *A General Theory of Exploitation.* Cambridge: Harvard University Press

Roethlisberger, F. J. and Dickson, W. J. 1939. *Management and the Worker.* Cambridge: Harvard University Press

Rogers, Everett 1962. *Diffusion of Innovations.* 5th edn. New York: Free Press, 2003

Romanes, George J. 1889. *Mental Evolution in Man.* New York: D. Appleton

Rosa, Eugene A. and Machlis, Gary E. 2007. 'Energetic Theories of Society: An Evaluative Review'. *Sociological Inquiry* 53, 2–3: 152–78

Rose, Michael 1975. *Industrial Behaviour: Theoretical Development Since Taylor.* London: Allen Lane

Rose, Niklas 1990. *Governing the Soul: The Shaping of the Private Self.* London: Routledge

Rose, Steven 2005. *The Future of the Brain.* Oxford: Oxford University Press

Rosenfield, Israel 1993. *The Strange, Familiar and Forgotten: An Anatomy of Consciousness.* New York: Vintage

Ross, Edward 1901. *Social Control.* New York: Macmillan
        1920. *Principles of Sociology.* New York: The Century Co.

Rostow, Walter Whitman 1960. *The Stages of Economic Growth.* Cambridge: Cambridge University Press

Roy, Donald 1952. 'Quota Restriction and Goldbricking in a Machine Shop'. *American Journal of Sociology* 67, 2: 427–42

Rudé, George 1959. *The Crowd in the French Revolution.* London: Oxford University Press
        1964. *The Crowd in History, 1730–1848.* London: Oxford University Press

Russell, Charles and Lewis, Harry S. 1900. *The Jew in London: A Study of Racial Character and Present Day Conditions.* London: T. Fisher Unwin

Russett, Cynthia E. 1966. *The Concept of Equilibrium in American Social Thought.* New Haven: Yale University Press

Rüstow, Alexander 1950–7. *Freedom and Domination: A Historical Critique of Civilization.* Princeton: Princeton University Press

Rylance, Rick 2000. *Victorian Psychology and British Culture, 1850–1880.* Oxford: Oxford University Press

Ryle, Gilbert 1949. *The Concept of Mind.* London: Hutchinson

Sacher, Eduard 1881. *Grundzüge einer Mechanik der Gesellschaft, Teil 1.* Jena: Gustav Fischer

Sack, Robert D. 1980. *Conceptions of Space in Social Thought.* Minneapolis: University of Minnesota Press

Sahlins, Marshall and Service, Elman (eds.) 1960. *Evolution and Culture.* Ann Arbor: University of Michigan Press

Sampson, Geoffrey 1997. *Educating Eve: The Language Instinct Debate.* London: Cassell

Sanderson, S. K. 1990. *Social Evolutionism.* Oxford: Basil Blackwell

Sapir, Edward 1921. *Language.* New York: Harcourt Brace

Sassen, Saskia 1991. *The Global City: New York, London, Tokyo*. Princeton: Princeton University Press

Sauer, Carl 1925. 'The Morphology of Landscape'. *University of California Publications in Geography* 2, 2: 19–53

Saussure, Ferdinand de 1916. *Course in General Linguistics*. New York: McGraw-Hill, 1966

Sayer, Andrew 1984. *Method in Social Science: A Realist Approach*. London: Hutchinson

Schäffle, Albert 1875–80. *Bau und Leben des Sozialen Körpen*. Tübingen: Laupp, 1906

Scheff, Thomas J. 1966. *Becoming Mentally Ill: A Sociological Theory*. New York: Aldine, 1984

   1990. *Microsociology: Discourse, Emotion and Social Structure*. Chicago: University of Chicago Press

   2006. *Goffman Unbound: A New Paradigm for Social Science*. Boulder: Paradigm Press

Schelling, Thomas 1960. *The Strategy of Conflict*. Cambridge: Harvard University Press

   1978. *Micromotives and Macrobehaviour*. New York: W. W. Norton

Schluchter, Wolfgang 1979. *The Rise of Western Rationalism: Max Weber's Developmental History*. Berkeley: University of California Press, 1981

   1989. *Rationalism, Religion, and Domination*. Berkeley: University of California Press

   1996. *Paradoxes of Modernity: Culture and Conduct in the Theory of Max Weber*. Stanford: Stanford University Press

Schmauss, Warren 1994. *Durkheim's Philosophy of Science and the Sociology of Knowledge*. Chicago: University of Chicago Press

Schreiner, Olive 1899. 'The Woman Question' in C. Barash (ed.), *An Olive Schreiner Reader*. London: Pandora Press, 1987

Schütz, Alfred 1932. *The Phenomenology of the Social World*. London: Heinemann Educational Books, 1972

   1943. 'The Problem of Rationality in the Social World' in A. Schütz (ed.), *Collected Papers, vol. II, Studies in Social Theory*. Dordrecht: Martinus Nijhoff, 1964

   1953. 'Common-Sense and Scientific Interpretation of Human Action' in A. Schütz (ed.), *Collected Papers, vol. I, The Problem of Social Reality*. Dordrecht: Martinus Nijhoff, 1962

Scott, John 1995. *Sociological Theory: Contemporary Debates*. Cheltenham: Edward Elgar

   1997. *Corporate Business and Capitalist Classes*. Oxford: Oxford University Press

   1998. 'Relationism, Cubism, and Reality: Beyond Relativism' in T. May and M. Williams (eds.), *Knowing the Social World*. Buckingham: Open University Press

   2000. *Social Network Analysis*. 2nd edn. London: Sage (1st edn 1991)

   2001. *Power*. Cambridge: Polity Press

   2005. *Social Theory*. London: Sage Publications

2010. 'Sociology and the Sociological Imagination: Reflections on Disciplinarity and Intellectual Specialisation' in J. Burnett, S. Jeffers, and G. Thomas (eds.), *New Social Connections: Sociology's Subjects and Objects*. London: Palgrave

Scott, John Finlay 1971. *Internalization of Norms: A Sociological Theory of Moral Commitment*. Englewood Cliffs: Prentice-Hall

Scott, Marvin B. and Lyman, Stanford 1968. 'Accounts'. *American Sociological Review* 33, 1: 46–62

Searle, John 1995. *The Construction of Social Reality*. Harmondsworth: Penguin

1997. *The Mystery of Consciousness*. London: Granta

2010. *Making the Social World: The Structure of Human Civilization*. Oxford: Oxford University Press

Semple, Ellen Churchill 1911. *Influences of Geographic Environment, on the Basis of Ratzel's System of Anthropo-Geography*. London: Constable, 1933

Sewell, William H. 2005. *Logics of History*. Chicago: University of Chicago Press

Shand, Alexander F. 1896. 'Character and the Emotions'. *Mind, NS* 5: 203–26

Shapiro, Meyer 1962. 'Style' in S. Tax (ed.), *Anthropology Today*. Chicago: University of Chicago Press

Sharma, Simon 1995. *Landscape and Memory*. London: HarperCollins

Shibutani, Tamotsu 1955. 'Reference Groups as Perspectives'. *American Journal of Sociology* 60: 562–9

Shilling, Chris 1993. *The Body in Social Theory*. London: Sage

Shils, Edward A. 1961. 'Centre and Periphery' in E. A. Shils (ed.), *Centre and Periphery: Essays in Macrosociology*. Chicago: University of Chicago Press, 1975

1981. *Tradition*. Chicago: University of Chicago Press

Sighele, Scipio 1891. *La Folla Delinquente*. Venice: Marsilio, 1985

Silverman, David 1970. *The Theory of Organisations: A Sociological Framework*. London: Heinemann

Simmel, Georg 1903. 'The Metropolis and Mental Life' in K. H. Wolf (ed.), *The Sociology of Georg Simmel*. New York: Free Press

1908a. *Soziologie: Untersuchungen Über die Formen der Vergesselshaftung*. Berlin: Duncker und Humblot, 1968

1908b. 'The Stranger' in K. Wolff (ed.), *The Sociology of Georg Simmel*. Glencoe: Free Press, 1950

1916. *Rembrandt: An Essay in the Philosophy of Art*. London: Routledge, 2005

Simon, Herbert 1945. *Administrative Behaviour*. New York: Macmillan

Skocpol, Theda 1979. *States and Social Revolutions*. Cambridge: Cambridge University Press

Small, Albion 1905. *General Sociology*. Chicago: University of Chicago Press

Smedley, Audrey 1993. *Race in North America: Origins and Evolution of a Worldview*. Boulder: Westview Press

Smelser, Neil J. 1959. *Social Change in the Industrial Revolution*. London: Routledge and Kegan Paul

Smith, Adam 1766. *The Wealth of Nations*. London: J. M. Dent, 1910

Smith, Anthony 1976. *Social Change: Social Theory and Historical Process*. Harlow: Longman

1986. *The Ethnic Origins of Nations*. Oxford: Basil Blackwell

Smith, Charles Hamilton 1851. *The Natural History of the Human Species*. Boston: Gould and Lincoln

Smith, Dorothy E. 1987. *The Everyday World as Problematic*. Milton Keynes: Open University Press

1990. *The Conceptual Practices of Power*. Toronto: University of Toronto Press

Soddy, Frederick 1922. *Cartesian Economics*. London: Henderson's

1926. *Wealth, Virtual Wealth and Debt*. London: George Allen and Unwin

Soja, Edward W. 1989. *Postmodern Geographies: The Reassertion of Space in Critical Social Theory*. London: Verso

Solvay, Ernest 1904. *L'energétique consideré comme principe d'orientation rationelle pour la sociologie*. Bruxelles: Misch et Thron

Sombart, Werner 1902. *Der Modernen Capitalismus*. Berlin: Duncker und Humblot

Somers, Margaret R. 1998. '"We're No Angels": Realism, Rational Choice, and Rationality in Social Science'. *American Journal of Sociology* 104: 722–84

Sorokin, Pitirim 1927. *Social Mobility*. New York: Harper and Row

1928. *Contemporary Sociological Theories*. New York: Harper and Row

1937–41. *Social and Cultural Dynamics*. London: G. Allen and Unwin

Sorokin, Pitirim and Merton, Robert K. 1937. 'Social Time: A Methodological and Functional Analysis'. *American Journal of Sociology* 42, 5: 615–29

Spencer, Herbert 1860. 'The Social Organism' in H. Spencer (ed.), *Illustrations of Universal Progress*. New York: D. Appleton and Co., 1873

1862. *First Principles*. London: Williams and Norgate, 1910

1870–2. *The Principles of Psychology*. London: Longman, Brown, Green, and Longmans

1873. *The Study of Sociology*. London: Kegan Paul, Trench and Co., 1889

1873–93. *Principles of Sociology*. London: Williams and Norgate

Spengler, Oswald 1918–22. *The Decline of the West*. New York: Alfred A. Knopf, 1932

Sprott, W. J. H. 1958. *Human Groups*. Harmondsworth: Penguin

Stacey, Margaret 1960. *Tradition and Change: A Study of Banbury*. Oxford: Oxford University Press

1969. 'The Myth of Community Studies'. *British Journal of Sociology* 20, 2: 34–47

Stamp, L. Dudley 1946. *Britain's Structure and Scenery*. London: Collins

1948. *The Land of Britain: Its Use and Misuse*. Harlow: Longman

Stevens, Anthony 2002. *Archetypes Revisited: An Updated Natural History of the Self*. London: Brunner-Routledge

Steward, Julian 1955. *The Theory of Cultural Change: The Methodology of Multilinear Evolution*. Urbana: University of Illinois Press

Stinchcombe, Arthur L. 1968. *Constructing Social Theories*. New York: Harcourt, Brace and World

Stones, Rob 2005. *Structuration Theory*. Basingstoke: Palgrave

Stout, G. F. 1896. *Analytical Psychology*. London: Macmillan
  1898. *A Manual of Psychology*. London: W. B. Clive
Strauss, Anselm 1978. *Negotiations*. San Francisco: Jossey Bass
  1993. *Continual Permutations of Action*. New York: Aldine, De Gruyter
Strauss, Anselm, Schatzman, Leonard, Ehrlich, D., Bucher, Rue, and Sabshin, M. 1963. 'The Hospital and its Negotiated Order' in E. Friedson (ed.), *The Hospital in Modern Society*. New York: Free Press
Straw, Will 1991. 'Systems of Articulation, Logics of Change: Communities and Scenes in Popular Music'. *Cultural Studies* 5, 3: 368–88
Sullivan, Harry Stack 1939. *Conceptions of Modern Psychiatry*. New York: W. W. Norton, 1947
Sully, James 1884. *Outlines of Psychology*. London: Longman's Green
Summerfield, Margaret A. 1991. *Global Geomorphology*. Harlow: Longman
Sumner, William Graham 1906. *Folkways*. Boston: Ginn and Co.
Sutherland, Edwin 1939. *Principles of Criminology*. Chicago: J. B. Lippincott
Swidler, Ann 1986. 'Culture in Action: Symbols and Strategies'. *American Sociological Review* 51: 273–86
Sztompka, Pyotr 1993. *The Sociology of Social Change*. Oxford: Basil Blackwell
Takata, Yasuma 1922. *Principles of Sociology*. Tokyo: University of Tokyo Press, 1989
Tarde, Gabriel 1890. *The Laws of Imitation*. New York: H. Holt and Co., 1903
  1898a. *Social Laws*. New York: Macmillan, 1899
  1898b. 'Sociology' in T. N. Clark (ed.), *Gabriel Tarde on Communication and Social Influence*. Chicago: University of Chicago Press, 1969
  1901. *L'opinion et la foule*. Paris: Presses Universitaires de France, 1989
Tarling, Donald H. and Tarling, Maureen P. 1971. *Continental Drift*. New York: Doubleday
Tarrow, Sydney 1994. *Power in Movement*. Cambridge: Cambridge University Press
Tayler, J. Lionel 1904. *Aspects of Social Evolution*, First Series, *Temperaments*. London: Smith, Elder
  1921. *Social Life and the Crowd*. Boston: Small, Maynard
Taylor, Ian R., Walton, Paul, and Young, Jock 1975. *The New Criminology, for a Social Theory of Deviance*. London: Routledge and Kegan Paul
Thibaut, John W. and Kelley, Harold H. 1959. *The Social Psychology of Groups*. New York: Wiley
Thom, René 1972. *Structural Stability and Morphogenesis*. London: Benjamin, 1975
Thomas, Franklin 1925. *The Environmental Basis of Society*. New York: Johnson Reprint, 1965
Thompson, F. M. L. 1963. *English Landed Society in the Nineteenth Century*. London: Routledge and Kegan Paul
Thornhill, Randy and Palmer, Craig T. 2000. *A Natural History of Rape: Biological Bases of Sexual Coercion*. Cambridge: MIT Press
Thrasher, F. 1927. *The Gang*. Chicago: University of Chicago Press
Tilley, Christopher 1994. *A Phenomenology of Landscape*. Oxford: Berg
Tilly, Charles 1978. *From Mobilization to Revolution*. Reading: Addison-Wesley

Tobler, Waldo R. 1963. 'Geographic Area and Map Projections'. *Geographical Review* 52: 59–78

Tong, Howell 1990. *Non-Linear Time Series: A Dynamical Systems Approach.* Oxford: Clarendon Press

Tönnies, Ferdinand 1889. *Community and Association.* London: Routledge and Kegan Paul, 1955 (based on the 1912 edn)

Tooby, J. and Cosmides, L. 1992. 'The Psychological Foundations of Culture' in J. H. Barkow and L. C. J. Tooby (eds.), *The Adapted Mind: Evolutionary Psychology and the Generation of Culture.* Oxford: Oxford University Press

Touraine, Alain 1964. 'Towards a Sociology of Action' in A. Giddens (ed.), *Positivism and Sociology.* London: Heinemann, 1974
    1965. *Sociologie de l'action.* Paris: Editions de Seuil
    1978. *The Voice and the Eye: An Analysis of Social Movements.* Cambridge: Cambridge University Press, 1981

Toynbee, Arnold J. 1934–9. *A Study of History.* London: Oxford University Press

Trewartha, Glen 1968. *The Earth's Problem Climates.* Madison: University of Wisconsin Press

Troeltsch, Ernst 1912. *The Social Teaching of the Christian Churches.* London: George Allen and Unwin, 1931

Trudgill, Stephen T. 1977. *Soil and Vegetation Systems.* Oxford: Oxford University Press

Trueman, Arthur E. 1949. *Geology and Scenery in England and Wales.* Harmondsworth: Penguin, 1967

Tuan, Yi-Fu 1974. *Topophilia.* Englewood Cliffs: Prentice-Hall
    1977. *Space and Place: The Perspective of Experience.* Minneapolis: University of Minnesota Press

Turk, Austin T. 1969. *Criminality and the Legal Order.* Chicago: Rand McNally

Turner, Jonathan 1988. *A Theory of Social Interaction.* Cambridge: Polity Press
    2000. *On the Origins of Human Emotions.* Stanford: Stanford University Press
    2007. *Human Emotions.* London: Routledge

Turner, Ralph 1962. 'Role-Taking: Process Versus Conformity' in A. Rose (ed.), *Human Behaviour and Social Processes.* Houghton Mifflin
    1969. 'The Theme of Contemporary Social Movements'. *British Journal of Sociology* 20, 4: 390–405

Turner, Ralph H. and Killian, Lewis 1957. *Collective Behaviour.* New Jersey: Prentice-Hall

Turner, Stephen P. 1994. *The Social Theory of Practices: Tradition, Tacit Knowledge and Presuppositions.* Cambridge: Polity Press

Tylor, Edward 1871. *Primitive Culture.* London: John Murray, 1920

Ullman, E. L. 1941. 'A Theory of Location for Cities'. *American Journal of Sociology* 46: 853–64

Urry, John 2000. *Sociology Beyond Societies: Mobilities for the Twenty-First Century.* London: Routledge
    2003. *Global Complexity.* Cambridge: Polity Press

Vacher de la Pouge, Georges 1896. *Les sélections sociales.* Paris: M. Rivière

Van Gennep, Arnold 1909. *The Rites of Passage.* London: Routledge and Kegan Paul, 1960

Vansina, Jan 1961. *Oral Tradition*. Harmondsworth: Penguin

Vidal de la Blache, Paul 1917. 'La répartition des hommes sur la terre'. *Annales de Geographie* 26

1922. *Principles of Human Geography*. New York: H. Holt and Co., 1926

Vidich, Arthur J., Stein, Maurice R., and Bensman, Joseph 1971. *Reflections on Community Studies*. New York: Harper and Row

Vierkandt, Alfred 1923. *Gesellshaftslehre*. Stuttgart: F. Enke

Virilio, P. 1977. *Speed and Politics: An Essay on Dromology*. New York: Semiotext(e), 1986

von Bertalanffy, Ludwig 1940. 'The Organism Considered as a Physical System' in L. von Bertalanffy (ed.), *General System Theory*. New York: Harper and Row, 1968

1945. 'Some System Concepts in Elementary Mathematical Consideration' in L. von Bertalanffy (ed.), *General System Theory*. New York: Harper and Row, 1968

1956. 'The Meaning of General System Theory' in L. von Bertalanffy (ed.), *General System Theory*. New York: Harper and Row, 1968

1964. 'Some Aspects of System Theory in Biology' in L. von Bertalanffy (ed.), *General System Theory*. New York: Harper and Row, 1968

1967. 'The Model of Open Systems' in L. von Bertalanffy (ed.), *General System Theory*. New York: Harper and Row, 1968

1968. 'The System Concept in the Sciences of Man' in L. von Betalanffy (ed.), *General System Theory*. New York: Harper and Row

von Hayek, Friedrich 1942. 'Scientism and the Study of Society' in F. von Hayek (ed.), *The Counter-Revolution of Science*. Glencoe: Free Press, 1952

1962. 'Rules, Perception and Intelligibility' in F. von Hayek (ed.), *Studies in Philosophy, Politics and Economics*. London: Routledge and Kegan Paul, 1967

von Helmholtz, Hermann 1847. *Über die Erhaltung der Kraft, eine physikalische Abhandlung*. Berlin: G. Reimer

von Humboldt, Wilhelm 1836. *On the Diversity of Human Language Construction and its Influence on the Mental Development of the Human Species*. Cambridge: Cambridge University Press, 1999

von Linné, Carl 1806. *The System of Nature*. London: Lackington, Allen

von Mises, Ludwig 1949. *Human Action*. New Haven: Yale University Press

von Stein, Lorenz 1850. *History of the Social Movement in France from 1789 to Our Day*. Totowa: Bedminster Press, 1964 (a translation of the 3rd edn of 1856)

von Thünen, Johann Heinrich 1826. *The Isolated State*. Oxford: Pergamon, 1966

von Wiese, Leopold 1924–9. *Allgemeine Soziologie als Lehre von dem Beziehungen und Beziehungsgebilden*. München: Duncker und Humblot

1931. 'Outlines of the "Theory of Social Relations"' in L. von Wiese (ed.), *Sociology*. New York: Oskar Piest, 1941

Vygotsky, Lev 1930–4. *Mind in Society*. Cambridge: Harvard University Press, 1978 (first translated 1962)

1934. *Thought and Language*. Cambridge: MIT Press, 1986

Wallas, Graham 1908. *Human Nature in Politics*. London: Constable, 1948

Wallerstein, Immanuel 1974. *The Modern World System I: Capitalist Agriculture and the Origins of the European World-Economy in the Sixteenth Century.* New York: Academic Press
  1980. *The Modern World System II: Mercantilism and the Consolidation of the European World-Economy, 1600–1750.* New York: Academic Press
  1989. *The Modern World System III: The Second Era of Great Expansion of the Capitalist World-Economy, 1730–1840s.* New York: Academic Press
Walras, Léon 1868. *Recherche de l'idéal social, leçons publiques faites à Paris, par Léon Walras. Première série (1867–68). Théorie générale de la société.* Paris: Guillaumin
  1874. *Elements of Pure Economics.* London: George Allen and Unwin, 1965
Ward, James 1918. *Psychological Principles.* Cambridge: Cambridge University Press
Ward, Lester 1883. *Dynamic Sociology.* New York: D. Appleton, 1913
  1903. *Pure Sociology.* New York: Macmillan, 1914
Watkins, J. W. N. 1952. 'Ideal Types and Historical Explanation' in J. O'Neill (ed.), *Modes of Individualism and Collectivism.* London: Heinemann, 1973
  1957. 'Historical Explanation in the Social Sciences' in J. O'Neill (ed.), *Modes of Individualism and Collectivism.* London: Heinemann, 1973
Weber, Alfred 1909. *Theory of the Location of Industries.* Chicago: University of Chicago Press, 1929
  1920. 'Die not der geistigen arbeiter'. *Schriften des Vereins für Sozialpolitik*
  1920–1. *Fundamentals of Culture-Sociology: Social Process, Civilization Process and Cultural Movement.* New York: Columbia University Press, 1939
Weber, Max 1904–5. 'The Protestant Ethic and the Spirit of Capitalism' in P. Baehr and G. C. Wells (eds.), *Max Weber: The Protestant Ethic and the 'Spirit' of Capitalism, and Other Writings.* Harmondsworth: Penguin, 2002
  1909. '"Energetische" Kulturtheorie'. *Archiv für Sozialwissenschaft und Sozialpolitik* 29: 575–98
  1913–14. 'The Economy and the Arena of Normative and De Facto Powers' in G. Roth and C. Wittich (eds.), *Economy and Society.* University of California Press, 1968
  1920. 'Conceptual Exposition' in G. Roth and C. Wittich (eds.), *Economy and Society.* University of California Press, 1968
Wegener, Alfred 1912. *The Origin of Continents and Oceans.* London: Methuen, 1966
Werlen, Benno 1993. *Society, Action and Space.* Cambridge: Polity Press
Westermarck, Edvard 1891. *The History of Human Marriage.* 2nd edn. London: Macmillan, 1894
White, Harrison C. 1970. *Chains of Opportunity.* Cambridge: Harvard University Press
  1992. *Identity and Control.* Princeton: Princeton University Press
White, Harrison C., Boorman, Scott A., and Breiger, Ronald L. 1976. 'Social Structure from Multiple Networks: I'. *American Journal of Sociology* 81: 730–80
White, Leslie A. 1949. *The Science of Culture.* New York: Grove Press
Whitrow, G. J. 1988. *Time in History.* Oxford: Oxford University Press

Whorf, Benjamin Lee 1936. 'A Linguistic Consideration of Thinking in Primitive Communities' in B. L. Whorf (ed.), *Language, Thought and Reality*. Cambridge: MIT Press, 1956

1937. 'Grammatical Categories' in B. L. Whorf (ed.), *Language, Thought and Reality*. Cambridge: MIT Press, 1956

1940a. 'Linguistics as an Exact Science' in B. L. Whorf (ed.), *Language, Thought and Reality*. Cambridge: MIT Press, 1956

1940b. 'Science and Lingustics' in B. L. Whorf (ed.), *Language, Thought and Reality*. Cambridge: MIT Press, 1956

1941. 'The Relation of Habitual Thought and Behaviour to Language' in B. L. Whorf (ed.), *Language, Thought and Reality*. Cambridge: MIT Press, 1956

Wiener, Norbert 1948. *Cybernetics: or, Control and Communication in the Animal and the Machine*. New York: Wiley

Wiese-Becker 1932. *Systematic Sociology, on the Basis of the Beziehungslehre and Gebildelehre of Leopold von Wiese, adapted and amplified by Howard P. Becker*. New York: Wiley

Wilde, Lawrence 1989. *Marx and Contradiction*. Aldershot: Avebury

Wilkins, Leslie T. 1964. *Social Deviance: Social Policy, Action and Research*. London: Tavistock

Williams, Raymond 1958. *Culture and Society, 1780–1950*. London: Chatto and Windus

1976. *Keywords*. Glasgow: Fontana

1977. *Marxism and Literature*. Oxford: Oxford University Press

1981. *Culture*. Glasgow: Fontana

Williams, Robin M. 1960. *American Society: A Sociological Investigation*. 2nd edn. New York: Alfred A. Knopf

Williams, Simon J. 2005. *Sleep and Society: Sociological Ventures into the (Un)known*. London: Routledge

Williams, William M. 1956. *The Sociology of an English Village: Gosforth*. London: Routledge and Kegan Paul

1963. *A West Country Village: Ashworthy*. London: Routledge and Kegan Paul

Wilson, Edward O. 1975. *Sociobiology: The New Synthesis*. Cambridge: Belknap Press

Winch, Peter 1958. *The Idea of a Social Science*. London: Routledge and Kegan Paul

Wittgenstein, Ludwig 1953. *Philosophical Investigations*. Oxford: Basil Blackwell

Wolff, Kurt H. 1950. *The Sociology of Georg Simmel*. New York: Free Press

Wood, Ellen Meiksins 1986. *The Retreat from Class: A New 'True' Socialism*. New York: Schocken Books

Wood, Margaret Mary 1934. *The Stranger*. New York: AMS Press, 1969

Worsley, Peter 1957. *The Trumpet Shall Sound: A Study of 'Cargo' Cults in Melanesia*. London: McGibbon and Kee

Wrong, Denis 1961. 'The Oversocialized Conception of Man in Modern Sociology'. *American Sociological Review* 26: 183–93

1994. *The Problem of Order*. New York: Macmillan Press

Wundt, Wilhelm 1897. *Outlines of Psychology*. St. Claire's Shore: Scholarly Press, 1902

1912. *Elements of Folk Psychology*. London: George Allen and Unwin, 1916

Yinger, J. Milton 1960. 'Contraculture and Subculture'. *American Sociological Review* 25, 5: 625–35

Young, Jock 1971a. *The Drugtakers*. London: McGibbon and Kee

1971b. 'The Role of Police as Amplifiers of Deviancy, Negotiators of Reality and Translators of Fantasy' in S. Cohen (ed.), *Images of Deviance*. Harmondsworth: Penguin

Young, Michael 1988. *The Metronomic Society*. London: Thames and Hudson

Zald, Meyer and McCarthy, J. D. (eds.) 1979. *The Dynamics of Social Movements*. Cambridge: Winthrop

Zerubavel, Eviator 1981. *Hidden Rhythms: Schedules and Calendars in Social Life*. Berkeley: University of California Press

1985. *The Seven Day Circle*. Chicago: University of Chicago Press

2003. *Time Maps: Collective Memory and the Social Shape of the Past*. Chicago: University of Chicago Press

Zimbardo, Philip 2007. *The Lucifer Effect: Understanding How Good People Turn Evil*. New York: Random House

Znaniecki, Florian 1919. *Cultural Reality*. Chicago: University of Chicago Press

1935. *Social Actions*. New York: Farrar and Reinhart

Zorbaugh, Harvey 1929. *The Gold Coast and the Slum*. Chicago: University of Chicago Press

Index